TEACHING JAMES JOYCE IN THE TWENTY-FIRST CENTURY

The Florida James Joyce Series

UNIVERSITY PRESS OF FLORIDA

Florida A&M University, Tallahassee
Florida Atlantic University, Boca Raton
Florida Gulf Coast University, Ft. Myers
Florida International University, Miami
Florida State University, Tallahassee
New College of Florida, Sarasota
University of Central Florida, Orlando
University of Florida, Gainesville
University of North Florida, Jacksonville
University of South Florida, Tampa
University of West Florida, Pensacola

Teaching James Joyce in the Twenty-First Century

Edited by Barry Devine and Ellen Scheible

Foreword by Sam Slote

UNIVERSITY PRESS OF FLORIDA

Gainesville/Tallahassee/Tampa/Boca Raton
Pensacola/Orlando/Miami/Jacksonville/Ft. Myers/Sarasota

Cover: *Bloom Smelling the Flower*, watercolor by artist Robert Berry. *Inset*: Detail from The Heaventree of Stars, by artist Robert Berry. Used with permission.

Copyright 2025 by Barry Devine and Ellen Scheible

All rights reserved

Published in the United States of America

30 29 28 27 26 25   6 5 4 3 2 1

DOI: https://doi.org/10.5744/9780813079479

The Library of Congress Cataloging-in-Publication Data
Names: Devine, Barry (Associate Professor of English) editor | Scheible, Ellen editor
Title: Teaching James Joyce in the twenty-first century / edited by Barry
Devine and Ellen Scheible.
Description: Gainesville : University Press of Florida, 2025. | Series: The
Florida James Joyce series | Includes bibliographical references and
index.
Identifiers: LCCN 2025024427 (print) | LCCN 2025024428 (ebook) | ISBN
9780813079479 hardback | ISBN 9780813081267 paperback | ISBN
9780813075105 ebook | ISBN 9780813074153 pdf
Subjects: LCSH: Joyce, James, 1882–1941—Study and teaching | LCGFT:
Literary criticism
Classification: LCC PR6019.O9 Z8274 2026 (print) | LCC PR6019.O9 (ebook)
| DDC 823/.912—dc23/eng/20250527
LC record available at https://lccn.loc.gov/2025024427
LC ebook record available at https://lccn.loc.gov/2025024428

The University Press of Florida is the scholarly publishing agency for the State University System of Florida, comprising Florida A&M University, Florida Atlantic University, Florida Gulf Coast University, Florida International University, Florida State University, New College of Florida, University of Central Florida, University of Florida, University of North Florida, University of South Florida, and University of West Florida.

University Press of Florida
2046 NE Waldo Road
Suite 2100
Gainesville, FL 32609
http://upress.ufl.edu

GPSR EU Authorized Representative: Mare Nostrum Group B.V., Mauritskade 21D, 1091 GC Amsterdam, The Netherlands, gpsr@mare-nostrum.co.uk

For
Claire Culleton and Michael Groden—
two deeply missed friends and mentors

CONTENTS

List of Figures   ix

Foreword   xi

Acknowledgments   xiii

Introduction   1
Barry Devine and Ellen Scheible

I. Curricular Joyce

1. Teaching Joyce's *Portrait* to High School Students   17
   Barbara M. Hoffmann

2. ". . . the real Oxford manner": Teaching *Dubliners* on the Foundation Year   31
   Lloyd Meadhbh Houston

3. Teaching Joyce's Backstories   44
   Julieann Veronica Ulin

4. Black Lives and Irish Lives: Teaching and Reading Deesha Philyaw and Joyce in 2021   62
   Mary M. Burke

5. To Cause Students to Stop in Wonder: Using/Teaching Popular Culture in Joyce   75
   Garry Leonard

6. Reading (and Loving) *Ulysses* While Black   92
   Zoë L. Henry

7. Decolonial Pedagogy and Teaching Joyce in a Liberal Arts College Classroom   116
   Shinjini Chattopadhyay

8. Eating with Joyce: *Ulysses* and the Cultural Discourses That Shape Personal Nutrition   131
   Talia Abu

9. Teaching the Wakean Sentence   148
   Paul Fagan

10. Teaching *Finnegans Wake:* Reading, Performing, and Creating   161
    Gregory Erickson

11. Preparing to Teach *Exiles*   181
    A. Nicholas Fargnoli

II. Extracurricular Joyce

12. Teaching Joyce's Poetry   199
    Margot Norris

13. Teaching *Ulysses* in Nonacademic Spaces   214
    Jonathan Goldman

14. "At their joggerfry": Joyce, Dublin, and City-as-Text   229
    Greg Winston

15. Teaching Art Through the Prism of *Ulysses*   250
    Robert Berry

16. Teaching *Dubliners* in Prison   266
    Michael Patrick Gillespie

    List of Contributors   281

    Index   285

FIGURES

5.1. Brooke's Soap advertisement (1891)   85
5.2. Brooke's Soap advertisement (1900)   87
5.3. PinkCherry billboard (2020)   87
6.1. Pole on which Will Brown was hanged   101
6.2. The burning of Will Brown's body by a lynch mob   102
6.3. "Hanging and burning a negro in Clarkson Street" (1863)   103
10.1. "Knitbook" by Hannah Baek, New York University Class of 2017   178
14.1. Dublin city centre *Ulysses* sidewalk plaque   231
14.2. "Learning Geography," *United Irishman,* September 2, 1899   233
14.3. The former St. Joseph's National School, Dorset Street   233
14.4. Poolbeg Stacks seen from Sandymount Strand   241
14.5. The Pigeon House   243

FOREWORD

Since it was launched thirty years ago, the Florida James Joyce Series has published almost fourscore volumes on an impressive array of Joycean research. But this volume marks the first time the series has published a book on teaching and pedagogy, research's counterpart within academia. Such an unfortunate lacuna is perhaps symptomatic of the ways in which teaching is often marginalized or even forgotten, even though teaching is supposedly central to the mission of academia. Barry Devine and Ellen Scheible, the editors of this volume, address this problem in their introduction as they argue how teaching Joyce is—or rather should be—enmeshed within Joyce studies as a whole. The teaching of Joyce is where scholarship and reception intersect—whether that teaching be in a university classroom, a coffee shop, or a Zoom reading group. Rather than ignore or take for granted Joyce's canonical status, the teaching of Joyce is exactly the space where this can be interrogated and reevaluated. The editors take a suitably multiperspectival approach to the question of how Joyce is and can be taught. Together, the contributions in this volume advocate for a rich plurality of reading and teaching Joyce.

The volume is not limited to third-level education, and the volume's first section includes chapters on teaching Joyce in a variety of ways in a variety of classrooms including high school. For example, Joyce's texts can be made to sing in the classroom through popular culture just as much as through postcolonial and decolonial pedagogy. The complexities of *Finnegans Wake* can be grappled with creative as well as with more conventional academic means. Likewise, Joyce's texts can be used to address contemporary concerns, such as Black Lives Matter. The chapters in this section are admirably eclectic and propose multiple ways of engaging with Joyce's texts in the contemporary classroom.

The second section looks at teaching Joyce outside traditional academic settings, such as in reading groups and in correctional facilities. Teaching is not and should not be limited to the classroom, and this section illustrates how professional academics can—and even should—ply their trade beyond an ivory tower. Taken together, this collection very much expands our sense of who reads Joyce and why. In a very real sense, this volume makes Joyce new (again).

Sam Slote
Series Editor

ACKNOWLEDGMENTS

The editors would like to thank University Press of Florida, specifically Sam Slote, editor of UPF's the Florida James Joyce Series, and Stephanye Hunter, editor-in-chief at UPF.

We gratefully acknowledge funding assistance from Bridgewater State University. Ellen Scheible was awarded a 2022–23 Presidential Research Fellowship from BSU that allowed her the opportunity to work on this project.

Thanks to our contributors: Talia Abu, Robert Berry, Mary M. Burke, Shinjini Chattopadhyay, Gregory Erickson, Paul Fagan, A. Nicholas Fargnoli, Michael Patrick Gillespie, Jonathan Goldman, Zoë L. Henry, Barbara M. Hoffmann, Lloyd Meadhbh Houston, Garry Leonard, Margot Norris, Julieann Veronica Ulin, and Greg Winston. It was an absolute pleasure to work with this dynamic group of scholars and educators.

Barry Devine: Long before I ever thought about graduate study, I obsessively read the major works of James Joyce as a novice reader who just wanted to understand the genius of his prose. It was not until I was taking postbaccalaureate courses for fun at the University of Oregon that I decided to dedicate much of my future life to Joyce in general and to *Ulysses* specifically. George Wickes at UO helped this first-generation student learn how to apply for graduate programs and still serves as a tireless mentor, despite the fact that he recently celebrated his one-hundredth birthday. In grad school at University College Dublin, I met Luca Crispi, who served as my MA thesis adviser and who patiently introduced me to genetic criticism and guided my early practice working with manuscripts. Later at the University of Miami, I had the pleasure of working with Patrick McCarthy, who guided my dissertation research and gave me freedom to explore and to discover and to make mistakes. These many mistakes were certainly not acts of volition, but instead valuable learning experiences that I might have missed with another mentor. Pat remains my first reader for much of my research, and I am forever grateful for his unlimited support and guidance, from my first visit to the Miami campus as a prospective student to the present day.

I owe an eternal debt to Michael Groden, who needs no introduction in a volume like this. As an eager undergrad looking for grad school advice, I boldly emailed Mike out of the blue, and he patiently took the time to explain my options for graduate study. Over the years, I touched base with Mike occasionally for advice or sometimes just for lunch when we happened to be in the same city. He later agreed to be the external reader for my dissertation and offered me his help throughout that process. Once I began teaching, I sought his advice for introducing Joyce to undergrads: how to best organize the semester, how much time to spend on each work, and, most importantly, how to embrace the difficulty students will have with his work and use it as a pedagogical tool. Mike's passing in 2021 was felt throughout the Joycean world, and I, like many others, would not be the scholar and educator I am without his generosity and passion for James Joyce and for his students.

I owe thanks to my parents, Bruce and Carol, for their enthusiastic support of my studies, even when they had no idea what I was doing; to my wife and partner Heleana for understanding why this book took so many weekends away from other things, and who helped me think through the challenges of editing a collection; and to Ellen for her enthusiasm about this project and for guiding me, Virgil-like, through the world of academic publishing.

Ellen Scheible: My love for James Joyce began at Claremont Graduate University under the mentorship of Paul Saint-Amour, who was at Pomona College at the time, and Colleen Jaurretche, who was at University of California, Los Angeles. Through Colleen and Paul, I met and read some of the most intelligent and provocative scholars I have ever encountered. I played charades with superstars I never dreamed of seeing in real life (John Bishop, Margot Norris, Kim Devlin, Vince Cheng), sang songs, learned the importance of single words in the act of reading complicated texts, and was generally embraced by a community that I continue to dearly love. Thank you, Joyceans, for your appreciation and support of junior scholars.

This book would not be possible without Claire Culleton, who we lost much too soon. Claire was a devout Joycean, a feminist, and a mentor to young academics who did not see themselves in the image of traditional scholars. I am forever in her debt. Her interest in my work and support for my writing gave me the confidence to be the academic I am now. She is deeply missed by so many.

For many years I taught a senior seminar titled "Wilde, Joyce, Beckett." Almost every semester, I teach *Dubliners*. I am grateful to all the students I have had the opportunity to learn from during my career including those from Harvey Mudd College, Stonehill College, and Bridgewater State University.

As always, thank you to my parents, Bruce and Sally, my husband, Bill, and my baby bugs, Astrid and Quinn. Barry Devine: you are divine, my friend.

Introduction

Barry Devine and Ellen Scheible

James Joyce appreciated the art of passionate teaching. Even at a young age, he recognized the impact education could have on his perception and understanding of the world. According to Richard Ellmann, he told the sculptor August Suter that his time at Clongowes Wood College helped him "'arrange things in such a way that they become easy to survey and to judge,'"[1] a prowess he would use to build and deconstruct an unrivaled repertoire of Irish modernist fiction. Of Joyce's early years at Clongowes, Ellmann points out that "if Joyce retained anything from his education, it was a conviction of the skill of his Jesuit masters, the more remarkable because he rejected their teaching."[2] Joyce would go on to become a teacher himself, memorialize his time as a student in *A Portrait of the Artist as a Young Man*, and depict teaching as a necessarily compassionate and humanistic enterprise in *Ulysses*. When Stephen Dedalus evolves from a tortured adolescent student into a benevolent, but awkward educator, Joyce must have known that he would capture the heart of the professoriate for many years to come.

Today's urgent and ongoing conversations about relevant pedagogy during a time of flux and change in the academy show that Joyce's view of education as foundational to the expansion of individual and national empathy was as prophetic as it was cautionary. At the 2021 Modern Language Association (MLA) conference, the International James Joyce Foundation sponsored a panel on teaching Joyce. While each panelist presented a different approach to teaching Joyce's texts—showing first-generation college students' depictions of class and race in *Dubliners;* co-teaching *Ulysses* to non-English majors through the visual arts; and simultaneously leading multiple *Finnegans Wake* reading groups[3]—the most telling and provocative component of the panel was the audience. This meeting of the MLA was entirely online, and the panel was held via Zoom. Even with the disappointment and alienation generated by the technological distance of a global pandemic, the 2021 Teaching Joyce MLA panel had enough attendees to fill more than one Zoom screen. Such a large audience reinforced and validated the panel's overall purpose: to consider Joyce's lingering presence in college classrooms, cultural debates, and contemporary art and fiction.[4]

The recognizable interest of educators and scholars from various levels of institutional work at such a specific literature panel underscored the devotion many readers still feel toward Joyce's works and the challenges teaching such complicated texts bring to any contemporary understanding of the processes of teaching and learning. Many questions were asked about approaches and content, but the panel discussion specifically addressed how, as educators, we manage the paradoxical feelings of aesthetic pleasure and ethical resistance many young readers experience when first encountering Joyce's characters and their early twentieth-century biases and flaws. The panel did not resolve this issue; there were no clear answers to the repeated question of how we help students accept that they can love to read Joyce and, at the same time, question and interrogate the textual politics of his work. The collection that follows, however, attempts to address that concern, and others, from the multifaceted perspectives of seasoned Joyceans, moonlighting modernists, and emerging writers and thinkers. The collection sprung from a series of organic and digital academic experiences shared during the COVID-19 lockdown. Predictably, technology and social media are quite compatible with Joyce studies.

The conversation about how and why we teach Joyce, though, began long before Facebook posts or Zoom rooms. Margot Norris affirmed Joyce's evergreen stature as a teacher of sentient experience in the foreword to her 1998 *A Companion to James Joyce's "Ulysses."* At the end of the opening pages, she thanks her students for showing her "the strange effect this radically innovative novel has on its readers," noting that *Ulysses* might present as "an elite artifact," but it "eventually becomes a living experience—a lifestyle almost—that knits its readers into sympathetic communities."[5] The extensive list of impactful modern and contemporary intellectuals who consider themselves part of the Joyce community is long and widely diverse. Yet, one of Joyce's most devoted students was also one of the strongest advocates for the dissemination of his work to a larger, less erudite, populace. Irish writer Edna O'Brien viewed Joyce as a teacher with unparalleled influence over her life and paid her debt to Joyce's progressive politics and experimental creativity with her own innovative mastery of the writing craft.[6] In O'Brien's penultimate chapter of *James Joyce: A Life*, her eclectic biography of Joyce, she points out,

"The battle as to who owns James Joyce infiltrates many a Joycean occasion, a claim so proprietary and absurd that it deserves no answer. Genius is singular" (171).[7]

In 1999, it made sense to dive into the fight about ownership and claims to Joyce's intellectual property, especially since the American Joyce Industry was producing some of the most canonical literary criticism to date on Joyce, and the larger field of Irish modernism was flourishing during Ireland's economic boom of the Celtic Tiger. But now, in 2026, it might make more sense to ask "who is willing to own James Joyce" as we move through an unprecedented reconfiguration of the university environment. The much-contested "end" of the COVID-19 pandemic has not generated greater retention rates in college classrooms as administrators had hoped, and the combined need for increased awareness of social justice issues and collective embrace of intersectional pedagogy and DEI (diversity, equity, and inclusion) has exposed the tenets of white supremacy underlying the infrastructure of the Western world's academic legacies. Where does Joyce fall in this complicated and often irresolvable milieu of contemporary discursive critique? Unsurprisingly, he falls right in the middle of all of it.

Joyce was writing about sexual difference, neurodiversity, physical disability, racism, classism, reproduction, death and dying, among many other controversial and progressive platforms, before women's and gender studies, disability studies, medical humanities, critical race theory, transgender studies, and reproductive rights were named as undeniable social concerns and much-needed interdisciplinary fields for students, activists, and scholars alike. He was not alone; Virginia Woolf, Zora Neale Hurston, Nella Larsen, Charlotte Perkins Gilman, and a slew of other writers on both sides of the Atlantic were addressing social issues with a candor that we now recognize as one of the many innovative tropes of literary modernism. Yet, Joyce had many personal struggles that set him apart from other writers of his period. He endured poverty during most of his years in Trieste; chose exile from a country and a revolution that defined his fiction; remained angry at the church that marginalized his intellect in favor of the institutions of marriage and nationalism; and lived in poorer health with each new project. As O'Brien describes:

> *Ulysses* took seven years of unbroken labor, twenty thousand hours of work, havoc to brain and body, nerves, agitation, fainting fits, numerous eye complaints—glaucoma, iritis, cataract, crystallized cataract, nebula in the pupil, conjunctivitis, torn retina, blood accumulation, abscesses and one-tenth normal vision. That Joyce has risen above so much mis-

understanding is surely a testament to those wounded eyes and the Holy Ghost in that ink bottle.[8]

Joyce called for Western humanity to reconsider the ideologies of religion and heteronormativity at the cost of personal isolation and physical pain during Ireland's very public fight for independence (a fight he did not always support, but almost always wrote about).[9] Joyce, as O'Brien proclaims, engendered the belief "that the artist who stakes his life is on his own," even though he had patrons, editors, and publishers, all mostly women, who eventually made him world famous.[10] He lived his art enough to never quite recover from the suffering it brought him or see the critical legacy it produced, but he reveled in the controversy it provoked.

Deciphering Joyce's personal opinions on cultural diversity continues to produce a spectrum of critical arguments about his progressive politics, or lack thereof, and, as many of us can testify, serves as one of the strongest catalysts for classroom discussion. Although a young, undergraduate Joyce told Henrik Ibsen that "we always keep the dearest things to ourselves," a mature Joyce overtly and publicly celebrated inconsistency and indecision in his work.[11] Free, indirect discourse forever changed the scope of modern writing and placed irreducible paradox, simultaneity, and epiphanic failure at the core of seminar exploration when world wars were threatening to annihilate democracy and limit the creativity of free thinking. Joyce's texts emulate the irresolvable experience of living in an inherently bifurcated, recycled, and fluid world, what ALP calls a "jigsaw puzzle of needles and pins and blankets and shins" in *Finnegans Wake*.[12] Gabriel and Gretta Conroy, Stephen Dedalus, Leopold and Molly Bloom, and HCE and ALP embody the fundamental incapacity of white, Western humanity to attain perfection; they are personifications of suffering, mistakes, pain, and frivolity—and they might anger us just about as much as they entertain us. To feel discomfort when facing such imperfection but still recognize the seduction of language and syntax freed from Victorian constraints, generates a palpable fervor among students, leading to rigorous debate and producing many eventual reclamations of the act of misreading. In short, Joyce is still important because learning to hold and interrogate two oppositional ideas in our minds at the same time is timelessly relevant and urgently critical, especially in our present cultural moment.

Even if we are willing to "own" Joyce in our classrooms and our scholarship, we still do not have an answer to the question of how to manage student responses to the lack of resolution that emerges from the inconsistencies and conundrums mentioned above. While we cannot claim that this collection successfully answers that question either, we can promise that it is the motivating conversational piece behind the chapters included here. Moreover, the contributions do not all approach teaching from the same perspective or methodology, and, at times, the tactics discussed are unconventional. Readers may consult this collection for a myriad of reasons and in a nonsequential fashion, employing the recommendations and reflections provided by the contributors at different times in their instructional and scholastic careers. In focusing on those specific concerns, we join a series of publications from the past two decades that have offered unconventional approaches to teaching Joyce in the contemporary era. Moreover, *Teaching James Joyce in the Twenty-First Century* owes its critical inception to a long line of scholars who have been working on Joyce and pedagogy for many years.[13]

Dylan Emerick-Brown's *As One Generation Tells Another: Teaching James Joyce in the Secondary Classroom* (2020),[14] a handbook for teaching Joyce to high school students, launched a contemporary conversation that includes responses akin to those of our contributors. In chapter 4 of Emerick-Brown's book, "*Ulysses* . . . yes! *Ulysses!*" in particular, he persuasively advocates for teaching *Ulysses* to fifteen- and sixteen-year-olds, arguing that with clear and concise instructions, any student, at almost any age, can enjoy an experience with Joyce's fiction. Emerick-Brown's expansive pedagogy, particularly his belief that Joyce's work can extend to readers from nontraditional ages, is an influential text for this collection, where you will find chapters on teaching Joyce in alternative spaces, such as senior centers and prison cells.

Before Emerick-Brown's work, in the early 2000s, *Eureka Studies in Teaching Short Fiction*, a journal supported by the English department at Eastern Kentucky University, published a series of essays on teaching *Dubliners*.[15] Contributors' affiliations spanned a global network of teaching Joyce including graduate assistants, lecturers, and creative writers. The collection offered a range of approaches for implementing Joyce into short story classes including references to lesson plans and collaborative learning. Later, in 2007, Janine Utell published "Are You Experienced? Teaching and Reading Joy(ce) through the Body" in *Feminist Teacher*,[16] where she uses feminist pedagogy to ask many of the same questions about teaching *Ulysses* as we are asking here: "What about those students who have been put off by Joyce's 'difficulty' and 'inaccessibility'? What about those whose training has up to that point been 'inadequate'? What about the 'common reader'?" (143). And recently, in 2017, Sarah Townsend discussed her utilization of social media when teaching Joyce in "*Ulysses* Here and Now: Using Twitter to Teach Experimental Literature," in which she discusses how one assignment "led students to engage with the novel's form and locale by creating a series of tweets that imitated Joyce's form and updated the content to reflect contemporary life in Albuquerque. A subsequent critical essay assignment prompted students to reflect analytically upon the process. Twitter served as a crucial foundation for the project. It provided a user-friendly platform for sharing student work, and it facilitated alternative routes of communication that complemented those forged in the classroom."[17] While we hope the following collection adds to the already existing rich pedagogical debates about how we share Joyce with others while making space for objection, criticism, and discontentment, we also hope it brings new perspectives and cutting-edge approaches into our contemporary classrooms.

This collection is part of a growing field of study known as the scholarship of teaching and learning academic writing that emphasizes the overlapping discourses of student and educator experiences. Students and their interests, reactions, discoveries, and interpretations are often the reason many of us do what we do. We love to teach because our students love to learn. Consequently, this book assumed its current shape determined by those on the learning end of the teacher-student relationship even though many contributors see themselves more as facilitators or guides when it comes to Joyce's texts, than teachers in the traditional sense. For the same reason, the essays in the collection do not refer to standard editions of Joyce's works. Teachers often use whatever texts they can access, or sometimes prefer a particular edition, and we celebrate that diversity of approach in the spectrum of editions consulted by our authors.

While the collection focuses on pedagogy, classrooms, and engagement with students, we also sought to include supplemental materials that reveal the breadth and reach of Joyce's impact on our literary community and more completely illustrate the scholarship of teaching and learning across a wide range of approaches and settings. Fittingly, a special cluster of resources including additional essays, syllabi, interviews, and a heartfelt tribute to the late John Bishop by two of his former students, Sarah Townsend and John Lurz, will appear in a 2026 forthcoming issue of *Joyce Studies Annual*. Townsend and Lurz recount their collective experience in John's classroom, out-of-class get-togethers, and times spent with him at his home. They describe a dedicated teacher, a world-class scholar, and a dear friend. These are qualities to which all of us who teach aspire, and the memories of John held by his students are how we would all like to be remembered by our own students. In its essence, the tribute to John touches at the heart of this collection of essays in which dedicated scholars and teachers share their classroom experiences so that we all might benefit.

We also include in the *JSA* special cluster an interview with Catherine Flynn, editor of *The Cambridge Centenary "Ulysses"* (2022), a reissue of the original 1922 text with introductory essays and a podcast, led by student readers and Flynn, to accompany a first-time reader's journey through the novel.[18] We ask

Flynn about the inspiration for this new teaching edition of *Ulysses* and encourage her to elaborate on the connection between her scholarship and her teaching in her relationship with Joyce's works. Her responses not only echo sentiments expressed by others in this collection but also capture the unique experience she offers to her students, her readers, and those who simply talk to her about Joyce. The interview format provides an unfiltered and heartfelt look into the life of a dedicated scholar and teacher that could only be captured by sitting down and having a casual conversation. The chapters in this collection provide a variety of pedagogical approaches and personal styles that all emphasize a common desire to share the passion for Joyce studies with others and hopefully inspire them to embrace reading as part of the interminable pursuit of self-knowledge.

We have divided this collection into two sections we call "Curricular Joyce" and "Extracurricular Joyce." The first section "Curricular Joyce," focuses on the teaching of Joyce's works in the traditional or conventional classroom including American high school students in New England, secondary students in Oxford's Astrophoria Foundation Year program, and undergraduates and MA students at various universities. With the exception of A. Nicholas Fargnoli's chapter on *Exiles* (see below), each chapter provides detailed pedagogical reasoning and practical descriptions of how each author approaches and teaches Joyce's texts. The second section, "Extracurricular Joyce," looks at pedagogical approaches to Joyce's works outside of the context of what most would usually consider a typical literature classroom. These chapters demonstrate that pedagogical approaches and strategies to Joyce's works are not limited to institutions of higher education but provide models for bringing them into unexpected spaces to reach more and different readers.

The two opening chapters address teaching Joyce's works to secondary students. Barbara M. Hoffmann opens the collection with "Teaching Joyce's *Portrait* to High School Students." Hoffmann details her experience of teaching *A Portrait of the Artist as a Young Man* to students in her Advanced Placement (AP) courses in her former career as a high school teacher. She presents a strong justification for teaching *Portrait* to high school students in lieu of other, more contemporary or more diverse texts. The second half of the chapter offers examples of practical solutions to some of the common difficulties high school teachers might face in the classroom.

In chapter 2, "'... the real Oxford manner': Teaching *Dubliners* on the Foundation Year," Lloyd Meadhbh Houston recounts their experience teaching underserved students in Oxford's Foundation Year program aimed at encouraging students, who might not otherwise, to earn a university degree. In this course they explore representations and implications of "the body" throughout *Dubliners. Houston's approach brings the stories into conversation with Judith Butler's ideas of the body expressing possibilities yet conditioned and restrained by historical situations.

Chapter 3, "Teaching Joyce's Backstories," by Julieann Veronica Ulin, moves the setting to the more familiar college classroom by providing details on securing her students' deep engagement in the stories from *Dubliners*. Inspired by a passage from Marcel Proust's *Swann's Way*, Ulin details the ways in which she encourages her MA students to focus critically on the backstories of the characters provided either by themselves or by the narrator. While aimed at her graduate students, we placed this chapter here because Ulin's methods of engagement can be applied at any level.

Chapter 4, by Mary M. Burke, "Black Lives and Irish Lives: Teaching Philyaw and Joyce in 2021," pairs Deesha Philyaw's short story collection, *The Secret Lives of Church Ladies*, set in contemporary Black evangelical America, with Joyce's colonial Catholic Dublin. The specificity of this course being taught in 2021 takes into consideration the challenges Burke's students faced in returning to the classroom after the COVID-19 lockdowns while simultaneously addressing the #MeToo and Black Lives Matter movements.

Garry Leonard, in chapter 5, "To Cause Students to Stop in Wonder: Using/Teaching Popular Culture in Joyce," continues the conversation of using popular culture as a pedagogical tool. Leonard describes his process of showing elements of popular culture to his students as a method of engagement with the text of *Ulysses*. Leonard takes readers on a journey to the pedagogical use of popular culture by way of two bookended student exercises based on the Saussurean sign system and the differences in two publications of "The Sisters."

Certain contributors approach teaching Joyce as an experience in diverse practices. In chapter 6, "Reading (and Loving) *Ulysses* While Black," Zoë L. Henry explores James Joyce's complex representations of Blackness in *Ulysses* alongside the hermeneutic experience of reading and teaching this text as a scholar of color. Henry explores the ways in which readers of color must negotiate competing forms of modernist difficulty in the novel, considering how this difficulty can become fruitful by attending to the ways in which Black figures are conceptualized, racialized, and (dis)incorporated at varying moments.

In chapter 7, "Decolonial Pedagogy and Teaching Joyce in a Liberal Arts College Classroom," Shinjini Chattopadhyay argues that the teaching of Joyce's works in the present college classroom requires the implementation of inclusive methods to execute the decolonial teaching that Joyce had envisioned. She discusses how the colonial epistemologies, which "Nestor" critiques, can be dismantled in the present college classroom through teaching Joyce's works and how inclusive pedagogies can be implemented broadly to forge a path toward decoloniality in English college curricula.

Talia Abu's chapter 8, "Eating with Joyce: *Ulysses* and the Cultural Discourses That Shape Personal Nutrition," investigates the glaring contradictions in Bloom's eating habits. In the morning Bloom delights in the idea of consuming a pork kidney after joyfully visiting the butcher shop, and yet at about two o'clock he finds flesh-eating unbearably offensive. Abu employs elements of food studies and the history of vegetarianism as a means of engaging students in Tel Aviv who are linguistically and culturally very distant from 1904 Dublin.

In chapter 9, "Teaching the Wakean Sentence," Paul Fagan provides a well-practiced outline for approaching the challenging language in *Finnegans Wake* with the simplest of concepts: the individual sentence as a grammatical unit. Fagan provides an updated and finely detailed version of his grammatical approach first presented as a plenary lecture at the Trieste Joyce School in 2009.

Gregory Erickson's chapter 10, "Teaching *Finnegans Wake*: Reading, Performing, and Creating," brings literature and art together. The chapter describes a pedagogy that is part interdisciplinary seminar, part reading group, and part arts workshop. Erickson combines the reading of short sections of the *Wake* in concert with artistic pieces that have been inspired by or that incorporate elements of the novel including visual art, film, music, sound art, theater, and dance. He then has his students create artistic works of their own based on their readings.

The chapter we chose to close out this section, chapter 11, "Preparing to Teach *Exiles*" by A. Nicholas Fargnoli, provides readers with an informative yet flexible framework for teaching Joyce's only surviving, and seldom taught, play, and which he leaves open and adaptable to many pedagogical styles. This chapter serves as a collaborative invitation of sorts for instructors to combine their own practiced pedagogies with Fargnoli's textual expertise in order to encourage more of us to teach Joyce's only play. Fargnoli uses his deep knowledge of the play to illustrate the ways in which Joyce achieves one of his major tenets of the purpose of drama, namely, to fasten attention away from the characters themselves and onto the recognition of a profound truth that lies behind the conflicts they face. His analysis of the play concentrates on the demands that unconditional freedom imposes on those in intimate relations and on the unsettling conflicts caused by doubt and betrayal.

The second section of the collection, "Extracurricular Joyce," provides readers with examples of pedagogical approaches that highlight the concept of the community writ large in the sharing of Joycean texts by focusing on Joyce outside of traditional academic institutions. These chapters deliver readers to cafés, a senior center, a prison, online forums, and the streets of Dublin. Margot

Norris writes about her experience preparing to teach Joyce's poetry to members of a senior center in Laguna Beach, California, in chapter 12, "Teaching Joyce's Poetry." She provides a touching account of the experiences that led her to this teaching opportunity as well as a justification and pedagogical model for teaching Joyce's infrequently taught poems.

In chapter 13, "Teaching *Ulysses* in Nonacademic Spaces," Jonathan Goldman expands the tenets of Joyce studies by widening our view of the spaces of Joyce pedagogy. He provides details of his experiences serving as a facilitator of several *Ulysses* reading groups, both in person and, more recently, online.

Geography and art also inform essays in this section. In chapter 14, "'At their joggerfry': Joyce, Dublin, and City-as-Text," Greg Winston combines memoir and pedagogy in a discussion about reading and teaching James Joyce in the context of Dublin geography. Drawing from his own experience of Dublin from the late 1980s to the early 2020s, Winston's pedagogy considers the role of local geography and urban environment in Joyce's texts. It also serves as a very handy model for student study abroad trips.

Robert Berry's chapter 15, "Teaching Art Through the Prism of *Ulysses*," discusses his self-proclaimed "outsider's" perspective as an artist who teaches *Ulysses* to three very different audiences: English undergraduates, the public via an online course, and art students. In these courses he uses his background to teach art inspired by readings from the novel. Despite the fact that two of these categories might place this chapter in the context of the first section of the collection, we present it here due to Berry's training as an artist and his removal of Joyce's works from what most would consider to be a traditional English literature classroom.

The final chapter is Michael Patrick Gillespie's chapter 16, "Teaching *Dubliners* in Prison." Gillespie describes his experiences teaching at the Everglades Correctional Institution in South Florida. He provides great detail about both his dialectical pedagogy as well as the strikingly nontraditional facility and classroom in which he teaches. Gillespie outlines the logistic and pedagogical challenges of teaching in a correctional institution and also the power of art to reach across cultural, structural, and physical boundaries.

The essays in this collection openly wrestle with the dissonance between teaching content and teaching critical thinking. Goldman, in "Teaching *Ulysses* in Nonacademic Spaces," offers a wise alteration of the oft-used aphorism about fishing: "teach a reader *Ulysses*, they read it for one day; teach a reader to read *Ulysses*, they read it for life." He encourages us to recognize the differences between delivering content and teaching students how to think critically about that content. If the goal is to "learn" Joyce, one might simply take up residency in the PR section of their local library and settle in for an afternoon or decade of reading secondary criticism. For many of us, this sounds like a dream holiday. But, if one's goal is to learn how to "read" Joyce, the stakes are higher because, as the essays in this collection show, the process is communal. Reading James Joyce with others is not only a shared act of intellectual engagement but an opportunity to build tribal inclusion and ritualistic experience back into our otherwise solitary modern lifestyles. What that inclusion entails and how it reinforces the rituals we embrace continue to mold our contemporary pedagogy. We hope the conversations in this collection add to that already rich dialogue.

Notes

1 Richard Ellmann. *James Joyce: New and Revised Edition* (Oxford: Oxford University Press, 1982), 27.
2 Ellmann, *James Joyce*, 27.
3 The panel was chaired by Sean Latham, then still the editor of the *James Joyce Quarterly*, and the panelists included Ellen Scheible, Paul Saint-Amour, and Tim Conley.
4 Modern adaptations of Joyce's works abound, such as Tramp Press's *Dubliners 100: Fifteen New Stories Inspired by the Original* (2014), ed. Thomas Morris.
5 Margot Norris, ed. *A Companion to James Joyce's "Ulysses"* (New York: Bedford, 1998), ix.
6 O'Brien has published over fifty creative works including novels, short story collections, drama, nonfiction, and children's books.
7 Edna O'Brien. *James Joyce: A Life* (London: Penguin, 1999).
8 O'Brien, *James Joyce: A Life*, 171.
9 See Andrew Gibson, *The Strong Spirit: History, Politics, and Aesthetics in the Writings of James Joyce 1898–1915* (Oxford: Oxford University Press, 2013).
10 O'Brien, *James Joyce: A Life*, 171.
11 Letter to Henrik Ibsen, March 1901, in Richard Ellmann, *Selected Letters of James Joyce* (New York: Viking, 1975), 7.
12 James Joyce, *Finnegans Wake* (New York: Penguin, 1999), 210.6–12. Originally published in 1939 by Faber and Faber (London) and Viking Press (New York).
13 See Kathleen McCormick and Erwin R. Steinberg's edited collection, *Approaches to Teaching Joyce's "Ulysses"* (1993), which includes pedagogical discussions by Hugh Kenner, Bonnie Kime Scott, Cheryl Herr, Vicki Mahaffey, and more. See also Margot Norris's *Suspicious Readings of Joyce's "Dubliners"* (2003).
14 Dylan Emerick-Brown, *As One Generation Tells Another: Teaching James Joyce in the Secondary Classroom* (Lulu.com, 2020).
15 *Eureka Studies in Teaching Short Fiction* (Richmond, Eastern Kentucky University).
16 Janine Utell, "Are You Experienced? Teaching and Reading Joy(ce) through the Body," *Feminist Teacher* 17, no. 2 (2007): 136–50.

17 Sarah Townsend, "*Ulysses* Here and Now: Using Twitter to Teach Experimental Literature." https://cuny.manifoldapp.org/read/ulysses-here-and-now-using-twitter-to-teach-experimental-literature-55aa0c47-523b-4677-a663-3dddac18950f/section/a36b20a8-c506-413c-b935-032105f4b4b8

18 Catherine Flynn, *The Cambridge Centenary* Ulysses: *The 1922 Text with Essays and Notes* (Cambridge: Cambridge University Press, 2022).

Bibliography

Blythe, Hal, and Charlie Sweet. "The Romance of 'Araby.'" *Eureka Studies in Teaching Short Fiction* 9, no. 2 (Spring 2009): 102–8.

Blythe, Hal, and Charlie Sweet. "Using the Pop Culture Bridge to Get to 'Araby.'" *Eureka Studies in Teaching Short Fiction* 7, no. 2 (Spring 2007): 75–81.

Cole, Catherine. "Teaching James Joyce's Short Fiction: *Dubliners* in the Creative Writing Classroom." *Eureka Studies in Teaching Short Fiction* 7, no. 2 (Spring 2007): 45–52.

Doyle, Maggie. "Teaching James Joyce's 'The Dead' within the Confines of the Lecture Hall." *Eureka Studies in Teaching Short Fiction* 7, no. 2 (Spring 2007): 53–60.

Ellmann, Richard. *James Joyce: New and Revised Edition*. Oxford: Oxford University Press, 1982.

Ellmann, Richard. *Selected Letters of James Joyce*. New York: Viking, 1975.

Emerick-Brown, Dylan. *As One Generation Tells Another: Teaching James Joyce in the Secondary Classroom*. Lulu.com, 2020.

Flynn, Catherine. *The Cambridge Centennial* Ulysses: *The 1922 Text with Essays and Notes*. Cambridge: Cambridge University Press, 2022.

Gibson, Andrew. *The Strong Spirit: History, Politics, and Aesthetics in the Writings of James Joyce 1898–1915*. Oxford: Oxford University Press, 2013.

Goldman, Jonathan. "Teaching Ulysses in Nonacademic Spaces," in *Teaching James Joyce in the Twenty-First Century*, Editors Barry Devine and Ellen Scheible (Gainesville: University Press of Florida, 2025).

Hunter, Cheryl. "The Coming of Age Archetype in James Joyce's 'Araby.'" *Eureka Studies in Teaching Short Fiction* 7, no. 2 (Spring 2007): 102–4.

Joyce, James. *Finnegans Wake*. New York: Penguin, 1999. Originally published in 1939 by Faber and Faber (London) and Viking Press (New York).

Kalish, Catherine S. "Finnegan for Freshmen: Why Joyce's Most Difficult Work May Be Easiest for Students to Grasp." *Eureka Studies in Teaching Short Fiction* 7, no. 2 (Spring 2007): 114–18.

Kirby, Alan. "Why James Joyce Celebrated 'Ivy Day': Teaching a Case Study in Authorial Intent." *Eureka Studies in Teaching Short Fiction* 7, no. 2 (Spring 2007): 19–30.

Kleypas, Kathryn. "Teaching Narrated Monologue through James Joyce's 'A Little Cloud.'" *Eureka Studies in Teaching Short Fiction* 7, no. 2 (Spring 2007): 124–27.

Kosse, Jeffrey P. "'He Saw Himself as a Ludicrous Figure': Commodifications and Epiphanies in James Joyce's 'Araby' and 'The Dead.'" *Eureka Studies in Teaching Short Fiction* 11/12 (2015): 1–13.

Logsdon, Loren. "Leading Freshmen College Students Through a Discussion of Joyce's 'A Little Cloud.'" *Eureka Studies in Teaching Short Fiction* 9, no. 2 (Spring 2009): 167–76.

Mack, Elizabeth. "James Joyce's 'The Dead': A Three-Tiered Approach." *Eureka Studies in Teaching Short Fiction* 9, no. 2 (Spring 2009): 118–24.

Mayer, Charles W. "*Dubliners:* The Marriage Center and 'A Little Cloud.'" *Eureka Studies in Teaching Short Fiction* 7, no. 2 (Spring 2007): 6–18.

McCormick, Kathleen, and Erwin R. Steinberg, eds. *Approaches to Teaching Joyce's "Ulysses."* New York: Modern Language Association of America, 1993.

McKenna, Bernard. "'Fragrant Necrophilia': Empires and Revivals in 'The Dead.'" *Eureka Studies in Teaching Short Fiction* 7, no. 2 (Spring 2007): 31–44.

McKenna, Bernard. "Maria, Allegory, and Humanity: Teaching James Joyce's 'Clay.'" *Eureka Studies in Teaching Short Fiction* 9, no. 2 (Spring 2009): 27–42.

McKenna, John J. "A Guardian's Dilemma: Keirsian Temperament in James Joyce's 'Eveline.'" *Eureka Studies in Teaching Short Fiction* 9, no. 2 (Spring 2009): 43–54.

Norris, Margot, ed. *A Companion to James Joyce's "Ulysses."* New York: Bedford, 1998.

Norris, Margot. *Suspicious Readings of Joyce's "Dubliners."* Philadelphia: University of Pennsylvania Press, 2003.

Norris, Margot, ed. *A Companion to James Joyce's* Ulysses. New York: Bedford, 1998.

O'Brien, Edna. *James Joyce: A Life.* London: Penguin, 1999.

O'Reilly, Nat. "'I Could Interpret These Signs': Adventures in Teaching James Joyce's 'Araby.'" *Eureka Studies in Teaching Short Fiction* 7, no. 2 (Spring 2007): 82–89.

Ostrander, Luke B. "The Paralytic Affect in James Joyce's 'The Dead.'" *Eureka Studies in Teaching Short Fiction* 7, no. 2 (Spring 2007): 61–66.

Ropp, Terry Merrill. "AP English: Making Room for Joyce's 'Araby' and 'Eveline.'" *Eureka Studies in Teaching Short Fiction* 7, no. 2 (Spring 2007): 94–101.

Schultz, Matthew. "The Multiple Contexts of Joyce: Why New Historicism Works." *Eureka Studies in Teaching Short Fiction* 7, no. 2 (Spring 2007): 119–23.

Schwarze, Tracey. "James Joyce's *Ulysses* Meets Jon Stewart's *America (The Book):* What Do We Teach When We Teach Joyce?" *Eureka Studies in Teaching Short Fiction* 7, no. 2 (Spring 2007): 105–13.

Sharkey, Rodney. "'Araby': A Universal Story?" *Eureka Studies in Teaching Short Fiction* 7, no. 2 (Spring 2007): 67–74.

Snart, Jason. "Detached and Empty: Subtexts of the Unoccupied House in James Joyce's 'Araby.'" *Eureka Studies in Teaching Short Fiction* 7, no. 2 (Spring 2007): 90–93.

Snart, Jason. "In Aid of Teaching James Joyce's 'Araby.'" *Eureka Studies in Teaching Short Fiction* 9, no. 2 (Spring 2009): 89–101.

Townsend, Sarah. "*Ulysses* Here and Now: Using Twitter to Teach Experimental Literature." https://cuny.manifoldapp.org/read/ulysses-here-and-now-using-twitter-to-teach-experimental-literature-55aa0c47-523b-4677-a663-3dddac18950f/section/a36b20a8-c506-413c-b935-032105f4b4b8.

Utell, Janine. "Are You Experienced? Teaching and Reading Joy(ce) through the Body." *Feminist Teacher* 17, no. 2 (2007): 136–50.

I

Curricular Joyce

1

Teaching Joyce's *Portrait* to High School Students

Barbara M. Hoffmann

Why Teach *Portrait* to High School Students?

This question—why teach *A Portrait of the Artist as a Young Man* to high school students—asks many things.[1] Taken one way, the question asks why we should teach the novel to *high school* students as opposed to keeping books by notoriously difficult authors (whose works require a good deal of scaffolding) safely ensconced in college-level English courses, especially in classes that students actively choose, as opposed to the required-for-every-student high school English class. The question also refers to the choice of what texts end up in the curriculum: Why teach *Portrait* and not another novel—a newer novel, a novel by a marginalized writer, or a novel not staunchly embedded in the Western canon? There is also the practical question of why and how teaching *Portrait* helps achieve certain learning outcomes; putting aside the debate about standardized testing and state standards, decisions about what to include in the curriculum should responsibly consider how to prepare students for tasks that test them on such learning outcomes.[2]

The last question of practicality is a good place to start. In this chapter, I will be calling on my experiences teaching *Portrait* specifically in Advanced Placement Literature and Composition classes (hereafter "AP Lit").[3] The AP Lit class as it is practically implemented in high schools across the country can be very wide-ranging in what literature it includes, and teachers assign a variety of works, all of which can be used to prepare students for the exam. Briefly, the exam consists of two sections. The first is multiple choice, with five passages—two prose fiction (including drama), two poetry, and one either prose or poetry—each followed by a question set. The second section of the exam is the "free response" or essay section made up of three essay prompts: the first prompt asks students to do a literary analysis of a provided poem; the second a literary analysis of a passage of prose fiction; the third an analysis of a theme or idea in a text of their choosing. It is the third essay prompt (usually referred to as "Question 3") on which I will here focus for our practical *Portrait* purposes. For Question 3, the student may select any work of fiction to analyze in their response, but the exam also includes a list of suggested works the student may opt to write about. From 1970 to 2023, *Portrait* is tied with a few other books as the eighth most frequently cited book for Question 3 on the exam.[4] Is this, in itself, a good enough reason for teaching *Portrait?* Of course not, but it does point to the qualities of the novel that make it an excellent practical selection for a high school literature class.

The topic or theme that the exam's third open response question asks students to consider changes every year; the fact that *Portrait* has appeared on it so many times reveals how rich for analysis the novel is, how students can find so many things to respond to in the novel—particularly topics that high school students would have spent their high school English experience preparing to consider deeply by the time they get to the end of their AP Lit courses. For example, Question 3 on the 2010 exam quoted Edward Said that "'Exile is strangely compelling to think about but terrible to experience'" but also "can become 'a potent, even enriching' experience," and asked students to write about "a character [who] experiences such a rift and becomes cut off from 'home.'"[5] The 2011 exam asked students to "choose a character . . . who responds in some significant way to justice or injustice"; the 2005 exam asked students to consider a character who, akin to Kate Chopin's description of Edna Pontellier, "conforms outwardly while questioning inwardly"; the 2013 exam asked *the* question for *Portrait* enthusiasts: "select a single pivotal moment in the psychological or moral development of the protagonist of a bildungsroman. Then write . . . [an] essay that analyzes how that single moment shapes the meaning of a work as a whole."[6]

This 2013 question's reference to the term *Bildungsroman* highlights the excellent work that teaching *Portrait* can do for students later in their high school careers. Certainly, they may have learned the term *Bildungsroman* at some point and have read novels in that genre (*To Kill a Mockingbird; Kite Runner; Catcher in the Rye; The Adventures of Huckleberry Finn;* even *Harry Potter*). So, *Portrait* not only fits in with the trajectory of their literary education thus far but also provides the perfect vehicle to pivot into the higher-level academic work of interrogating some concepts they have been learning since middle school. For example, students may have learned and memorized a list of different points of view from which novels are told: first person, third person omniscient, third person limited omniscient, etcetera. *Portrait* provides students the opportunity to question a static notion of a text's point of view; students can discover moments that shift between Stephen's inner thoughts and the narrator's descriptions and can question why these shifts happen and what the relationship is between character and narrator.

In other words, *Portrait* is an opportunity to move from what Paulo Freire famously defined as the banking model of education "in which the students are the depositories and the teacher is the depositor" to a model in which teachers "must be partners of the students in their relations with them."[7] With *Portrait*, simple questions, such as "What is the point of view of this novel?" can no longer be answered with memorization/regurgitation or multiple-choice-style answers (first-person peripheral, say, or third-person omniscient); the answer must be explored and teased out (the point of view shifts, there are multiple points of view, there are overlapping points of view, etcetera). While there is still much scaffolding that the high school teacher of *Portrait* must provide, which will be addressed shortly, it is a novel that can put the student in the position of a scholar, equal to their teacher. The teacher can show them that scholars are still writing whole books on *Portrait*, still publishing on it regularly—and in particular that Joyce is exemplary of a writer whose work asks to be studied and re-studied. (High school students do love that famous line from Joyce about *Ulysses*: "I've put in so many enigmas and puzzles that it will keep the professors busy for centuries arguing over what I meant.")[8] There is still plenty to say about the novel and they can be the ones to say it: to find that moment no one has noticed before, that connection between two lines, that confluence of images, that embedded reference to a motif. This is not to denigrate their experiences in earlier English classes. *Portrait* can feel like the moment they've been preparing for throughout high school, the moment when they can take all of those terms and ideas they've learned and really apply them: They can interpret every line, every word!

As it turns out, the students themselves enjoy that feeling of accomplishment that comes from doing the work of inquiry and not merely regurgitating. Every year, I asked my students to complete a survey/reflection about the readings and assignments in AP Lit so I could adjust the course for future classes. One of the questions asked students what their favorite piece of writing was that they produced for the class. The answers from those who selected their *Portrait* essays reflect this satisfaction with true close reading. Several students mentioned the real enjoyment that came from looking at small details from the book, from finding so much to write about, from having the opportunity to be creative and to connect different parts of the novel together. They felt the analytical payoff that comes from intense close reading.

Therefore, *Portrait* can be an excellent opportunity for students to develop comfort in not immediately knowing—a chance to learn the patience that scholarship takes. High school teachers take it for granted now that students will look up whatever text they are reading online; in fact, there is such pressure for grades that students' desire to get the so-called right answer often has them Googling books before even trying to think about the texts on their own. The way that *Portrait* encourages and rewards deep, close reading of individual lines and passages helps them move away from the desire to find a single, big-picture "answer" or "meaning" (this desire often puts me in mind of the Billy Collins poem "Introduction to Poetry": "I want them to waterski / across the surface of a poem / waving at the author's name on the shore. // But all they want to do / is tie the poem to a chair with rope / and torture a confession out of it").[9] The complexity of Joyce's work is the antidote to students' desire for the "right" answer, and it is the ideal time to introduce them to John Keats's idea of "negative capability."[10] *Portrait* allows high school students a taste of the way that the study of any individual text or topic can be an inquiry into the way that knowledge is formed.

Finally, for me, the most important reason to teach *Portrait* to teenagers is because it is about them—in many ways, it was written for them. Discovering who you are and what your identity is separate from your parents or from the place and people you grew up with is what high school is for. That inquiry is their lived experience. Another question on the aforementioned end-of-the-year survey was always: "What was your favorite novel or play we read this year and why?" For the students who answered *Portrait* to this question, the idea that came up over and over was relatability. They related to Stephen's struggles, his identity crisis, his rebellion. This feeling students have of seeing themselves in Stephen can be the first point of access into a novel that certainly presents many teaching challenges.[11]

Problems and Solutions

While there are many good reasons to include *Portrait* in the high school curriculum, teachers will still face many pedagogical obstacles with such a complex book. Here, I hope to highlight some practical solutions to teaching *Portrait*. Students may have basic trouble following or understanding the narrative and, related to that, trouble with the complexity of the language. Teachers may wonder how much context they need to provide for students to understand the novel: Irish revolutionary history; Joyce's personal life; Greek mythology. One of the most important things for high school teachers of Joyce to remember—

one that almost goes without saying—is that this is one class of many that the students are taking. At the college level, taking a class on Joyce would likely indicate a self-selection bias of students particularly interested in literature. In high school, English is a requirement; even if a student is taking AP Lit, chances are they are doing it as part of a well-rounded schedule, not because they plan to be an English major. This may be especially true if the teacher and school advocate for inclusivity in AP classes.

Keeping in mind the diversity of interests of students in the high school English classroom, I suggest that my students' aforementioned responses form the basis of the overall foci of the unit: the excitement that can come from really delving into a complex text and the connection students feel between Stephen's experiences and their own. These two main foci reflect a confluence of two curriculum theories: the scholar-academic model and the learner-centered model. While curriculum theories are complex, have evolved over time, and have overlap in their approaches, it can be helpful to identify the underlying reasons for structuring a unit, such as the teaching of a certain novel, in a particular way. Briefly, in the scholar-academic curriculum model, the "teacher emphasizes that students should be very excited" because they "can explore the same questions scholars in [academic] fields ask."[12] The learner-centered approach "endeavors to educate people in the manner most appropriate to their stage of development."[13] Used together, these two curriculum theories can help balance a study of the Joyce who reveled in complex wordplay and the Joyce who captured what it means to exist as a human (and a teenage human at that).

Part of preparing students to tackle the complexity of Joyce's language comes from careful scaffolding not only of the novel itself but also of its larger place in the curriculum. Ensuring that students already know and have practiced recognizing and analyzing certain techniques in texts taught earlier in the school year will help them when they look at the torrent of techniques Joyce employs on every page of *Portrait*. For example, when students read *Macbeth* earlier in the semester, I had them carefully and methodically trace a single word throughout the text; this prepares them for an ongoing motif assignment they complete while reading *Portrait* (which I describe below). During the short unit on Greek tragedies that began the school year, I taught the myth of Icarus and Daedalus as part of the general background on Greek myth and culture. And the entire first quarter of the school year focused on close reading and on identifying and analyzing tropes, schemes, and other literary techniques.

High school is especially conducive to large-scale scaffolding: thanks to the collaborative curriculum planning that typically happens to some extent in high school English departments, a teacher can know exactly what the students have read before they come to their classroom. To refer to an earlier example, the high school teacher can know which books students read in previous classes that are examples of *Bildungsroman*. Outside of the curriculum, high school teachers often have more opportunities to see multiple sides of their students: the sports and activities they are involved in, the people they sit with at lunch, even their family situations. All of this background can help teachers engage in both the scholar-academic and learner-centered approaches.

Beyond this large-scale scaffolding, much can be done to help students connect to and understand the novel as they read it. To foreground the focus on students' personal connection with Stephen, starting with some learner-centered pre-reading questions can be helpful. Listing several and allowing students to respond to a few that they select gives them authority through choice; as their answers are discussed in class, students may choose to respond to some questions aloud even if they did not complete a written response. Some possible examples of pre-reading questions include:

1. What is your very first memory? When you picture it in your head, how does it appear—what can you remember?
2. Do any of your family members disagree about politics? Have you ever overheard, perhaps at a holiday dinner, your family argue about politics?
3. Do you have any habits that are exactly like your parents'? How do you feel about that?
4. What would be some good and some bad things about continuing to live in (name of town/city/state) for the rest of your life?
5. Can you remember an incident from your early childhood—even a small, minor incident—that is still affecting you now?
6. Do you have an idea of what you want to do after high school/after college? What made you decide that?

These questions are clearly designed to help students identify with Stephen's experiences, especially in the early part of the novel. But, as David Pierce reflects in *James Joyce's "Portrait": A New Reading*, "my initial difficulties ... were not so much about references to the world outside the novel as to tracking the course of the narrative."[14] Pierce recalls the types of questions he had on first reading the novel—"What has the boy done to merit such a punishment?"[15]—that the high school students might also have.

The difficulty students will face in understanding what is even happening in the novel can be mitigated by focusing students' attention on things they *can* see or notice. As David Bartholomae and Anthony Petrosky advise their students in *Ways of Reading*:

> When you read, you hear an author's voice as you move along; you believe a person with something to say is talking to you. You pay attention, even when you don't completely understand what is being said, trusting that it will all make sense in the end, relating what the author says to what you already know.... Even if you don't quite grasp everything you are reading at every moment (and you won't), and even if you don't remember everything you've read (no reader does—at least not in long, complex pieces), you begin to see outlines of the author's project, the patterns and rhythms of that particular way of seeing and interpreting the world.[16]

To help students with that difficulty of following the narrative, a motif-tracing project can focus students' attention on those "patterns and rhythms" even when they do not "completely understand what is being said."

Here is an example of what such a novel-long project looks like; such a project can then become a focus of an essay at the end of the unit.

> Background: Throughout *Portrait*, many recurring motifs help to unify this rather disjointed novel of a young man's inner thoughts as he becomes who he is—an artist. Pay attention to the following motifs that recur throughout the novel.
>
> Assignment: Choose three of the following motifs and note their occurrence throughout the novel. Note where the reference is and the context, and, if necessary, how this is an example of that motif. Make sure that you're not only looking for the *word*, but for images or feelings of the *idea* (for example, don't just note when something is literally made of ivory, but perhaps when something is white and cold, or perhaps a reference to a statue can call ivory to mind—see?).
>
> I ask you to do only three, but please read through this list, and if you note others, please feel free to jot it down. This is a very informal assignment: handwritten and sketchy is fine.

The assignment then lists several possible motifs from which to choose, including birds, ivory, smells, father figures, applause and performance, *The Count of Monte Cristo*, and others. Giving students a foothold they can return to throughout the novel helps them get through difficult parts without anxiety; they will focus on what they *can* understand, even if it's just a reference to a motif, and know that class discussion will help with the rest.[17]

In terms of the importance of class discussion, it doesn't help students' confusion about the narrative that the novel starts with one of its most difficult-to-follow sections. Spending a good deal of time unpacking that first section of Stephen's earliest impressions is worthwhile in grounding their understanding of the rest of the novel. Students can already see many of the motifs on the list in that first section. Beginning with an in-class close reading of the first forty-one lines also offers an opportunity to introduce some of the historical background on Irish politics, jumping off from the brushes in Dante's press and Stephen's punishment regarding his Protestant neighbor.

While there are many ways to go over this background, one excellent teaching tool for high school teachers looking to give students quick background information on just about any topic is YouTube. It takes some vetting, but there are wonderful videos out there that can give the necessary background in an easily accessible way. A few good ones include: "History Summarized: Ireland" (12 minutes)[18] and "The Animated History of Ireland" (10 minutes);[19] if you have time and want to give a bit of deeper background after these more general histories, add "Charles Stewart Parnell (Documentary)," which really gets into the background on Davitt and Parnell (17 minutes).[20] Beyond the historical background, teachers can use the first section to lay out what is at stake in the rest of the novel, while connecting back to students' own lived experiences of early childhood.

In line with directly introducing students to the history of Ireland, it can be helpful to be forthcoming about some things rather than to expect students to figure them out on their own. This leaves time for them to do deep, close reading of other moments of their choice. For example, giving students a list of difficult or obscure vocabulary is not denying them the chance to look things up on their own; it allows them to spend their time doing other work.[21] Because, as mentioned above, students will certainly look the book up online, it can also help to be forthcoming about the famous lines of the novel—such as the ones SparkNotes will list in the "important quotes" section. This gets the analysis of those out of the way in class so students can focus their own analytical work on sections and lines they are personally drawn to, allowing them to say something new about the novel rather than feeling like they must reiterate some "right" answer.

Scaffolding each section of the novel helps direct students in their personal discovery of lines they find rich for interpretation. Focused group work is an excellent way to enact the scholar-academic curriculum model. Productive group work should be modeled all year so that students are ready to work collaboratively by the time they get to reading *Portrait*; they trust that by collaborating with peers they will achieve more than by working alone. A sample in-class group work assignment looks like this:

Please discuss all the points listed below. Select one person in your group to record the thoughts/discussion of the group.

- Reread from the beginning of chapter 3 to the entrance of the rector ("Here he is!")
- Summarize *briefly* (for your own benefit; not mine) what is happening in these scenes. Look up and define any words that you don't know. Differentiate between what Stephen is thinking/reflecting on, and what is actually happening.
- Exploring the literary techniques Joyce employs from the beginning of the chapter to "Well now, Ennis," explain whether or not Stephen is enjoying his sins. Do not merely cite details; explore tropes, schemes, and other techniques. Feel free to refer to the many lists of literary techniques we've discussed over the year.
- Explore and discuss the imagery surrounding Mary.
- Discuss any symbols/images/diction/etcetera that recall earlier scenes. What concerns from our first day of discussion are recalled in this scene?
- Select two short passages within this larger passage (a short passage can be a phrase, a line, a few lines—whatever). Focus specifically on style: What weird things does Joyce do with his writing? What is the significance? What rhetorical schemes are employed? To what end? What tone is thus revealed? Look at syntax, diction, etcetera.

Each group is assigned a different small part of the chapter and asked a similar series of questions about it; the class then comes together, and each group shares its answers. Questions like this ask students to notice specific details on their own while also directing them toward the types of details that might be fruitful to explore.

While such heavily scaffolded activities help students see the richness of the text, more open activities can show students the way that Joyce makes every line in the novel worthy of close, careful attention. One such activity is the Word Dip;[22] it does take a lot of on-the-spot thinking on the part of the teacher as well as the students, and by its nature cannot be prepared for in any formal way other than knowing the novel quite well. In this activity, a student is selected at random and told to close their eyes, open to a random page, and select a random line/word. The class then analyzes that line. I would personally not do this activity with any other novel, and I tell the students that. I know that Joyce's writing works well with this kind of activity.

Beyond Close Reading

As mentioned above, students' enjoyment in reading *Portrait* comes not only from this detail-oriented engagement with the words of the text but also from students' personal connections with Stephen's experiences. One way of helping students make connections to their own lives is to engage with community resources, whether formal Irish heritage institutions or informal conversations with the people in their lives. I was fortunate to teach the novel in the Boston area, where there are many resources related to Irish heritage, such as the Irish Famine Memorial in Downtown Crossing.[23] But engaging with whatever resources you have available can create this connection. When I was teaching *Portrait,* another teacher at my school happened to be from Ireland, and I asked him to come speak to my class about growing up in Ireland or whatever else he wanted to talk about. He came in with a map of Ireland and a guitar and a hurling stick; he read sections of the novel in different regional accents as he pointed to those areas of the map; he sang a few Irish songs. Students were able to ask him questions about what it was like to grow up in Ireland, to read Joyce as an Irish person, and to understand more about different character types, such as Davin. In addition to grounding the novel in the lived experiences of Irish people, this serendipitous assistance from my colleague benefited student attentiveness, engagement, and learning by offering them a variety of teaching and learning modes: lecture, class discussion, videos, group work, and guest speakers.

While I am grateful that I had such a wonderful resource in that colleague, there are many ways to tap into community resources and students' experiences. The aforementioned strongly scaffolded reading of the first section of the novel that introduces students to Stephen's connection between personal identity and national identity can be supplemented by students' discussion of their own connection to their national identities or cultural heritages. Stephen's departure from Ireland at the end of the novel can initiate a discussion about students' parents or grandparents who may have left their homelands. Whether or not the teacher chooses to introduce postcolonial theory formally in these instances, the conversation itself is an introduction to the ideas thereof.

These lessons in the broader cultural connections to be made from Joyce's novel introduce another curricular theory that can help guide a teaching of *Portrait*: social reconstruction theory. Social reconstructionist teachers "assume that education is the social process through which society is reconstructed. They have faith in the ability of education, through the medium of curriculum, to teach people to understand their society in such a way that they can develop a vision of a better society and act to bring that vision into existence."[24] Social reconstructionists "begin with the assumption that the survival of our society is threatened by many problems" and that "underlying many of these problems are deep social structures—many based in Eurocentric conceptions of knowledge, culture, and values—that through the school's hidden curriculum subtly shape student beliefs and behavior in such a way that they, as both students and future adults, will contribute to the continuation and worsening of these problems."[25]

As Vincent Cheng highlighted in 1997, there was a shift happening from "the academy's estimation of Joyce as a revolutionary prose innovator within a high modernist context" to a "representing" of Joyce as "an anti-canonical, anti-imperialist, and even nationalist writer—via the lenses of contemporary postcolonial theory and cultural criticism."[26] Cheng asked if, by reading an author as canonical as Joyce as a postcolonial, subaltern voice "speaking against the discourse of empire," scholars were "displacing other subaltern, colonial, native voices."[27] Teaching Joyce's *Portrait* to AP Lit students and emphasizing these two sides of reading Joyce throughout the unit—the linguistic virtuosity and the commentary on colonial oppression—can open a discussion of canonicity and of the "school's hidden curriculum."

A great entry point for high school students on these issues is an open discussion of what books are included on that aforementioned list of works given along with Question 3 on the AP Lit exam. The list has shifted considerably in recent years, including more diverse and newer voices, so a teacher can ask her students why they think *Portrait* has remained a relatively consistent option. Pointing out that the most frequently cited novel on the Question 3 list is Ralph Ellison's *Invisible Man* can help students question the rigidity of the line between canonical and subaltern voices. As Cheng concludes, scholars can "use a postcolonial Joyce as a means to pry open, to shift, the criteria and perspectives for canonical inclusion—to make some room also for other, but *different* (and not previously canonized) texts from other cultures, as part of a process that can help illuminate a constant (if uncomfortable) awareness that imperialism and colonialism are still a fact of life."[28] It need not only be scholars who take on that task: it can start in the high school classroom.

Finally, while teaching *Portrait* to high school students might seem a daunting task with so much scaffolding and so much background that can be covered, teachers of Joyce might do well to summon the delight they felt the first time they read *Portrait*. I recall vividly my own first reading of *Portrait*, assigned to me in my AP Lit class over winter break, while on vacation with my family: little did my sister know, as she was trying to get me to come to the pool with her, that I was sitting in a classroom watching the dean of students lighting a fire and wondering what Stephen's answer will be to the call of the priesthood. With no background or knowledge of Irish history, I still fell in love with the novel, and I told my students as much. Openly sharing your own excitement and enthusiasm for a text with your students is often the first point of entry into a challenging work. While careful lesson planning is key to a successful unit, those comments from students who felt that they really related to Stephen hopefully reinforce that this is a very teachable novel for the high school curriculum.

Notes

1. I would like to acknowledge my own AP English teacher, Carla Stockton, who introduced me to *Portrait* while I was still in high school and thus prepared me to believe it is an excellent novel to teach to high school students, as well as AP Literature expert Tim Averill.
2. The debate about standardized testing is wide-ranging. In general, proponents suggest that they offer objective measures to help guide student improvement. Detractors suggest that they are classist, racist, and sexist, and that they only measure how good students are at taking tests.
3. This focus is not meant to be elitist or to suggest that students at all levels cannot benefit from reading *Portrait*; my AP class had no prerequisite level requirements other than students' expressing a desire to take the class and willingness to put in the hard work.
4. Several teachers and schools have, using the past exam questions made available on the College Board's website, amassed lists of the books that appear on Question 3. Here is one such list including the Most Frequently Cited books at the bottom: https://mseffie.com/AP/AP_Titles.html.
5. College Board, "AP English Literature and Composition Past Exam Questions," *AP Central*, 2022. https://apcentral.collegeboard.org/courses/ap-english-literature-and-composition/exam/past-exam-questions.
6. College Board, *AP Central*, 2022.
7. Paulo Freire, *The Pedagogy of the Oppressed: 30th Anniversary Edition* (New York: Bloomsbury, 2014), 75. ProQuest EBook Central.
8. Richard Ellmann, *James Joyce* (New York: Oxford University Press, 1982), 521.
9. Billy Collins, "Introduction to Poetry," *Poetry Foundation*. https://www.poetryfoundation.org/poems/46712/introduction-to-poetry.
10. John Keats to George and Tom Keats, December 27, 1817, in *Selected Letters of John Keats*, ed. Grant F. Scott (Cambridge: Harvard University Press, 2002), 60. ProQuest Ebook Central.
11. In the interest of full disclosure and appropriately tempered expectations, one student responded that she liked everything we read except *Portrait*.
12. Michael Stephen Schiro, *Curriculum Theory*, 2nd ed. (Los Angeles: Sage, 2013), 17–18.
13. Schiro, *Curriculum Theory*, 111.
14. David Pierce, *James Joyce's "Portrait": A New Reading* (Brighton: Edward Everett Root, 2019), 3.

15 Pierce, *James Joyce's "Portrait,"* 4.
16 David Bartholomae and Anthony Petrosky, *Ways of Reading: An Anthology for Writers,* 7th ed. (Boston: Bedford/St. Martin's, 2004), 2.
17 I also used this lesson to continue introducing students to literary criticism. I assigned the excerpt from Thornton Weldon's essay "The Bird Motif" so students can see, again, that the work they are doing is the same real, scholarly work that academics are doing on Joyce.
18 Overly Sarcastic Productions, "History Summarized: Ireland," November 22, 2019, video, https://youtu.be/RCCUEt8S61k.
19 Suibhne, "The Animated History of Ireland," May 24, 2017, video, https://youtu.be/dQvaGt9B6H0.
20 Protestant Irish Republican, "Charles Stewart Parnell (Documentary)," August 28, 2014, video, https://youtu.be/TaoMKQXx8co.
21 Providing students with an appropriately footnoted version of the book can also be helpful, but most high school teachers are constrained by what is available in the bookroom. I recommend that teachers have at hand the excellent Norton Critical Edition edited by John Paul Riquelme.
22 I admit that I first borrowed this technique's name after learning what a Bible dip was from Augusten Burroughs's memoir *Running with Scissors,* with a nod to the bibliomancy practiced in Wilkie Collins's *The Moonstone.*
23 For a list of Irish Famine Memorials in the United States, see: https://irishfaminememorials.com/united-states/.
24 Schiro, *Curriculum Theory,* 6.
25 Schiro, *Curriculum Theory,* 151.
26 Vincent J. Cheng, "Of Canons, Colonies, and Critics: The Ethics and Politics of Postcolonial Joyce Studies," *Cultural Critique* no. 35 (Winter 1996–97): 81.
27 Cheng, "Canons, Colonies, and Critics," 84.
28 Cheng, "Canons, Colonies, and Critics," 102.

Bibliography

Bartholomae, David, and Anthony Petrosky. *Ways of Reading: An Anthology for Writers.* 7th ed. Boston: Bedford/St. Martin's, 2004.

Cheng, Vincent J. "Of Canons, Colonies, and Critics: The Ethics and Politics of Postcolonial Joyce Studies." *Cultural Critique* no. 35 (Winter 1996–97): 81–104. https://jstor.org/stable/1354572.

College Board. "AP English Literature and Composition Past Exam Questions." *AP Central.* 2022. https://apcentral.collegeboard.org/courses/ap-english-literature-and-composition/exam/past-exam-questions.

Collins, Billy. "Introduction to Poetry." *Poetry Foundation.* https://www.poetryfoundation.org/poems/46712/introduction-to-poetry.

Effinger, Sandra. "MsEffie's List of Titles from Open Response Questions for Advanced Placement® English Literature Exams, 1970–2023." https://mseffie.com/AP/AP_Titles.html.

Freire, Paulo. *The Pedagogy of the Oppressed: 30th Anniversary Edition.* New York: Bloomsbury, 2014.

Joyce, James. *A Portrait of the Artist as a Young Man: A Norton Critical Edition.* Edited by John Paul Riquelme. New York: Norton, 2007.

Keats, John. "Letter to George and Tom Keats 27 December 1817." In *Selected Letters of John Keats,* edited by Grant F. Scott, 59–61. Cambridge: Harvard University Press, 2002. *ProQuest Ebook Central.*

Overly Sarcastic Productions. "History Summarized: Ireland." November 22, 2019, video, https://youtu.be/RCCUEt8S61k.

Pierce, David. *James Joyce's "Portrait": A New Reading.* Brighton: Edward Everett Root, 2019.

Protestant Irish Republican. "Charles Stewart Parnell (Documentary)." August 28, 2014, video, https://youtu.be/TaoMKQXx8co.

Schiro, Michael Stephen. *Curriculum Theory.* 2nd ed. Los Angeles: Sage, 2013.

Suibhne. "The Animated History of Ireland." May 24, 2017, video, https://youtu.be/dQvaGt9B6H0.

Thornton, Weldon. "The Bird Motif." In *Readings on "A Portrait of the Artist as a Young Man,"* edited by Clarice Swisher, 130–37. San Diego: Greenhaven Press, 2000.

2

"... the real Oxford manner"

Teaching *Dubliners* on the Foundation Year

Lloyd Meadhbh Houston

When the call for submissions for the present volume was circulated in the online Joyce-o-sphere, a senior figure in the field (in both years and standing) responded by commenting, "in the context of volumes such as these," they were "never sure precisely what was meant by 'teaching.'" While the comment may well have been meant dismissively—to "teach" Joyce in a didactic and programmatic way is, we might infer, a sleeveless errand, or an affront to the spirit of such protean and polyvocal writing—but, taken in good faith, the question it poses, or begs, merits consideration: What, precisely, do we mean by "teaching" in relation to Joyce's writing? What constitutes a sufficient account of it for readers? And what skills might we use it to cultivate along the way?

Such questions were thrown into relief for me in 2017, when a colleague and I selected *Dubliners* to serve as one of the core texts we would be teaching as part of a Foundation Year scheme being piloted at Lady Margaret Hall, one of the forty-four colleges that, along with the various subject faculties, comprise the University of Oxford. Modeled after a similar access scheme at Trinity College, Dublin, the Foundation Year was introduced under the auspices of the college's then recently appointed principal—the former *Guardian* editor, Alan Rusbridger—with the intention of offering young people from backgrounds traditionally underrepresented at Oxford (and in UK higher education more broadly) the opportunity to cultivate independent study skills, extend their subject knowledge, and increase their personal and academic confidence, with the hope of ultimately facilitating their entry into Oxford or another university as an undergraduate.[1] The participants were drawn from state schools with little or no history of putting students forward to study at Oxbridge, and encompassed students of color, students from migrant backgrounds, queer students, students with disabilities, neurodivergent students, students in care or estranged from their families, and students with disrupted educational histories. These young people were offered fully funded places at the college for one academic year, with free accommodation and meals, and a stipend to facilitate their studies and socializing. During the course of the year, they would be supported in applying to study their chosen subject at Oxford or at any other higher education institution they wished to attend.

For each of the four years in which I was involved with the course, two of the dozen or so students who participated in the Foundation Year elected to study English. Fifty percent of their timetable in each of the three eight-week terms that comprise the academic year in Oxford would be devoted to subject-specific tutorials involving the two English students and myself or my colleague—a permanent member of staff at the college with whom I was developing the module—while the other 50 percent would be given over to study skills and enrichment sessions involving the larger Foundation Year cohort.

We settled on a format in which the students would begin the week with a half-hour meeting, to which they would bring a paragraph or two of writing produced in response to a stimulus document we would provide, during which we would discuss the topic and workshop ideas for the essay. They would then spend the rest of the week developing an essay of 1,000 to 1,500 words, which we would reflect and share feedback on in a second, hour-long tutorial. The stimulus documents would feature two or three potential essay topics, combined with excerpts from relevant pieces of theory and criticism, and a suggested reading list. The intention was to provide the students with a robustly scaffolded but relatively open space in which to get to grips with the assigned material, allowing their interests and intuitions to guide them, while at the same time providing them with the primary and secondary materials necessary to give their insights nuanced and persuasive articulation.

A number of caveats are necessary here. Most obviously, I am conscious that these unusually small class sizes, and the intensive, highly personalized engagement they facilitate, are far removed from the lecture and seminar environments in which most readers of this chapter will experience teaching *Dubliners*. The idea of having one-and-a-half direct contact hours with two students every week for the better part of two months is a luxury few of us in contemporary higher education are able to enjoy. Nevertheless, I hope that the intensity and intimacy of the pedagogical encounters that undergird this chapter—and the inescapable presence of questions of privilege, gatekeeping, and elitism that the institutional setting in which these encounters took place made so acutely legible—will yield insights that can be usefully applied in other contexts. I also wish to make it clear at the outset that the following chapter will be as much a catalog of things I wish I had done—or had the insight, confidence, energy, and, above all, time to attempt—as it will be an account of what I actually did, and that most of what is valuable in what follows emerges, as is so often the case, from things my students taught me, rather than the other way around.

Why *Dubliners*?

A deliberate consideration in framing the course was not only the pedagogical value of close engagement with the literary material we would be studying—and the analytical and compositional skills the students would cultivate in the process—but the cultural capital they would accrue through their familiarity with the material in question. Confronted with a cohort of conventionally recruited Oxford candidates, we wanted the Foundation Year students to feel able to hold their own in conversation, speaking with confidence and insight about material that would be familiar, and perhaps even faintly intimidating, to their peers.[2] Yet, this necessarily begged its own considerations, particularly concerning canonicity, ingrained hierarchies of cultural value, and the degree of intellectual agency we wished to afford our students. What was needed, we thought, was a text that was:

a) widely known and well regarded,
b) short enough to be manageable in the time available, but,
c) sufficiently aesthetically rich and intellectually stimulating to merit a term's-worth of sustained scrutiny, and,
d) sufficiently internally variegated to offer multiple thematic pathways for students to explore in line with their own evolving interests and from a range of theoretical perspectives, while,
e) addressing a range of personal, social, and political issues that would be sufficiently interesting and relevant to students to inspire enthusiasm and encourage critical engagement, and,
f) affording the students the raw materials necessary to interrogate and problematize the framing of the course itself.

Like many educators before us, we found that *Dubliners* was one of the few texts to meet and, indeed, exceed every one of these criteria.

It is also a text that seems not only to invite but actively mandate a degree of reflective practice in how it is taught. Famously, *Dubliners*, as a collection, is patterned after the intellectual and psychological processes of *Bildung* with which modern notions of education and pedagogical philosophy, are closely implicated.[3] More specifically, as a wide body of scholarship has attested, it is a collection that takes as its subject the frustration, distortion, and malfunction of that process under the conditions of colonial rule: the forms of apparent arrested development that beset the "gratefully oppressed" (5.6–7) Irish subject as a result of, and in response to, British imperialism.[4] Hence one of the structuring paradoxes of *Dubliners*: it is a collection framed in deliberate relation to a normative paradigm of social, cultural, and psychological "development" that consistently contests the validity and perceived self-evidence of the assumptions and structures upon which such a developmental model rests.

Teaching *Dubliners* in the context of the Foundation Year—and, indeed, in any higher education context—actualizes a similar paradox. Put simply, how does one teach a text about the distorting effects of an elitist, materialistic, imperial culture—and a social, cultural, and political hierarchy that privileges elite, imperial intuitions—in an institution that exemplifies just such a culture and hierarchy, to students from marginalized social and educational backgrounds, without reproducing the same distortions, imbalances, and oppressions that the text documents? Our response was to take a cue from *Dubliners* itself, and to focus our attention on one of the key means by which the collection registers and dramatizes these distortions and the forces that enact them: its handling of the human body.

Literature and the Human Body: Teaching *Dubliners*

References to bodies abound in *Dubliners*. Few figures in Joyce's Dublin are as fortunate (or fastidious) as Maria in "Clay," who, notwithstanding "its years," finds herself possessed of a "nice tidy little body" (10.84–85), which she can regard "with quaint affection" (10.83). Some feel their bodies exceed their conscious control, manifesting an agency seemingly of their own, like Farrington's "great body" in "Counterparts," which aches to "rush out" of the office that confines it and "revel in violence" (9.145–46) or return to the "comfort of the publichouse" (9.203–4). Others, like the ascetic Mr. Duffy in "A Painful Case," seek to escape their body and its claims, endeavoring to live "at a little distance" from it, and regarding its acts "with doubtful sideglances" (11.40–42).

Many, especially among the collection's female cast, find their bodies the subject of (often unwelcome) approbation and desire, such as the "slavey," whose "stout short muscular body" is "noted approvingly" by the voyeuristic Lenehan in "Two Gallants," or Greta Conroy in "The Dead," whose "musical and strange and perfumed" body sends a "pang of lust" (15.1327–28) through her husband that "only the stress of his nails against the palms of his hands"

(15.1340–41) can keep in check. Every character in the collection, to some extent or another, confronts the reality of Judith Butler's assertion that "the body is always an embodying *of* possibilities both conditioned and circumscribed by historical convention" and, thus, constitutes "a manner of doing, dramatizing, and *reproducing* a historical situation."[5] Our hope in inviting students to approach the collection through this frame was to equip them to catalog these possibilities, identify the conventions that condition and circumscribe them, and explore the literary means by which Joyce dramatizes the historical situations in which the bodies of his narrative subjects find themselves, and which those bodies serve to reproduce.

To facilitate this approach and to ensure that students sampled a range of theoretical frameworks and methodological approaches across the course of the module, we decided to structure our sessions around a range of different bodily "situations" and differently situated bodies. Within these thematic clusters, we invited students to read the *Dubliners* stories in conversation with a handful of thematically cognate literary and nonliterary texts intended to illuminate the specificities of Joyce's approach, while simultaneously extending the students' frame of cultural and critical reference and giving our discussions a foothold in a range of social and historical contexts. Our session on "Gothic Bodies, Naturalist Bodies" paired "The Sisters" (in both its *Irish Homestead* and *Dubliners* iterations) with a translation of Guy du Maupassant's "Auprès d'un mort" ["Beside a corpse"] (1883) and Elizabeth Bowen's "The Demon Lover" (1945); "Disciplined Bodies, Deviant Bodies" examined "An Encounter" and "A Painful Case" in the light of George Moore's *Celibates* (1895) and selected sections of *"The Man Who Thought Himself a Woman" and Other Queer Nineteenth-Century Short Stories* (2016); "Bordered Bodies, Unbounded Bodies" brought together "Araby" and "Eveline" with sections of Bernardine Evaristo's *Girl, Woman, Other* (2019) and Rosaleen McDonagh's *Unsettled* (2021); "Desiring Bodies, Commodified Bodies" invited students to read "Two Gallants" and "The Boarding House" alongside extracts from Melissa Gira Grant's *Playing the Whore: The Work of Sex Work* (2014); "Producing Bodies, Consuming Bodies" placed "Counterparts" and "Clay" in conversation with Herman Melville's "Bartleby, the Scrivener" (1853) and David Graeber's "On the Phenomenon of Bullshit Jobs" (2013); while our final session on "The Dead" invited students to combine elements of all these approaches in whatever manner they found most productive.[6]

Each session was scaffolded with a selection of discussion prompts (short stimulus quotations and a question) and a range of extracts from relevant theoretical, critical, and contextual sources, and was paired with the corresponding chapters of Margot Norris's *Suspicious Readings of Joyce's "Dubliners"* and *Collaborative Dubliners: Joyce in Dialogue*, edited by Vicki Mahaffey, which served as companion handbooks to the module. Thus, for instance, our "Gothic Bodies, Naturalist Bodies" session was framed in relation to extracts from Joyce's famous May 5, 1906, letter to Grant Richards concerning the form and content of *Dubliners;* John Paul Riquelme's chapter on "Modernist Gothic" in *The Cambridge Companion to Modern Gothic;* Cathy Caruth's *Trauma: Explorations in Memory;* Sigmund Freud's "The Uncanny"; chapter 10 of Oscar Wilde's *The Picture of Dorian Gray;* chapter 2 of Bram Stoker's *Dracula;* Émile Zola's *Le Roman Experimental* [*The experimental novel*]; and Joseph Valente's *The Myth of Manliness in Irish National Culture, 1880–1922*—a selection I would now supplement with material from the opening chapters of Margot Gayle Backus and Valente's *The Child Sex Scandal and Modern Irish Literature: Writing the Unspeakable* and Catherine Flynn's chapter on "*Dubliners* and French Naturalism" in *The New Joyce Studies*.

In adopting this approach, we hoped to do justice to those "deceptively simple" elements of *Dubliners* that, in Norris's view, serve to make it so eminently teachable, even as they render the collection so pointedly resistant to didactic exegesis:

> For getting students to go beyond considerations of theme, and beyond considerations of style, even, to think about how textuality itself works, it would be difficult to find a better curriculum than *Dubliners*. The stories can be taught in a way that makes narration opaque rather than transparent to them and obliges them to interpret the narrative operation itself. The stories can help them see fiction as a text, as a bundle of dynamic meaning-producing strategies that put various possible, and often conflicting, interpretations into destabilizing and productive play. And the stories can help students to read self-reflectively, to think about how the text positions them as readers and provides them with prompts or invites their resistance. *Dubliners* can lead students into the act of reading as a meaning-producing *process* rather than as merely confrontation with a meaning-laden *product*. (16)

Of course, Norris's assertion that the stories *can* be taught in this way necessarily begs the question of how we in fact *should* be teaching them to achieve this effect. In the concluding section of this chapter, I will offer an account of how we approached our "Gothic Bodies, Naturalist Bodies" session, as a representative example of the challenges and opportunities *Dubliners* afforded in the context of the Foundation Year.

Case Study: "The Sisters"

In practical terms, then, how did we seek to encourage and equip students to engage meaningfully and productively with these deliberately "enigmatic" aspects of *Dubliners*, particularly as they pertained to the presentation of bodies in the text? One exercise we found productive in helping students to register and account for this tendency toward strategic elision, at both the level of literary technique and implication, was to have them compare the version of "The Sisters" that first appeared in the *Irish Homestead* on August 13, 1904, with the more familiar version that now opens *Dubliners*. While this comparison can be facilitated by assigning students Norris's commendably edited Norton Critical Edition of *Dubliners*, which usefully reproduces the *Irish Homestead* renderings of "The Sisters" and "Eveline" alongside an array of other contextual and critical matter, it also affords a valuable opportunity to introduce students to the *Modernist Journals Project*.[7] As Sean Latham has argued, reading Joyce's work "in the context of the articles, advertisements, illustrations and treatises amid which it first appeared generates a new sense of cultural richness and connection," which productively locates Joyce "within the very flows and contingencies of modern life which he so powerfully explores."[8] In our experience, providing students with the publication details for the story, but withholding the URL or PDF itself, and instead instructing them to locate it independently, yielded an often stimulatingly chaotic romp through the *MJP* archive that afforded a fruitful starting point for a discussion of modernist literary culture, its networks of circulation and reception, and its relationship to its paratexts.[9]

What sorts of things did our students uncover when they contrasted the *Irish Homestead* and *Dubliners* iterations of the story? In the context of a discussion of the body and the historical circumstances that condition it, the most readily apparent difference between the two versions concerns the depiction of the malady that besets Father Flynn, and the narrator-protagonist's relationship to it.[10] In its *Irish Homestead* form, "The Sisters" presents Flynn as the sufferer of a mental illness ("Upper storey ... gone" ["Stephen Daedalus," 676]) whose effects were exacerbated by his "scrupulousness" and brought to a head by the shattering of a chalice.[11] While this incident is undoubtedly replete with sexual connotations, these remain relatively oblique, the cause of Flynn's death is elided, and the word "paralysis" remains absent from the story. By contrast, when revising "The Sisters" to open *Dubliners* in the summer of 1906, Joyce introduced three instances of "paralysis" and its cognates into the narrative, in each case having the young narrator collocate the malady with references to "sin" (1.83) and Flynn's pathological need to confess.[12]

As most editions of *Dubliners* note (and as I would tend to inform students who expressed an interest in this element of the story), in contemporary clinical discourse "paralysis" served as a metonym for syphilis in its most infamous and debilitating manifestation: General Paralysis of the Insane (GPI).[13] Provided with contextual information on the symptomology, etiology, and sociocultural stakes of GPI in the late nineteenth and early twentieth centuries, students were quickly able to identify the ways in which Joyce's revisions reinforce the venereal connotations of Flynn's "paralysis" through the introduction of a range of physical details that closely resemble the symptoms of neurosyphilis: Flynn's trembling hands (1.105), grotesque smile (1.80), involuntary drooling (1.81), and mumbled speech (1.76), all of which could be taken to indicate a failure of muscular coordination consistent with advanced tertiary syphilis; Eliza's description of regularly discovering her brother "with his breviary fallen on the floor, lying back in the chair with his mouth open" (1.255–56), which suggests that the priest suffered from seizures caused by cerebral syphilitic lesions; the succession of strokes (1.1) that readers are informed have sealed the priest's fate.

Framing the story in this manner necessarily entailed asking students to think about the ways in which medical science was informing how late nineteenth- and early twentieth-century culture understood and depicted the human body and its relationship to its environment.[14] This approach was not without its potential pitfalls. As anyone who has invited students to read texts in the light of the history of medicine will know, such an invitation has a tendency to bring out a diagnostic impulse in students, who will seek to overcome or resolve the ambiguities of an obscure text through the reassuring certainties of nosology. *Dubliners*, with its beguiling combination of strategic opacity and legible debts to naturalism's "case study" approach to character and environment, seems particularly to invite (and utterly frustrate) this sort of reading.[15]

This empiricist impulse, with its emphasis on linear relationships of cause and effect and its tendency to over-reify characters, sometimes prompted students to produce responses to the stimulus texts that were, at best, reductive, and, at worst, unwitting inheritors of a turn-of-the-century impulse to pathologize perceived deviance: How do we know Flynn has abused the protagonist of "The Sisters"? Because he has syphilis. Why does Farrington beat his son in "Counterparts"? Because he is an alcoholic. And so on. However, when asked to explore what would happen if we were to read the stories of *Dubliners*, as Norris suggests, not as case studies of real people with actual ailments, but as representations and simulacra, rooted in codes and conventions that can be identified and analyzed, these students began to see how the collection could be used to interrogate and problematize this diagnostic impulse, and to identify the normative structures that underpinned the vision of health with which both the stories and their own critical exegeses were in conversation.

Encouraged, in the light of such conversations, to consider the ways in which GPI was held to violate the robust, continent, and well-regulated masculine body fetishized by both late nineteenth-century English muscular Christianity and advanced-nationalist organizations such as the Gaelic Athletic Association, students linked these revisions to the additions Joyce made to the story concerning the young protagonist's apparently deficient masculinity: Old Cotter's advocacy of outdoor play "with young lads his own age" (1.52–53), in implied contrast with the less salubrious forms of indoor "play" with which he associates Flynn; the boy's uncle, who teases him for his "rosicrucian" esotericism (1.55) before instructing him to "take exercise" (1.56), "box his corner" (1.54–55), and have "a cold bath" every morning (1.57); and so on.[16] As in many of our subsequent sessions, this element of the story—its intersectional engagement with the construction and inculcation of a normative masculinity—was one that proved particularly compelling to students, many of whom productively analyzed the relationship between gendered socialization, implied abuse, and trauma in the story in conversation with Bowen's handling of similar issues in "The Demon Lover." In both instances, students wrote passionately about the ways in which institutions and social formations apparently intended to vouchsafe the development of the subject along conventional, hetero-patriarchal lines—the Catholic Church and nationalist physical culture in the case of "The Sisters"; militarism, marriage, and motherhood in the case of "The Demon Lover"—ultimately frustrate and undermine their own ends, and, in the process, expose the artificiality of the supposedly "natural" categories upon which they are premised. Put another way, as my colleague and I had done when we first began to assemble the course, our students found in Joyce's writing a welcome invitation to reflect on the stakes of education (and miseducation) and the social, political, and cultural forces that inflect it.

Conclusion

As this overview illustrates, and as the skeptical senior Joycean I mentioned at the outset would, no doubt, be reassured to hear, our approach to teaching *Dubliners* was not, in itself, particularly radical or programmatic: we focused on one of the collection's key conceptual throughlines and used it to frame relevant clusters of stories in relation to a range of thematically cognate, but aesthetically and methodologically heterogeneous, literary and critical material. No wheels were reinvented here. Indeed, though I began this chapter with questions about how best to teach a text like *Dubliners*, ultimately, as the editors of the present collection suggested during one of our conversations about the project, the more salient consideration in the context of the Foundation Year was not so much "how" to teach *Dubliners*, as *why* to adopt it as the focus of our students' attention.

As this chapter has sought to demonstrate, *Dubliners* is an ideal text to teach in the context of an access and outreach program like the Foundation Year, not only because it is a canonical "classic" comprised of discrete yet interconnected units that reward close analytical scrutiny both individually and collectively but because it foregrounds and problematizes many of the issues with which access and outreach are bound up in an educational context. It obliges educators to reckon with the social structures and systems of power and prestige into which they are ushering students, or, at the very least, through which they are helping them to navigate, and it empowers students to reflect upon and critique those structures, even as it rewards their curiosity, attention, and insight. To echo the words of Margot Norris I quoted earlier, especially when placed in conversation with texts that allow its interrogation of the development of the normative subject to resonate beyond the confines of turn-of-the-century Dublin, it remains difficult to find a better curriculum than *Dubliners*.

Notes

1. Alan Rusbridger, "Alan Rusbridger on Building a More Inclusive University of Oxford," *Times Higher Education* (blog), April 20, 2016, https://www.timeshighereducation.com/blog/alan-rusbridger-building-more-inclusive-university-oxford.
2. For an overview of Oxford's selection procedures for undergraduates, see "How to Apply," *Faculty of English* https://www.english.ox.ac.uk/how-to-apply-undergraduate. For an outline of its tutorial-based teaching system, see "Personalized Learning," *University of Oxford*, https://www.ox.ac.uk/admissions/undergraduate/student-life/exceptional-education/personalised-learning. Historically, both processes have tended to favor candidates from elite, fee-charging schools with long traditions of sending candidates to Oxbridge.
3. For a recent critical reflection on the relationship between modernism and pedagogical philosophy and the implications of that relationship for our teaching of modernist texts, see Peter Howarth, "Introduction: Modernism and/as Pedagogy," *Modernist Cultures* 14, no. 3 (August 2019): 261–90.
4. James Joyce, *Dubliners: A Norton Critical Edition,* ed. Margot Norris, Hans Walter Gabler, and Walter Hetcche (New York: W. W. Norton, 2006). All citations to the collection will be given parenthetically by story number and line number.
5. Judith Butler, "Performative Acts and Gender Constitution: An Essay in Phenomenology and Feminist Theory," *Theatre Journal* 40, no. 4 (December 1988), 519–31 (521; emphasis in the original).

6 As the publication dates for some of these titles suggest, this selection of materials evolved and was subject to revision across the period in which I was involved with teaching the module.
7 Modernist Journals Project (searchable database), Brown and Tulsa Universities, ongoing, https://modjourn.org.
8 Sean Latham, "Twenty-First-Century Critical Contexts," in *James Joyce in Context*, ed. John McCourt, 148–59 (Cambridge: Cambridge University Press, 2009), 151. Also, Latham notes that a useful secondary resource for facilitating students' engagement with these contexts is David M. Earle's *Re-Covering Modernism: Pulps, Paperbacks, and the Prejudice of Form* (Burlington: Ashgate, 2009).
9 I have also found this exercise to have a salutary professionalizing effect, making students feel like they are engaged in "proper" research, in a manner that makes them more conscious of questions of evidence and provenance.
10 My handling of this material was inflected by my own research on the topic. See Lloyd (Meadhbh) Houston, *Irish Modernism and the Politics of Sexual Health* (Oxford: Oxford University Press, 2023), 107–15.
11 Stephen Daedalus [James Joyce], "The Sisters," *Irish Homestead*, August 13, 1904, 676–77 (676; 677).
12 Hans Walter Gabler contends that Joyce's most substantial revisions to "The Sisters" took place between June 23 and July 9, 1906. See introduction to *Dubliners: A Norton Critical Edition*, xxix.
13 Resources I found useful in introducing students to the nature, effects, and cultural connotations of tertiary syphilis in this period include Jennifer Wallis's "'Atrophied,' 'Engorged,' 'Debauched': Muscle Wastage, Degenerate Mass, and Moral Worth in the General Paralytic Patient," in *Insanity and the Lunatic Asylum in the Nineteenth Century*, ed. Thomas Knowles and Serena Trowbridge (London: Pickering and Chatto, 2015), 99–114; and Elaine Showalter's *Sexual Anarchy: Gender and Culture at the Fin de Siècle* (London: Virago, 1992), chap. 10 and "Syphilis, Sexuality, and the Fiction of the Fin de Siècle," in *Sex, Politics, and Science in the Nineteenth-Century Novel*, ed. Ruth Bernard Yeazell (Baltimore: Johns Hopkins University Press, 1990), 88–115.
14 Significant efforts to read Joyce's work in the light of the history of medicine and medicalization and the emergence of the critical medical humanities include Enda Duffy, "Corrigan's Pulse, Medicine, and Irish Modernism," in *Science, Technology, and Irish Modernism*, ed. Kathryn Conrad, Cóilín Parsons, and Julie McCormick Weng (Syracuse: Syracuse University Press, 2019), 183–202; J. B. Lyons, *James Joyce and Medicine* (Dublin: Dolmen Press, 1973); several works by Vike Martina Plock: "Joyce and the (Critical) Medical Humanities," in *The New Joyce Studies*, ed. Catherine Flynn, 208–21 (Cambridge: Cambridge University Press, 2022), *Joyce, Medicine, and Modernity* (Gainesville: University Press of Florida, 2010), and "Medicine," in *James Joyce in Context*, ed. John McCourt (Cambridge: Cambridge University Press, 2009), 250–61.
15 For an account of the collection's debts to French naturalism, see Catherine Flynn, "*Dubliners* and French Naturalism," in *The New Joyce Studies*, ed. Catherine Flynn (Cambridge: Cambridge University Press, 2022), 50–63.

16 The introduction to Valente's *Myth of Manliness* was a useful resource for helping students to think critically about these elements of the text.

Bibliography

Primary Sources

Bowen, Elizabeth. *The Collected Stories of Elizabeth Bowen.* London: Vintage, 1980.
Evaristo, Bernardine. *Girl, Woman, Other.* London: Penguin, 2019.
Graeber, David. *Bullshit Jobs: A Theory.* London: Penguin, 2018.
Grant, Melissa Gira. *Playing the Whore: The Work of Sex Work.* London: Verso, 2014.
Joyce, James. *Dubliners: A Norton Critical Edition.* Edited by Margot Norris, Hans Walter Gabler, and Walter Hetcche. New York: W. W. Norton, 2006.
Joyce, James. *The James Joyce Archive.* Vol. 4. Edited by Hans Walter Gabler, Michael Groden, David Hayman, A. Walton Litz, and Danis Rose. New York: Garland, 1977.
Joyce, James. *Letters of James Joyce.* Vol. 2. Edited by Richard Ellmann. London: Faber and Faber, 1966.
Looby, Christopher, ed. *"The Man Who Thought Himself a Woman" and Other Queer Nineteenth-Century Short Stories.* Philadelphia: University of Pennsylvania Press, 2017.
Maufrigneuse [Guy de Maupassant]. "Auprès d'un mort," *Gil Blas,* January 30, 1883, 1.
McDonagh, Rosaleen. *Unsettled.* Dublin: Skein Press, 2021.
Melville, Herman. *The Piazza Tales.* New York: Dix and Edwards, 1856.
Moore, George. *Celibates.* London: Walter Scott, 1895.
Stephen Daedalus [James Joyce]. "The Sisters," *Irish Homestead,* August 13, 1904, 676–77.
Stoker, Bram. *Dracula: A Norton Critical Edition.* 2nd ed. Edited by John Edgar Browning and David J. Skal. New York: W. W. Norton, 2021.
Wilde, Oscar. *The Picture of Dorian Gray: A Norton Critical Edition.* 3rd ed. Edited by Michael Patrick Gillespie. New York: W. W Norton, 2019.
Zola, Émile. *Le Roman Experimental.* Paris: Charpentier, 1880.

Secondary Sources

Backus, Margot Gayle, and Joseph Valente. *The Child Sex Scandal and Modern Irish Literature: Writing the Unspeakable.* Bloomington: Indiana University Press, 2020.
Butler, Judith. "Performative Acts and Gender Constitution: An Essay in Phenomenology and Feminist Theory." *Theatre Journal* 40, no. 4 (December 1988): 519–31.
Caruth, Cathy, ed. *Trauma: Explorations in Memory.* Baltimore: Johns Hopkins University Press, 1995.
Duffy, Enda. "Corrigan's Pulse, Medicine, and Irish Modernism." In *Science, Technology, and Irish Modernism,* edited by Kathryn Conrad, Cóilín Parsons, and Julie McCormick Weng, 183–202. Syracuse: Syracuse University Press, 2019.
Earle, David M. *Re-Covering Modernism: Pulps, Paperbacks, and the Prejudice of Form.* Burlington: Ashgate, 2009.
Flynn, Catherine. "*Dubliners* and French Naturalism." In *The New Joyce Studies,* edited by Catherine Flynn, 50–63. Cambridge: Cambridge University Press, 2022.

Freud, Sigmund. "The Uncanny." In *The Standard Edition of the Complete Psychological Works of Sigmund Freud*. Vol. 17. Translated and edited by James Strachey, 217–56. London: Hogarth Press, 1953–73.

Houston, Lloyd (Meadhbh). *Irish Modernism and the Politics of Sexual Health*. Oxford: Oxford University Press, 2023.

Howarth, Peter. "Introduction: Modernism and/as Pedagogy." *Modernist Cultures* 14, no. 3 (August 2019): 261–90.

Latham, Sean. "Twenty-First-Century Critical Contexts." In *James Joyce in Context*, edited by John McCourt, 148–59. Cambridge: Cambridge University Press, 2009.

Lyons, J. B. *James Joyce and Medicine*. Dublin: Dolmen Press, 1973.

Mahaffey, Vicki, ed. *Collaborative Dubliners: Joyce in Dialogue*. New York: Syracuse University Press, 2012.

Norris, Margot. *Suspicious Readings of Joyce's "Dubliners."* Philadelphia: University of Pennsylvania Press, 2003.

Plock, Vike Martina. "Joyce and the (Critical) Medical Humanities." In *The New Joyce Studies*, edited by Catherine Flynn, 208–21. Cambridge: Cambridge University Press, 2022.

Plock, Vike Martina. *Joyce, Medicine, and Modernity*. Gainesville: University Press of Florida, 2010.

Plock, Vike Martina. "Medicine." In *James Joyce in Context*, edited by John McCourt, 250–61. Cambridge: Cambridge University Press, 2009.

Riquelme, John Paul. "Modernist Gothic." In *The Cambridge Companion to Modern Gothic*, edited by Jerrold E. Hogle, 20–36. Cambridge: Cambridge University Press, 2014.

Rusbridger, Alan. "Alan Rusbridger on Building a More Inclusive University of Oxford." *Times Higher Education* (blog), April 20, 2016. https://www.timeshighereducation.com/blog/alan-rusbridger-building-more-inclusive-university-oxford.

Showalter, Elaine. *Sexual Anarchy: Gender and Culture at the Fin de Siècle*. London: Virago, 1992.

Showalter, Elaine. "Syphilis, Sexuality, and the Fiction of the Fin de Siècle." In *Sex, Politics, and Science in the Nineteenth-Century Novel*, edited by Ruth Bernard Yeazell, 88–115. Baltimore: Johns Hopkins University Press, 1986.

Valente, Joseph. *The Myth of Manliness in Irish National Culture, 1880–1922*. Urbana: University of Illinois Press, 2011.

Wallis, Jennifer. "'Atrophied,' 'Engorged,' 'Debauched': Muscle Wastage, Degenerate Mass, and Moral Worth in the General Paralytic Patient." In *Insanity and the Lunatic Asylum in the Nineteenth Century*, edited by Thomas Knowles and Serena Trowbridge, 99–114. London: Pickering and Chatto, 2015.

3

Teaching Joyce's Backstories

JULIEANN VERONICA ULIN

Early in Marcel Proust's *Swann's Way*, the narrator considers the "familiar figure" of Charles Swann as part of a larger meditation on the limitations of knowledge:

> [E]ven in the most insignificant of details of our daily life, none of us can be said to constitute a material whole, which is identical to everyone, and need only be turned up like a page in an account-book or a record of a will; our social personality is a creation of the thoughts of other people. Even the simple act which we describe as "seeing someone we know" is to some extent an intellectual process. We pack the physical outline of the person we see with all the notions we have already formed about him, and in the total picture of him which we compose in our minds those notions have certainly the principal place. In the end they come to fill out so completely the curve of his cheek, to follow so exactly the line of his nose, they blend so harmoniously in the sound of his voice as if it were no more than a transparent envelope, that each time we see the face or hear the voice it is these notions which we recognize and to which we listen.[1]

During my most recent experience teaching James Joyce's *Dubliners*, I've considered the above passage as both an invitation and a warning. As a metaphor for how one sees what one deems the familiar, Proust's transparent envelope captures both how a constructed narrative can conceal and fail to acknowledge what we do not see and cannot know and how narratives promising to convey the "total picture" circulate.

The backstory in Irish literature is given extraordinary predictive and explanatory power. In *Medieval Invasions in Modern Irish Literature*, I examined the construction and circulation of the twelfth-century origin story for the English presence in Ireland by twentieth-century writers returning to and reimagining the events of that period as a means to consider and critique the power of causal narratives. In what follows, I want to share how emphasizing the backstories within *Dubliners,* in which a character or the text itself accounts for a character's present or projects a future by way of a past, and attending to the limits imposed by these structures in some stories and to the narrative possibilities they release in others, creates a space where contemporary students begin to recognize the gaps in assumed total narrative or critical knowledge. In my own teaching of these familiar stories, those moments in *Dubliners* where the text encourages skepticism toward the explanatory backstory offered by the narrative or its characters serve as a warning against too complete a reliance on those interpretative frameworks that I recognize most fully and to which I have assigned a "principal place." Foregrounding these narrative or critical backstories and inviting students to question their impositions allow students to see themselves as "genuinely valuable . . . to the critical and interpretive production."[2]

As a collection, *Dubliners* opens and closes with stories that focus on the revelation of a character's backstory and serves as a particularly rich example of Joyce's use and subversion of this narrative technique. At times these backstories are self-constructed, as when the narrator's uncle in "The Sisters" accounts for his own vitality by declaring, "Why, when I was a nipper every morning of my life I had a cold bath, winter and summer. And that's what stands to me now."[3] Elsewhere, the narrative voice provides the backstory, incorporating the attempted murder of Mrs. Mooney by her husband in "The Boarding House" and a young Miss Devlin secretly eating Turkish delight and becoming aware of social gossip in "A Mother." "Ivy Day in the Committee Room" offers a number of instances that reflect a strong communal desire to fashion and affix backstories, knitting potential treachery in the present to betrayals centuries earlier. Elsewhere, characters are accounted for by way of a familial history. In "Grace," for example, Mr. Power declares emphatically of one family that "None of the Grays was any good" (*D* 170).

What interpretative and critical possibilities are released when we encourage students to notice these backstories? When we move them to the forefront? When we consider not only their efforts to contain and control interpretation but, often, their failures to do so? When we treat these moments in the text as more than ornament and instead as narrative surprises encoding possibility and demonstrating the limits of what can be predicted? Such an approach, in my experience, encourages students to look at the margins of literary texts, to question structures that seek to explain (in the text itself and, by extension, in criticism on that text), and to speculate in discussions of even the most canonical stories.

Here I focus on teaching *Dubliners* in spring 2023 in one of the two required courses for the master's in art degree in English students at Florida Atlantic University, Advanced Research Methods in English. The course must prepare first-year students in the program to write seminar papers and an MA thesis of forty to sixty pages. This was my sixth time teaching the course since spring 2018. The students complete six practical field challenge assignments designed to introduce them to research in literary studies (working with key library databases and special collections, locating archives and funding travel, responding to current calls for papers, finding author and literature journals and joining societies, choosing scholarly models for making critical interventions, and considering the state of the profession).[4] In each previous version of the course, I had used Joyce as the focal author and *Ulysses* as the core case study, pairing each episode with an article representing a specific critical approach. Terence Brown noted in his introduction to the Penguin Classics edition of *Dubliners* that it tends to "languish somewhat in the shadow of Joyce's other fictions" and that "[m]any critics of course tend to read *Dubliners* as an apprentice work by the master who produced *Ulysses*" (*D* viii, xxxi). In these earlier courses, despite the number of book-length studies not only of *Dubliners* but of individual stories that have appeared in the decade leading up to and through the centenary of its publication, the one or two classes devoted to *Dubliners* had inevitably made it feel like a backstory itself to Joyce's novels. Even with Brown's introduction elevating *Dubliners*, the appendix to the edition contains a list of the characters from *Dubliners* who appear in *A Portrait of the Artist as a Young Man* and *Ulysses*, with Brown writing that, "It can . . . be useful in reading *Dubliners* to know how the characters fare in the later work" (229). In the Spring 2023 version of the course, I was curious to see how *Dubliners* would fare on its own. Though I had taught *Ulysses* in graduate, undergraduate, and independent study courses for the centenary of its publication in 2022, this switch to *Dubliners* was less motivated by my own desire for a change and more inspired by recent exit surveys from the MA program's students and what I had noticed about student research interests in those *Ulysses* centenary courses.

Florida Atlantic University is the most diverse institution in Florida's State University System, is recognized as a Hispanic Serving Institution by the U.S. Department of Education, and is ranked no. 32 by *U.S. News and World Report* on the list for Top Performers on Social Mobility. With a few exceptions, the students in my courses do not enter the classroom with extensive knowledge of James Joyce or the approaches to his work that would be well known to anyone likely to read this volume. It is rare that a student in one of my classes has visited Ireland and rarer still that one of them mentions the mythic method, epiphany, or paralysis. It is not difficult for me to imagine teaching "a readership that does not know the critical history or the famous quotations from Joyce's letters to Grant Richards, that has not yet engaged with paralysis or any other critical lens."[5] While I provided extensive critical background and multiple interpretative frameworks for understanding *Ulysses* during my spring 2022 courses, my students' discussion, interests, and final research projects departed significantly from these approaches.

The three spring 2022 *Ulysses* courses I taught had, at the undergraduate, independent study, and graduate levels, produced especially strong student projects on neurodivergence in Joyce. During the semester, I had been struck by the change this brought to classroom discussions about Stephen Dedalus in both *Portrait* and *Ulysses*. In my experience, his character had posed significant challenges to students put off by his philosophically dense thinking, his fixation on religious structures obscure to most of them, and his standoffishness and isolation from peers and potential romantic partners. Now I had three levels of students excited to talk about him: his sensitivity to sound, smell, touch; his fixation on language; his repetition of phrases that soothe him; his detachment from those around him; his immersion into imaginative and fictional worlds from the opening page of the novel to *The Count of Monte Cristo* in the end; his difficulty in interpreting sexual or social cues.[6] More broadly, our strongest discussions during the 2022 semester were on topics like consent in Circe, "gifted kid burnout syndrome," student debt and Nestor, r/antiwork and the representation of labor in *Ulysses*. A strong interest in ecocriticism among the graduate cohort was evident in the enthusiasm for discussing Proteus and Cyclops. More than once, this left me holding my notes on twelfth-century Irish history or Great Famine memory and finding myself in the midst of a conversation on local beach cleanup efforts and the history of deforestation in Ireland.[7] Of the courses in which I have taught *Ulysses* over the past fourteen years, these students would not complete the course with the most thorough knowledge of the critical backgrounds for understanding Joyce that in my own writing and research I have found most illuminating. But the spirit of collaboration in their classroom close readings, the urgency in their discussions as they articulated the connections between the text and their own contemporary moment, their excitement for their research projects and presentations, and their belief in the stakes of these arguments made teaching those classes a truly distinctive experience, especially coming after the two preceding years of pandemic teaching, and, as it would turn out, before the availability of ChatGPT.

This experience was foremost in my mind as I turned to *Dubliners* for the MA graduate course. I wanted to do more to cultivate what I had sensed in the *Ulysses* courses by using the text of *Dubliners* itself to encourage students to try out interpretations of the text that they were less likely to encounter in a cursory internet search or, as the semester progressed, in their critical research. In *Suspicious Readings of Joyce's "Dubliners,"* Margot Norris writes that "For getting students to go beyond considerations of theme, and beyond considerations of style, even, to think about how textuality itself works, it would be difficult to find a better curriculum than *Dubliners*. The stories can be taught in a way that makes narration opaque rather than transparent to them and obliges them to interpret the narrative operation itself."[8] Focusing on the backstories provided by the narrative voice, by characters about others, and by characters about the self, encourages readers to arrive at "various possible, and often conflicting, interpretations."[9]

I had in mind Claire A. Culleton and Ellen Scheible's edited collection *Rethinking Joyce's "Dubliners"* and its call to "reconsider traditional tropes of paralysis and stagnation in favor of movement and change" as I thought about the possibilities present in backstories.[10] To that end, I wanted to approach *Dubliners* as a text that internally demonstrates the inadequacy of existing explanations, predictive causal narrative structures, and character backstories. In doing so, I hoped to facilitate "a full encounter with the individual story itself," inviting students to recognize these moments of disruptive tension within the text and to view any totalizing critical approach and explanation with a similar sense of skepticism (*D* xxxiii). An approach that foregrounds the backstory can estrange and energize the text in ways that resist the imposition of a predictive causal narrative structure and can be one way to shift discussions of *Dubliners* from the "stock" to the speculative.

Whether or not to be satisfied with explanatory frameworks is both an internal question for the characters from "The Sisters" through "The Dead" as well as one that we may pose to beginning students of literary research. *Dubliners* rewards reading aloud because it registers and inspires skepticism toward received narratives and invites its readers to question whether they have yet been told "all the story" (*D* 223). We began by reading "The Sisters" aloud in our first class meeting, and we continued to read aloud throughout the semester, not only for the pleasure of it but as an acknowledgment of the students' labor outside the classroom that may well mean that the texts have not been read at a pace that enables the best understanding and deep thinking. The most common Graduate Teaching Assistant assignment here involves teaching two nineteen-student sections of Writing Across the Curriculum composition courses while taking three graduate courses. Teaching two courses as a first-year master's student represents a significant undertaking, and most of the students struggle to balance their own coursework with their teaching assignment. In addition, the cost of living in the Boca Raton area means that many graduate students take on additional jobs to supplement their stipends. For these reasons that I know, and countless others I do not, reading aloud in class can be the best way to ensure an engaged classroom discussion. In beginning our course with "The Sisters," and by facilitating the students' auditory recognition of the pauses within the constructed backstories for Father Flynn's decline, I initiated our discussion of *Dubliners* in a way designed to encourage them as curious readers and questioning researchers. Rather than seeking to deny their feeling of dissatisfaction at the offered explanation at the conclusion of "The Sisters," I frame that sense of something missing as the spark of many research journeys.

Backstories, not unlike established interpretative frameworks, can exert extraordinary pressure. "The Sisters" allows the reader to witness the narrator's solidifying belief in the power of language and the stories one tells about the self from its opening paragraph: "[Father Flynn] had often said to me: *I am not long for this world*, and I had thought his words idle. Now I knew they were true" (*D* 1). This moment demonstrates how the narrator is already beginning his own process of assembling the story of Father Flynn's decline. But a story is simultaneously being constructed about him that joins him with the priest. The narrator is held "under observation," told how he will feel ("you'll be sorry to hear"), and aligned with the priest ("The youngster and he were great friends") (2). He is a nearly silent listener as his uncle and old Mr. Cotter classify him as affiliated with Father Flynn due to the narrator's disinclination to "take exercise" and to "run about and play with young lads of his own age."

Well before the most significant backstory constructed in "The Sisters," the narrative told by Father Flynn's sister of the reason for his decline, we watch the shaping of other stories and the narrator's powerlessness over them and dissatisfaction with them. Mr. Cotter's account of the priest's peculiarity is marked by ellipses, and the narrator is forced to try to "extract meaning from his unfinished sentences" (*D* 3). In pausing to think about another meaning of "sentence" here, the class can start to consider the relationship between the assembling of narratives and the judgment and pronounced rulings by internal characters, the narrative voice, and the reader. The use of ellipses in the two backstories for Father Flynn offered by Mr. Cotter and Father Flynn's sister Eliza resists the construction of an explanatory structure that would "sentence" Father Flynn according to Old Cotter's suggestive pauses and Eliza's own attempt to exert some narrative control over how her brother came to be a "disappointed man," his life "crossed" (9). Eliza states, "It was that chalice he broke. . . . That was the beginning of it. [. . .] That affected his mind" (9–10). The emphasis here is on locating the "beginning of it," the start of a backstory that will answer the narrator's mother's question "And was that it?" with the phrase in "The Sisters" final sentence, "of course" (10).

In a graduate classroom, "of course" is a phrase that can often inspire shame rather than skepticism. As one graduate student noted, their own experience of reading Joyce as an undergraduate was alienating precisely because his work was introduced solely in terms of its canonical status: "Without any background information or context about the text aside from that it was considered a great work of fiction in the literary canon, I felt embarrassed to ask questions about the history of the text and what to expect from the text. I got the feeling that it was assumed that I would already know, and as such, I was ashamed to ask."[11] When we finished reading "The Sisters" aloud, nearly all the students believed that what they have registered as missing in these attempted backstories may be found in the text somewhere. Mr. Kernan's question in "Grace," "How did it happen at all?" can be a difficult one to ask aloud as a graduate student; the pressure not to expose a limited understanding of a concept or a text can be significant (*D* 159). Reading the story together allows for the pauses to be heard by all. In this case a student's question immediately after our reading concluded, "What happened?" generated a productive discussion about how the offered backstories fail to fill in the gaps of those ellipses. Yet even this recognition could not prevent speculation as to what could, definitively, prove a solid backstory. On the first day of the course, with no advanced notice that we would be reading and discussing the story, the students assembled a range of possibilities for Father Flynn's decline ranging from a crisis of faith to Parkinson's disease—and for the narrator's retrospective return to this moment in his childhood from the formative power of early encounters with death to trauma from sexual abuse. Even in a text that provokes suspicion in explanations, we continue to search for them. If one lesson of "The Sisters" is to distrust the "of course," to understand that while it promises finality it leaves them in the dark (one of the many reasons the story teaches beautifully alongside Seamus Deane's novel *Reading in the Dark*), the discussion of this story can invite them not only to speak up when they do not understand something but also to point out the tensions, the gaps, and the elisions, within both the text and the criticism on it (*D* 10).[12] Foregrounding the backstories in *Dubliners* pushes readers into the margins and disrupts some of the more entrenched interpretations of these stories.

Throughout *Dubliners*, we witness the communal desire to affix causal narratives and fashion them into backstories that sentence their fellow Dubliners. As an exercise, asking students to locate moments in the text where such narratives are created can focus attention on a story that may otherwise challenge those without an in-depth knowledge of Irish politics. In "Ivy Day in the Committee Room," Mr. Henchy hands a young man a bottle of stout and remarks, "That's the way it begins," predicting future alcoholism (*D* 126). One suspected informer is characterized as "a lineal descendent of Major Sirr," the man responsible for the arrest of Lord Edward Fitzgerald and Robert Emmett (120). Candidate Richard J. Tierney is insulted by Mr. Henchy by way of his father, suggesting his trickery comes by way of a genetic predisposition: "But Tricky Dickey's little old father always had a tricky little black bottle up in a corner. Do you mind now? That's That" (120). The finality of "that's that," like the "of course" in "The Sisters," seeks not only to explain but to conclude discussion. While students can begin to connect the imposition of these structures with a kind of predestination or doom for the characters, they are also able to recognize that in a number of cases, no sooner are these convincingly stated causal backstories advanced than they are exposed as inadequate.

If Dublin is, in the oft-quoted descriptions from "After the Race," "a channel of poverty and inaction" occupied by the "gratefully oppressed," it nonetheless encodes change and surprise in a manner that resists the predetermined structure of the backstory (D 35). For all the critical emphasis on paralysis, for all the seemingly predictive power exerted by the backstory, *Dubliners* is rife with surprises that emerge in side remarks and micronarratives that show characters who have eluded a range of predictions. When inviting students to locate and consider how the presence of these nested backstories affects the stories, it comes to matter deeply that "An Encounter" opens not with Mahoney and the narrator, the two boys who will go on to have the title's encounter, and not even with Leo Dillion "the idler," who surrenders both his adventure stories and the adventure itself, but with Leo Dillion's older brother Joe:

> It was Joe Dillion who introduced the Wild West to us. [...] But however well we fought, we never won siege or battle and all our bouts ended with Joe Dillion's war dance of victory. His parents went to eight o'clock mass every morning in Gardiner Street and the peaceful odour of Mrs. Dillion was prevalent in the hall of the house. But he played too fiercely for us who were younger and more timid. He looked like some kind of an Indian when he capered around the garden, an old tea-cosy on his head, beating a tin with his fist and yelling: Ya! yaka, yaka, yaka! Everyone was incredulous when it was reported that he had a vocation for the priesthood. Nevertheless it was true. (D 11)

Why is this backstory introduced if not to imply a contrast between a wild, warring, fierce, and yelling boy and the priest he would become? To build in the possibility of a change that would inspire incredulity? And yet, a reader might equally invest the backstory with significance not as a contrast but as releasing the possibility of a wild, warring, fierce, and yelling priest. Even if Joe Dillion's choice comes as no little surprise to a reader inclined to give considerable weight to the influence of parents who "went to eight o'clock mass every morning," how Joe Dillion "turns out" does shock the narrator and his peers. And he is by no means the only character whose development takes an unexpected turn away from a seemingly predestined path.

When these backstories are moved to the foreground, *Dubliners* reveals its narrative surprises. We might think here of Jimmy's father in "After the Race," "who had begun life as an advanced Nationalist, [and] had modified his views early. He had made his money as a butcher in Kingston and by opening shops in Dublin and in the suburbs he had made his money many times over. He had also been fortunate enough to secure some of the police contracts and in the end he had become rich enough to be alluded to in the Dublin newspapers as a merchant prince" (*D* 36). Jimmy's father "in the end" occupies a position not predictable for one who began life as "an advanced Nationalist." Speaking of his son, the old caretaker Jack, in "Ivy Day in the Committee Room," asks "Who'd think he'd turn out like that!" and this sense of surprise at how people "turn out" works against the finality of the "private and candid opinion[s]" that are anything but private and that seek to explain people by way of their family histories (116, 121). Joe Hynes is no sooner described by Mr. O'Connor as "a decent skin" than Mr. Henchy counters this assertion by emphasizing not the familial association but the change from father and son: "His father was a decent respectable man. [. . .] Poor old Larry Hynes! Many a good turn he did in his day! But I'm greatly afraid our friend is not nineteen carat" (121). This unexpected turn, as in Jack's question "What's the world coming to [. . .]?" encodes the sense that, as Eveline thinks as she hears a neighbor walk along the path where once there had been a field, "Everything changes" (116, 29).[13]

When a character eludes a seemingly predestined path, it can "upset the equipoise" in the text (*D* 75). As he walks to Corless's for his reunion with Ignatius Gallaher, Little Chandler wrestles with how his "inferior in birth and education" (75) has outpaced him. Their impending meeting forces Little Chandler to adjust his perception of Gallaher by rewriting his backstory: "Ignatius Gallaher on the London press! Who would have thought it possible eight years before? Still, now that he reviewed the past, Little Chandler could remember many signs of greatness in his friend" (67). For Little Chandler, the present requires an adjustment to the past. He gives up his initial commitment to success stories rooted in being superior in birth and education and instead reckons with Ignatius Gallaher as "wild," "bold," and as having "a certain . . . something" (67). We have here another promised conclusion that opens rather than closes down possibilities: "*In the end* he had got mixed up in some shady affair, some money transaction: at least, that was one version of his flight" (67; emphasis mine). Subverting "the end" as just "one version" resists a definite account, returns us to the Proust quote at the start of this chapter, and exposes the instability of the constructed backstory. As Little Chandler begins to shape an alternate narrative explaining Ignatius Gallaher's success, he is confronted with his old friend's "new gaudy manner" that immediately places him at odds with Little Chandler, his "old chap" and "old man" and with "old jog a long Dublin" in the "old country" (72, 73, 74). We might be tempted to read this story as Ignatius Gallaher's declaration that Ireland is the country for old men, except that he breaks off his rendezvous with Little Chandler to seek better company in Dublin alongside his travel companion, a "clever young chap" (74). This appointment, which may not even be real, nonetheless creates possibility. There are other Dublins, and other Dubliners, here.[14]

If the speculative resides in the gaps and omissions of the agreed upon narrative, then *Dubliners* is a text that continually registers the inadequacy of the backstory and urges its readers to attend to the narrative potential that exists in imagining something that exceeds its attempt to impose limits. Perhaps nowhere in *Dubliners* is the gap clearer between the causal backstory and the end it is designed to explain than in "A Painful Case." Structurally, nearly half of "A Painful Case" is taken up with the backstory to Mr. Duffy reading the newspaper account of Mrs. Sinico's death. The newspaper account takes up another 15 percent of the story. The story, in other words, is weighted with imposed explanations.

Joyce most clearly flags the limits of the predictive power of the backstory by leaving a two-year gap between the end of Mrs. Sinico's relationship with Mr. Duffy and the start of her troubles. Four years pass from the time Mr. Duffy cuts off contact with Mrs. Sinico until he reads of her death in a newspaper. At the inquest reported in the paper after her death, Mr. Sinico reports that he and his wife "lived happily until about two years ago when his wife *began* to be rather intemperate in her habits" (*D* 111; emphasis mine). Their daughter moves the timing of Mrs. Sinico's decline up even further, noting that "of late her mother had been in the habit of going out at night to buy spirits. She, witness, had often tried to reason with her mother and had induced her to join a league." The multiple temporal words used here ask the reader to consider a problem that "began" two years ago, a "habit" that develops "of late" and that led her daughter to "often" try to reason with her mother, and Mr. Duffy's own supplied backstory of Mrs. Sinico's death.

For Mr. Duffy, the testimony that something causes a change in Mrs. Sinico's behavior within the period of the last two years is completely ignored. For him, the story that ends with Mrs. Sinico's death starts four years earlier, when he abruptly cuts off communication with her. But if the timeline offered in the newspaper account doesn't provoke Mr. Duffy's speculation, it can certainly invite our own. Two years are missing. Neither Mr. Duffy's offered backstory—

nor the backstories provided in the newspaper account—satisfy us. The reasons behind the sudden changes in Mrs. Sinico's behavior remain inscrutable. And this, I would suggest, is the point. Mr. Duffy asks, "Why had he withheld life from her? Why had he sentenced her to death?" (*D* 113). He later states with confidence "He had sentenced her to . . . a death of shame." Mr. Duffy has indeed "sentenced" Mrs. Sinico to a death of shame, but only because in his narrative construction of the backstory to her drinking and her death, he is the principal cause. But in the unaccounted for gap of two years, the text invites us to speculate.

In her essay "Redefining Ornament: An Argument for the (Seemingly) Inessential," my colleague Ayşe Papatya Bucak cautions against a too rigid commonplace in creative writing pedagogy that seeks to eliminate anything seen as inessential, ornamental, and not necessary for the forward progression of the plot: "No matter how short or long the piece, if it narrows its focus too much then surely some necessary context has been eliminated along with a portion of life's complexity and life's plurality. Ornament can be a surprisingly good way to remind readers of complexity and plurality. It can add contrast and it can add context."[15] *Dubliners* is hardly the first Joyce work to come to mind when thinking about a potentially excessive level of detail, but the backstories present in *Dubliners* offer an opportunity both for craft-focused discussions on the use of ornament and the (seemingly) inessential and for places where the presence of character and narrative-constructed backstories complicate and even resist the more conventional approaches to these stories that dominate the online summaries. Pragmatically, as I revise this chapter exactly two years after Open AI's release of ChatGPT, it strikes me that directing student attention to moments at the periphery of the text, to narrative microhistories assigned to the characters, and to backstories present throughout the collection, is all the more important as a way to encourage them to develop their own interpretative skills beyond what an AI-generated summary would be most likely to aggregate, hallucinate, or fabricate.[16]

So what effect did this focus on backstories and their troubling of the text have on the students' in-class discussions and submitted writing on *Dubliners*? First, discussing the backstories in the text and their impact on the characters in the present seemed to create a space for more personal discussions. Increasingly since 2020, I've been struck by the deeply personal connections students have made to modernism through our discussions of fragmentation, loss, pain, isolation, and subjectivity. Perhaps the focus on backstories in the text implicitly invites students to share their own. This was most evident in an early discussion of "An Encounter." Writing of a "forced and unwelcomed obedience" experienced by children in *Dubliners*, one student linked the moment in "The

Sisters" where the boy is "forced to bite his tongue and curb his anger at their remarks and slights" to the silence of the boy in "An Encounter," enduring the man's talk as his discomfort grows.[17] This led to a longer discussion about the boy's slow and outwardly calm response to the danger in which he finds himself in the moments before he leaves: "Lest I should betray my agitation I delayed a few moments pretending to fix my shoe properly and then, saying that I was obliged to go, I bade him good-day" (*D* 20). The narrator has been, as one student characterized it, "indoctrinated in politeness." After all, he is not one of those "National School boys" (19). But these behaviors are also strategies directed at not provoking anger that felt very familiar to those who had experienced terror in a moment of vulnerability. The narrator's overwhelming feeling of relief at Mahoney's recollection of their chosen aliases and willingness to play along brought up connections to moments of danger averted when someone—another person on the late bus, a bartender, someone who answered the door to a frightened random knocking, a stranger in a club, a shopkeeper—has gone along with a "paltry stratagem" and played along to offer some measure of protection (20).

When I asked students to consider the question posed by the editors of this volume, about how teaching Joyce can create moments of radical change, their answers focused on emphasizing the text's "representation of various struggles" and connections to today. A student used "Two Gallants" as an example and suggested focusing on the "marginalized and exploited," particularly those who "have been exploited in order to provide a profit for another."[18] The servant in "Two Gallants," she suggested, may end up feeling just as "real life victims end up feeling—alienated and dispensable" while exploitative behavior against them is "overlooked" and seen only as the basis for accessing a reward. Two decades ago, in *Suspicious Readings of Joyce's "Dubliners,"* Margot Norris wrote that "The narrative voice seems to promote a highly complacent representation of turn-of-the-century bourgeois Dublin life that papers over all manner of conflict, oppression, unhappiness, and injustice."[19] I've found that today's students respond far less complacently to what a narrative voice may relegate to the margins.

Second, compared to other courses in which I have taught *Dubliners*, there was far more attention paid to character change and transformation within the stories. In his chapter in *Rethinking Joyce's "Dubliners,"* Jim LeBlanc claims that the narrator in the opening story experiences an existential freedom following the death of Father Flynn, but that "the stories that follow 'The Sisters' in Joyce's collection depict an increasing disregard for, or at least a growing apathy toward, this sensation of freedom" and that in these later stories the "limits to personal freedom are usually self-imposed or intentionally unchallenged."[20] In their class discussions of "The Boarding House" and "A Mother" in particular, neither of which is discussed in LeBlanc's chapter, three students countered the trajectory he implies. These students considered how the characters' backstories indicate a drive to navigate and utilize existing religious structures to attain freedom from domestic violence ("The Boarding House") and demonstrate a capacity for transformation in the face of injustice ("A Mother").

In his writing on "A Mother," one of these three students used the textually supplied backstory in "A Mother" to locate a moment of transformation in which Mrs. Kearney resists the predictive power of her backstory, imagines, and attempts an escape from her circumstances. Joyce offers the reader several paragraphs of backstory in which we learn that Miss Devlin, who becomes Mrs. Kearney, eventually marries in order to silence gossip and speculation: "when she drew near the limit and her friends began to loosen their tongues about her she silenced them by marrying Mr. Kearney" (D 134). This student asked us to consider how the woman who so desires to silence gossip becomes by the end of the story the source of what Mr. O'Madden Burke calls "the most scandalous exhibition he had ever witnessed" (146). He viewed "A Mother" as tracing "a move from paralysis to (attempting to) break free of limitations. Initially, she succumbs: by mentioning the spite out of which Mrs. Kearney has chosen to marry, accompanied with information about her class surroundings, the text has provided the conditions under which Mrs. Kearney must negotiate her own freedom."[21] That the earlier Miss Devlin, secretly eating her Turkish delight and fixated on what is being said about her, transforms into the Mrs. Kearney we meet in the present indicates for this student both the inadequacy of the supplied backstory to predict Mrs. Kearney's present actions and her attainment of what LeBlanc describes as a Sartaean imaginative freedom in his chapter in *Rethinking Joyce's "Dubliners."* In class, another of these three students argued that in these two stories in particular, Joyce offers powerful visions of mothers raising adolescent daughters who, whatever our view of their methods, seem more than capable of adaptation and action. Rather than seeing these stories as ones in which characters "bemoan and wallow in their social, political, and religious circumstances," and in which they "refused to struggle effectively against, aim to transcend, or try to escape from the conditions that seemed to confine and paralyze them," these students found moments of resistance that joined with the sensation of freedom LeBlanc locates in the earlier narratives.[22]

Finally, attending to the textual presence of backstories is one way to create space in the classroom to question received literary and critical narratives and to focus on what remains opaque, an encouragement perhaps for students encountering a writer with a critical history as extensive as Joyce's. I encourage them to look for the gaps, to listen for the "silent discourse . . . that invites us to consider its obverse, to wonder if the story could be otherwise, or at least be told in another way. What the narrators fail or refuse to tell, as well as how they tell things, is always significant because it opens a silent counter-discourse that presses the possibility of an interpretation in opposition to that prompted by the narrative voice."[23] This acknowledgment can have the effect of conveying to students that there remains much for them to explore. I tell them that as readers and the times and places in which Joyce is read change, different moments in the text will appear to shift into prominence. I acknowledge that their preoccupations and questions upon reading these stories will be different from my own. The acceptance of this, which is really a relinquishing of my own interpretative control over these stories in the classroom, has allowed for conversations, connections, and critical interpretations that I could not have anticipated.

One such example may be seen in then-MA student Kate Wolfe's research, which builds on her undergraduate honors thesis at West Virginia Wesleyan College and seeks to discover a canon of asexual representations in literature and to develop an "asexual literary lens... that aims to rebel against compulsory sexuality."[24] Wolfe's research is focused on characters "described as 'backward' or 'odd,' since asexuality has long been understood as a social ineptitude or even an abnormality. The assumptions that asexual people do not love correctly, or that they are less than, prudish, or late bloomers, are all common in literary history and are thus prominent hints that a character may be asexual." Her first sustained reading of Joyce occurred during this semester. Her initial submission on "An Encounter" interpreted it as the narrator's encounter with compulsory sexuality. As she writes, "The story of 'An Encounter' is that of a young boy feeling [compulsory sexuality's] oppressive presence for the first time. In a compulsively sexual society, romance is often pushed on children before they are even old enough to understand the real concept of it. This is evident in how the old man is asking about the two boys' sweethearts. He asked the boy how many he had, and the boy answered none: 'He did not believe me and said he was sure I must have one. I was silent.'"[25]

Wolfe subsequently advanced an asexual interpretation of James Duffy in "A Painful Case," building on Ela Przybylo's work in *Asexual Erotics* in seeking "an alternative language for discussing forms of intimacy that are not reducible to sex and sexuality" but which is asexually affirming, recognizing the "ways in which compulsory sexuality is detrimental not only to asexual and nonsexual people but to all."[26] Wolfe argues for viewing James Duffy not as emblematic of paralysis, stagnation, failed *Bildungsroman*, or repression but as an ace character, one whose pleasure comes from "finding resonating and emotional attachments to things other than sexual relations. Through asexual erotics, one can find the same (or even more) happiness from things that ignite the soul. This is true for James Duffy."

Continuing to teach Joyce in a way that cultivates student interest in his work today requires that my own discoveries do not "in the end... come to fill out so completely" my approach to teaching the text that they come to suggest "that's that" (*D* 120). Writing this essay has caused me to recall some of my own experiences as a graduate student. In one memory, we have been asked why an author keeps returning to a particular number in a short story we have just read. Around the seminar table, speculation abounds. Abruptly, the professor declares that the answer is that the author had that number of siblings. All these years later, the silence that followed that declaration has stayed with me. The memory of that moment has stopped me on a number of occasions, though not all, of course, from intervening in a way that closes discussion on a textual moment. In another memory, we are sitting in Maud Ellmann's class when she asks us, "Is the James Joyce who wrote *Finnegans Wake* the Joyce who wrote *Dubliners*? What happens when we read Joyce backwards?" She had a reputation for posing these kinds of questions in class, and we recognized how they were designed to open our thinking, to surprise us, and to get us to speculate with her. Indeed, I recall a number of productive discussions outside of her class that began with one or more of us posing a "Maud question."

Sitting in the silence that follows an invitation to speculate can be challenging. The readers of and contributors to this volume have many answers at hand, many notions that we recognize, and many voices to which we have listened. There's a moment at the end of "The Dead," after Gretta has delivered a backstory of her own and fallen asleep, when Gabriel looks at her fallen boot and thinks to himself, "Perhaps she had not told him all the story" (*D* 223). It's a moment of humility for him, a recognition and acceptance that there are untold stories and backstories within and beyond the one he has heard. It is a valuable lesson from a fellow professor for those of us teaching Joyce in this contemporary moment.

Notes

1 Marcel Proust, *In Search of Lost Time, Volume I: Swann's* Way, trans. C. K. Scott Moncrieff and Terence Kilmartin (New York: Modern Library, 2003), 23–24.
2 Margot Norris, *Suspicious Readings of Joyce's "Dubliners"* (Philadelphia: University of Pennsylvania Press, 2003), 15.
3 James Joyce, *Dubliners,* intro. and notes by Terence Brown (New York: Penguin, 1993), 11. References to *Dubliners* are hereafter cited parenthetically in the text.
4 If you would like to see what these assignments look like, reach out to the author at julin@fau.edu.

5   Victor Luftig, "Review: Rethinking Joyce's *Dubliners*," *James Joyce Quarterly* 54, no. 3/4 (Spring-Summer 2017): 440.
6   In her undergraduate honors thesis, Nicole Rogers argued that *A Portrait of the Artist as a Young Man* was not only "one of very few authentic and unapologetic literary representations of the neurodiverse experience, but it serves as a testament to the historical presence, and undeniable importance of what remains a very underrepresented community today." Nicole Rogers, "A Neurodivergent Approach to James Joyce: Reimagining the Character of Stephen Dedalus" (undergraduate honors thesis, Florida Atlantic University, 2022).
7   Jacqueline Mullen completed an MA thesis in Spring 2023 focused on the Cyclops episode in *Ulysses*, building on the work of Yi-Peng Lai in *Eco-Joyce: The Environmental Imagination of James Joyce* (Cork, Irl.: Cork University Press, 2014). In addition to her GTA assignment, she worked as a tutor for a local company, where she read *Dubliners* with a tenth grade English Honors Student with a strong interest in creative writing: "He wrote an extended ending to Araby, which so far has been his favorite. He has also been working on a screenplay through Joyce's eye. . . . He really wanted to know about my thesis so I showed him my old term paper and what I had been working on now, and he was like, 'I want to read Joyce.' I'm like, 'okay then, we will start slow!'" (Jacqueline Mullen email to author, February 4, 2023). The majority of our MA students take teaching positions after graduation. I include this as an illustration of how one such student, deeply committed to her ecocritical approach, is open to exploring creative projects as a way of engaging a high school student with the work of Joyce.
8   Norris, *Suspicious Readings*, 14.
9   Norris, *Suspicious Readings*, 14.
10 Claire A. Culleton and Ellen Scheible, eds., *Rethinking Joyce's "Dubliners"* (New York: Palgrave Macmillan, 2017), 2.
11 Student Response A, "*Dubliners*: Submission One," January 18, 2023, Research Methods in Advanced Literary Studies, Florida Atlantic University.
12 Seamus Deane, *Reading in the Dark* (New York: Vintage International, 1998). For more on the intersections between "The Sisters" and Deane's *Reading in the Dark*, see Ulin, "'No sign of improvement anywhere': Phantom Development in Seamus Deane's *Reading in the Dark*," in *The Postcolonial Bildungsroman: Narratives of Youth, Representational Politics, and Aesthetic Reinventions*, ed. Arnab Dutta Roy and Paul Ugor (Edmonton: University of Alberta Press, 2025).
13 While the discussion here focuses primarily on character backstories, the history of place can also offer alternatives to paralysis and stagnation. The opening of "Eveline" makes for a good introduction to an exercise for students that asks them to locate such character, place, or historical backstories in *Dubliners* to consider how such seemingly ornamental backstories resist, complicate, or support a reading thematically focused on the main characters. She listens to a neighbor walk on the "cinder path before the new red houses." She recalls that "One time there used to be a field there in which they used to play every evening with other people's children. Then a man from Belfast bought the field and built houses in it—not like their little brown houses but bright brick houses with shining roofs. [. . .] Everything changes" (*D* 29).

The narrative's temporal signals (one time, then) suggest a fixed structure that the final sentence resists concluding. The beginnings of backstories, too, can prove troubling. The question "What is he exactly?" asked about Father Keon in "Ivy Day in the Committee Room" recurs in various iterations throughout Joyce (*D* 123). We might think here of how often Stephen Dedalus is asked to identify or define himself. At one point, Temple challenges Stephen by suggesting that a twelfth-century text provides a backstory that explains something about him in the present: "I know all the history of your family too, Temple said, turning to Stephen. Do you know what Giraldus Cambrensis says about your family?" (*Portrait*, ed. Seamus Deane [New York: Penguin, 1993], 250). Temple's boast ultimately proves empty; there is no mention of the Dedalus family in Cambrensis. Joyce gives Stephen the most potentially liberating backstory of all, an unwritten one. The Dubliners of *Ulysses* regularly attempt to define Leopold Bloom by constructing stories around him. The question of who or what someone is provokes considerable conversation and occasional anxiety for many of the Dubliners generating backstories.

14 "A Little Cloud" reveals how the speculative can torture; the knowledge of Ignatius Gallaher having exceeded his potential based upon his assigned backstory fills Little Chandler with a sense of dread. I've often paired this story with Philip Larkin's "Poetry of Departures," and it has led to some of the most revealing discussions on *Dubliners* I've encountered, with students talking about familial pressures for first-generation students, the inescapable curated online vision of the rise of one's peers, and fears of landing in a life both "Reprehensibly perfect" and soulless.

15 Ayşe Papatya Bucak, "Redefining Ornament: An Argument for the (Seemingly) Inessential," *Fiction Writers Review*, May 9, 2022, https://fictionwritersreview.com/essay/redefining-ornament-an-argument-for-the-seemingly-inessential/.

16 As an exercise, I entered a number of prompts into ChatGPT about specific embedded backstories in *Dubliners,* and the responses generated fused the backstories into the main narrative. When asked, for example, "What is the significance of the man from Belfast in 'Eveline'?," ChatGPT responded, "In James Joyce's short story *Eveline,* the man from Belfast—Frank—is a significant character, albeit one who is only partially developed in terms of backstory and presence." When asked about the former tenant of the narrator's house in "Araby," ChatGPT referred to the former tenant as the narrator's uncle in one answer, again collapsing the backstory into the main narrative. Its response to the question of the tenant's significance replaces his death in the back drawing-room with a different leave-taking: "The former tenant's departure without explanation could be seen as symbolic of the narrator's own eventual loss of innocence and idealism. Just as the former tenant has left the house, the narrator too will soon leave behind his youthful dreams and romantic fantasies." In its current form, at least, ChatGPT struggles to differentiate the backstory.

17 Student Response B, "*Dubliners:* Submission One," January 18, 2023, Research Methods for Advanced Literary Study, Florida Atlantic University.

18 Student Response C, "*Dubliners:* Submission One," January 18, 2023, Research Methods in Advanced Literary Studies, Florida Atlantic University.

19 Norris, *Suspicious Readings,* 9.

20 Culleton and Scheible, *Rethinking Joyce's "Dubliners,"* 55, 56.

21 Jamel West, "*Dubliners:* Submission Two," January 26, 2023, Research Methods in Advanced Literary Studies, Florida Atlantic University.
22 Culleton and Scheible, *Rethinking Joyce's "Dubliners,"* 64.
23 Norris, *Suspicious Readings,* 9.
24 Kate Wolfe, "Reading Asexually" (undergraduate honor's thesis, West Virginia Wesleyan University, 2022).
25 Kate Wolfe, "*Dubliners:* Submission One," January 18, 2023, Research Methods in Advanced Literary Studies, Florida Atlantic University.
26 Kate Wolfe, "*Dubliners:* Submission Two," January 26, 2023, Research Methods in Advanced Literary Studies, Florida Atlantic University.

Bibliography

Bucak, Ayşe Papatya. "Redefining Ornament: An Argument for the (Seemingly) Inessential." *Fiction Writers Review.* May 9, 2022. https://fictionwritersreview.com/essay/redefining-ornament-an-argument-for-the-seemingly-inessential/.

Culleton, Claire A., and Ellen Scheible, eds. *Rethinking Joyce's "Dubliners."* New York: Palgrave Macmillan, 2017.

Joyce, James. *Dubliners.* With an introduction and notes by Terence Brown. New York: Penguin, 1993.

Joyce, James. *A Portrait of the Artist as a Young Man.* Edited with an introduction and notes by Seamus Deane. New York: Penguin, 1993.

Luftig, Victor. "Review: Rethinking Joyce's *Dubliners.*" *James Joyce Quarterly* 54, no. 3/4 (Spring-Summer 2017): 437–41.

Norris, Margot. *Suspicious Readings of Joyce's "Dubliners."* Philadelphia: University of Pennsylvania Press, 2003.

Proust, Marcel. *In Search of Lost Time. Volume I: Swann's* Way. Translated by C. K. Scott Moncrieff and Terence Kilmartin. New York: Modern Library, 2003.

Rogers, Nicole. "A Neurodivergent Approach to James Joyce: Reimagining the Character of Stephen Dedalus." Undergraduate honors thesis, Florida Atlantic University, 2022.

Wolfe, Kate. "Reading Asexually." Undergraduate honors thesis, West Virginia Wesleyan University, 2022.

4

Black Lives and Irish Lives

Teaching and Reading Deesha Philyaw and Joyce in 2021

Mary M. Burke

I am a white Irish-born professor of English at the University of Connecticut, and my scholarly training, research, and publications are in the fields of Irish and Irish-American literature, cultures, and minority identities. For the most part, I am lucky enough to be able to teach the upper-level undergraduate Irish and Irish-American literature offerings on my campus in Storrs, Connecticut (as well as graduate seminars in these fields). I am also able to occasionally offer lower-level undergraduate genre courses, primarily Drama and the Short Story. In the fall semester of 2021, I was assigned to teach my university's 2000-level genre course on the latter. The following essay unfolds a collaborative engagement with James Joyce and Deesha Philyaw between instructor and students in the class concerned. In addition, the dialogue between the Joyce and Philyaw short story collections described below emerged to a huge extent from the writing and contributions of students. As such, this is their publication too, and I have listed their first names in the dedication at the close.

2021: Contexts

Before I delve into the specifics of the Short Story course and those who took it and the role the work of Joyce played therein, I want to draw attention to the date just mentioned. It was, on my campus and on many others, effectively our first fully "in-person" semester after the disruption of the previous three semesters due to the COVID-19 pandemic, during which most campuses made a sudden pivot to online teaching and, later, hybrid online-in-person formats. Just as relevant was that the semester was also only a year after the worldwide demonstrations against police killings of civilians in response to the May 2020

George Floyd case. Everywhere one went in the US Northeast in the months after, Black Lives Matter posters were on display. Alongside the disquiet of the lockdown and the demonstrations in support of BLM, the memory of the worldwide Women's March of January 2017 in response to Trump's inauguration also hovered. That eruption, in turn, had laid the groundwork for the #MeToo movement, named for a viral hashtag in response to the Harvey Weinstein sexual abuse case in late 2017.

The recent political urgency on multiple fronts combined with an awareness of students' ensuing fragility impacted what I wanted to achieve with the in-person Short Story course that semester. Such was my own over-vigilance going into that fall that I created an "online classroom" space for the course of the sort that had been my only "classroom" during lockdown as a safety net should we have to pivot online suddenly—for whatever reason. Nevertheless, in the fall 2021 course, I wanted to hold onto something of the tenor of my online and hybrid classes, which I hope is conveyed in the "special note" I appended to syllabi during lockdown:

> A syllabus is an aspirational statement of what we could and should do, but its usual promise of stability cannot account for the challenges we might face in the coming months: some may be attending class from different time zones, or experiencing physical or mental health issues, additional caretaking or work responsibilities, struggles with employment, inconsistent or inadequate internet access or workspace, or difficulty juggling multiple online and in-person formats. For these reasons, I will approach our time together with flexibility and empathy as it is inevitable that circumstances will arise that cannot be anticipated. We will focus as much on motivation and well-being as on course content as my priority is our physical, mental, and emotional well-being. To that end, the workload is lighter than usual for this offering. Altogether, I will be flexible about deadlines when required by individual or collective circumstance. Please be in touch if you are facing issues that impact your ability to participate fully. I want our virtual classroom to be a community for all of us in these unprecedented times.

Pairing Philyaw with Joyce

I have no deep expertise in the short story but enjoy teaching it because it is a form in which Ireland has excelled, so I can always justify including Irish writers on the syllabus. When I have taught that course in the past, I have assigned various editions of Ann Charters's anthology, *The Story and Its Writer*.[1]

Alongside writers from every corner of the globe, that volume also covers Irish practitioners of the form, from James Joyce and Frank O'Connor to Mary Lavin. Altogether, Charters's anthology facilitated a conventional and chronological survey, which could make for a perfectly adequate class. The semester of 2021 called for something beyond adequate, however.

In response to what was almost certainly going to be the continuing needs of students to have the classroom reflect and reflect upon recent collective experience, I went looking for new short story collections in the prior spring, when book orders are made for the fall semester. I was seeking something that was of its moment and had forwarded the short story form in some way. It occurred to me that Deesha Philyaw's *The Secret Lives of Church Ladies* (*SLCL*), an award-winning breakthrough collection centered on queer Black women that had been published in September 2020, was the book that the fall 2021 course needed.[2] Reviews suggested that the stories were loosely interconnected and all set in a very specific Southern Black Protestant community shaped by religion and in which identities had been forged by a shared troubled history. In short, here was a volume that could pair beautifully with James Joyce's *Dubliners,* a collection I knew inside-out from teaching it repeatedly in my Irish literature classes and from publishing on two of its stories, "The Dead" and "Clay."[3] *Dubliners* could be assigned alongside *SLCL* to make for a dynamic class that pulled contemporary Black evangelical America into conversation with colonial Catholic Dublin.

Philyaw's 2020 collection was of its specific cultural moment, particularly with regard to the wake of the #MeToo movement and the even more immediate context of Black lives (and deaths).[4] Indeed, in an interview, Philyaw herself referred to 2020 as the year of "'alleged racial reconciliation that wasn't.'"[5] In assigning these two collections to be read together, I hoped that the class could attempt to answer the very questions that Ellen Scheible listed in her May 2022 email to me regarding the present volume: "How do we consider marginalized readers, particularly women of color, queer folx, and Indigenous peoples, while teaching Joyce?"[6]

I should note at this juncture, before I delve into the specifics of Philyaw's collection and its reception in my classroom, that this essay assumes a certain degree of knowledge of *Dubliners* and Joyce. I also assume that other essays in this collection will discuss such specifics. In the interest of rebalancing the consideration given historically to white male authors at the expense of women authors of color, this essay will pay attention to Philyaw's stories and will mostly refer only in passing to Joyce's themes and the publication history of *Dubliners.* Furthermore, many references to reviews of *SLCL* and interviews with Philyaw in newspapers are provided. This is necessary in the absence of a body of critical engagements with a collection that emerged during a pandemic that slowed down the usual timeline of scholarly publication.[7]

Who Were My Students?

My Short Story class was offered for honors credit in the fall of 2021. I was the director of honors for English at the time, so I will admit to having been disappointed initially when not one English major or Honors English major signed up for the class. Instead, the students were overwhelmingly STEM majors of color. I remember only a small handful of students who identified as white during discussions in a class of twenty-three enrollees, the bulk of whom spoke of their Asian, South Asian, Latinx, African, and African American identities during discussion. Moreover, as I discovered when students were connecting stories to their own lives during discussions, many were either foreign born or the children of recent immigrants. Additionally, almost all came from beyond the usual relatively moneyed Catholic and mainline Protestant backgrounds of the students who tended to take my upper-level Irish literature classes. I suspect that this contributed to the tenor of openness and ease that soon took hold in the classroom, since that semester students born abroad, students for whom English was a second language, or students of color were not, as they sometimes have been in my Irish literature classes, the classroom's faces and voices of difference. Indeed, I, and the handful of white students in the class, were the faces and voices of difference.

In the fall of 2021, I was in the final stages of preparing a manuscript on race and Irish America that encompassed Irish Americans of color as well as a reading of "The Dead" through William Faulkner,[8] and believe that this experience was immensely helpful in that creative process. The presence of so many STEM students also meant that the gender balance was a little better than I was used to in teaching heavily English major enrollee classes, which always skew predominantly female. Altogether, I was just about to discover the answer to yet another question that Ellen Scheible listed in a 2022 email to me regarding this volume, namely: "How does Joyce appeal to savvy users of technology, scientists, and generalists who may not pursue the study of literature willingly?"[9]

Despite my keenness that the class materials might help us process recent collective trauma, they also needed to be fun. Joy, too, could be a weapon with which we could slay dragons, and reviews of Philyaw consistently drew attention to the joy in her work. My approach was to aim to spark joy in students for whom the college experience seemed to be—beyond any consideration of recent global trauma—a daily grind, according to their own testimonies: they were majoring in one or sometimes two challenging subjects and had to fit in the extra work necessitated by honors program requirements, all while thinking about graduate school for those in their final year. I wanted the classroom to be a small respite from the pressure—a space in which they could connect with wonderful writing and each other and gain confidence in their ability to appreciate fiction.[10]

Overlaps of Philyaw and Joyce

In a classroom dominated by STEM majors, I could not rely on a grounding in literary history of the sort I can assume when I teach classes populated mainly by English majors. There was freedom of sorts in this, since I began with a blank slate when introducing the short story tradition in the early weeks of class using Charters's anthology. I kept the narrative arc simple so that the emphasis would be on the joy of narrative and connection between texts, authors, and traditions. As such, the "story" of the short story in the opening weeks emphasized two strands: the formally and thematically conventional, "closed," didactic, and commercial tradition that peaked in the nineteenth and into the twentieth century as exemplified by Guy de Maupassant, and the innovation, open-endedness, and relative disregard for commercial success of the style inaugurated by Anton Chekhov. After getting grounded in these basics, we turned to Joyce's collection for the second part of the course and Philyaw for the third and final portion. Throughout the course, I set up discussion prompts and suggestions for the open-topic micro and long response papers so that one writer or text readily built upon what had already been covered. Therefore, by the time we turned to Philyaw, students were knowledgeable about Joyce and the short story form and were able to interpret her work in terms of precedence as well as on its own terms.

Philyaw's collection was rewarding in the context of the course's early emphases as she encompassed both traditions. *SLCL* was approachable and quite commercial in its straightforward naturalism and first-person voice, but there was a thematic freshness to the attention given to Black and queer women in the specific context of African American evangelicalism in the US South. (Philyaw's most formally innovative story is "Instructions for Married Christian Husbands," a list of written rules for the married men with whom the narrator is unapologetically conducting affairs.) One reviewer explicitly named *SLCL* a "collection of linked stories,"[11] and the implication that these lives lived in the same milieu could or did intersect echoed Joyce; although certain characters repeated across Philyaw's stories, students were often excited to speculate—

based on overlaps of setting, period, and other specifics—that an unnamed character in one story was possibly one and the same as a named character in another. One insightful essay also compared the roughly chronological order of Joyce's stories to how, in Philyaw's collection, "characters range in age . . . , but each story [moves progressively] closer to the present tense." Another saw the controlling trope of *Dubliners*, "paralysis," as being equally present in Philyaw's stories, concluding that "while Joyce ties religious belief . . . to mental paralysis, Philyaw focuses on organized religion" as the source of paralysis, "rather than belief itself." In short, students identified that *SLCL* was (however distantly) a descendant of *Dubliners*. They enjoyed plucking out the thematic overlaps of Joyce and Philyaw but could also see how the interconnectedness of the worlds built by both authors allowed the collections *themselves* to intersect.

Dubliners exposes the compromises required to conform to social, gender, sexual, spiritual, denominational, and political norms in the early twentieth-century Irish capital city. Philyaw, a Jacksonville, Florida, native who went to Black Protestant church services every Sunday alongside neighbors and family members right into her college years,[12] paints a similar picture of how church culture creeps into every aspect of existence for those raised in its orbit. It is striking that an Irish author whose own upbringing mirrors that of Philyaw's characters wrote one of the most incisive reviews of *SLCL:* Jan Carson, whose own acclaimed novel, *The Raptures* (2022), explores the similar territory of the effect of male-dominated evangelical Protestantism on rural and small-town Ulster women, penned what she knowingly called an "evangelistic" review of the 2022 Pushkin Press UK edition of *SLCL* in *The Irish Times:*

> [Philyaw's] stories resist lazy tropes at every turn. Her characters are complicated, messed up and easy to warm to. Her plots, tight little nuggets of tragicomedy. Each story feels like Philyaw has pulled the curtain back and allowed us to glimpse something private and intimate. Yet the gaze is never voyeuristic so much as affirming and empathetic. It's rare to read short stories which so generously reward the reader's curiosity.[13]

Carson concludes that Philyaw's "stories of dissent" will resonate "with any woman who's grown up in a community marked by religion and conservative values." For Carson, Philyaw's collection is "a defiant laugh in the face of dour religion and the men who use religion as a form of control." The women of *SLCL*, Carson concludes approvingly, "challenge the patriarchal constraints of their communities, question the more hypocritical aspects of both organised religion and the patriarchy, and ultimately demand the freedom to be themselves."[14] As Carson implies, Philyaw's gift was in drawing attention to the intersections of sexual and religious "non-conformism."[15]

The pairing of Philyaw with Joyce drew out their thematic and structural overlaps, making an early twentieth-century white male author from the edge of Western Europe much more approachable and comprehensible than he might otherwise have been. Joyce's stories respond to a Catholic and colonial Ireland dominated by both Rome and London, while racism, sexism, and homophobia are backdrops to Philyaw's sustained celebration of the lives, loves, and religious identities of queer or otherwise nonconformist Black women. The focus upon characters from a similar milieu could have become tiresome, but the *Dubliners*-like generosity regarding human failings renders each *SLCL* story a distinct gem. Like Joyce, Philyaw sets stories in a narrow social milieu where money is often tight and among characters who may well know each other. Like Joyce, it is a world in which many are connected by the pressures that shared religious culture creates. Respectability and churchgoing are entwined in both Joyce's Catholic Dublin and Philyaw's Black Southern Protestant America. Like Joyce, Philyaw depicts a world from which it is hard to escape, both physically and psychologically. Most strikingly, Philyaw's characters remain attached to the South even when they leave it. This allows that location to function (as Dublin does in Joyce) as a domineering presence across stories.

The inferiority complex of Joyce's poor, colonized, sectarian, class-conscious Dublin (so evident in "After the Race") challenged any presumptions students may have had about white privilege in that unfamiliar setting. Soon they began making connections between the hierarchies of empire implied in Joyce and oppressive American structures of race and heteronormativity that served as the background hum of Philyaw's stories. The hide-bound class and denominational divides of Joyce's stories led spontaneously to discussions of the Indian caste system by South Asian students and to the color divide of Protestant America by both African American and African students of that heritage. Students of churchgoing background gleefully seized upon Philyaw's often subversive nods to the Old Testament,[16] and used the Bible to refine readings of the authors: one essay comparing "the pernicious influence of parental and religious authority figures" in Philyaw's "Peach Cobbler" and Joyce's "Eveline" and "The Sisters" used the commandments "Thy desire shall be to thy husband, and he shall rule over thee" (Genesis 3:16) and "Honour thy father and thy mother" (Exodus 20:12) to center the discussion (KJV). Altogether, I found myself learning much in witnessing how students joined the dots between the worlds created by Philyaw and Joyce and the world from which they or their families originated.

Both Joyce and Philyaw depict how secrecy and suppression thrive in an overweening religious culture. Nevertheless, Philyaw attends to the inner lives of African American women, and the solace they find in each other, even in interdicted ways: the collection's opening story, "Eula," portrays two ostensibly straight forty-something female friends who spend every New Year's Eve in bed together. They have been having an affair for years, though the eponymous Eula is hoping to marry a man one day. She has internalized the heteronormative expectations of her church despite her queerness, as Philyaw implied in an interview:

> She is terrified of this idea of hell and eternal damnation. She doesn't want to acknowledge this relationship with her best friend, even when they are sitting there naked. That's how much of a hold that the dogma has on her. It's the shame, it's the fear, it's the guilt.[17]

Philyaw has described her stories as "the kinds of things that Black women whisper amongst ourselves. So, those are the secrets about how we navigate our full humanity, our full sexuality, our full sexual lives in the face of the church's teachings, which are, in many ways, antithetical to freedom, in particular, sexual freedom."[18] Religious hypocrisy and the seesaw from sin to repentance (and back again) emerges in Philyaw's tales as in Joyce's "Grace." For instance, the narrator of Philyaw's closing story, "When Eddie Levert Comes," remembers being perplexed by her mother's behavior in her earlier years:

> One Saturday night, you've got every blanket in the house draped over your head to drown out the sound of your mother's headboard banging against the bedroom wall as she hollers her soon-to-be-ex-best friend's husband's name. And the next Saturday night, she's snatching the softened deck of playing cards out of your hands because "Games of chance are from the devil." (*SLCL*, 167)[19]

Of course, the church is also a source of solace and community for many of Philyaw's older women characters, just as Catholicism sometimes allows for a consolatory loyalty to Rome above London within Joyce's colonial Ireland. For some students of South Asian heritage, the refusal of the British colonial master that inhered in practicing an "othered" religion was readily understood.

If Joyce's dysfunctional male-centered world references alcohol many times, then food could be said to serve a similar role in Philyaw's stories. In "Peach Cobbler," Olivia has been raised by a mother who saves her sweetness for a married pastor lover who comes by weekly for the homemade dessert of the title. (The revelation some way into the action that the young Olivia conflated the man of God *with* God explains the story's sassy opening: "My mother's peach cobbler was so good, it made God himself cheat on his wife" [*SLCL*, 39].) Olivia's mother dumps any leftovers rather than offering them to her emotionally neglected child. Food offerings are complicated in the stories: they serve both as marker of female servility in the context of heterosexual relationships and of female liberation and love offerings in tales centered on queer women. (Students were tickled when we discovered that the cover of what was then the forthcoming UK edition of SLCL was a close-up of a luscious and highly suggestive peach!)[20] In the aforementioned "Instructions for Married Christian Husbands," the grown Olivia is now the owner of a bakery that sells a renowned peach cobbler (SLCL, 147–49). However, like her mother before her, the damaged young woman makes do with other women's husbands for lovers, whom she treats with efficient froideur. Although comfort food often emerges as a salve to life's difficulties and a nostalgic link to Southern childhoods in Philyaw's stories, across "Eula" and "Peach Cobbler" sweetness is poisoned by inherited dysfunction and emotional unavailability.

A further overlap to which students gravitated was the slow and difficult journey to publication of both Dubliners and SLCL. Philyaw was published by West Virginia University Press only after several major New York publishers turned her down.[21] These rejections led her to fear that a book as "unapologetically black" as hers would never see the light.[22] Students also enthusiastically drew out the parallel complexity of the authors' attitude to their places of birth. Just as Joyce's fiction obsessively portrayed a Dublin from which he had long exiled himself, Philyaw now resides in Pittsburgh but still sets her stories in the South, a location for which she continues to feel "a deep nostalgia."[23] (Indeed, when the then fifty-year-old Philyaw returned to Florida to do a reading in the fall of 2021, it was the first time she had visited her home state since she left it in the 1980s.)[24] A further similarity that students drew out was that just as Joyce offered a portrait of Dublin that he claimed to be new to the world, Philyaw was hailed as a writer of stories "about Black women that haven't been told with this level of depth, wit or insight before."[25]

The contrasts between Dubliners and SLCL in terms of the depiction of family relationships and sexuality also inspired much lively class discussion and incisive written work. Whereas Joyce foregrounds *ostensibly* straight young and middle-aged men and fathers in the main,[26] SLCL portrays the complex connections between grandmothers, mothers, and queer or otherwise "nonconformist" daughters and sisters. In Philyaw, that nonconformity is generally linked to daughters' resistance to the politics of respectability and gender conformity of African American "church lady" culture.[27] One essay compared her story, "Snowfall," about a queer woman who chooses to abandon "the relationship she had with her mother because she decided to pursue happiness with her spouse," with Joyce's character Eveline, "forced to decide between a relationship or taking care of her family."

Nevertheless, and as many students examined in class and in the open-topic essays, Joyce and Philyaw overlapped in their attention to the damage done to children by adult caretakers who did not demonstrate care. The aforementioned "When Eddie Levert Comes" explores a daughter who grudgingly accepts the burden of looking after her senile elderly mother while remembering past trauma inflicted by that parent. Likewise, as with the unhappy husbands, fathers, priests, and uncles in Joyce, fathers, pastors, and male lovers are generally absent, ineffectual, short-lived, or disloyal in Philyaw's stories. For all of this, and in contrast to Joyce, Philyaw's tenor is rarely bleak, however. As an example, in "Dear Sister," a letter from Nichelle on behalf of her sisters to the half sister they've never met is prompted by the death of the feckless father they share. It is typical of Philyaw's woman-centered warmth that the story becomes a celebration of the successes of the sisters rather than dwelling on the failings of the wastrel father.

The sequence in which we read in fall 2021 enacted a kind of emotional restoration. Except for the uplift afforded by the close of "The Dead," for many students Joyce's stories stirred gloom. Philyaw's protagonists have often emerged from similarly dysfunctional and blighted histories, but her stories tended to celebrate female characters' resilience, strength, and the community found in other women. Altogether, as a class, we confronted trauma with Joyce but found healing with Philyaw.

Dedication

For the reasons described at the outset, the fall of 2021 had the potential to be disastrous in terms of my engagement and that of students. Instead, the work of James Joyce and Deesha Philyaw and their dialogue when placed side by side on the Short Story syllabus led to one of the most enjoyable classes I have ever taught. Therefore, I dedicate this essay to the members of class who made that happen, week after week, and with whom I plan to share this piece: Alijah, Alyssa, Anika, Anjeli, Ashanti, the two Carolines, Erika, Jiss, Julianne, Karina, Kyle, Luna, the two Mayas, Nick, Niyati, Olivia, Sahana, Sara, Sunaina, Vivian, and Wilona.

I hope that you all thrive in every way in the years to come.

Notes

1. Ann Charters, *The Story and Its Writer*, 10th ed. (Boston: Bedford/St. Martin's, 2019). In fall 2021, I used the tenth edition but have used earlier editions in previous years.
2. Deesha Philyaw, *The Secret Lives of Church Ladies* (Morgantown: West Virginia University Press, 2020). Hereafter cited as *SLCL*. Philyaw's debut marked "the emergence of a *bona fide* literary treasure." It was a finalist for the 2020 National Book Award for Fiction, received the Story Prize, the *Los Angeles Times* Art Seidenbaum Award for

First Fiction, and the PEN/Faulkner Award for Fiction. Marion Winik, "Unabashed breakers of rules," *Star Tribune* (Minneapolis), September 6, 2020.

3 Mary Burke, "Disremembrance: Joyce and Irish Protestant Institutions for Women and Children," *Éire-Ireland* 55, no. 1–2 (2020): 201–22; Mary Burke, "Forgotten Remembrances: The 6 January 'Women's Christmas' and the 6 January 1839 'Night of the Big Wind' in 'The Dead,'" *James Joyce Quarterly* 54, no. 3–4 (2017): 241–74.

4 Reviews nodded to these contexts: "In this year of constriction and pain, juicy goodness bursts from every page"; "Philyaw's stories are addictive while also laying bare the depth and vulnerability of Black women." Winik, "Unabashed breakers of rules." Lauren LeBlanc, "The Must-Reads of 2020's National Book Awards Shortlist," *New York Observer*, November 12, 2020.

5 Helen Ubinas, "The secret to success was in rejection," *Philadelphia Inquirer*, June 6, 2021.

6 Ellen Scheible, personal email, May 2022.

7 At the time of writing (August 2023), a search for the author in the MLA International Bibliography produces no results. Given Philyaw's success, this is likely to change.

8 Mary Burke, *Race, Politics, and Irish America: A Gothic History*, which came out in the United States with Oxford University Press in March 2023.

9 Scheible, personal email, May 2022.

10 I realized that we were getting there when one student's running joke during discussions about spotting emotionally vampiric relationships everywhere in our reading created the unforgettable essay title, "Please Tell Me Someone Else Noticed the Vampires in *Dubliners!*"

11 Alex Preston, "Fiction to look out for in 2022," *Observer* (London), December 26, 2021.

12 Marylynne Pitz, "Wilkinsburg Author Reveals 'The Secret Lives of Church Ladies,'" *Pittsburgh Post-Gazette*, November 1, 2020.

13 Jan Carson, "Sassy Sisterhood Stories" (review of Philyaw's *The Secret Lives of Church Ladies*), *Irish Times*, May 7, 2022, 17.

14 Carson, "Sassy Sisterhood Stories," 17.

15 In English church history, nonconformists were Protestants who did not "conform" to the governance and usages of the state church, the Church of England. In the Irish colonial context, northern Presbyterians (in which denomination Carson was raised) were considered nonconformist by the British authorities at certain junctures.

16 In "Jael," a teenage girl who covets her pastor's wife and takes violent revenge upon a lascivious older man is named for an Old Testament woman who hammered a tent peg through a male enemy's skull as he slept.

17 Pitz, "Wilkinsburg Author Reveals."

18 Brittany Brown, "How Black women and the church shaped Deesha Philyaw's writings," *Newstex Blogs/Mississippi Today*, June 23, 2021.

19 The double entendre of the verb in the story title "When Eddie Levert Comes," typifies Philyaw's impish humor.

20 See https://pushkinpress.com/books/the-secret-lives-of-church-ladies/.

21 Hillel Italie, "Deesha's Deal: Wilkinsburg Author Signs 7-Figure Contract for Next Two Books," *Pittsburgh Post-Gazette*, September 15, 2023.

22 John Self, "*The Secret Lives of Church Ladies* by Deesha Philyaw review—big characters with bigger appetites," *Times* (London), April 30, 2022.
23 "University of Mississippi: National Book Award Finalist Named 2022 Grisham Writer-in-Residence," *Targeted News Service*, August 19, 2021.
24 Julia Croston, "Jacksonville Author Deesha Philyaw Shares Her Inspirations," *Spinnaker* (University of North Florida), November 15, 2021.
25 Tony Norman, "A List of Things to Love in 2020," *Pittsburgh Post-Gazette*, August 7, 2020.
26 Recent criticism has argued for the queerness of many of Joyce's characters in *Dubliners*. However, the overwhelmingly STEM major class hardly delved beyond a surface reading of sexuality in *Dubliners*, possibly because queerness was so upfront in Philyaw that it was more readily engaging. Nevertheless, for a class of different makeup in which both Philyaw and Joyce were assigned, queerness could become a node of comparison too.
27 The most telling moment regarding this politics of respectability is in the Philyaw story in which the narrator's "church lady" mother lambasts her daughter for going without a girdle: "God forbid you are soft and unbridled." Philyaw, "How to Make Love to a Physicist," 108. Philyaw has noted in an interview that in the churches of her youth, "[women] did all the work, but the leaders were predominantly male." Peter Smith, "Majority in U.S. Belong to No Religion," *Pittsburgh Post-Gazette*, May 16, 2021. For the optics of church lady "respectability," see https://www.pinterest.com/murriellstokes/church-ladies/. For intersections of religion, respectability, prosperity gospel theologies, and gender that produce "church lady" culture and the allied disempowerment of Black women, see Eboni Marshall Turman, *Toward a Womanist Ethic of Incarnation: Black Bodies, the Black Church, and the Council of Chalcedon* (New York: Palgrave Macmillan, 2016) and Keri Day, *Unfinished Business: Black Women, the Black Church, and the Struggle to Thrive in America* (Maryknoll, NY: Orbis, 2012).

Bibliography

Brown, Brittany. "How Black women and the church shaped Deesha Philyaw's writings." *Newstex Blogs/Mississippi Today*, June 23, 2021. https://advance-lexis-com.ezproxy.lib.uconn.edu/api/document?collection=news&id=urn:contentItem:630C-Y471-F03R-N0GH-00000-00&context=1516831.
Burke, Mary. "Disremembrance: Joyce and Irish Protestant Institutions for Women and Children." *Éire-Ireland* 55, no. 1–2 (2020): 201–22. https://dx.doi.org/10.1353/eir.2020.0008.
Burke, Mary. "Forgotten Remembrances: The 6 January 'Women's Christmas' and the 6 January 1839 'Night of the Big Wind' in 'The Dead.'" *James Joyce Quarterly* 54, no. 3–4 (2017): 241–74. https://jjq.utulsa.edu/issue-54-3-4/.
Burke, Mary. *Race, Politics, and Irish America: A Gothic History*. Oxford: Oxford University Press, 2023.
Carson, Jan. "Sassy Sisterhood Stories" (review of Philyaw's *The Secret Lives of Church Ladies*). *Irish Times*, May 7, 2022, 17. Document IRTI000020220507ei570003e
Charters, Ann. *The Story and Its Writer*. 10th ed. Boston: Bedford/St. Martin's, 2019.

Croston, Julia. "Jacksonville Author Deesha Philyaw Shares Her Inspirations." *Spinnaker* (University of North Florida), November 15, 2021. https://advance-lexis-com.ezproxy.lib.uconn.edu/api/document?collection=news&id=urn:contentItem:6439-TVB1-DY7P-T0N9-00000-00&context=1516831.

Day, Keri. *Unfinished Business: Black Women, the Black Church, and the Struggle to Thrive in America.* Maryknoll, NY: Orbis, 2012.

Italie, Hillel. "Deesha's Deal: Wilkinsburg Author Signs 7-Figure Contract for Next Two Books." *Pittsburgh Post-Gazette,* September 15, 2023. https://advance-lexis-com.ezproxy.lib.uconn.edu/api/document?collection=news&id=urn:contentItem:695T-16S1-JC8R-336T-00000-00&context=1516831.

LeBlanc, Lauren. "The Must-Reads of 2020's National Book Awards Shortlist." *New York Observer,* November 12, 2020. https://advance-lexis-com.ezproxy.lib.uconn.edu/api/document?collection=news&id=urn:contentItem:618P-YMY1-DY6Y-M2D8-00000-00&context=1516831.

Norman, Tony. "A List of Things to Love in 2020." *Pittsburgh Post-Gazette,* August 7, 2020. https://advance-lexis-com.ezproxy.lib.uconn.edu/api/document?collection=news&id=urn:contentItem:60HY-X411-JC8R-318T-00000-00&context=1516831.

Philyaw, Deesha. *The Secret Lives of Church Ladies.* Morgantown: West Virginia University Press, 2020.

Pitz, Marylynne. "Wilkinsburg Author Reveals 'The Secret Lives of Church Ladies.'" Pittsburgh Post-Gazette, November 1, 2020. https://advance-lexis-com.ezproxy.lib.uconn.edu/api/document?collection=news&id=urn:contentItem:616B-KC91-JC8R-30CD-00000-00&context=1516831.

Preston, Alex. "Fiction to look out for in 2022." *Observer* (London), December 26, 2021. https://advance-lexis-com.ezproxy.lib.uconn.edu/api/document?collection=news&id=urn:contentItem:64CX-3401-JBNF-W355-00000-00&context=1516831.

Self, John. "*The Secret Lives of Church Ladies* by Deesha Philyaw review—big characters with bigger appetites." *Times* (London), April 30, 2022. https://advance-lexis-com.ezproxy.lib.uconn.edu/api/document?collection=news&id=urn:contentItem:65BG-B4N1-JBNF-W4FX-00000-00&context=1516831.

Smith, Peter. "Majority in U.S. Belong to No Religion." *Pittsburgh Post-Gazette,* May 16, 2021. https://www.post-gazette.com/news/faith-religion/2021/05/09/No-congregation-church-synagogue-or-mosque-no-problem/stories/202104290173.

Turman, Eboni Marshall. *Toward a Womanist Ethic of Incarnation: Black Bodies, the Black Church, and the Council of Chalcedon.* New York: Palgrave Macmillan, 2016.

Ubinas, Helen. "The secret to success was in rejection." *Philadelphia Inquirer,* June 6, 2021. https://advance-lexis-com.ezproxy.lib.uconn.edu/api/document?collection=news&id=urn:contentItem:62VK-V2N1-JC3R-B49V-00000-00&context=1516831.

"University of Mississippi: National Book Award Finalist Named 2022 Grisham Writer-in-Residence." *Targeted News Service,* August 19, 2021. https://advance-lexis-com.ezproxy.lib.uconn.edu/api/document?collection=news&id=urn:contentItem:63DD-0G81-DYG2-R0DS-00000-00&context=1516831.

Winik, Marion. "Unabashed breakers of rules." *Star Tribune* (Minneapolis), September 6, 2020. https://advance-lexis-com.ezproxy.lib.uconn.edu/api/document?collection=news&id=urn:contentItem:60SH-WB81-DYRH-900M-00000-00&context=1516831.

5

To Cause Students to Stop in Wonder

Using/Teaching Popular Culture in Joyce

GARRY LEONARD

In taking up the question "how to teach Joyce?" the follow-up question is bound to be "which work by which Joyce?" For the purposes of this essay, I am going to imagine a semester-long class covering *Dubliners, A Portrait of the Artist as a Young Man,* and *Ulysses.* The difference between preparing lesson plans for "Araby" and lesson plans for Joyce's two subsequent novels, might appear to be very different. But is this necessarily so? Whether I am teaching *Dubliners* to undergraduates, or *Ulysses/Finnegans Wake* in a graduate seminar, I often begin with the same question: "What is the difference between the word 'tree' and a tree?"

I explain this is intended as a "freewrite," which is to say, they are being asked to write, without stopping, for two minutes. I emphasize the phrase "without stopping" and unpack its implications: Do not pre-think. Do not formulate—just write. "Ambush your own thinking," I suggest. "This is not about right or wrong, better or worse, it is about spontaneous rather than premeditated." I then briefly leave the room to make this seem even less like an "academic" exercise. When I return, I draw a line on the board, designating two columns—one with the word "tree"—in quotes—and the other with a simple sketch of a tree.

Some among you will recognize this is an approximate copy of Ferdinand de Saussure's famous diagram illustrating his argument that the world is not the "word," and that the relationship between the signifier ("tree") and a signified (a tree, in fact) is arbitrary. Saussure goes on to draw an analogy to the game of chess: "The respective value of the pieces depends on their position on the chessboard just as each linguistic term derives its value from its opposition to all the other terms.... Language is a system of interdependent terms in which the value of each term results solely from the simultaneous presence of the others. . . . Signs function, then, not through their intrinsic *value* but through their relative *position*."[1] This allows me to suggest an initial way to "map" the apparently aimless quality of the boy's internal ruminating in the opening paragraph of "The Sisters": How, I ask, is he "positioned"? The boy acts like a pawn on a chessboard: someone with limited movement whose relative value is determined by other pieces (Old Cotter, his aunts, and most especially the recently deceased Father Flynn who has been "removed from the board," so to speak).

When his aunt takes him to visit "the house of mourning," presided over by Flynn's sisters, he sits in the corner of the room, his back to the wall, even refusing the crackers offered to him out of fear he "would make too much noise eating them."[2] The boy's behavior does not yet rise to the level of "silence, exile and cunning"—Stephen Dedalus's mantra in *A Portrait of the Artist as a Young Man*—but by highlighting for students his frightened, even paranoid, behavior, I am able to draw their attention back to Saussure's point that our relative value is both determined by, and dependent upon, the unresolvable tension between those words we use to identify ourselves, and those which identify us for others.[3] As I ask them to read aloud from their freewrites, I write their key word choices on the blackboard until, here too, there is a similar "chessboard" of contested space among competing positions.

I point out what I call, to coin a phrase, "the anxiety of the pawn"—and suggest it describes character after character throughout *Dubliners*, whose anxiety is so much about how they experience their "position" relative to words, relative to others. It is most pronounceable, perhaps, in the skittish Gabriel, who, indeed, seems unable to defend his "square" against the unmanageable encroachment of first Lily, then Molly Ivors, then his own wife, and then, finally, even the long-dead Michael Furey. Joyce conjures up, in story after story, this incalculable confluence of ineffable words on a wide variety of "anxious pawns." And this, I tell my students, is what makes Joyce a *modern* writer and, even more to the point, what makes Joyce *Joyce*. The determined lack of a traditional plot in the stories, for example, which they, as first-time readers might find so dismaying, is not regrettable, it is unavoidable because it is *modern*: "losing the plot" is what the story is about—it is, if we can manage to pause long enough to wonder, what *we* are about—forever stabilizing the perpetual slippage between the word and the world, which is to say between the "I" that speaks, and the "I" that is spoken, both by ourselves and by others. Or, as Jacques Lacan put it, "I identify myself in language, but only by losing myself in it like an object."[4]

The Joycean text, from the outset, cannot say what anything "means" because it wants to explore *how* meaning itself is *generated*, and how, in turn, that mystical signification—both malevolent and fascinating—modulates our struggle to signify ourselves to others. Words, because they are positioned in signifying chains, *generate* meaning(s). A word like "paralysis," in the existential sense, might *actually* paralyze. In the case of Father Flynn, it appears to have done so. The young narrator tells us he had thought the priest's words "*idle,*" but now he "knows them to be true" (*D* 7; emphasis mine). This causes him to reflect further on other odd-sounding words like "gnomon" and "simony"; it is not the single words he fears as much as the power they take on, when placed in a signifying chain. Their placement seems to summon a "maleficent and sinful being" and, from that point on, these deceptively "idle" words, through an imperceptible alchemy, begin their "deadly work" (*D* 7).

Of course, the freewrite is not intended as an introduction to the work of Saussure (though I usually do mention him in passing). Rather, this exercise, and this particular question, taken together, are intended to activate the students' awareness that somewhere between the word and the world is their own self-consciousness—in both senses of this hyphenated word: that is to say, on the one hand, their construction of self, and, on the other, its (rather vexed) relationship to their unstructured consciousness. When I invite them to read their freewrite aloud, ad-libbing as they go, if they wish, I steel myself to be an alert listener. What I am listening for is *word choice,* not sentences, and this is for two reasons: One, I can't hope to jot down whole sentences on the board as they read (nor would there be room). Two, I am most interested in single word choices, words they selected in haste, arranged with a high degree of spontaneity, such that a certain degree of unintended je ne sais quoi floats above and around their intended meaning.

The unmoored words offered up by my students gather and stir, detach and converge. I repeat the question that spawned this constellation: How are the word and the thing the same? How are they different? Silence, hesitation, then: "The word tree has *letters,*" someone points out. "A tree has *leaves,*" notes another student. "You can *read* the word 'tree,' but you can't climb it," says another. Or "you can *climb* a tree, but you can't read it," I add. Their citation of the act of "reading" as an active verb that, unlike "climb" cannot actually move, will prove useful in the discussion that follows. More follow: "You can *cross-out* the word tree, but you have to *cut-down* a tree." And "the word 'tree' can be put into *a mailbox,* but an actual tree would not even fit into *a house.*" And so on. By now, I have generated, both in their thoughts and in their feelings, what Stephen calls, approvingly, "a thought-enchanted silence," or more to my purpose, and with apologies to Billy Joel, "a Joycean state of mind."

In this potential state, one might go anywhere in Joyce (I leave the readers of this essay to test that out in the laboratory-conditions of their own classroom). But for now, and for the purposes of this essay, I am concerned with showing, more specifically, how I draw the students' attention to the presence, importance, and effect, in its many iterations, of popular culture in Joyce: billboards, newspapers, songs, advertisements, shop windows, half-completed thoughts, the half-realized fantasies of Stephen Dedalus and Leopold Bloom, and even the verbal fever-dreams of the epic sleepers in *Finnegans Wake*, a work where the letter becomes litter, and vice versa.

Allow me to pause and make a pedagogical point: This freewrite takes time to execute; but it also creates a learning atmosphere that carries forward beyond the specific class where it is initially launched, all the way to the end of the semester. And this is for the simple reason that, when successful, it meets the criteria of a proverb attributed to Confucius: "Tell me and I will forget, show me and I may remember; involve me and I will understand." In education, involvement is the key. As the teacher, just because you said it does not mean they heard it, much less that they will give it any further thought (beyond asking "is this going to be on the final?"). After seeing fragments of signifying chains scattered on the board, the students now may be said to have (to use a contemporary metaphor), "skin in the game." Whatever permutations arise going forward, they are part of it and can (justly) lay claim to having helped start it.

I then draw their attention to subtle differences in the two published versions of "The Sisters," the first version that appeared in the *Irish Homestead* in 1904, the second, and final version, a decade later, in the collection *Dubliners*. There are, as it happens, more than a few differences; but my intention in juxtaposing the two versions is to establish the rapidly growing emergence of popular culture in Dublin as something Joyce brought into his fiction to meet his stated goal of showing his fellow Irish citizens the pervasiveness of "moral paralysis" in Dublin. To begin, I juxtapose these two sentences, one from the first version, the next from the second:

> As I stood *looking* up at the crape and the card that bore his name *I could not realise* that he was dead. (*Irish Homestead*; emphasis mine)[5]

> The *reading* of the card *persuaded me* that he was dead and I was disturbed to find myself at check. (*D* 12; emphasis mine)

In both cases, the boy ruminates about the death of the priest. But in the first instance, though he looks at the card, it makes no impression: He still cannot "realize" Father Flynn is dead. In the second, however, he *reads* the card and is "persuaded" that, in fact, the priest is dead. An apparently small point in a single story, but it speaks volumes: In one instance the boy stands apart from words, alienated; in the next version, however, they "persuade."

Furthermore, in the *Irish Homestead* version, his mobility is arrested at this point: We get no report of him walking away. Instead, at the end of the rumination, we are told, in a sort of narrative jump-cut "[t]hat evening my aunt visited the house of mourning and took me with her" (677). This is still very much in the passive voice. Despite *looking* at the card, he is *unable* to "realise he was dead." In the amended version of the story, however, he does not "look" at the card, he *reads* it and, in contradiction to the first version of the story, he is (active voice) "persuaded . . . that he was dead" (*D* 12). Looking at the word "tree" is not the same as reading it (encountering it as part of a larger signifying chain). The difference between the signifier and the signifying chain is the difference between a static awareness of one's own consciousness, and a sense that the world is affecting consciousness—actually invading it—via the word. "Language," as Hugh Kenner put it, "is a Trojan horse through which the universe gets into the mind."[6]

I then draw their attention to Joyce's actualization of another felt moment of the narrator presented in the *Dubliners*' version, without equivalent in the *Irish Homestead* version: "He had often said to me: 'I am not long for this world,' *and I had thought his words idle*. Now I knew they were true" (*D* 9; emphasis mine). When printed words persuade him of the priest's death, he is experiencing what he thought to be "idle words" coming to life! As I mentioned earlier, the *Irish Homestead* version stops at this point, jumps forward in time, and picks up again in the evening. But in the final version in *Dubliners*, this interregnum is filled in. The effect the reading of the card had on him persists and dictates a somewhat compulsive behavior as he walks down the street:

> I wished to go in and look at him but I had not the courage to knock. I walked away slowly along the sunny side of the street, *reading all the theatrical advertisements in the shop-windows as I went*. (*D* 12; emphasis mine)

Having read the word, and seeing the word was true, and that the word was "death"—Father Flynn's, his, everyone's—he walks away from the holy hush of the moment, over to "the sunny side of the street," in search of other words, different words; he starts *"reading"*—not looking—at the advertisements in the shop-window; and not this or that ad, but *all* of them. Whatever content they have is subsumed under the urge to read, to be immersed, to stretch out the signifying chain along a perpetual axis, so it does not stop at the word "death." Instead of words persuading him of the finality of death—words that *involve him* in that sense of finality—he immerses himself in words, thereby expanding for himself a sensation of an ever-expanding present moment. This movement from mortality to vitality, from deprivation to compensation, lifts his spirits: "neither I nor the day seemed in a mourning mood" (*D* 12). Popular culture, posters, entertainment, enter, all at once, both the boy's mind and Joyce's fiction, like a ray of sunshine, banishing, even if only for the moment, the fear instilled in him as he passed by the priest's house, "night after night," hoping, but hoping in vain, to see lighted candles in the window, informing him of the priest's passing, but also, at the same moment, pushing back the night.

I ask my students: "What has happened to Joyce's narrative style in the interval between the first version of the story and this rewriting?" Students often note that, in the first version, the boy's state of mind seems unaffected by words—which is to say, the effect of individual words on his state of mind is not mentioned in the narrative; but, in the revision, the effect words have on his state of mind *is* the story. I now amend the freewrite question from "what is the difference between the word 'tree' and a tree?" to "what is the difference between the word and the world?" The word is not the world, and yet the world we know comes to us through words.

And what of the world not in the words? It haunts the outer reaches of what we know of the world.[7] We cannot say what it is, but we can sense it is there, much like another young boy in Joyce's fiction, Stephen Dedalus:

> [H]e remembered the song about the wild rose blossoms on the little green place. But you could not have a *green* rose. *But perhaps somewhere in the world you could.* (*P* 24; emphasis mine)

But where? And how? We cannot summon a green rose into the world with the use value of words, but perhaps in their exchange value—in what they imply. As the capacity to mass-produce commodities engendered the economic necessity of mass-producing a desire for them, a new discourse emerged: advertising. Objects, previously identifiable by their use value, become objects of desire, radiating their exchange value. I put a slogan on the board the students know: "Coke Is It!" I ask, "What is *it*"? "Coke!" they exclaim. "What is Coke?" "A soda!" Then I ask, "Why not say 'Coke is a soda'"? "Because Coke is not just a soda," they answer. "What else is it"? I ask. "Whatever you want," is the general response. So, perhaps, somewhere in the world—the world of advertised commodities—there could be a green rose, or even an omniscient soda!

This provides a segue to "Araby" where I can point to how neatly the story divides in half: the first half where the boy walks through the market in the daytime, jostled by the crowd, pining for love of Mangan's sister, feeling as though he "bore his chalice safely through a throng of foes" (*D* 29). And then the second half—the moment where the young man has heard the question of

Mangan's sister: Would he be going to the Araby Bazaar? It is not just the fact that she has spoken to him but rather that her question is prompted by her own disappointment: Would he be going to the bazaar, because she has to go on a retreat. In that moment he feels transformed by her thwarted desire from a dutiful, frustrated boy, into her knight errant: "—If I go, I said, I will bring you something" (32). Far from a mere promise, this is a troth. The all-too-apparent world of school routines becomes the undifferentiated blur of "tedious intervening days," all of which he wishes to "annihilate," so he might bring back from the nighttime bazaar—if not the Holy Grail itself—at least "something."

Of course, he still must pass over the threshold of his aunt's permission and, more difficult still, acquire funds from his unreliable uncle. After that, it is just a matter of climbing aboard "a *special* train for the bazaar," stepping out onto an "*improvised* wooden platform" (D 34; emphasis mine), and finding himself standing before "a large building which displayed the *magical* name" (34; emphasis mine). I stress to the students the duality of the emphasized words—special, improvised, magical—how they mean what they mean, but, taken altogether, seem to transport the boy to another place (quite literally in the case of the "special" train), to a "somewhere" of green roses and whatever he imagines will serve (he has no idea what) as the "something" he will bring back to his love, proving thereby both his valor and the steadfastness of his love.

Once again, as with the young boy narrating "The Sisters," he falls into the gap between a longing to be near words, and a deep fear of their "deadly work":

> I recognised a silence like that which pervades a church after a service.... I heard a voice call from one end of the gallery that the light was out. The upper part of the hall was now completely dark.
>
> Gazing up into the darkness I saw myself as a creature driven and derided by vanity; and my eyes burned with anguish and anger. (D 35)

I point out to the students that the bazaar is likened to a church, the name of which appears as "magical"; but the only magic in this tawdry, makeshift affair is its use of a combination of theatrics and electric light to transform mere objects into commodities. The bazaar itself would have been advertised in posters in shop windows such as the ones so exhaustively perused by the narrator of "The Sisters."

From there, I plunge (no doubt unexpectedly) into a passage from Karl Marx, the one where he famously struggles to find an analogy to explain how it is possible for something to be an object, but also, at the same time, inexplicably, much more than that:

> [T]he commodity-form, and the value-relation of the products of labour, within which it appears, have absolutely no connection with the physical nature of the commodity and the material relations arising out of this.... In order, therefore, to find an analogy, *we must take flight into the misty realm of religion.*[8]

Mangan's sister must forgo attending the bazaar because she is required to go on a religious retreat, but it is the boy's trip to the bazaar, on her behalf, which seems, at least initially, much more like a pilgrimage to a Holy Land than the retreat of Mangan's sister. In Joyce's fiction, advertising, as I have suggested elsewhere in my work, is "The New [improved!] Testament." It is a discourse every bit as dominant as the innumerable allusions to the Bible and classical literature.

Advertising, much like Stephen's definition of God, is a "shout in the street."[9] Stephen offers this metaphor to Mr. Deasy when pushing back against that old man's wheezy definition of history as a movement "towards one great goal, the manifestation of God" (*U* 28). Whereas Deasy's teleology canonizes imperialism, while at the same time denigrating its colonial subjects, Stephen collapses both history and God into the singular experience of "now." In doing so, he is aligning his cosmology with his equally quotidian aesthetics, whereby any given object is reduced to a moment of *quidditas*—a term Stephen re-purposes from St. Thomas of Aquinas, referring to that basic quality or nature of something that makes it not only *what it is*, but also what *distinguishes it from everything else*:

> You see that it is that thing which it is and no other thing. The radiance of which he speaks is the scholastic *quidditas,* the *whatness* of a thing. (*P* 185; emphasis in the original)

While quidditas is an important term, borrowed by Stephen from Catholic theology and philosophy, it is also a term that pinpoints the goal and intent of all advertisers who insist their shampoo, or coffee, or soda is uniquely itself ("accept no substitutes!"). In Joyce's fiction, the momentary is always momentous, in direct contrast to the august apparatus of hegemonic discourse.[10] For instance, Bloom admires how effectively the Catholic Church utilizes complex slogans to market the Communion wafer: "Good idea the Latin. Stupefies them first" (*U* 66). The uniqueness of any given moment, in other words, is not contained *in* any particular event, but rather in the momentary effect *of* the event. And, yes, as I hope the attentive reader has surmised, I have now engineered the entry point to introduce to the class that Rosetta Stone of all Joyce scholarship: THE EPIPHANY.

In his description of Bloom witnessing Communion, Joyce insists on the easy slippage from spiritual ecstasy to ordinary climax. The same dynamic will be on display, literally, when Bloom encounters Gerty McDowell on Sandymount Strand. As litanies chanted to the Virgin Mary sound faintly from a church in the distance, Gerty, her mind ruminating on what she is wearing, where she bought it, how much it cost, and how well it accords with the latest dictates of fashion, leans back, clasping her knee, thus granting the silently beseeching Bloom a vision that inspires him to engage vigorously in his alternative form of worship.[11]

Advertising and other forms of popular culture have pride of place in Joyce's fiction because they feature words that purport to correspond to a mystical world. And is this not, I ask them, when we have moved on to a discussion of *A Portrait of the Artist as a Young Man*, a defensible and useful description of what a young Stephen does, fated as he is, to move on, every year or so, to increasingly squalid surroundings, driven inexorably toward domestic chaos and financial ruin, by his progressively alcoholic father?:

> *Words* which he did not understand he said over and over to himself till he had learnt them by heart: and through them he had glimpses of the real *world* about them. (*P* 64; emphasis mine)

But this "real" world, conjured up by words, is always being transformed by more words, this time by his reading of *The Count of Monte Cristo*:

> [H]e pored over a ragged translation of *The Count of Monte Cristo*. . . . At night he built up on the parlour table an image of the wonderful island cave out of transfers and paper flowers and coloured tissue paper and strips of the silver and golden paper in which chocolate is wrapped. . . .
> Outside Blackrock, on the road that led to the mountains, stood a small whitewashed house in the garden of which grew many rosebushes: and in this house, he told himself, another Mercedes lived. (*P* 65)

Once again, Stephen longs for and fears the "deadly work" by which words cast a spell over the world—his world. Dear, dirty Dublin becomes sunny Marseille—no small feat. Are there like instances in the majestic labyrinth of *Ulysses*?

For a man tasking himself with walking around all day, and most of the night, neither interfering with, nor thinking about, his wife's appointment with a lover, we see the Joycean touch, traceable all the way back to the boy in "The Sisters," of advertising words, as omnipresent as Bloom himself, that pose as capable of affording one transcendence:

> What is home
> Without Plumtree's Potted Meat?
> Incomplete
> With it an abode of bliss. (*U* 61)

When preparing students to analyze the important role of popular culture in *Ulysses*, I remind them how the effect of Joyce's prose is such that it often evokes an unmappable place somewhere *in-between* between "word" and "world." The point is made explicitly, if not intentionally, in the letter written to Bloom by the well-meaning Martha Clifford:

> I called you naughty darling because I do not like that other world.
> Please tell me what is the real meaning of that word? (*U* 63)

Presumably Bloom is citing specific words he wants her to use when she writes to him, so as to produce an effect on him. But Martha substitutes "naughty darling" because, she explains, "I do not like that other *world*," which is to say she does not like the effect using that word might have on her.

In *Ulysses*, I suggest to my students, eighteen chapters appear to revolve around a single day, but the shift in perspective and style is so radical as to suggest eighteen different days. The real meaning of the word is the world, and the real meaning of the world is the word—but this is a Möbius strip—neither the word nor the world can represent what Lacan calls the "Real," which is the inevitable remainder of the incomplete formula word/world, or signifier/signified.[12] The world of *Ulysses* "happens" as much *in between* and among the eighteen chapters as it does *in* them.

This is a term Bloom mulls over throughout the day—a term used in Astronomy—"parallax." In the most general terms, parallax refers to the phenomena whereby the distance of a star must be measured twice, six months apart, to determine its actual distance from the sun. Such a doubled over calculation will account for, and factor out, the curvature of the earth. Is this not like the interrelationship of subjectivity and language? We measure consciousness by the word, and then again by the world, and attempt to factor out the curvature in-between—that is, what Lacan calls the Real. Joyce has produced the narrative equivalent of this phenomenon in his eighteen chapters registering eighteen different shifts relative to a single star: June 16, 1904.

When Bloom is pointing out constellations to Stephen, the question is posed "[w]ith what meditations did Bloom accompany his demonstration to his companion . . . ?" (*U* 573). And the answer is: "Meditations of . . . the parallax or parallactic drift of socalled fixed stars, in reality evermoving wanderers"

The "parallactic drift of... evermoving wanderers" is interrupted by "one sole unique advertisement to cause passers to stop in wonder"—and here my blackboard covered with a constellation of words becomes "the heaventree of stars hung with humid nightblue fruit" set before the wandering attention of my students (*U* 573). My association of the commodity with planetary bodies is not just an interpretation on my part. In the "Circe" episode, where objects become anthropomorphized on a regular basis, Bloom's bar of "new clean lemon soap arises, diffusing light and perfume"; the chemist Sweny's face "appeals in the disc of the soapsun.... Three and a penny, please." It would appear Joyce found the jingle in an ad for Brooke's Soap (fig. 5.1).

But it is the second iteration of the soap ad, which I have placed beside it, that starkly illustrates Marx's contention that although the commodity "appears at first sight an extremely obvious, trivial thing.... its analysis brings out that it is a very strange thing, abounding in metaphysical subtleties and theological niceties."[13] In the second Brooke's Soap ad, the apes paint a Platonic ideal of themselves as though it were a planetary face beaming down, what Lacan would call "an ideal ego" (fig. 5.2). Advertisements are the public discourse of what Lacan called "the mirror stage." When a child sees his image, this constitutes a specular ego construction—an ideal ego—that will henceforth drive the child to emulate, and strive to achieve, this ideal of perfection he misrecognizes as equivalent to himself—much the way the two apes in the ad strive to paint a highly idealized semblance of how they would wish to imagine their own face.

Here we seem to have traveled a long way from our initial class discussion, but, I suggest to the students, it is a matter of degree, and not of kind. And here I give my students a new assignment—"homework" in every sense of the word—one which involves role-playing as the boy who crossed to the sunny side of the street to read all the theatrical posters in the shop windows:

Assignment: Find a billboard that is part of your daily journey—a journey that might involve walking, or taking the bus, or subway, or driving, or some combination of all of these. Address yourself to your chosen billboard—to what extent does it meet the requirements of Bloom's final meditation upon all the necessary qualities of a perfect advertisement? How does it associate the product with the mystical? How is the message it puts forth to you posed as transcendent? How might it be said to offer to converge and fix the word and the world into one stable ideal moment, commensurate with your (imagined) ideal ego? I found my billboard on Highway 401 East, leading out from the Pearson International Airport, here in Toronto.[14] (fig. 5.3)

Figure 5.2. An advertisement for Brooke's Monkey Brand Soap from 1900, featuring two macaques painting. Nash Collection of Primates in Art and Illustration. https://digital.library.wisc.edu/1711.dl/BPEHLJQE7OZML8K.

Figure 5.3. Billboard advertisement in Toronto, Canada, near Pearson Airport. Photography by Garry Leonard, March 10, 2020.

It ticks off all the boxes:

—excludes all extraneous accretions (devoid of context)
—reduces itself to its simplest and most efficient terms (in this case, a scream)
—does not exceed the span of casual vision (one simply encounters what one sees, without having to look for it, and without knowing to look away from it)
—is congruous with the velocity of modern life (the speed and direction of the promised release is in harmony with the speed and direction of the observer in their car passing by)
—and causes the passerby to stop (or in my case, pull over to take a picture) in wonder

The "magical name" is no longer "Araby"; it is "your own name."[15] At a glance, this seems different—but is it? Every ordinary object (bread and wine), through being transubstantiated by the liturgy of advertising, transcends into Marx's "mystical realm" where it shines forth as the commodity. The apotheosis of the completion of the fantasy of the self is simultaneous with the advertised object rising up as a commodity—like the sun. Such a transformation can only be presented literally in the "Circe" chapter (that chapter devoted to all manner of phantasmagoric transformation) when Bloom's lemon soap rises in the sky and shines:

(He points to the south, then to the east. A cake of new clean lemon soap arises, diffusing light and perfume.)
THE SOAP
We're a capital couple are Bloom and I;
He brightens the earth, I polish the sky. (*U* 360)

The ever-intensifying fantasy to achieve self-completion drives commodity culture; one feels an urge to purchase the advertised commodity in order to actualize its promise to move us from "incomplete" to "an abode of bliss." On the one hand, in Joyce's earliest work, the boy in "Araby" seeks "something" commensurate with his blissful fantasy of himself as a knight errant—rather than his chronically incomplete iteration of himself as a perpetually apprehensive boy in turn-of-the-century Dublin. But despite the "magical name" at the entrance to the Araby Bazaar, none of the objects for sale *in* the bazaar have achieved their quidditas, none of them have risen up into the mystical realm as a commodity/sun. Besides, he intended to bring Mangan's sister something commensurate with *her* desire, so that she might desire him.

What is different about "my" billboard ad, ostensibly for a mechanical device, is that a woman is invited to foreclose her role as the object of a man's desire, by becoming the object of her own desire. Such a closed loop, were it to be made available to Mangan's sister, and were she to choose it, would also foreclose the boy's self-generated quest: How could he even imagine obtaining for her the object of her desire, if it is always, already, herself?

Here, I am able to illustrate for the class (with another nod toward Lacanian theory) that the "parallactic effect" in *Ulysses* (if not in all Joyce's fiction) is that *what* we want is not what we want, but what *makes us* want.[16] And what we want is to complete our fantasy of ourselves. As such, it is the circulation of the commodity that drives the structuring principle of capitalism Marx calls "commodity fetishism." Commodities continually masquerade as "what we want," but, in fact, function as the (further) cause of our desire.[17] It is a truism of advertising that "sex sells," and "my" billboard might seem to be a case in point, except that what it offers for sale, like all (successful) ads is not a fantasy of sex "with" someone, but a fantasy of self-completion with oneself.

In fact, the boy who falls apart at the end of "Araby" does so because he dares to set forth on a path he imagines will grant him self-completion, but only if he can find and bring back to Mangan's sister "something" that will do the same for her—a holy grail, of sorts, a chalice. But a chalice is not what she wants (in fact, she never says she wants anything); rather, this never-named object, this holy grail, nowhere to be found, represents, for him, *who he imagines himself becoming*, the equivalent of "shouting out his own name," a point made earlier when he experienced the noise and jostle of the crowded street market as a place that required him to bear his ideal ego, or as he imagines, his "*chalice through a throng of foes*" (*D* 29; emphasis mine).

In light of these discussions, the students become eager to look, once again, at whatever billboard *they* chose to photograph and bring to class—which is to say, what *they* have brought back from the market. As they stand before the "magic names" of their respective billboards, the lights go out, one by one, and they can almost hear, somewhere, the sound of money being counted. They, too, can look up into the darkness and see themselves, at least in the capitalist marketplace, as creatures derided by vanity. In this way, perhaps, I am able to illustrate for them Richard Ellmann's famous observation, written in 1959 but still pertinent today: "[W]e are still learning to be James Joyce's contemporaries, to understand our interpreter."[18]

Notes

1. Ferdinand de Saussure, "From Course in General Linguistics," in *Critical Theory Since 1965*, ed. Hazard Adams and Leroy Searle (Tallahassee: Florida State University Press, 1986), 650, emphasis mine.
2. James Joyce, *Dubliners* (New York: Penguin, 1983), 9. Hereafter cited parenthetically in the text as *D* followed by page number.
3. James Joyce, *A Portrait of the Artist as a Young Man,* ed. Seamus Deane (New York: Penguin, 1993). Hereafter cited parenthetically in the text as *P* followed by page number.
4. Jacques Lacan, *Four Fundamentals of Psycho-Analysis,* ed. Jacques-Alain Miller, trans. Alan Sheridan (New York: Routledge, 2018).
5. *Irish Homestead,* August 13, 1904, 676.
6. In Hugh Kenner, *Dublin's Joyce* (London: Chatto and Windus 1955).
7. I draw on Lacanian theory in making this analogy. For a thorough application of Lacanian theory to *Dubliners* see my book: *Reading Dubliners Again: A Lacanian Perspective* (Syracuse: Syracuse University Press, 1993).
8. Karl Marx, "From 'The Fetishism of the Commodity and Its Secret,'" in *Social Theory: A Reader* (Edinburgh: Edinburgh University Press, 2005), 19–20, emphasis mine.
9. James Joyce, *Ulysses* (New York: Random House, 1984), 28. Hereafter cited parenthetically in the text as *U* followed by page number.
10. For an in-depth analysis of advertising and commodity culture in Joyce's fiction, see my book *Advertising and Commodity Culture in Joyce* (Gainesville: University Press of Florida, 1998). For a collection of essays on the same topic see *James Joyce Quarterly*, Special Issue: Joyce and Advertising, ed. Garry Leonard and Jennifer Wicke, vol. 30/31, 1993.
11. For a full discussion of this scene, see my essay "The Virgin Mary and the Urge in Gerty: Advertising and Desire in the 'Nausicaa' Chapter of *Ulysses*," *University of Hartford Studies* 23 (1991): 3–23.
12. For a detailed application of Lacan's formulation of the Real to "The Sisters," see my essay "The Freeman's Journal: The Making of His/Story in Joyce's 'The Sisters,'" *Modern Fiction Studies* 36, no. 4 (Winter 1990): 455–82. Also, note how this discussion of Martha's "slip of the pen" returns us to the earlier freewrite without having to force the issue. As I pointed out earlier, the freewrite conducted in the class often becomes the gift that keeps on giving, throughout a given class, and even throughout the semester. Granted, there is a high degree of improvisation and thinking on one's feet, but it is this that makes class discussion lively!
13. Karl Marx, *Capital: A Critique of Political Economy,* vol. 1, trans. Ben Fowkes (New York: Penguin, 1990).
14. Personal photo, taken by me with an Apple iPhone, March 10, 2020.
15. In my current work-in-progress, "Capitalist Discourse and Subjectivity in Joyce's Fiction," I trace this shift from "Araby" to "your name" as equivalent to the transposition Lacan notes in the shift from the Master Discourse to the Capitalist: it is no longer the Subject (S1) in the position of agent, but the cause of desire itself (the *objet petit a*); which is to say, it is now the commodity that interpellates the subject, not the subject imagining the transcendence of the commodity.

16 It is well beyond the scope of this essay, but I have found this paradox of desire goes a long way toward elucidating a fact that puzzles first-time readers: How is Bloom able to avoid interfering with the assignation of Molly and Blazes, and still return to her later in the evening? Both he and Molly, each in their different ways, seem to come to terms with the danger of pursuing the illusion of absolute self-completion.
17 In Lacanian theory, human desire is fundamentally structured around a sense of lack. The *objet petit a* represents the unattainable object that we believe will complete or fulfill us. By definition, it is apparently elusive and entirely unattainable—a constantly substitutable thing that we perpetually seek, but which, even if attained, fails to complete us.
18 Richard Ellmann, *James Joyce* (London: Oxford University Press, 1984), 9.

Bibliography

Ellmann, Richard. *James Joyce*. London: Oxford University Press, 1984.
Joyce, James. *Dubliners*. New York: Penguin, 1983.
Joyce, James. *A Portrait of the Artist as a Young Man*. Edited with an introduction and notes by Seamus Deane (New York: Penguin, 1983).
Joyce, James. "The Sisters." *Irish Homestead*. August 13, 1904.
Joyce, James. *Ulysses*. Edited by Hans Walter Gabler, et al. New York: Random House, 1984.
Kenner, Hugh. *Dublin's Joyce*. London: Chatto and Windus, 1955.
Lacan, Jacques. *Four Fundamentals of Psycho-Analysis*. Edited by Jacques-Alain Miller. Translated by Alan Sheridan. New York: Routledge, 2018.
Leonard, Garry. *Advertising and Commodity Culture in Joyce*. Gainesville: University Press of Florida, 1998.
Leonard, Garry. "The Freeman's Journal: The Making of His/Story in Joyce's 'The Sisters.'" *Modern Fiction Studies* 36, no. 4 (Winter 1990): 455–82.
Leonard, Garry. *Reading Dubliners Again: A Lacanian Perspective*. Syracuse: Syracuse University Press, 1993.
Leonard, Garry. "The Virgin Mary and the Urge in Gerty: Advertising and Desire in the 'Nausicaa' Chapter of *Ulysses*." *University of Hartford Studies* 23 (1991): 3–23.
Leonard, Garry, and Jennifer Wicke, eds. *James Joyce Quarterly, Special Issue: Joyce and Advertising*. Vol. 30/31, 1993.
Marx, Karl. *Capital: A Critique of Political Economy*. Vol. 1. Trans. Ben Fowkes. New York: Penguin, 1990.
Marx, Karl. "From 'The Fetishism of the Commodity and its Secret.'" In *Social Theory: A Reader*. Edinburgh: Edinburgh University Press, 2005.
Saussure, Ferdinand de. "From Course in General Linguistics." In *Critical Theory Since 1965*, edited by Hazard Adams and Leroy Searle. Tallahassee: Florida State University Press, 1986.

6

Reading (and Loving) *Ulysses* While Black

Zoë L. Henry

To bear witness to Blackness in James Joyce's *Ulysses* is a complicated task. On its surface, the novel espouses familiar forms of anti-Black racism. Racist language and stereotypes are rendered natural in the minds of its central characters, and portraits of Black people feel reductive and incomplete, as "throwaway" as the horse on which Leopold Bloom is rumored to have bet. References to historical Black figures are inaccurate, suggesting that Joyce's meticulous fact-checking may not have extended to our particular margins. Molly Bloom—albeit racialized for her Gibraltan upbringing throughout the novel—is arguably the most problematic figure of all, lusting, Bloom thinks, after Black servants in livery.[1] Where *Finnegans Wake* has been lauded for turning racism on its head—making racial Otherness a redeeming feature that creates a "solidarity of the marginalized"—*Ulysses* is a decidedly more ambivalent read.[2] It seems clear to me, a mixed-race woman, that this novel was not written with a reader of color in mind. What, then, does it mean to love a book that was not written for you? One that, at crucial moments, gives you reasons *not* to love it?

By way of an answer, this essay intervenes in much postcolonial and genetic criticism of the novel, which tends to circle around the broader *question of Blackness* without addressing the embodied and psychic experience of the *Black reader*, for whom there lies a fundamental conundrum in such representations: *Ulysses* is replete with racist imagery, surely, but Joyce also seems dedicated to addressing racism in Ireland. Given these contradictory elements, critics have tended to either dismiss the novel for being too embedded within racist culture or, alternatively, praise the elements that challenge racist tropes while leaving unaddressed the more problematic effects. Here I offer a different solution, suggesting how people of color—those most attuned to the contradictions of racism—are potentially privileged readers of *Ulysses*, because their understanding of the complexities of racist discourse has prepared them to be the kind of acute and subtle readers that Joyce's text calls for.

For instance, such a reader might return to the novel with an obsessive attention to racializing details, searching for alternate readings to defy those initial affronts. Seen from another angle, *Ulysses* is invested at key, transitional moments in representing—not always effectively—a persistent, Africanist presence in turn-of-the-century Ireland. Despite assumptions within the Celtic Revival that the category "Irish" depended on racial purity, the novel takes great pains to think through the racially mixed nature of a country on the brink of Independence and Civil War. Joyce himself addressed the obsession with Irish "purity" in his 1907 lecture, "Ireland: Island of Saints and Sages," wherein he states: "Our civilization is an immense woven fabric in which very different elements are mixed[. . . .] What race or language [. . .] can nowadays claim to be pure? No race has less right to make such a boast than the one presently inhabiting Ireland."[3]

As contemporary organizations such as Black and Irish and Roots in Africa-Ireland (RAINetwork) will attest, Black presence in Ireland was and remains far more pervasive than we might imagine, an important, if neglected feature of said Irish "fabric," as of what Paul Gilroy has termed the Black Atlantic.[4] Against one scholar's assertion that blackface minstrelsy would have been the Irishman's only recourse to Blackness, historians indicate that Black people were, in fact, present throughout Ireland beginning in the eighteenth century, and Dublin had, after London, among the largest population of African or East Asian peoples of any European city.[5] We find in *Ulysses* Black performers, Black American victims of lynching, and North African immigrants.

Bloom is culturally marked as Jewish, finding himself the target of xenophobic comments throughout his day (most memorably in his encounter with the nameless Citizen in "Cyclops," a figure based on Irish nationalist Michael Cusack). Although Bloom's Jewishness is decidedly *not* a marker of Blackness, he is still positioned as Other to the Irish nationalists' fantasies of white homogeny, where those figures trade on racist epithets to keep Unionists at arms' length. The irony is that such figures were replicating the racializing lexica of the English, whose representations of the Irish as simianized figures—as in caricatures published in the satirical *Punch*—theoretically justified Ireland's continued subjugation.[6]

Indeed, for Joyce, part of the problem with the Gaelic League's obsession with whiteness lay in the reality that enslaved Africans and Irish subjects had more in common than staunch nationalists seemed to think. In "Ireland: Island of Saints and Sages," he argues that the Irish would naturally want revenge for England's brutality, for "How could he forget? Can the back of a slave forget the rod?" and he explicitly likens England's tyranny over Ireland to Belgium's conquest of Congo.[7] To insist upon racial purity as fitness for citizenship was in his view problematic, because the master's tools can never dismantle the master's house.

If the signal term associated with *Ulysses* is difficulty—in the classically hermeneutic and formal senses—then this becomes triply freighted for Black readers. Seduced and frustrated as anyone else by the cadence, effluvia, and unpredictability of the novel's language, readers of color are also subjected to the pain of being misrepresented and deprived of humanity in the very minds we have worked so hard to inhabit. Interpretive labor takes on new meaning when the line in question involves "smackfatclacking nigger lips" (*U* 15.419), fantasies of trying a Black penis, or an uncritical reverence for Eugene Stratton. At the same time, *Ulysses* cannot simply be reduced to a catalog of racist thought, a point on which minoritized scholars tend to agree. Vincent Cheng asserts that the novel is deeply invested in forging cross-cultural connections, and reminds us that Joyce was opposed to anti-Semitism, blind nationalism, male aggression, and imperialism in all guises.[8] Thus emerges a third difficulty, of holding two contradictory realities at once: *Ulysses* is a product of Ireland's racial blind spots, and an imperfect effort to respond and move beyond them.

Given these challenges, readers may respond by scanning the novel for imminent danger, steeling themselves for the possibility of emotional harm while hoping for, and being rewarded with, pleasures in the journey. To read *Ulysses* while Black is to inhabit a public sphere: the literal publics that Joyce conjures—from Sandymount Strand to the Ormond Hotel—but also the *psychological publics* where one feels routinely unstable in another's consciousness. It is to feel the "existential deviation" that Frantz Fanon theorizes of colonial Blacks to white culture, to be surveilled in the novel and, at the same time, to surveil *oneself* as a reader possibly complicit with the storyworld's worst tendencies.[9] It is to do all of this as a labor of love, for the moments of affirmation echoed in Molly Bloom's last word, and for the rare instances when such figurations turn tender, profound, and essentially, impossibly true.

Indeed, such readers are more well versed than most in precisely the forms of hermeneutic scanning—reading, rereading, signifying, resisting—that the novel ultimately encourages, if not demands of any audience. It is in this sense that we can feel at home in *Ulysses*, even if that home is an uncanny one: the neuroses of Bloom, Stephen, and Molly, reflected in the anxiety of (attempting) to inhabit them fully, are also reminiscent of the kinds of psychological self-fashioning that a person of color feels compelled to perform daily, *if only to remain safe that day*. (Hands up, it wasn't me, don't shoot.)[10] If Blackness is, by definition, a public ontology, as Aliyyah Abdur-Rahman has suggested, then negotiating forms of illegibility—learning to skirt around an aggressive interlocutor—precipitates for the Black reader a different mode of closeness, wherein certain textual figurations are kept at a distance.¹¹ In refusing to read so closely that the novel's racism leaves me burned, in learning to resist while also allowing myself to be seduced by its unutterable beauty, I am able to "yield, with love, to the pleasures of [its] ignorance."¹²

In a rare academic treatise, author Toni Morrison mines for the ignored, yet persistent Africanist presence in twentieth-century U.S. fiction, arguing that Blackness—far from incidental or peripheral in the minds of lauded white American authors—is actually central to our understanding of literary culture.¹³ Morrison is attuned to instances of racism that repel her from such texts, but also grasps literature's potential to "explode and move beyond" this: "Much more important," she writes, "was to contemplate how Africanist personae, narrative, and idiom moved and enriched the text in self-conscious ways, to consider what the engagement meant for the work of the writer's imagination."¹⁴ In what follows, then, I heed Morrison's directive to unearth a persistent, yet largely obfuscated feature of *Ulysses*, as of Irish history writ large: the unassailable presence of Black figures, as they are conceptualized, racialized, and (dis)incorporated at varying moments from Dublin's city streets. This chapter will explore three, key scenes where Black figures operate in the novel's world, as in the imaginations of its central characters: the lynching of Will Brown in "Cyclops," the Bohee Brothers troupe in "Circe," and the birth of a Black child from a white mother in "Penelope." My readings attend to the crucial, underexplored presence of Africanism in Joyce's work, and to the hermeneutic experience of encountering these figures as a mixed-race reader, writer, and teacher. Taken together, these can provide a more layered analysis of how Blackness exists, persists, and speaks to an Ireland on the brink of change, in 1922 as it is today. Such an orientation carries important implications for how educators should approach a text that remains challenging for our students (of color) in multiple senses, including those we do not yet grasp. First, I provide a brief overview of how postcolonial scholars have appraised the novel with respect to race and resistance, indicating where my own readings marry and depart therefrom.

Subaltern *Ulysses:* Joyce, Race, and Postcolonialism

James Joyce's works were once considered apolitical, uninterested in offering cross-cultural affiliations or representing (however partially) figures of different races. The canonizing of Joyce as a high modernist, one who fomented stylistic revolution in Europe and America, rather softened, scholars suggest, the political edge of his writing. Joyce was certainly a master stylist, pioneering forms such as stream of consciousness while including allusions to everything from anglophone letters and British history to turn-of-the-century music culture.

Nonetheless, Joyce was also himself responding to the tyranny of colonial rule in Ireland, crafting *Ulysses* in the very period—1914 to 1921—in which the nation gained its independence from England in a violent uprising.

This is precisely the case that Enda Duffy makes for recuperating *Ulysses* as the signal text of Irish independence, one that is "preoccupied [...] with both the means by which oppressed communities fight their way out of abjection and the potential pitfalls of anticolonial struggle."[15] This dualism remains important for Duffy, because figures like the Citizen and Bloom emerge as deeply flawed and worthy of our readerly sympathy. As he argues, it is the very clashing of styles in this episode—the realist mode that recounts Bloom and the Citizen's face off, and the polysemic interjections from newspaper headlines, radio broadcasts and the like—that allow for an appreciation of its larger commitment to racial diversity, "upturning stereotypes as they are created."[16]

For Vincent Cheng, in his landmark *Joyce, Race, and Empire,* attending to the "subalternity" of *Ulysses* and *Finnegans Wake* allows us to see how Joyce forged connections between Ireland and the larger decolonizing world, in effect "universaliz[ing] the colonial relationship" between oppressor and oppressed.[17] Building on work by scholars such as Dominic Manganiello, Seamus Deane, Cheryl Herr, Margot Norris, and Vicki Mahaffey, Cheng re-casts *Ulysses* as both politically engaged and "ideologically progressive," a space across which, as Herr has it, "ideologies perform."[18] Seen through this lens, it is no wonder that Joyce's unique blend of political fang and stylistic virtuosity influenced marginalized writers across the globe, from Ralph Ellison and Wallace Thurman to Salman Rushdie, Gabriel García Márquez, and Wole Soyinka. (In the late 1960s, Soyinka wrote the poem "Ulysses: Notes From Here to My Joyce Class" as a meditation on resistance while incarcerated as a political prisoner during Nigeria's Civil War.) And, as Paul Saint-Amour notes, *Ulysses*'s more "elastic" delineation of the complexities of history may actively anticipate the mid-century writings of Négritude artists Aimé Césaire and Léopold Senghor, each of whom "attempted to invent novel frameworks that could link political universality and cultural multiplicity."[19]

More recent criticism, however, has been skeptical of sanguine recuperations of *Ulysses* as an insurgent text of global, anticolonial sweep. Leonard Orr expresses hesitancy with the emerging paradigm of a postcolonial Joyce, reminding us that Joyce remained at odds with Ireland and its people, leaving the nation permanently in 1904 (his last visit to the Isle was in 1912, a full decade before the publication of *Ulysses*).[20] Heralded by other modernists such as T. S. Eliot and Ezra Pound, Joyce was surely different from those negotiating coloniality in Africa, India, or the Middle East. "Postcolonial studies," Orr writes, "has been happily appropriated by American and European academics to be applied to European writers of particular situations of political exile and oppression," without recognizing their incongruities.[21] In response, a proliferation of terms to qualify Joyce's postcoloniality have emerged in recent years, including "semicolonial" and "white postcolonial," while others reject the notion that Joyce offers anything useful to the decolonizing world at all.[22] Amadi Ozier's account of his representations of minstrelsy in *Ulysses*—and of what they term "lynching modernism" more generally—suggests that Joyce leveraged American cultural iconography, and spectacular racial violence in particular, in order to mark himself as modern and cosmopolitan. More broadly, Ozier suggests, Joyce thematizes a version of the problem that Orr earlier identified: that generally white, non-American global writers "situate themselves within a global discursive network by commenting on spectacular American racism," thereby distancing themselves from it.[23]

My own sense of Joyce's politics—and his approach to representing Blackness more specifically—falls in the middle ground articulated by Aarthi Vadde. For Vadde, modernist "internationalism" can allow the political aspirations of literature across cultures to flourish, without seeking to overcome the "real illegibilities, distortions and affective conflicts that pervade attempts to think through [global] collectivity."[24] In her reading of "Cyclops," the Linati schema's "alternating asymmetry" reveals a latent critique of international parallelism—of the kind espoused by the Citizen—and Joyce's own suspicion of "overstated solidarity" across cultures.[25] The episode thus brings "colonial subjectivity into relief through comparisons with other sides of racial oppression not entirely explained by the representational regime of the British Empire," giving attention to convergences while leaving room for rupture.[26] This is the sense in which I understand Joyce's recourse to Blackness across *Ulysses:* Such presence can emerge as politically useful in connection to the Irish situation, but there is also disjuncture between "Black" and "Irish" that the novel sometimes reflects, and sometimes falls victim to collapsing. Joyce was certainly, in my view, a postcolonial writer, though one who—from a U.S. postbellum perspective—often failed to grant his Black figures the rich interiority so readily accorded to others. The affective experience of witnessing this failing is worth bearing out in our scholarly readings, and in our teaching of Joyce in the twenty-first century.

I. Reckoning and Anachronism: Will Brown as "Black Beast" in Georgia

Competing narrative voices in "Cyclops" make this an especially useful episode for exploring questions of authority, oppression, subjugation, and resistance. It is here that tensions between Irish nationalism and British apologism, whiteness and ethnic Others, rise to their highest pitch. "Cyclops" references the capture of Odysseus and his men by the one-eyed monster in Homer's *Odyssey* and their subsequent escape through blinding. (Famously, Odysseus tells the Cyclops that his name is "Noman," so that when the giant asks for help, he insists that "Noman" has hurt him.) The weight of this allusion lies most powerfully, I would argue, in Odysseus's final, fated flaw: His decision to shout back his true name to the Cyclops, thus invoking the wrath of the monster and his father, Poseidon, by extension.

The events of this myth map rather neatly onto Joyce's text: The nameless narrator is "Noman," Bloom—whose final ascension to "heaven" mirrors flight from the cave—is Odysseus, and the Citizen, a vehement Irish nationalist, corresponds to the central villain. Even so, there are other, disembodied voices that frustrate the neatness of this schema, and our sense of who gets to speak (and whether their speech should be taken seriously). Newspaper headlines, revivalist sagas, death notices, medical journals, soapy romance novels, court transcripts, and biblical prose permeate the scene, thwarting readerly desire to make moral sense of the racially charged standoff. These additions seemingly render "Cyclops" a comedy, wherein the dissonance and polysemy of public discourse is the backdrop against which graver political concerns are cast.

If the crust of the episode is humor, however, its yeasty core is abject terror—a reality that recalls the content of its mythic parallel. Odysseus's self-positioning as "Noman" is clever in the classically comedic sense—there is something ridiculous about Odysseus's lie—but his final revelation directly causes the deaths of many members of his crew. Whereas Terence Killeen argues that the "sheer linguistic exuberance" of "Cyclops" works against the more political, official program as articulated by the Citizen, I think the logic of the episode actually works in reverse: The trite nature of the political positions being claimed—by Bloom and the Citizen both—is counterbalanced, in awful seriousness, by relentless images of death, mutilation, and execution.[27] Most postcolonial readings of "Cyclops" narrow in on the Citizen's exaggerated agenda—one that replicates, via fantasies of whiteness, the logic of British colonialism—or, alternatively on Bloom's morally soporific appeals to "love" as an inadequate antidote thereto (*U* 12.1485).

I am interested in how the parodic voices operate as a kind of insurgency, flooding the text's farcical circuits with an insistence that death—the visceral loss of human life—is the reality at stake behind surface-level ideological debates. As Patrick Mullen suggests, the question of liberation on a *global scale* mediates both "narrative conventions and political realities" in "Cyclops," such that the "clash of passions and forces [characterize] the struggle for freedom" in a manner not unlike a dramatic play.[28] (Indeed, it is worth remembering that the "Cyclops" chapter was meant to inspire an opera that Joyce was planning with the American director George Antheil, underscoring the performative context of the debates connecting Bloom, the Citizen, and Noman. The opera was arranged for electric motors, buzzers, amplified voices, gramophones, and sixteen piano players, replicating the din of the city and of its major political speakers.)[29] These are realities that Black readers might also be uniquely attuned to: Suspicion lies not in the loftiness of political claims—for certainly, those are everywhere and will not be going away—but rather in the insistence that *here* lies the seriousness, and not the deaths that reverberate, like breath notes for the performer, in the text's grim interstices.

Allow me to inhabit such an incident, an inaccurate reference to an American lynching. Violence has thus far framed the Citizen's speech, setting the macabre background against which the humor of the episode unfolds. We get descriptions of hangings (Alf Bergan producing letters from hangmen obtained during his time as a sheriff), a catalog of public executions of Irish patriots (as in the Galway lynchings), and detailed depictions of atrocities enacted by the British navy: "a young lad brought out, howling for his ma, and they tie him down on the buttend of a gun[.] ... the master at arms comes along with a long cane and he draws out and he flogs the bloody backside off of the poor lad til he yells meila murder" (*U* 12.1336–37, 1343–45). Just before this moment— one which seems to reach forward, a touch across time, to George Floyd and Tyre Nichols's breathless screams for their own mothers—Joyce includes the following from the perspective of the narrator:

> Hanging over the bloody paper with Alf [Bergan] looking for spicy bits instead of attending to the general public. Picture of a butting match, trying to crack their bloody skulls, one chap going for the other with his head down like a bull at a gate. And another one: *Black Beast Burned in Omaha, Ga.* A lot of Deadwood Dicks in slouch hats and they firing at a Sambo strung up in a tree with his tongue out and a bonfire under him. Gob, they ought to drown him in the sea after and electrocute and crucify him to make sure of their job. (*U* 12.1321–28)[30]

Scholars have debated this reference for some time. Robert Adams points out that no lynching ever took place in the small, 217-person town of Omaha, Georgia, though one did occur in Lumpkin, Georgia, in 1897.[31] For Weldon Thornton, the headline refers to a brief description of a lynching in Springfield, Ohio, that appeared in *The Freeman's Journal* on Wednesday, March 9, 1904.[32] In 1982, sixty years after the novel's publication, Timothy Weiss set the record straight: The *Black Beast* headline, he shows, was taken from a 1919 London *Times* report of September 30, referencing the Omaha, Nebraska, race riot in which Will Brown, a Black man accused of raping a white woman, was tortured, lynched, and burned in a manner similar to the image discussed.[33]

Yet for Weiss, the "cardinal importance" of this allusion lies not in the connection Joyce makes between lynching of the Irish and of Black Americans—nor the redundant logic by which the Noman, wishing to further "drown him in the sea after and electrocute and crucify him," establishes his bloodlust for an Independent Ireland that matches that of its former colonizers—but in the provenance of the episode as material artifact.[34] Surely, it is interesting and worth noting that the inclusion of this event suggests that Joyce finished writing "Cyclops" in October 1919, rather than in August or September, before sending it off to Ezra Pound for feedback. And yes, Weiss can be said to correct both Richard Ellmann and Michael Groden in their previous dating of the Rosenbach Manuscript. Yet to say that this remains *the* significance of the allusion replicates the problematic logic of white exceptionalism that Joyce was, to my mind, not actually endorsing but rather, in this moment, critiquing. If anything, it is the whiteness of the critics themselves—as of the Joyce industry writ large—that would allow Weiss to shunt the particulars of Brown's death in the context (and content) of the novel's episode. As those most sensitive to Black history well know, this was just one of many, bloody encounters across the infamous Red Summer that blazed on as Joyce was writing, an American extension of the Somme's atrocities at home. Weiss's mistake was to view *Ulysses* as a puzzle—and nothing more than a puzzle—rather than an intimate, if partial, reflection of the daily terrors of Black life, terrors which had something important to say to twentieth-century Ireland.

So let me tell the story from a different angle, one in which the gruesome, anachronistic particulars of Will Brown's death incite an important shift in the narrative of "Cyclops" and the novel as a whole.[35] On the afternoon of Sunday, September 28, 1919, two hundred boys gathered near the Bancroft School in Omaha, Nebraska, to decry the assault of Agnes Loebeck, a nineteen-year-old, white former classmate. The boys marched to the courthouse where Brown, the Black man Agnes claimed as her assailant, was being held. (Brown worked as a coal hustler at the time of his arrest, and was in feeble physical condition due to rheumatism, which makes it unlikely that he was the attacker.) As local historian Daniel Greunig describes in an oral history of the event, thousands of whites joined the schoolboys in front of the courthouse and began shooting at its windows, demanding Brown be released to them.[36]

The rioters poured gasoline on the building and set fire to it. They threw bricks and sticks, and wrested revolvers, badges, and caps from policemen. Others pillaged hardware stores and pawnshops in search of firearms, with as many as one thousand revolvers and shotguns stolen over the course of

Figure 6.1. The pole on which Will Brown was hanged. From UNO Digital Commons: Educational Publishing Company, "Omaha's riot in story and picture" (1919). *Digitized Books* 20, p. 19. https://digitalcommons.unomaha.edu/ascdigitizedbooks/20

the night. Women were thrown to the ground and trampled. Black men were dragged from their cars and beaten. The mayor, in his attempts to placate the mob, was seized and nearly hanged. (This—the mayor's near-death experience, rather than Brown's actual death—is the subject of the *Times* brief.)

Back in the courthouse, as the flames crept up to the fifth floor where Brown was being held, the Sheriff led all 121 prisoners to the roof of the building. Eventually, he handed Brown over to the mob. They shot Brown and hanged him from a telephone poll, where his lifeless body was struck with hundreds more bullets (fig 6.1). They cut the rope, tied the corpse to an automobile, and dragged it for four blocks. Then they poured red lantern oil over the body and set fire to it. Some of the men smiled and posed for a picture in front of the carnage, before hauling pieces of the charred remains through Omaha's business district into the early morning hours (fig. 6.2).

The resonances that emerge between Brown's death and the episode are compelling. The phrase "Deadwood Dicks in slouch hats" is a canny description of the leering Omaha lynchers as they are captured in photograph behind Brown's burning corpse, and a nod to the violence that escalates during the scene. (It is possible, though perhaps not likely, that Joyce had seen the photograph as he was crafting the episode.) Bloodthirsty in their search for justice—and gruesomely excessive in its execution—the faces of these men further reflect the "Cyclops" narrator's subsequent assertion that they should have continued

Figure 6.2. Charred corpse of Will Brown. From the University of Washington, "Omaha courthouse lynching," September 28, 1919. https://en.wikipedia.org/wiki/Omaha_race_riot_of_1919#/media/File:Omaha_courthouse_lynching.jpg.

to drown and crucify the body (U 12.1328). This is, historically speaking, an expression of bombast that leads to the Omaha men's punishment: the photograph was subsequently used by the authorities to identify and capture several perpetrators. The image also reflects the flawed logic of "force-against-force" that British imperialists, the Citizen, Noman, and finally Bloom himself are all, to varying degrees, guilty of enacting (U 12.464).[37]

There is, however, a further anachronism on display here, complicating any easy association of Irish subjects with Black Americans in the South. The picture that Bergan and his ilk are looking at matches a widely circulated illustration, "Hanging and burning a negro in Clarkson Street," by the American political cartoonist Thomas Nast, originally published in the 1863 issue of *Harper's Weekly* (fig. 6.3). That illustration depicts an event during the New York Draft Riots, in which many Irish immigrants in New York protested against new conscription laws to replenish Union soldiers fighting in the American Civil War.[38] The mob ultimately attacked and brutally lynched an innocent Black man, later identified as William Jones. Through the Nast images and the reference to Will Brown—Is it incidental that he is also William? Does he reach across time to

Figure 6.3. Hanging and burning a negro in Clarkson Street. Thomas Nast. Appears in Joel Tyler Headley, *Pen and Pencil Sketches of the Great Riots: An illustrated history of the Railroad and other great American Riots* (1882), 228. https://commons.wikimedia.org/wiki/File:HEADLEY(1882)_-p228_New_York_-_hanging_and_burning_a_negro_in_Clarkson_Street.jpg. Nast's image originally appeared in *Harper's Magazine,* August 1, 1863.

an innocent brother?—Joyce is actually conflating two anachronistic events, one that predates 1904 and another that postdates it.

If the second reference connects Irish victims to Black ones, however, the first reminds us that the Irish, too, could be perpetrators of precisely the mob violence they later resisted. Anachronism here allows Joyce to achieve the thickness of historical complexity, one that cannot cut easily across the political lines established by Bloom and the Citizen but may rather be indicated by the emergent mob violence that surrounds their debate. For as Saint-Amour notes of Joycean histories, "events do not have their meaning alone [. . .] their importance inheres not in their singularity but in their multiplicity, their being made up of echoes and distortions of like and unlike events."[39]

Furthermore, Black readers—at once repelled by the mention of a "Sambo," but then intrigued by its likely connection as atrocity to the violence of American lynching (on the part of the Irish no less than Southern whites)—might hear echoes of the riot that erupted in Omaha (as in Chicago, as in Tulsa), as a similar mob mentality emerges in Barney Kiernan's pub. Could Will Brown be a Joycean harbinger of precisely the public violence and vitriol that Bloom, exiting the pub "like a shot off a shovel," narrowly avoids and, it should be said, partially stokes? Or, as Ozier has it, does the spectacle of Brown's death—the violated Black body on display—rather fashion a "caustic joke out of the execution's vulgar excesses," in another instance of Irishmen leveraging American racism to center themselves on the world stage?[40] I would suggest that through the formal confusion and brutal escalation of "Cyclops," both can actually be true at once. These competing, anachronistic retellings and reshapings enable *Ulysses* to mine the "multiplicity" of historical events, amplifying the tenor of racial violence without reducing the complexities of the moment.

The lynching reference directly precedes descriptions of the British navy's atrocities, and it also occurs as the energy of the pub shifts from spirited debate to an awareness of potential, even likely bodily harm. The Citizen spits at Bloom, when he asserts, a few pages later, that he, too, belongs to Ireland. The pub patrons' animosity is roused when it is rumored that Bloom gave a tip on a horse race, leading them to surmise—erroneously—that it was Bloom who gave Arthur Griffith the idea for Sinn Féin. As the Citizen's anger reaches its peak, Bloom is ushered out of the pub and into a nearby coach, only to be chased by the Citizen and his dog, the former insisting he will "crucify" Bloom (*U* 12.1812), as the Noman wishes they would have done to Will Brown (and which the depicted racist mob *did* to William Jones).

It is in this sense that plural Black *readings*, like the plural histories and futures the text recounts, enhance our understanding of *Ulysses*: Aware that death is the episode's fulcrum, exploding the comedic frame that the language of the parodies suggests, readers can inhabit the visceral lacunae that "Cyclops" only appears to paper over. In this, then, Will Brown *is* of cardinal importance—a key allusion—with more far-reaching implications than the dating of a manuscript, implications that speak powerfully to a nation in the midst of social and political reckoning, then as now. It is our responsibility as teachers, I advance, to make room for the possibility of these competing interpretations, such that the space of the classroom might ultimately come to mirror the contradictions and reprisals of the history it conveys. Yet we must do so with an awareness of those who are left out of traditional historical narratives—and the harm that can be perpetuated when racial stereotypes are left uninterrogated, as the rich, interior lives of Black people go so frequently unimagined in *Ulysses*. A path forward, as this reading of "Cyclops" suggests, may be to entertain and even duplicate the force of anachronism: to see the disjointed relevance of current events—our history in process—in the pages of a novel that imperfectly wrestles with its own, ambivalent place in its present.

II. (Mis)Recognition: The Bohee Brothers in Nighttown

In a similar fashion to the historical reduplication found in "Cyclops," the boundaries between subjectivity and realist action are delightfully blurred in the later "Circe" episode, making it a famously challenging episode for readers to interpret. The recourse to the conventions of a stage play—speakers, stage directions, scene changes, prop use—further subverts our total immersion into the inner worlds of our protagonists, Bloom and Stephen, who have only recently come together as figural father and son in the preceding events at the National Maternity Hospital. If the allusion to Will Brown's lynching in "Cyclops" forces readers to reckon with the prevalence of death and violence—the real-world stakes of the political positions claimed by Bloom, the Citizen, and Noman—forms of intercultural *misrecognition* proliferate in "Circe," a world already preoccupied with the discrepancy between appearances and reality. I want to consider a key moment of mistaken identity—a possible (mis)reading on Joyce's part—that hovers behind the exaggerated performance of minstrelsy. On the one hand, the racializing and racist language of this performance deters Black readers from the novel, as the conventions of minstrelsy—a position created and staged by predominantly white practitioners—voids Black subjects of humanity and specificity. On the other hand, the particularity of this troupe has the potential to subvert the caricature, because some Black actors resisted stereotypes by mocking minstrelsy's generic conventions. It might offer a window into Black cultural formations, allowing subjects to maintain their "right to opacity."[41] The gap between these readings is one that I wish to preserve, to remain with the hermeneutic difficulties that loving *Ulysses* while Black involves.

Upon entering Nighttown, Joyce's name for Dublin's brothel district, Bloom experiences a series of hallucinations in which sexual desire—and the possibility of intercourse—are mixed up with fantasies of Blackness. Nowhere is this more apparent than in Bloom's encounter with Mrs. Breen, Molly's close friend, whom he finds en route to Bella Cohen's establishment. Mrs. Breen mocks Bloom for his appearance in the neighborhood but also encourages his sexual advances toward her; if Bloom's presence in Nighttown is conspicuous, Mrs. Breen's is never fully explained to the reader, leaving open the possibility that she, too, has relations beyond her marriage (and in this is similar to Molly). When Mrs. Breen threatens to tell Bloom's wife—"O just wait till I see [her]!"—of his escapades, Bloom responds by insisting that Molly herself has said she'd like to visit Nighttown, has a taste for the "exotic," and would go so far as to hire "Negro servants in livery too if she had the money" (*U* 15.406–10). The scene as a whole—with its insistence upon *women's* psychosexual autonomy in a (white) and male-dominated landscape—telegraphs Molly's final soliloquy, in which orgasm and Blackness are also powerfully, if disturbingly, intertwined. As Mrs. Breen says before disappearing: "Yes, yes, yes, yes, yes, yes, yes," a verbal foreshadowing of the novel's final lines (*U* 15.575).

It is in this context that hallucinated minstrel performers take center stage. As Bloom reflects that Molly is attracted to "Othello black brute"—a linguistic call back to Will Brown's sensationalizing headline as "Black Beast" three episodes ago—stage directions tell of the following apparition:

> (*Tom and Sam Bohee, coloured coons in white duck suits, scarlet socks, upstarched Sambo chokers and large scarlet asters in their buttonholes, leap out. Each has his banjo slung. Their paler smaller negroid hands jingle the twingtwang wires. Flashing white kaffir eyes and tusks they rattle through a breakdown in clumsy clogs, twinging, singing, back to back, toe heel, heel toe, with smackfatclacking nigger lips.*)
>
> TOM AND SAM:
> There's someone in the house with Dina,
> There's someone in the house, I know,
> There's someone in the house with Dina
> Playing on the old banjo.
> (*They whisk black masks from raw babby faces: then, chuckling, chortling, trumming, twanging, they diddle cakewalk dance away.*)
> (*U* 15.412–26)

Thus emerges the first, most painful form of misrecognition for Black readers: arguably the most detailed evocation of Blackness in *Ulysses* relies upon the conventions of minstrelsy, a projection of Black life on the part of white audiences. Here we get the infantilizing language of "raw babby faces," the animalistic rendering of "white kaffir eyes and tusks," and the blundering incompetency of "clumsy clogs," "chortling, trumming, twanging, [as] they diddle diddle cakewalk dance away." My initial response—as a reader and teacher of color—is to reject the text, to refuse to repeat such language—and the racist ideologies it belies—in the classroom, or even to myself.

But then, look closely, and there is also this: The Bohee Brothers were themselves Black, a powerful and self-sufficient performance duo that, in a generous reading, appropriated the tools of white oppression in order to *perruque* the conditions of their public visibility.[42] Black performers featured on Irish stages across the nineteenth century, and certainly Joyce would have been familiar with them.[43] Ira Aldridge, for example, performed in Belfast and Dublin as early as the 1820s, making history by becoming the first African American to perform the role of Othello in the titular play that Bloom thinks of as a precursor to this moment. George and James Bohee were celebrated banjoists, born in New Brunswick, who got their start in Boston beer halls in the 1870s. They arrived in Britain in 1881 to form their own, eponymous troupe, which included Black and white musicians. They toured the British Isles for many years, playing Dan Lowrey's music hall and the Gaiety.

While their repertoire did include imitation plantation acts—of which the "cakewalk," a mockery of white plantation owners, formed a part—the brothers were widely credited with elevating the banjo to fashionable drawing rooms and even, according to one review, "social gatherings on the West End."[44] While performances did include sentimental songs meant to appease European audiences, they also included antislavery songs and spirituals. They were among the earliest Black musicians to record their music on a phonograph. More than this, they built a career around their repertoire. The Bohee Brothers manufactured and sold banjos; taught laymen how to play the instrument; tutored Queen Victoria's son; managed theatrical productions; and promoted concerts.[45] If readers are initially disgusted by Joyce's seemingly careless reference, our curiosity is piqued by the empowering vision of Black self-possession and perseverance indexed by "Bohee" as a name. Might this be an olive branch extended, a performance that—like the genre it mimes—is meant to satirize, not whet, the appetite of white supremacists?[46]

One of the uses of minstrelsy, from the perspective of Black performers, may be to resist—by way of the caricature itself—any truer form of self-revelation to a hostile world.[47] They allow themselves to be misrecognized, because misrecognition can afford some safety. If *Ulysses* does not offer its Black characters the interiority accorded to others, there remains the possibility that the novel sometimes replicates stereotypes precisely to remind readers that Black humanity, indeed all human specificity, is essentially invisible to another's eye; moreover, that this is a good, necessary thing for those whose bodies remain vulnerable to surveillance, capture, and mutilation, as in "Cyclops." What if we read the Brothers Bohee, emerging in an episode meant to offer interior truths, but circumvented by conventions of theatricality, as just another instantiation of minority self-performance? A performance that belies, as Circe's stage directions do, secure knowledge of an inner life that remains, fundamentally, the performer's own? As Bert Williams is rumored to have said: "Nobody in America knows my real name, and, if I can prevent it, nobody ever will."[48]

The slippage between these readings is important. We should be wary of giving Joyce too much credit. (Bohee, after all, might simply *be* throwaway; the first names in the above passage, Tom and Sam—and the resultant portmanteaus "Sambo" and "Tambo"—tell us a very different story than the historical George and James Bohee do.) At the same time, our knowledge of *Ulysses* is clearly impoverished if we fail to mine this archive of Black historical integrity, style, and self-sufficiency. To take both readings, separately and together, as moments of conflict and potential release, is the intervention of the Black reader, who reorients the text to simultaneously confront and work through its racializing legacy. If we, as historically attuned critics, must remain stuck in this hermeneutic impasse—itself a reflection of the mental and emotional kinesthetics that Black readers are implicitly asked to perform in English classes that assign canonical texts—then here is the place to involve our students, to model and encourage equivocation. And what better place to do so than the novel's final episode, and its most famously obscure one: a polylogue of conflicting voices animating a fictional, mixed-race woman's thoughts?

III. Seduction: Molly Bloom's Last Word

> Molly has a sass about her.
> Did she get down with a Priest?
> Molly is [established as] different and "exotic"
> I feel this was written in a way that would be moving for someone more neurotypical than me.
> My first thought of "Penelope" is that it sounded like a kid who completely lost track of his words while speaking to someone.[49]

In spring 2023, I assigned a small portion of "Penelope" in an introductory survey course on global fiction. At Indiana University in Bloomington, teachers get a (sort of) diverse crop of students: Many come from rural towns across Southern and Central Indiana, where they've had little exposure to Black professors. (I once had a student who told me, sheepishly, upon learning that a class was focused on Black authors, that he had never met a person of color before coming to college.) Some have graduated from elite, private high schools in metropolitan areas like Chicago and Indianapolis and take Introduction to Fiction with a clear sense of the prose "greats" (though *Ulysses* is rarely on their list of texts devoured). Most, however, are lay readers: Very few describe themselves as enjoying fiction at all, and still fewer claim to have read much beyond *Lord of the Rings* and *Harry Potter* or required high school texts like *The Catcher in the Rye*. In this particular semester, I had eight non-white students out of twenty-five, only one of whom identifies as Black. In the third week of school, on a snowy January afternoon, we came together to discuss what may—to this day—remain among the most difficult, experimental pieces of literature written in English. I was elated and terrified.

Ahead of the conversation, I had asked the students to post on an online discussion board in response to the following prompt: *What do we learn about Molly Bloom as a character from this remarkable first "sentence" of the final episode of* Ulysses? I am of the belief that *Ulysses* should of course be read as a unified entity; the languor and serendipity of a single day as a slice of life can otherwise be lost. I also think certain episodes do stand on their own. In the context of this course, I felt remiss not giving my students an example of the most radical kinds of linguistic exuberance they could encounter in fictional universes. I provided some necessary context for their reading in the preceding class: This is a novel that follows two men, Leopold Bloom and Stephen Dedalus, over the course of a single June day in Dublin, Ireland, in 1904. Molly, Bloom's unfaithful wife, has been discussed throughout the novel, but her own perspective has been withheld from readers until this final, unpunctuated chapter. Here, we might say, is Molly Bloom's last word, her thoughts on everything that has come before, her experience of being watched and discussed (and moreover of watching herself *being* watched), and also her memories, urges, dreams, and desires as gender roles were shifting in turn-of-the-century Europe. It is a white, male author's imperfect, yet genuine attempt to inhabit and portray the lilting contours of a (racialized) female psyche. Or maybe not. You decide.

At the beginning of class, I gave a note on problematic language: Racist diction appears throughout the novel, as it does in Molly's consciousness, though whether Joyce actually held these views, I cautioned, remains up for debate and our discussion. I caught eyes with my one Black student. He perhaps knew the worst moment from Penelope's first "sentence" to which I implicitly referred: Meditating on women's roles as machines of reproductive futurity, Molly's thoughts travel to one of Mina Purefoy's many children: "the one they called budgers or something *like a nigger with a shock of hair on it Jesusjack the child was a black*" (*U* 18.162–63; emphasis mine). To my knowledge, no criticism has yet alighted on this particular moment in the episode as worthy of extended analysis.[50]

As in "Circe," thoughts of sex and reproduction are connected to representations of racial Otherness. Readers sense Molly's own fear of miscegenation—the child, "like a nigger with a shock of hair on it," has come from a white mother, suggesting the possibility of Mina Purefoy's extramarital dalliance with a Black man. The significant Africanist presence in turn-of-the-century Ireland may help to explain the yoked fear and excitement that Molly brings to this observation. It also points back to the notion that Joyce was committed to exploding the racially "pure" doctrine of Irish nationalism, representing an Ireland that was already profoundly intermixed, and would only become more so over the course of the twentieth century.

Finally, as I had signaled to my class at the start of the discussion, we must remember that both Bloom and Molly are racialized throughout *Ulysses*: Molly—as she recalls in thunder just prior to this moment—was born in Gibraltar, the daughter of an Irish father and a mother of Jewish and Moroccan ancestry (*U* 18.137).⁵¹ Might this knowledge, I wondered, lend texture to our reading of what might be either a form of internalized racism *or* a pleasurable self-revelation on the part of a woman of color? Or is this simply another example of repellant textuality that Black readers should just press beyond, as we so often teach ourselves to do? A question for educators writ large: What about our reading and teaching of *Ulysses* might change if we foregrounded, from the outset, that Molly herself is among the Afro-Spaniard girls she remembers throughout the monologue? That her final, affirmative yes comes routed not despite, but directly through her ambiguous, yet persistent Blackness?

> and Gibraltar as a girl where I was a *flower of the mountain yes* when I put the rose in my hair *like the Andalusian girls used* or shall I wear a red yes and how he kissed me under *the Moorish wall* and I thought well as well him as another and then I asked him with my eyes to ask me again yes and then asked me would I yes to say yes *my mountain flower* and first I put my arms around him yes and drew him down to me so he could feel my breasts all perfume yes and his heart was going like mad and *yes I said yes I will Yes.* (*U* 18.1602–9; emphasis mine)

When I was nineteen, I sat huddled, breathless, finishing these lines in a yellow armchair. I was probably heartbroken—I always was—but this I remember less than the shudder that passed through me like the shock of an electric eel. *Ulysses* was not written for someone like me, so how was it that I could feel so reflected in its pages? Ten years later, as a scholar and teacher of modernism, I wanted to explain those feelings to myself by selling the passage to a group of nineteen-year-olds. Difficulty, I said—in all of its senses—can be repellant, but something else exists *simultaneous to and inside of the repulsion*. If you allow yourself to live in the uncertainty of language, then the novel has a way of seducing its reader, guiding us along its syntactical curves with a *Yes . . . yes . . . yes . . .* And in the seduction, we might also find a sort of shining, naked core—calcified in time—that moves beyond its subject. Did anyone, I ask, find pleasure in this passage? Does anyone feel seen this way, too?

The room was silent. Most did not. "Penelope" had failed them, or I had. Then my one Black student smiled, looked around, and raised his hand.

Notes

1 James Joyce, *Ulysses*, ed. Hans Walter Gabler (London: Vintage, 1986), 15.409. References to *Ulysses* are to this edition and hereafter cited in the text as *U* followed by episode and line number.
2 Vincent J. Cheng, *Joyce, Race, and Empire* (New York: Cambridge University Press, 1993), 27.

3   James Joyce, "Ireland: Island of Saints and Sages," in *Occasional, Critical, and Political Writing*, ed. Kevin Barry (New York: Oxford, 2000), 118.
4   Paul Gilroy, *The Black Atlantic: Modernity and Double Consciousness* (Cambridge: Harvard University Press, 1995).
5   Suzanna Chan, "'I Treated You White': *Ulysses*, Gender, and the Visual Culture of Race," in *Facing the Other: Interdisciplinary Studies on Race, Gender, and Social Justice in Ireland*, ed. Borbála Faragó and Moynagh Sullivan (Cambridge: Cambridge Scholars Press, 2008), 23. See also William Hart, "Africans in Eighteenth-Century Ireland," *Irish Historical Studies* 33, no. 129 (May 2002): 22.
6   L. Perry Curtis, *Apes and Angels: The Irishman in Victorian Caricature* (Devon: David and Charles, 1971).
7   James Joyce, *The Critical Writings of James Joyce*, ed. Ellsworth Mason and Richard Ellmann (New York: Viking, 1964), 168, 166.
8   Cheng, *Joyce, Race, and Empire*, 6.
9   Frantz Fanon, *Black Skin, White Masks* [1952], trans. Richard Philcox (New York: Grove, 2008), xviii.
10 The long history of Black incarceration—and the stakes of being outwardly resistant to police intervention—has tended to yield quieter (though not to say *quietist*) responses to racial interpellation and violence. See Kevin Quashie, *The Sovereignty of Quiet: Beyond Resistance in Black Culture* (New Brunswick: Rutgers University Press, 2012).
11 Aliyyah Abdur-Rahman, and Simone Brown, "Capture, Illegibility, Necessity: A Conversation on Black Privacy," *The Black Scholar* 51, no. 1 (2021): 67–72.
12 Merve Emre, "The Seductions of Ulysses," *New Yorker*, February 7, 2022. https://www.newyorker.com/magazine/2022/02/14/the-seductions-of-ulysses.
13 Toni Morrison, *Playing in the Dark: Whiteness and the Literary Imagination* (Cambridge: Harvard University Press, 1992).
14 Morrison, *Playing in the Dark*, 16.
15 Enda Duffy, *The Subaltern "Ulysses"* (Minneapolis: University of Minnesota Press, 1994), 1.
16 Duffy, *The Subaltern "Ulysses,"* 115.
17 Cheng, *Joyce, Race, and Empire*, 7.
18 Cheryl Herr, *Joyce's Anatomy of Culture* (Chicago: University of Illinois Press, 1986), 12. See also Dominic Manganiello, *Joyce's Politics* (London: Routledge, 1980); Margot Norris, *Joyce's Web: The Social Unraveling of Modernism* (Austin: University of Texas Press, 1992); Vicki Mahaffey, *Reauthorizing Joyce* (Cambridge: Cambridge University Press, 1988).
19 Gary Wilder, *Freedom Time: Negritude, Decolonization, and the Future of the World*, 255, quoted in Paul Saint-Amour, "Rising Timely and Untimely: On Joycean Anachronism," in *The Edinburgh Companion to Irish Modernism*, ed. Maud Ellmann, Siân White, and Vicki Mahaffey (Edinburgh: Edinburgh University Press, 2021), 46.
20 Leonard Orr, "From High Modern Aesthete to Postcolonial Subject," in *Joyce, Imperialism, and Postcolonialism*, ed. Leonard Orr, 1–11 (New York: Syracuse University Press, 2008).
21 Orr, "High Modern Aesthete," 8.

22 See Derek Attridge and Marjorie Howes, eds., *Semicolonial Joyce* (Cambridge: Cambridge University Press, 2000), as well as Marjorie Howes, *Colonial Crossings: Figures in Irish Literary History* (Dublin: Field Day, 2006). Cf. Saikat Majumdar, "Desiring the Metropolis: The Anti-Aesthetic and Semi-Colonial Modernism," *Postcolonial Text* 3, no. 1 (2007): 1–14.
23 Amadi Ozier, "Lynching Modernism: *Ulysses,* America, and the Negro Minstrel Abroad," *Modernism/modernity* 30, no. 3 (September 2023): 539.
24 Aarthi Vadde, *Chimeras of Form* (New York: Columbia University Press, 2017), 7.
25 Vadde, *Chimeras of Form,* 84.
26 Vadde, *Chimeras of Form,* 100.
27 Terence Killeen, *"Ulysses" Unbound: A Reader's Companion to James Joyce's "Ulysses"* (Gainesville: University Press of Florida, 2014), 140.
28 Patrick Mullen, *The Poor Bugger's Tool: Irish Modernism, Queer Labor, and Postcolonial History* (New York: Oxford University Press, 2012), 97.
29 Although this opera, "Mr. Bloom and the Cyclops," never materialized as such, Antheil did ultimately complete a musical setting to Joyce's 1927 poem "Nightpiece." See Morgan Library and Museum's online exhibition of One Hundred Years of James Joyces's *Ulysses,* "George Antheil," https://www.themorgan.org/exhibitions/online/ulysses/george-antheil.
30 Deadwood Dick was the fictional creation of dime novelist Edward Wheeler—a Wild West cowboy—from Deadwood, South Dakota.
31 Robert Adams, *Surface and Symbol* (New York: Oxford University Press, 1962), 204–5.
32 Weldon Thornton, *Allusions in "Ulysses"* (Chapel Hill: University of North Carolina Press, 1968), 283.
33 Timothy Weiss, "The 'Black Beast' Headline: The Key to an Allusion in *Ulysses,*" *James Joyce Quarterly* 19, no. 2 (Winter 1982): 183–86. Don Gifford corroborates Weiss's allusion. Gifford, *"Ulysses" Annotated,* with Robert J. Seidman (Berkeley: University of California Press, 1988 [1974]), 357.
34 Weiss, "'Black Beast' Headline," 185.
35 To be sure, I am not claiming that Joyce necessarily knew of, or intended to re-create, the *particulars* of this American tragedy, even as those particulars are worth revisiting.
36 Daniel Greunig, "Omaha Folklore Project: Interview with Daniel Greunig," University of Nebraska Omaha Libraries Oral History Collection (1976), https://revelation.unomaha.edu/ohms-viewer/viewer.php?cachefile=MSS0018_au033.xml. See also *Omaha's Riot in Story and Picture* (Omaha: Educational Publishing Company, 1919).
37 We might consider Bloom's final taunts as a mode of "force" that responds to the violent atmosphere of the pub.
38 See Sam Slote, Marc A. Mamigonian, and John Turner, eds., *Annotations to James Joyce's "Ulysses"* (London: Oxford University Press, 2022), 632.
39 Saint-Amour, "On Joycean Anachronism," 35–50. Saint-Amour suggests that "Cyclops" references the antisemitic boycott of Limerick's Jewish merchants in 1904—a third anachronism.

40 Ozier, "Lynching Modernism," 555. I concur with Ozier that the Irish nationalists represented in "Cyclops" may well be using the specter of U.S. racial violence to mark themselves as modern; I am less convinced that *Joyce* leveraged these narratives for similar gain, given the many, competing references (and their multiple villains).
41 Édouard Glissant, *Poetics of Relation*, trans. Betsy Wing (Ann Arbor: University of Michigan Press, 1997).
42 I take this formulation from Michel de Certeau, who offers the French *la perruque* as a means of describing how company employees can "steal back" time from their employer while appearing not to: "*La perruque* is the worker's own work disguised as work for his employer. It differs from pilfering in that nothing of material value is stolen. It differs from absenteeism in that the worker is officially on the job." De Certeau, *The Practice of Everyday Life*, trans. Steven Randall (Berkeley: University of California Press, 1988), 25. Extrapolated here, the minstrel performer *appears* to embrace the oppressive framework of white audiences, but actually *steals* its performative value as a means of calling attention to whiteness' failures of imagination.
43 Herr, *Joyce's Anatomy of Culture*, 195, quoted in Chan, "I Treated You White," 24. Cheng (*Joyce, Race, and Empire*) and Gifford ("*Ulysses" Annotated*) both erroneously assume that the brothers were white, 458.
44 *Bristol Times and Mirror*, November 20, 1888, quoted in Chan, "I Treated You White," 24.
45 See the University of Lincoln's Black musicians in the John Johnson Collection: The Bohee Brothers, https://library19.blogs.lincoln.ac.uk/tag/black-musicians/.
46 A similarly fraught allusion appears in Joyce's 1914 "The Dead," when Freddy Mallins makes reference to "a negro chieftain." Margot Norris points out several Black American performers sang on various stages in Dublin during the first week of January 1904, although none of them perfectly fit Mallins's description. Freddy then asks if the other guests dislike the singer from the Gaeity just because he is Black, a direct challenging of racist judgments.
47 Susan Gubar makes a version of this claim in *Racechanges: White Skin, Black Face in American Culture* (Oxford: Oxford University Press, 1997).
48 Quoted in Ann Charters, *Nobody: The Story of Bert Williams* (New York: MacMillan, 1970), 15.
49 The excerpts that precede this section come directly from the course online discussion board; I selected the ones that feel most true to the text. All student commentary reproduced with grateful permission.
50 Cheng mentions this in passing, referencing a brief annotated entry that "Jesusjack the child was a black" was a common Dublin saying (*Joyce, Race, and Empire*, 161), and Gifford ("*Ulysses" Annotated*), 611.
51 On Molly's mixed-race heritage and the melting pot of Gibraltar, see Carol Shloss, "Molly's Resistance to the Union"; Susan Bazargan, "Mapping Gibraltar: Colonialism, Time, and Narrative in 'Penelope,'" in *Molly Blooms: A Polylogue on "Penelope" and Cultural Studies*, ed. Richard Pearce, 119–38 (Madison: Wisconsin University Press, 1994); and Younghee Kho, "Moving Beyond the Famine: Joyce, Emigration, and Imagining a New Community in 'Penelope,'" *Joyce Studies Annual* (2017): 163–84.

Bibliography

Abdur-Rahman, Aliyyah, and Simone Brown. "Capture, Illegibility, Necessity: A Conversation on Black Privacy." *The Black Scholar* 51, no. 1 (2021): 67–72.
Adams, Robert. *Surface and Symbol*. New York: Oxford University Press, 1962.
Attridge, Derek, and Marjorie Howes, eds. *Semicolonial Joyce*. Cambridge: Cambridge University Press, 2000.
Bazargan, Susan. "Mapping Gibraltar: Colonialism, Time, and Narrative in 'Penelope.'" In *Molly Blooms: A Polylogue on "Penelope" and Cultural Studies*, edited by Richard Pearce, 119–38. Madison: Wisconsin University Press, 1994.
Chan, Suzanna. "'I Treated You White': *Ulysses*, Gender, and the Visual Culture of Race." In *Facing the Other: Interdisciplinary Studies on Race, Gender, and Social Justice in Ireland*, edited by Borbála Faragó and Moynagh Sullivan, 19–31. Cambridge: Cambridge Scholars Press, 2008.
Charters, Ann. *Nobody: The Story of Bert Williams*. New York: MacMillan, 1970.
Cheng, Vincent J. *Joyce, Race, and Empire*. New York: Cambridge University Press, 1993.
Curtis, L. Perry. *Apes and Angels: The Irishman in Victorian Caricature*. Devon: David and Charles, 1971.
De Certeau, Michel. *The Practice of Everyday Life*. Translated by Steven Randall. Berkeley: University of California Press, 1988.
Deane, Seamus. "National Character and National Audience: Races, Crowds, and Readers." In *Critical Approaches to Anglo-Irish Literature*, edited by Michael Allen and Angela Wilcox, 40–52. Totowa, NJ: Barnes and Noble, 1989.
Duffy, Enda. *The Subaltern "Ulysses."* Minneapolis: University of Minnesota Press, 1994.
Emre, Merve. "The Seductions of *Ulysses*." *The New Yorker*, February 7, 2022. https://www.newyorker.com/magazine/2022/02/14/the-seductions-of-ulysses
Fanon, Frantz. *Black Skin, White Masks*. [1952] Translated by Richard Philcox. New York: Grove, 2008.
Gifford, Don, and Robert J. Seidman. *"Ulysses" Annotated*. [1974] Berkeley: University of California Press, 1988.
Gilroy, Paul. *The Black Atlantic: Modernity and Double Consciousness*. Cambridge: Harvard University Press, 1995.
Glissant, Édouard. *Poetics of Relation*. Translated by Betsy Wing. Ann Arbor: University of Michigan Press, 1997.
Greunig, Daniel. "Omaha Folklore Project: Interview with Daniel Greunig." University of Nebraska Omaha Libraries Oral History Collection (1976). https://revelation.unomaha.edu/ohms-viewer/viewer.php?cachefile=MSS0018_au033.xml.
Gubar, Susan. *Racechanges: White Skin, Black Face in American Culture*. Oxford: Oxford University Press, 1997.
Hart, William. "Africans in Eighteenth-Century Ireland." *Irish Historical Studies* 33, no. 129 (May 2002): 19–32.
Herr, Cheryl. *Joyce's Anatomy of Culture*. Chicago: University of Illinois Press, 1986.
Howes, Marjorie. *Colonial Crossings: Figures in Irish Literary History*. Dublin: Field Day, 2006.

Joyce, James. *The Critical Writings of James Joyce,* edited by Ellsworth Mason and Richard Ellmann. New York: Viking, 1964.

Joyce, James. "The Dead." In *Dubliners,* edited by Margot Norris, Hans Walter Gabler, and Walter Hettche. New York: W. W. Norton, 2006.

Joyce, James. "Ireland: Island of Saints and Sages." In *Occasional, Critical, and Political Writing,* edited by Kevin Barry, 108–26. New York: Oxford, 2000.

Joyce, James. *Ulysses.* Edited by Hans Walter Gabler, et al. London: Vintage, 1986.

Kho, Younghee. "Moving Beyond the Famine: Joyce, Emigration, and Imagining a New Community in 'Penelope.'" *Joyce Studies Annual* (2017): 163–84.

Killeen, Terence. *"Ulysses" Unbound: A Reader's Companion to James Joyce's "Ulysses."* Gainesville: University Press of Florida, 2014.

Mahaffey, Vicki. *Reauthorizing Joyce.* Cambridge: Cambridge University Press, 1988.

Manganiello, Dominic. *Joyce's Politics.* London: Routledge, 1980.

Morrison, Toni. *Playing in the Dark: Whiteness and the Literary Imagination.* Cambridge: Harvard University Press, 1992.

Mullen, Patrick. *The Poor Bugger's Tool: Irish Modernism, Queer Labor, and Postcolonial History.* New York: Oxford University Press, 2012.

Norris, Margot. *Joyce's Web: The Social Unraveling of Modernism.* Austin: University of Texas Press, 1992.

Orr, Leonard, ed. *Joyce, Imperialism, and Postcolonialism.* New York: Syracuse University Press, 2008.

Ozier, Amadi. "Lynching Modernism: *Ulysses,* America, and the Negro Minstrel Abroad." *Modernism/modernity* 30, no. 3 (September 2023): 539–61.

Quashie, Kevin. *The Sovereignty of Quiet: Beyond Resistance in Black Culture.* New Brunswick: Rutgers University Press, 2012.

Saint-Amour, Paul. "Rising Timely and Untimely: On Joycean Anachronism." In *The Edinburgh Companion to Irish Modernism,* edited by Maud Ellmann, Siân White, and Vicki Mahaffey, 35–50. Edinburgh: Edinburgh University Press, 2021.

Shloss, Carol. "Molly's Resistance to the Union." *Modern Fiction Studies* 35, no. 3 (Autumn 1989): 529–41.

Slote, Sam, Marc Mamigonian, and John Turner, eds. *Annotations to James Joyce's "Ulysses."* London: Oxford University Press, 2022.

Thornton, Weldon. *Allusions in "Ulysses."* Chapel Hill: University of North Carolina Press, 1968.

Vadde, Aarthi. *Chimeras of Form.* New York: Columbia University Press, 2017.

Weiss, Timothy. "The 'Black Beast' Headline: The Key to an Allusion in *Ulysses.*" *James Joyce Quarterly* 19, no. 2 (Winter 1982): 183–86.

Wilder, Gary. *Freedom Time: Negritude, Decolonization, and the Future of the World.* Durham: Duke University Press, 2015.

7

Decolonial Pedagogy and Teaching Joyce in a Liberal Arts College Classroom

SHINJINI CHATTOPADHYAY

Modernist literature has a tense relationship with educational institutions and pedagogy. In *A Room of One's Own,* Virginia Woolf famously disparages how prestigious educational institutions have historically excluded women. Peter Howarth, in the introduction to a special issue of *Modernist Cultures* on "Modernism and/as Pedagogy," argues that works like Virginia Woolf's *Three Guineas* and Ezra Pound's *ABC of Reading* demand for educational reform and show that modernist writers were disconcerted with how "education had become one of the central ways in which liberal, democratic and industrial society was reproducing itself and shaping its citizens in its image."[1] Whereas Woolf and Pound critique the education system, D. H. Lawrence laments how exploitative and unrewarding the teaching profession is, noting that "We [the teachers] have prepared, and are not wanted. We are the nations [sic] servants."[2] The discontent of modernist writers with pedagogical practices is, however, not limited to the generation of critiques, but also leads to the formation of experimental pedagogical models.

Rachel Sagner Buurma and Laura Heffernan, in their phenomenal study of modernist pedagogy, *The Teaching Archive,* examine how T. S. Eliot developed a radical pedagogy in his teaching career to adequately address the distinct learning needs of his working-class students whom he taught from 1916 to 1919 at the Modern English Literature tutorial for the University of London Joint Committee for the Promotion of the Higher Education of Working People. They show that Eliot implemented various radical strategies in his teaching, such as compiling the course syllabus in collaboration with his students, revising essay prompts to better suit the work schedules of the students, reorienting the syllabus around interconnected themes and questions and decentering individual authors, and even drafting a syllabus that presented Elizabethan poets and playwrights as working writers, which would better resonate with his working-class students.³ Eliot not only creates an important instance of innovative pedagogy but also transfers his pedagogical philosophy to works of literary criticism when he converts the course syllabi into the essays of *The Sacred Wood*.

Similarly, James Joyce also combines his pedagogical principles with creative works, particularly in *A Portrait of the Artist as a Young Man*, "Nestor" in *Ulysses*, and "Nightlessons" in *Finnegans Wake*, where he illustrates how the shortcomings of contemporary educational methods inhibit the intellectual growth of individual students. Joyce supplements Woolf, Eliot, and Lawrence's gender, class, and profession-based critiques of pedagogy with a critique of coloniality, where he identifies colonialist structures of knowledge implicit in contemporaneous education systems that diminish Irish subjectivity to colonial stereotypes. In this chapter I argue that Joyce critiques British colonialist epistemologies undergirding pedagogical practices of his times in which he proleptically anticipates a decolonial pedagogy, and, therefore, the teaching of Joyce's works in college classrooms requires the implementation of inclusive methods to execute the decolonial teaching that Joyce had envisioned.

Decolonial Pedagogy: Definition and Implementation

The praxis of decolonial pedagogy is founded on the concept of decoloniality. The notion of decoloniality emerges from a critique of colonial and neocolonial practices that come into being during the period of colonization and endure even after the end of colonial regimes. Walter Mignolo defines decoloniality as the exercise of power that reveals how colonization inevitably engenders all-pervading and long-lasting colonial structures, such as colonial forms of governance, the notion of Western hegemony over other forms of cultures, and capitalist economy.⁴ He describes decoloniality as a project of epistemic reconstitution in essence that delinks (or detaches) from colonialist and Eurocentric structures of knowledge. He explains that decoloniality entails an epistemic reconstitution of "ways of thinking, languages, ways of life and being in the world that the rhetoric of modernity disavowed and the logic of coloniality implement."⁵ Since the aim of decoloniality is ultimately an epistemic reconstitution, its relevance for pedagogy is self-evident.

Morreira et al., in the introduction to *Decolonising Curricula and Pedagogy in Higher Education*, foreground the epistemic function of decolonial pedagogy defining it as "an inherently plural set of practices that aim to interrupt the dominant power/knowledge matrix that affects teaching and learning practices in higher education."⁶ In other words, decolonial pedagogy aims to disrupt the hegemony of colonial structures of knowledge in the college classroom.

Morreira et al. note that decolonial pedagogy impacts knowledge produced via research, content selected for curriculum, classroom practices of teaching said content, and modes of assessing student work.[7]

Since decolonial pedagogy encompasses a wide range of practices in higher education, it is especially essential for the English literature curricula. Ankhi Mukherjee and Ato Quayson rightly point out in their introduction to *Decolonizing the English Literary Curriculum* how colonialist structures still undergird the discipline, "[i]n departments of English, where we teach the history of literature and language from Anglo-Saxon to World Literature, chronology is Eurochronology to a large extent, and to situate oneself in literary tradition is to inhabit structures that are historically Eurocentric, patriarchal, classist, xenophobic, or racist."[8] Decolonial pedagogy particularly assists with revising the English curricula by foregrounding ontologies that have been hitherto suppressed within colonialist structures.

Despite our robust understanding of the theories of decolonial pedagogy, its practice remains relatively elusive.[9] The gap between theory and practice primarily arises from the apparent incommensurability of the theory of decoloniality with the practices of the formal college classroom. Mignolo explains that the challenge of implementing decoloniality in the classroom is a conundrum because when decoloniality is put into practice, it takes the form of disrupting the academy.[10] In defining decoloniality, he unequivocally states that "decoloniality is *not* an academic discipline."[11] However, he also notes that this does not mean that decoloniality cannot be enacted in the academy. In this chapter I show that reading and teaching the works of James Joyce shows us a way (among many others) of bridging the gap between decolonial theory and pedagogical practice. In the first part of the chapter, I examine how "Nestor," the second episode of Joyce's *Ulysses,* anticipates modes of decolonial pedagogy by critiquing the ways in which early twentieth-century education systems perpetuate colonial structures of knowledge. In the second part of the chapter, I draw on my own experience of teaching Joyce's "The Dead" in an upper-division undergraduate English literature course at a US liberal arts college in Georgia to examine how the teaching of Joyce's works in the college classroom can facilitate the incorporation of decolonial theory in pedagogical practices.

"Nestor" and Decolonial Pedagogy

James Joyce, similar to T. S. Eliot, Virginia Woolf, and D. H. Lawrence, had extensive firsthand experience with teaching. During his Triestine sojourn, Joyce taught English language to non-native speakers at Trieste's *Scuola "Revoltella"*

Superiore di Commercio and *Scuola Serale di Commercio* and gave private lessons to wealthy students of the city (Italo Svevo and his wife were among his notable students). Elizabeth Switaj, in *James Joyce's Teaching Life and Methods*, has extensively analyzed Joyce's experience of teaching English as a foreign language. She shows that Joyce started teaching English to non-native speakers primarily out of the necessity to cover essential expenses for himself and his family and not out of any particular commitment to or affinity for teaching. However, Switaj adds that, "[a]fter a few decades of teaching, the pedagogical role became key to who James Joyce was," and his pedagogy notably influenced his creative output.[12]

Joyce shared with his fellow modernists a dissatisfaction with extant practices of teaching. Switaj cites Joyce's education as a student at Clongowes Wood College and Belvedere College, where he was taught foreign languages in the grammar-translation method of language instruction. In this method, instruction focuses on grammatical rules and translations. But when Joyce taught English as a foreign language, he departed from this restrictive method and took up a more spontaneous conversational approach. Switaj interprets Joyce's rejection of grammar-translation methods as a "judgement" on the inefficacy of said method.[13]

Joyce extends his critique of extant pedagogical practices from his teaching to his writing. In *A Portrait of the Artist as a Young Man* he illustrates how within the Catholic educational framework of Clongowes, students are subjected to violent methods of being disciplined and punished that are detrimental to their learning. Father Arnall sentences Fleming to be on his knees before the whole class, and the prefect of studies strikes him with the pandybat because he "wrote a bad Latin theme" and "missed all the questions in grammar."[14] Instead of being taught with compassion and sympathy, Fleming is abused with painful corporal punishment and public humiliation. The prefect of studies justifies Fleming's punishment by declaring him "a born idler" in which he reinforces the British colonialist stereotype of condemning the Irish subjectivity inferior to British modernity. Thus, in *Portrait,* Joyce critiques how British colonialist biases lead to hostile educational environments that do not foster positive intellectual growth among Irish students.

Whereas in *Portrait* Stephen struggles with a colonialist education system as a student, in "Nestor," he grapples with a colonialist curriculum in the role of an instructor. In this episode, Stephen teaches (or tries to teach) history to a class of young boys at a private school in Dalkey. The opening of the episode, which begins in medias res showing Stephen quizzing one of his students about the class content, succinctly portrays the inefficacy of the lesson:

—You, Cochrane, what city sent for him?
—Tarentum, sir.
—Very good. Well?
—There was a battle, sir.
—Very good. Where?
   The boy's blank face asked the blank window.[15]

Here Stephen teaches about Pyrrhus (318–272 BCE), who resisted Roman imperial aggression against the Tarentines, a Greek colony in lower Italy.[16] But the history lesson is reduced to memorizing a collection of random facts where students are interrogated about events like "what city sent for him?" and where the battle was fought. The lesson involves little critical analysis of the historical context of Roman imperialism since students are not encouraged to critically inquire *why* Pyrrhus fought against the Romans or *why* the battles were ultimately futile. Students memorize facts and events by deracinating them from their historical context, and this decontextualization of history is mirrored in the abrupt opening of the episode, which provides little background about the lesson being taught. Students deposit the lessons in memory as arbitrary pieces of information that they recall and regurgitate during examinations without any critical reflection. Such lessons lead to little intellectual growth among students, and the lack of growth is reflected in Cochrane's "blank face" at the end of the scene.

The ineptitude of the pedagogical methods of Stephen's school is implicitly attributed to the school's colonialist foundations. At the end of the episode, Stephen's interaction with the school's headmaster, Mr. Garret Deasy, reveals the headmaster's pro-British sentiments, his anti-Semitism, and misogyny. In "Nestor" Joyce illustrates how a colonialist administration actively hinders the development of critical thinking among students. The curriculum followed at Mr. Deasy's school perpetuates hegemonic knowledge by emphasizing Eurocentric histories and colonialist triumphalism and obscuring histories of colonial resistance. Students learn about Roman history and remain ignorant about centuries-long English occupation of Ireland.

The history lesson does not assist students in drawing parallels between Roman imperialism in the past and British colonialism in the present, and the students do not develop intellectual faculties to apply their knowledge of the past to evaluate the colonial condition of early twentieth-century Ireland. Furthermore, the British colonialist bias implicit in the curriculum is continued, as Len Platt notes, when "[f]or no apparent reason, Stephen's lesson switches midway from classical history to literature, and students are asked to read from Milton's 'Lycidas,' a one-time standard of school poetry compilations."[17] Platt interprets that the choice of an English poet betrays the underlying Anglicization of the curriculum.[18] Thus, in this curriculum the Irish subjectivity is ignored, and histories of colonial disempowerment are framed before the students as the narrative of progress and modernity, which hinder them from challenging colonialist power structures.

Stephen attempts to depart from the British colonialist and anglicized curriculum toward the end of his lesson by switching to active-learning methods. When students implore him to tell them a story, he eventually presents them with a riddle to solve:

The cock crew,
The sky was blue:
The bells in heaven
Were striking eleven.
'Tis time for this poor soul
To go to heaven. (U 2.102–7)

Stephen produces a slightly different version of a well-known nonsense Irish riddle, which the students briefly puzzle over, but they admit soon enough that they are unable to find the solution and rely on Stephen to supply them the answer. The students' inability to find the answer is not entirely due to their lack of capacity in critical thinking as Robert Spoo rightly points out that "the riddle's solution can't be supplied by thoughtful guesswork; it must be known in advance."[19] The riddle is thus unanswerable and does not seem to stimulate active critical thinking among students. However, through the riddle Stephen hints at an Irish way of life. In *English As We Speak It in Ireland* (which has a slightly different version of Stephen's riddle), P. W. Joyce notes that riddles are an integral part of Irish identity, stating that "[a]mong fireside amusements propounding riddles was very general sixty or seventy years ago. This is a custom that has existed in Ireland from very early times."[20] Through the riddle, Stephen draws attention to everyday Irish history, which has no place in the curriculum that is primarily populated by lessons on Roman history or literature imported from England. Stephen's answer to the riddle, "the fox burying his grandmother under a hollybush" (*U* 2.115), further emphasizes the gap in the teaching of history in a colonial Irish classroom. His answer can be interpreted as the fox burying its past. In this sense the answer echoes a famous statement made by Stephen a little later in the episode: "[H]istory is a nightmare from which I am trying to awake" (*U* 2.377).

In the riddle Stephen not only expresses his discontent with Irish history but he also shows his dissatisfaction with the way in which Irish history is taught (or ignored) in curricula. The riddle provides veiled indications that the dominant narratives of history that the students are being taught need to be interrogated, because they remain silent about the complexities of the Irish colonial condition. The students' lack of familiarity with the popular Irish riddle reflects how their Irish identity is overshadowed by British colonialist structures of knowledge—they can read from Milton, but they do not know about a common Irish riddle. By exposing students to the Irish riddle, Stephen transcends the British colonialist canon and constructs an instance of decolonial pedagogy. He displaces the dominant anglicized and British colonialist curricula by giving voice to the Irish identity that otherwise remains suppressed in the classroom.

Teaching Joyce's "The Dead" with Decolonial Pedagogy

How does Joyce's critique of colonialist pedagogies impact the teaching of Joyce's works in the liberal arts college classroom at present? How does teaching Joyce's works impact the teaching of the broader English literature curriculum beyond modernism? These questions were crucial to me when I designed my course, Anglophone Literatures and Cosmopolitanism. This was an upper-division undergraduate English literature course, which I taught at a US liberal arts college in Georgia, in fall 2022. I included the following course description in my syllabus:

> What does it mean to be a cosmopolitan? Does it mean indulging in exotic trends? How is cosmopolitanism different from globalization? How does one truly become a citizen of the world? In this course we will explore how in these times of polarizations cosmopolitanism can show us an avenue of unity without forcing homogeneity. We will particularly focus on cosmopolitanism's relationship with places and study how it achieves a synergy between the local and the global. We will begin with analyzing how early twentieth-century literature revises cosmopolitanism as anticolonial and opposes the idea that cosmopolitanism is a privilege available only to the elite. Then we will turn to contemporary literature and examine how minority communities in postcolonial nations, such as Black Britons, Black African migrants in Ireland, and subaltern Indians among others, formulate unique forms of cosmopolitanisms, which they employ to subvert Western imperial hegemony, advance efforts of decolonization, preserve the uniqueness of their communities, and explore the diversity of global cultures. We will study novels, poetry, short stories, essays, graphic novels, movies, and documentaries to analyze how race, class, gender, citizenship status, and pathways of

immigration make cosmopolitanism part of our everyday lives. We will sharpen our skills in close reading, analytical thinking, and research.

It is evident from the above description that the course is not designed exclusively around Joyce's works. Instead, the central question of the course is how communities (and individuals) with marginalized race, class, gender identities, and precarious citizenship status forge multicultural connections in modern and contemporary global anglophone literatures. So where do Joyce's works fit in a course like this? The first primary text of the course is Joyce's "The Dead," because it helps ground discussions on the themes of anticolonialism, nationalism, and multiculturalism, all of which are central tenets for decolonial pedagogy.

The decolonial pedagogy of "Anglophone Literatures and Cosmopolitanism" begins with Joyce's position in the course syllabus. In "Nestor" Stephen challenges the colonialist underpinnings of a curriculum saturated with Roman history and English poetry by exposing students to a commonplace Irish riddle. Beginning a course on cosmopolitanism with Joyce's "The Dead" echoes Stephen's legacy of decoloniality by interrogating traditional notions of cosmopolitanism. Cosmopolitanism is often misunderstood as the act of elite international travel where tourists from the colonial center explore the exoticism of the colonized other.[21] Analyzing how the notion of cosmopolitanism is developed in "The Dead" challenges the dominant (and reductive) understanding of the concept.

"The Dead" decenters the point of origin of cosmopolitanism from the imperial center to the colonial outpost. It suggests that the colony is not just a subject of the exoticizing colonial gaze, but it also generates its own multicultural connections. The text shows how cosmopolitanism in Ireland is a product of the complex interplay of the forces of British colonization, Irish nationalism, and multicultural connections beyond Ireland and England. The story, in highlighting Ireland's colonial status within the British Empire, disrupts the notion of Eurocentrism. It shows that Europe is not a homogeneous unit of Western modernity, rather it is marked by internal colonial conflicts, where Ireland is made subservient to the imperial powers of England in the colonial imagination.

Shahjahan et al., in their review article on the implementation of decolonial curriculum and pedagogy in the college classroom, note that the disruption of hegemonic knowledge structures is integral to the execution of a decolonial pedagogy. They write that this disruption often takes the form of "decentering" or "destabilizing," and the objects of this disruption are "dominant," "imperialist," "colonial," "hegemonic," "Westernized," "Eurocentric," or "neoliberal" modes of knowledge production within higher education.[22] Foregrounding the context of the Irish colonial consciousness in teaching "The Dead" assists with the epistemic reconstitution of the notion of cosmopolitanism destabilizing dominant power/knowledge structures of the college curriculum. Beginning the course with "The Dead" creates the scaffolding to further analyze how multiple complex formations of cosmopolitanism are created with varied worldwide conditions of race, class, gender, and citizenship status as depicted in the subsequent texts in the course, such as Chimamanda Ngozi Adichie's *Americanah*, Melatu Uche Okorie's *This Hostel Life*, Joy Harjo's *Living Nations, Living Words*, and Bernardine Evaristo's *Soul Tourists* among other global anglophone texts.

Whereas planning to analyze the colonial crosscurrents in "The Dead" is the first step toward a decolonial pedagogy, the process of decolonial pedagogy is effectively executed when the textual analysis is performed with the help of inclusive classroom practices. Kelly Hogan and Viji Sathy, experts of inclusive teaching, note that inclusive classroom practices especially benefit "students who are underrepresented either at the institution or in a discipline, students who are first in their families to go to college, students who are introverts, minoritized students, those who experience imposter phenomenon, students holding a minority view on an issue, students with learning differences, those with physical disabilities, individuals who identify as LGBTQIA+, international students, and many others."[23] Thus, inclusive practices dismantle neocolonial power structures by decentering dominant voices, and empowering students with nontraditional identities.

Inclusive teaching was especially required for my class because I had a heterogeneous student population. In keeping with the small student-instructor ratio usually implemented at liberal arts colleges, I had a small class that was enrolled at capacity with twenty students, eighteen of whom were English literature or creative writing majors, one was a STEM major, and one was a social science major. The students varied from sophomores to seniors. Because of the variety of disciplinary backgrounds and unequal number of years spent in college education, the students had dissimilar levels of knowledge about modern literature and the sociohistorical context of British colonialism in Ireland and uneven skills in literary analysis. To create an inclusive environment in the classroom and promote active learning, I used a combination of lecturing, small-group discussions, and whole-group discussions.

I began my inclusive pedagogy with lecturing, and the goal of my lectures was to provide students with adequate scaffolding for understanding Joyce's works as a product of his colonial consciousness. The lectures prepared the groundwork for students to independently analyze the complex interplay of nationalism, colonialism, and cosmopolitanism in "The Dead." In my first lecture I provided an overview of Joyce's biographical information, introduced students to his notable works, and outlined the major themes of his works (urbanism, gender, religion, betrayal, and so on). In my second lecture I provided information on British colonization of Ireland and the construction of the west of Ireland in the Irish nationalist imaginary. I especially emphasized how Joyce critiqued British colonialism in Ireland in his works, and how he also opposed exclusionary Irish nationalism. I intentionally kept the lectures brief (fifteen to twenty minutes of lecturing in a seventy-five-minute class period) to allow students enough time to incorporate the information supplied in the lectures in their class discussions and critical thinking activities.

In their in-class discussion sessions, students applied the contextual information provided in the lectures and performed critical analyses of the text. "Nestor" critiques how merely committing information to memory does not help students develop actual intellectual capacity; for instance, Sargent fails to figure out how to solve the sums even after copying them off the board per Mr. Deasy's instructions (*U* 2.133–34). The episode thus advocates the necessity for new pedagogical practices that would cultivate independent thinking among students. Following the critique in "Nestor," I focused on developing critical analysis skills in students. Students in the course performed the initial stage of analysis by participating in Think-Pair-Share (TPS) activities in small groups. Students were given the following discussion prompts:

1. Why does Miss Ivors say that Gabriel should be ashamed of himself (*D* 187) and why does Gabriel have the urge to respond with the statement that literature is above politics (188)?[24]
2. Why does Gabriel emphasize the tradition of Irish hospitality in his dinner speech and why does he say that he will not linger on the past?
3. What does Gabriel mean when he says at the end of the story that "the time had come for him to set out on his journey westward" (*D* 223)?

The goal of the discussion prompts was to get students to begin thinking about how "The Dead" illustrates issues of early twentieth-century Irish nationalism and British colonialism in Ireland with relation to the contextual information provided in the lectures.

Hogan and Sathy note that TPS is a versatile tool to use in an active-learning environment. But they also warn that it is often poorly executed when instructors skip the think section and go directly to the share/discussion section of the activity, which puts certain students (such as students who need more time to process their ideas before they can articulate them, multilingual students, introverted students, and others) at a disadvantage in TPS activities. Not getting enough time to think may lead to diminished learning in students and even a sense of marginalization in the class community. Hogan and Sathy suggest that, to avoid such inequities in the classroom, in a properly implemented TPS activity "the instructor will prompt students to spend a specific amount of time thinking independently."[25] Following their advice, I allocated five minutes at the beginning of the TPS activity for students to reflect on the discussion prompts on their own. After five minutes I signaled to the class to begin their small-group discussions in groups of three to four students. The TPS activity was followed by a whole-group discussion where each group reported a summary of their discussions. Students discussed the dichotomy of the allegedly anti-modern west of Ireland in the nationalist imaginary of Miss Ivors, the purportedly modern west of continental Europe in Gabriel's cosmopolitan imaginary, and how each position operates on colonial stereotypes of modern/anti-modern.

I did not limit the whole-class discussion to the above discussion prompts. The class discussions eventually went beyond the discussion questions and students generated new points of reflection. Eighteen out of twenty students in the class identified as women, and a majority of students were interested in analyzing the depiction of women in the text. Many students raised the question why the two main women characters in the story, Miss Ivors and Gretta, are shown not to share Gabriel's obsession with Western Europe and have special bonds with the west of Ireland in their own distinctive ways. This led to a discussion on how women are differently impacted by colonialism and nationalism and how their cosmopolitan trajectories could potentially differ from what their male counterparts would experience. The students concluded the discussion by making observations on how Irish identity is not a homogeneous phenomenon, rather it takes up multiple forms in response to the individual's gender and class identities as well as intellectual and geographical backgrounds. The TPS activities and whole-group discussions helped to implement a decolonial pedagogy by assisting students in developing their autonomous analytical skills when examining ideas of coloniality, nationalism, and cosmopolitanism. They also created an inclusive and equitable environment in the classroom in which all students had a chance to voice their textual interpretations and participate in active learning in a collaborative environment.

Beyond classroom discussions, I continued my decolonial pedagogy in the modes of assessment to ensure that decoloniality is integral to my overall pedagogy. Elaine Showalter, in *Teaching Literature,* has expressed suspicion about the efficacy of consecutive writing assignments in literature courses. She writes, "[o]ne of my perpetual dilemmas in teaching literature is the convention of the paper assignment—two short and one long, or two medium and a final examination, spread out throughout the semester like a patient etherized upon a table."[26] She doubts if such writing assignments adequately stimulate in-depth critical engagement among students with the course content.

To inspire thoughtful critical responses to the text, I provided students options beyond writing a traditional research paper. I gave students the choice of doing a creative project if they were passionate about creative writing and not inclined to write a research paper. The assignment required students to write an accompanying reflection with their creative piece in which they would explain how they have creatively analyzed the tenets of cosmopolitanism. Since many students in the class were creative writing majors, they were eager to conduct creative projects that would be included in their final portfolios. Adding the creative assignment promoted student-centered learning, integral to the liberal arts environments, by providing students the flexibility to choose the mode in which they would like to critically engage with the course content and which they find the best suited with their learning preferences. The creative option made the assignment inclusive because it acknowledged the varied learning preferences of the students and it also decentered the dominant practice of writing research essays.

Two students performed creative rewritings of "The Dead," transporting the Irish context to the contemporary American South. One of the students reimagined the heated exchange between Gabriel and Miss Ivors in "The Dead" and composed a short story set in contemporary Georgia in which two characters had a similarly acrimonious conversation about the idea of patriotism in the United States. The author wrote in the reflection piece that they chose to transpose Joyce's story to the modern-day American South because the text reflected the present political climate. The assignment, thus, enabled students to not only critically analyze "The Dead" but also extend their analysis to the present to critically examine how ideas of nationalism and cosmopolitanism have evolved in the present sociopolitical context.

Joyce's critique of colonialist pedagogy helps us find ways in which the gap between decolonial theory and its pedagogical application can be reduced in the present college classroom. Joyce principally critiques how colonialist modes of knowledge suppress the histories of colonial disempowerment and discourage the analysis of the consequences of imperialism. The suppression of such forms of knowledge helps sustain the hegemony of colonial power and obscures minority voices. The teaching of Joyce's works helps us counter many of Joyce's critiques of colonialist pedagogies. Placing emphasis on how Joyce depicted the colonial condition of Ireland helps students disrupt the dominant power/knowledge matrix of British imperial triumphalism. This decolonial reading of Joyce can be further amplified by incorporating inclusive and equitable classroom practices. Executing active-learning practices that foster independent critical thinking among students is crucial for decolonial pedagogy. But such active-learning practices need to be implemented with a view to inclusivity and equity so that they benefit all students regardless of their race, gender, class, citizenship identities, intellectual abilities, and preparedness. Since Joyce is an essential part of undergraduate and graduate curricula at various universities, teaching Joyce's works with principles of decoloniality can provide a model of decolonial pedagogy for the larger curriculum of English literature. It can lead to the development of nontraditional classroom practices, new modes of assessment, and new ways of engaging students with the course content.

Notes

1 Peter Howarth, "Introduction: Modernism and/as Pedagogy," *Modernist Cultures* 14, no. 3 (2019): 266.
2 Quoted in Benjamin Hagen, *The Sensuous Pedagogies of Virginia Woolf and D. H. Lawrence* (Clemson: Clemson University Press, 2020), 44. Hagen argues that Lawrence, influenced by his experience as a schoolteacher in his early life, develops nontraditional models of teaching where he complicates "the very notion of pedagogy itself, focusing on problems that arise in the relation between people who play at being teachers and students with each other and the uncomfortable role that feeling (namely, touch) plays in their fragile relationships" (45–46).
3 Rachel Sagner Buurma and Laura Heffernan, *The Teaching Archive: A New History for Literary Study* (Chicago: University of Chicago Press, 2020), 18–19.
4 Walter Mignolo and Catherine E. Walsh, *On Decoloniality: Concepts, Analytics, Praxis* (Durham: Duke University Press, 2018), 114.
5 Walter Mignolo, "Interview—Walter Mignolo/Part 2: Key Concepts," int. *E-International Relations*, January 21, 2017, https://www.e-ir.info/2017/01/21/interview-walter-mignolopart-2-key-concepts/.
6 Shannon Morreira, Kathy Luckett, Siseko H. Kumalo, and Manjeet Ramgotra, introduction to *Decolonising Curricula and Pedagogy in Higher Education: Bringing Decolonial Theory into Contact with Teaching Practice*, ed. Morreira, et al. (New York: Routledge, 2021), 7–8.
7 Morreira, et al., introduction to *Decolonising Curricula*, 8.
8 Ankhi Mukherjee and Ato Quayson, introduction to *Decolonizing the English Literary Curriculum*, ed. Ankhi Mukherjee and Ato Quayson (Cambridge: Cambridge University Press, 2023), 14.
9 Morreira, et al., introduction to *Decolonising Curricula*, 6.
10 Mignolo and Walsh, *On Decoloniality*, 106.
11 Mignolo and Walsh, *On Decoloniality*, 106 (emphasis mine).
12 Elizabeth Switaj, *James Joyce's Teaching Life and Methods: Language and Pedagogy in "A Portrait of the Artist as a Young Man," "Ulysses," and "Finnegans Wake"* (London: Palgrave Macmillan, 2016), 1.
13 Switaj, *James Joyce's Teaching Life*, 15–17.
14 James Joyce, *A Portrait of the Artist as a Young Man*, ed. Jeri Johnson (Oxford: Oxford University Press, 2000), 40.

15 James Joyce, *Ulysses,* ed. Hans Walter Gabler, et al. (New York: Vintage, 1986), 2.1–6. Hereafter cited parenthetically in the text as *U* followed by episode and line number.
16 Don Gifford and Robert J. Seidman, *"Ulysses" Annotated: Notes for James Joyce's "Ulysses"* (Berkeley: University of California Press, 1988), 30.
17 Len Platt, *James Joyce and Education: Schooling and the Social Imaginary in the Modernist Novel* (London: Routledge, 2021), 90.
18 Platt, *James Joyce and Education,* 90.
19 Robert Spoo, "Nestor," in *The Cambridge Centenary Ulysses: The 1922 Text with Essays and Notes,* ed. Catherine Flynn (Cambridge: Cambridge University Press, 2022), 61.
20 P. W. Joyce, *English As We Speak It in Ireland* (Dublin: M. H. Gill and Son, Ltd., 1910), 185.
21 For more on how cosmopolitanism can be misunderstood see Angela Taraborrelli, *Contemporary Cosmopolitanism* (London: Bloomsbury, 2015).
22 Riyad A. Shahjahan, Annabelle L. Estera, Kristen L. Surla, and Kirsten T. Edwards, "'Decolonizing' Curriculum and Pedagogy: A Comparative Review Across Disciplines and Global Higher Education Contexts," *Review of Educational Research* 92, no. 1 (February 2022): 83, https://doi.org/10.3102/00346543211042423.
23 Kelly A. Hogan and Viji Sathy, *Inclusive Teaching: Strategies for Promoting Equity in the College Classroom* (Morgantown: West Virginia University Press, 2022), 111–12.
24 James Joyce, "The Dead," in *Dubliners,* ed. Robert Scholes and A. Walton Litz (New York: Penguin, 1996), 187–88.
25 Hogan and Sathy, *Inclusive Teaching,* 127.
26 Elaine Showalter, *Teaching Literature* (London: Blackwell, 2003), 100.

Bibliography

Buurma, Rachel Sagner, and Laura Heffernan. *The Teaching Archive: A New History for Literary Study.* Chicago: University of Chicago Press, 2020.

Ellmann, Richard. *James Joyce.* New and revised edition. Oxford: Oxford University Press, 1982.

Gifford, Don, and Robert J. Seidman. *"Ulysses" Annotated: Notes for James Joyce's "Ulysses."* Berkeley: University of California Press, 1988.

Hagen, Benjamin. *The Sensuous Pedagogies of Virginia Woolf and D. H. Lawrence.* Clemson: Clemson University Press, 2020.

Hogan, Kelly A., and Viji Sathy. *Inclusive Teaching: Strategies for Promoting Equity in the College Classroom.* Morgantown: West Virginia University Press, 2022.

Howarth, Peter. "Introduction: Modernism and/as Pedagogy." *Modernist Cultures* 14, no. 3 (2019): 261–90. https://doi.org/10.3366/mod.2019.0256.

Joyce, James. "The Dead." In *Dubliners,* edited by Robert Scholes and A. Walton Litz, 175–224. New York: Penguin, 1996.

Joyce, James. *A Portrait of the Artist as a Young Man.* Edited by Jeri Johnson. Oxford: Oxford University Press, 2000.

Joyce, James. *Selected Letters of James Joyce.* Edited by Richard Ellmann. London: Faber and Faber, 1975.

Joyce, James. *Ulysses.* Edited by Hans Walter Gabler, et al. New York: Vintage, 1986.
Joyce, P. W. *English As We Speak It in Ireland.* Dublin: M. H. Gill and Son, Ltd., 1910.
Mignolo, Walter. "Interview—Walter Mignolo/Part 2: Key Concepts." Interview by *E-International Relations,* January 21, 2017. https://www.e-ir.info/2017/01/21/interview-walter-mignolopart-2-key-concepts/.
Mignolo, Walter, and Catherine E. Walsh. *On Decoloniality: Concepts, Analytics, Praxis.* Durham: Duke University Press, 2018.
Morreira, Shannon, Kathy Luckett, Siseko H. Kumalo, and Manjeet Ramgotra. Introduction to *Decolonising Curricula and Pedagogy in Higher Education: Bringing Decolonial Theory into Contact with Teaching Practice,* edited by Morreira, et al., 1–18. New York: Routledge, 2021.
Mukherjee, Ankhi, and Ato Quayson. Introduction to *Decolonizing the English Literary Curriculum,* edited by Ankhi Mukherjee and Ato Quayson, 1–22. Cambridge: Cambridge University Press, 2023.
Platt, Len. *James Joyce and Education: Schooling and the Social Imaginary in the Modernist Novel.* London: Routledge, 2021.
Shahjahan, Riyad A., Annabelle L. Estera, Kristen L. Surla, and Kirsten T. Edwards. "'Decolonizing' Curriculum and Pedagogy: A Comparative Review Across Disciplines and Global Higher Education Contexts." *Review of Educational Research* 92, no. 1 (February 2022): 73–113. https://doi.org/10.3102/00346543211042423.
Showalter, Elaine. *Teaching Literature.* London: Blackwell, 2003.
Spoo, Robert. "Nestor." In *The Cambridge Centenary Ulysses: The 1922 Text with Essays and Notes,* edited by Catherine Flynn, 58–67. Cambridge: Cambridge University Press, 2022.
Switaj, Elizabeth. *James Joyce's Teaching Life and Methods: Language and Pedagogy in "A Portrait of the Artist as a Young Man," "Ulysses," and "Finnegans Wake."* London: Palgrave Macmillan, 2016.
Taraborrelli, Angela. *Contemporary Cosmopolitanism.* London: Bloomsbury, 2015.

8

Eating with Joyce

Ulysses and the Cultural Discourses That Shape Personal Nutrition

TALIA ABU

Ulysses is not easily digested by 2022 students. Across the globe, students grapple with the book's length, its perceived incomprehensibility, and scarce action, while teachers strive to guide them through the surplus of textual and thematic complications. But teaching *Ulysses* outside Western Europe and the United States involves further considerations, including differences in language, geopolitical context, history, and cultural associations. In the following pages, I discuss the challenges of teaching a lengthy novel from the 1920s in twenty-first-century Israel[1] and explore potential strategies for bridging the gaps between the students and the novel. While I have taught in both English departments and Hebrew-speaking classes, here I focus on teaching *Ulysses* in Hebrew-speaking classes: While English departments accommodate many international students, Hebrew-speaking classrooms consist of students who grew up within the Israeli educational system and are immersed in Israeli culture, and thus provide a more specific reflection on the ethnic and sociopolitical complexities of Israel and Palestine.[2] This environment presents unique challenges that require me to explore creative opportunities for introducing *Ulysses* to students.

Israeli classrooms are shared by several of the ethnicities populating this region. While the two main groups are of Jewish and Arab students, these two vast groups further divide into Orthodox, Muslim, Christian, Druze, as well as secular students of all ethnicities. National and cultural identity is especially complicated for Arab students, as some identify as Israeli-Arabs and others as Palestinians. For most students born and raised in Israel, of any religion or ethnicity, Dublin is too foreign, the experimental language is too alienating, and cultural references are unfamiliar. There are, to be sure, postcolonial readings of the novel that parallel local political realities, but students often express a stronger desire to engage with universal themes rather than being reminded again that they are defined by the Israeli-Palestinian conflict.[3] Other thematic concerns in *Ulysses,* such as racism, cultural imperialism, and critique of institutionalized religion, are appropriate for Israeli classrooms, and yet run the risk of reinforcing polarization.

However, a particular set of themes has proved to be especially compelling for students of all ethnicities and is best illuminated through food studies. As a secular Jew of Iranian and Moroccan descent, who is painfully aware of the segregating and discriminating policies of the Israeli government, I find Joyce's celebration of the human body and its functions in *Ulysses* a useful way of engaging students despite apparent political, cultural, and religious differences. I approach Joyce's preoccupation with bodily themes particularly through the prism of food and acts of eating, since consumption and digestion are intimately tied to the body, highlighting a shared physicality that goes beyond religion and ethnicity. Moreover, food-related themes in *Ulysses* resonate with the culinary interests of contemporary students, connecting them to global food culture. Streaming services, online media companies, and social media accounts are brimming with food-related images and content, with people eating and cooking, and with advice on how to eat well or cook well. Crucially, however, introducing *Ulysses* through the potentially appealing quality of food-related themes is not a teaching strategy aimed at simplifying Joyce's novel. Rather, inquiring into representations of food and eating unfolds a rich spectrum of themes that attest to the novel's complexity and to its enduring appeal.

Approaching literary analysis through the lens of food is often labeled as food studies. This academic discipline explores the interplay between food and the body in literature, while also exploring the historical contexts of foodstuffs and consumption. Significantly, an exploration of food-related themes in literature yields a political dimension: Seemingly personal choices about what to eat are shaped not only by individual tastes or health considerations but also by broader values and beliefs, as well as by sociopolitical forces. Ultimately, arguments made by food studies scholars that I apply in my reading and teaching of *Ulysses* provide the students with tools for journeying into the motives that guide their own nutritional preferences.

The introduction of Leopold Bloom, in "Calypso," is especially useful in teaching the novel through the framework of food studies. The depiction of Bloom preparing breakfast, feeding his cat, and daydreaming about meat, resonates with today's food-centric popular culture so familiar to students. Moreover, Bloom's gastronomical preferences, as portrayed in "Calypso," are particularly provoking, thus inviting deeper reflection:

> Mr Leopold Bloom ate with relish the inner organs of beasts and fowls. He liked thick giblet soup, nutty gizzards, a stuffed roast heart, liverslices fried with crustcrumbs, fried hencods' roes. Most of all he liked grilled mutton kidneys which gave to his palate a fine tang of faintly scented urine.[4]

The vivid descriptions of animal parts, and the appeal to the olfactory sense, evoke a visceral response that encourages students to reflect on culinary practices, such as eating meat for breakfast (uncommon in Israel), their personal opinion on consuming internal organs, and whether they associate specific smells—such as urine—with food.

Bloom's love for meat persists in the following passages, setting the stage for exploring broader concerns related to food and its consumption:

> Kidneys were in his mind as he moved about the kitchen softly, righting her breakfast things on the humpy tray. Gelid light and air were in the kitchen but out of doors gentle summer morning everywhere. Made him feel a bit peckish. [. . .] Another slice of bread and butter: three, four: right. She didn't like her plate full. Right. (*U* 4.6–11)

The insistence on the dismembering of animals and consuming their internal organs, together with the new detail informing that Bloom is in fact making breakfast for his wife, Molly ("righting her breakfast things on the humpy tray"), before eating his own breakfast (as implied by the description of Bloom as "peckish"), prompt the students to reflect on social and cultural issues related to food, such as the moral implications of consumption (Is it moral to eat animals?) and how food reflects or challenges gender roles (What is the significance of meeting Bloom in the kitchen, a space traditionally reserved for the woman? Does Molly's reluctance to have "her plate full" reflect the cultural expectation of women to eat sparingly?).

These questions show my students that despite temporal and spatial differences from their contemporary culture, *Ulysses* addresses social and ideological issues that are relevant in the twenty-first century. And while all the questions raised above are significant and can spark thought-provoking discussions, I often focus on Bloom's gastronomical preference to engage the students in one interpretive problem that is particular to Joyce's novel, namely Bloom's ambivalence toward meat consumption: at breakfast time, 8:00 a.m., Bloom's carnivorous tendencies are asserted with his stated love for "the inner organs of beasts and fowls" (*U* 4.1–2); later that day, between 1:00 and 2:00 p.m., Bloom enters the Burton restaurant during lunch hour only to find himself repulsed by a crowd of meat-eating men; he then resolves to seek a different restaurant, and at Davy Byrne's he enjoys a Gorgonzola sandwich and a glass of Burgundy; later that day, at the Ormond Hotel, Bloom's disgust with meat consumption is forgotten as the text resurfaces his love for "Steak, kidney, liver," and "bacon" (*U* 11.608, 614).

Bloom's contradictory attitude toward meat, and his choice of vegetarian lunch in "Lestrygonians," raises useful questions about culinary trends that appeal to the students. Vegetarianism is an especially popular topic nowadays, relating to such pressing matters as animal cruelty, global warming, and healthy lifestyle. As many vegetarians and vegans (including me) can testify, the reasons for these dietary preferences vary from ethical to health to financial considerations, and yet it is less intuitively obvious that a seemingly individual choice, such as eating or avoiding meat, is informed by cultural discourses.

The motivation for Bloom's seemingly displaced vegetarian impulse has been addressed by Joyce scholars, and this discussion provides a compelling example of the value of applying a food studies approach to *Ulysses*. Marguerite M. Regan contextualizes Bloom's decision to avoid meat within vegetarian discourses that equate the subjugation of animals to the social and political disadvantages of marginalized populations.[5] In Ireland especially, which in 1904 is still part of the British Empire, vegetarians cultivated a "conversation which draws connection [*sic*] between habits of meat-eating and habits of political and cultural dominance."[6] Peter Adkins addresses Bloom's vegetarian experience by underlining a conceptual correlation between Joyce's ethics and "contemporary attempts to theorize animal death and consumption."[7] With these two readings in mind, I employ food studies in the classroom to account for the possible sociopolitical reasons for Bloom's midday aversion from meat and to shed light upon the cultural discourses that prescribe personal nutrition. And yet, to maintain the richness of the text, I encourage the students to avoid reaching a definite conclusion to the conundrum of Bloom's fleeting vegetarian sensibility. The coexistence of several possible motives for Bloom's vegetarian lunch mirrors the abundance of cultural discourses that Joyce alluded to in his encyclopedic novel,[8] and that continue to influence and shape individual food intake.

The history of vegetarianism cannot be sufficiently recapped here. However, a brief overview of nineteenth- and early twentieth-century perspectives is essential for discussing Bloom's decision to avoid meat at lunch and for highlighting contemporary interests in meat avoidance. One prominent perception throughout history connects the slaughter and consumption of animals with aggressive and violent masculinity. Rod Preece, in his thorough historical account, traces this gendering of meat to the early stages of civilization, arguing that early civilizations learned to send their strongest members "to entrap larger animals"[9] for the community's sustenance, thus establishing hunting as a masculine vocation and signaling the constitution of food hierarchy by which animal flesh was deemed superior to other foodstuffs. Preece's account readily contextualizes Bloom's encounter with flesh-eating men in "Lestrygonians." His immediate response to the customers at the Burton restaurant, "Eat or be eaten, Kill! Kill!" (*U* 8.703), his disgust with the meat-eating "Men, men, men" (8.653) and of the "Smells of men" (8.670), that drives him out of the Burton, taps into the long-standing cultural discourse associating meat with aggressive masculinity.

In fact, the connection between carnivorous diet and aggressive masculinity grew stronger in the eighteenth and nineteenth centuries among those who believed that giving up meat was a key step in moral development for both individuals and societies. In another history of vegetarianism, Colin Spencer examines the rise of vegetarianism in correlation with the growth and spread of humanism and social reform as well as with the shift from humanism to radical humanism.[10] He reports that, during the eighteenth century, abstinence from meat was often associated with "anti-slavery campaigners, [. . .] the barbarity of the penal laws, the convict hulks or the use of child labour and the conditions in the factories."[11] The Vegetarian Society—whose first annual gathering took place in 1848 in Manchester, England—advocated avoidance of meat by appealing to the moral and ethical sensibilities of their contemporaries. As Preece notes, the members of the society deemed flesh-eating as an incentive to violence, a view elaborated in print in 1883 with Howard Williams's treaty against the cruel practice of flesh-eating, *The Ethics of Diet*.[12]

Bloom's potential rejection of dominant masculinity expressed in his avoidance of meat at lunch provides an agreeable analysis. Twenty-first century students enjoy the reading that deems the protagonist of the book as an opponent to traditional aggressive masculinity and consider him an ally in their own increasing struggle against fixed gender roles. They are especially delighted when I ask them to consider Molly's sexual encounter that is to take place at 4:00 p.m. with Blazes Boylan, whose intrusive virility is often objectionable. Interpreting Bloom's vegetarian inclination as undermining gender norms allows the students to compensate Bloom for the betrayal by sympathizing with his alleged defiance against masculine ideals. And yet, alas, Bloom's motivation for avoiding meat is not that easily pinned down. The history of vegetarianism is intertwined with several, even opposing, cultural discourses that resist any simple linking of Bloom with a single set of beliefs.

Leaving the Burton, Bloom betrays a significant value judgment that further complicates his motive.

> He backed towards the door. Get a light snack in Davy Byrne's. Stopgap. Keep me going. Had a good breakfast. (*U* 8.697–98)

Here, Bloom rationalizes his decision to avoid meat by admitting that he is not particularly hungry and would rather have a light snack. Moreover, seeing that Bloom ate flesh for breakfast, his statement about having had "a good breakfast" should not be overlooked. If Bloom is willing to skip a hearty lunch because he is still energized from his breakfast, then "a good breakfast" renders the denotation of "good" as "adequate": his breakfast was sufficient to provide him with the proper amount of energy. However, if we read "good" as "virtuous" then Bloom's comment proposes a moral judgment: "Had a *morally agreeable* breakfast." The latter denotation suggests that Bloom does not condemn flesh-eating and presents the students with a curious discrepancy between Bloom's ideological approval of carnivorous diet and his noontime avoidance of meat.

If Bloom does not challenge the moral and ethical premises attached to meat consumption, then our reading of his vegetarian adventure should be revised. Here, another historical perspective of vegetarianism, prevalent in America and in Victorian England, which did not condemn the consumption of meat as an expression of masculine aggressiveness, proves beneficial. In the nineteenth century, the newly established vegetarian identity invoked resistance, and for most people "the tendency was to think of vegetarians as decided misfits and oddballs."[13] Comments published in *Punch, or The London Charivari* magazine, in 1848, summarize the contempt expressed toward the practitioners of this diet:

> We look upon the Vegetarian humbug as a mere pretext for indulging a juvenile appetite for something nice, and we are really ashamed of those old boys who continue, at their time of life, to display such a puerile taste for pies and puddings.[14]

Spencer sums up the general attitude toward vegetarians during the Victorian era: "It verged upon the disreputable and [...] it was seen as downright scandalous and immoral. Vegetarians were therefore firmly outsiders and would remain so."[15] This view of vegetarians as eccentric personalities provides another compelling historical and ideological context to Bloom's vegetarian adventure.

If the historical association between meat consumption and masculine aggressiveness implies Bloom's subversive perception of masculine norms, the view of vegetarians as misfits suggests that Bloom's avoidance of meat reflects on how the community perceives him. Indeed, Bloom is perceived by fellow Dubliners as eccentric, even eerie, and is often shunned by his peers. His alienation from his community famously culminates in the "Cyclops" episode where he is mocked by the other man at the bar and subjected to an attempted physical attack by the Citizen. Bloom's ongoing alienation sheds light upon his position at the Burton as a detached observer, standing at the threshold of an establishment in which he is a stranger: "He gazed round the stooled and tabled eaters, tightening the wings of his nose" (*U* 8.678–79). Without fully assimilating with the crowd at the Burton, Bloom continues to be an outsider, a role easily explained by the common view of vegetarians as misfits.

The conundrum surrounding Bloom's disgust with meat intensifies; the question of motives persists. By taking to the history of vegetarianism, Bloom's avoidance of meat may suggest a condemnation of the masculine aggression associated with meat eating; in turn, it may reflect his inability to integrate within Dublin society on account of his peculiarity. This ambiguity of motives shows the students the interactive quality of the text that here is operative on the level of the word. The word itself is a changing and potent entity (what is the meaning of "good"?) that unleashes a flow of meanings through which the students are supposed to navigate with critical and interpretive tools. As lunchtime in "Lestrygonians" demonstrates, *Ulysses* facilitates different interpretations, historical contexts, and cultural perceptions that relate to food, and thus encourages the students' participation in the production of meaning.[16] The dynamic quality of the Joycean language in *Ulysses*, as illustrated by the complexity of "good" in "good breakfast," sets the grounds for a classroom discussion of vegetarianism that does not conclude with a stale observation that vegetarianism is better or morally superior, but that inquires into the values and mores that shape our plates. A productive question, therefore, is not why Bloom chooses to avoid meat at lunch, but who or what influences this choice?

Bloom shows an awareness of how cultural factors impact individual dietary habits when, shortly before entering the Burton, he spots George Russell and a female companion exiting a vegetarian restaurant. Upon seeing the Irish writer, a known vegetarian, he acknowledges the conventional association between vegetarianism and intellectuals:

> Those literary etherial people they are all. Dreamy, cloudy, symbolistic. Esthetes they are. I wouldn't be surprised if it was that kind of food you see produces the like waves of the brain the poetical. For example one of those policemen sweating Irish stew into their shirts you couldn't squeeze a line of poetry out of him. Don't know what poetry is even. (*U* 8.543–47)

Here Bloom reiterates a well-established perception of vegetable-based food as better suited for the visionary occupation of men of letters. Henry David Thoreau's views on vegetarianism, accounted for by Tristram Stuart, demonstrate the cultural endurance of this perception. Although not vegetarian himself, "Thoreau was convinced that eating meat was nutritionally unnecessary, that vegetable food was cheaper, easier to acquire and, being a lighter diet, was well suited to the contemplative life."[17] Thoreau was far from being the only one, and Bernard Shaw's conversion to vegetarianism comes to mind as an example for "prominent members of the literary establishment [that] lent their name to the cause" during the 1880s.[18]

Bloom's familiarity with Russell's diet usefully appeals to the students' awareness of food as a major cultural concern and one that often collaborates with celebrity culture. Russell, "the eminent poet" (*U* 8.526–27), whom Bloom recognizes for his distinguished status, exemplifies the link between individual nutrition and the personal dietary choices of famed persons. That Russell and his female companion are seen at a moment of exiting a vegetarian restaurant (8.534) explains prosaically why Bloom immediately contemplates Russell's preferred diet. And yet Russell's celebrity status is a key aspect in explaining Bloom's familiarity with Russell's diet, and interest in it, despite having no personal relationship with him. Bloom knows Russell is a vegetarian because the public takes interest in what famous people eat, to this very day.

Significantly, interest in celebrity diet exceeds mere curiosity and bears practical consequences. Emma-Jayne Abbots, in *The Agency of Eating*, explains that the connection between celebrity and food is one of authority: "The media, in the form of reality television [. . .], celebrity chefs [. . .] and social media [. . .] can all be seen as public pedagogical mechanism that inform and look to shape knowledge of what constitutes morally acceptable and 'healthy' bodies."[19] Celebrity culture has appropriated the authoritative perspective that supposedly provides an objective outlook on desirable nutrition, that in the medical field is reserved to health professionals and scientists.

Bloom's knowledge of Russell's diet triggers the association between nutrition and celebrities (a status that today is often gained by social media personalities) that is more than familiar to twenty-first-century students. The food they eat, the brands they consume, the reasoning behind their dietary choices are often influenced by an endless stream of dietary advice from celebrities, celebrity dietitians, YouTubers, and TikTok-ers. For example, *Vogue*'s YouTube channel (with 12.2 million subscribers) and *Harper's Bazaar*'s (with the modest count of 1.68 million subscribers) weekly upload videos of celebrities discussing their daily meals, cooking, or providing dietary advice for healthy and successful living. The *First We Feast* YouTube channel (with 11.7 million subscribers) produces several shows that regularly host celebrities eating and commenting on spicy foods (Hot Ones), burgers (Burger Scholar Sessions), or pizza (Pizza Wars). Celebrities offer young people grounds for identification with a desired class, culture, and values; one way of embracing the values and social discourses promoted by celebrities is by taking up their diet.

Bloom's reasoning here, that if one takes up a vegetarian diet one becomes inclined to aesthetic or poetic production, is shaped by the public figure of Russell. Bloom seems to think that the association between vegetarianism and literary pursuits originates with him ("I wouldn't be surprised [. . .]"), but the conception of this association cannot be separated from the public interest in celebrities' lifestyle. Even more so, this scene suggests that there is a close link between food and identity-construction that is influenced by celebrity culture. Bloom contrasts two types—of the "esthete," symbolized by Russell, with that of the sweaty "policemen"—and associates each with different dietary preferences: vegetarian diet creates the "Dreamy, cloudy, symbolistic" (*U* 8.543) type, while meat consumption creates the unhygienic and uneducated type ("Don't know what poetry is even" [*U* 8.547]). This connection between food and identity-construction is intuitively picked up by contemporary students, whose culture insistently reinforces the link between diet and identity.

One of numerous such platforms is BuzzFeed, a news and entertainment company, whose revenue in 2021 was estimated as 398 million USD.[20] On its website and apps, this internet media platform posts several Food Quizzes a day that ask web surfers to answer food-related questions that provide an insight about their personalities, unveil the future, or offer an allegedly personalized life advice. In 2022, several titles insisted on the mutuality between the food we consume and our lives and personalities: "Don't Be Weirded Out When We Know Exactly What Career You Should Pursue Based On Your Choice In Animated Food," "Which Plant-Based Milk Are You Based On What You Eat In A Day?," and the pompous "Choose Your Favorite Snacks And I'll Guess If You're An Old Soul Or Not."[21] The deeply ingrained association between food and identity-formation, often reinforced by celebrity culture, provides the students with familiar vocabulary for explaining why Bloom avoids meat after seeing Russell, despite personal reservations: "Tried it. Keep you on the run all day. Bad as a bloater. Dreams all night. Why do they call that thing they gave me nutsteak? [. . .] Absurd" (*U* 8.537–40).

Nevertheless, celebrities and the values they promote that inform individual diets are part of a greater web of principles and ideals that articulate social expectations. Tracing dietary reforms from the nineteenth century to the present day, Charlotte Biltekoff spells out two core sociopolitical considerations that influence personal nutrition:

> [D]ietary ideals primarily convey two interlocking sets of social ideals: one communicates emerging cultural notions of good citizenship and prepares people for new social and political realities; the other expresses the social concerns of the middle class and attempts to distinguish its character and identity.[22]

The two "sets of social ideals" determining private eating habits shed light upon Bloom's indecisive state of mind during lunch hour and may in turn illuminate the cultural values that shape the students' nutritional preferences. The first conceptual framework mentioned by Biltekoff relates to political considerations, and in Bloom's case may be explored through Anglo-Irish relations. Historically, vegetarianism was conceived as especially threatening in England because of the national, and patriotic, preference for meat. England's idealized personification, John Bull, celebrates the connection between beef and national loyalty and, according to Preece, has shaped the public perception of vegetarians as "a little unpatriotic!"[23] Bloom's disgust with meat-eaters may thus be interpreted as directed at England's nationwide taste for animal flesh, and his meat-defying moment as embodying the Irish struggle against British dominion.

That Bloom's vegetarian lunch is charged with aspects of Anglo-Irish relationship reiterates the claim that individual food intake is political. Bloom's Ireland, in 1904, is coping with the aftermath of the Great Famine of 1845–1852. The contamination of potato crops, by the fungus-like organism *Phytophthora infestans*, was so destructive for rural Ireland because, Alvin Jackson writes, "Irish dependence on the potato had been growing since the early eighteenth century, and by the mid-1840s it constituted the staple foodstuff of the labouring poor."[24] However, allegations were repeatedly made against the British government's failure to execute relief strategies to reduce starvation. Joyce subscribes to these allegations in his 1907 lecture, published as "Ireland, Island of Saints and Sages": "[I]n the years in which the potato crops failed, the negligence of the English government left the flower of the people to die of hunger."[25] In turn, imperialist narratives justified English policies by arguing that Irish reliance on potatoes, a vegetable, brought about this disaster and is proof of the need for England to rule and modernize Ireland. The predominantly vegetarian Irish diet was utilized by British colonial ideologies to fuel racist stereotypes.[26]

Vegetarianism retained its political connotations in turn-of-the-century Dublin. As Miriam O'Kane Mara indicates, an "understanding of famine as a political symbol for English oppression politicized Irish eating behaviors and intensified food as a way to mark identity."[27] Bloom's repulsion of the meat-eaters, therefore, may be interpreted as a performative gesture challenging British political and cultural dominion in Ireland. Indeed, earlier in the "Lestrygonians" episode, Bloom contemplates several staples of Irish nationalism, including the Invincibles (*U* 8.443), the group of Irish extremists associated with the Phoenix Park murders, and alludes to nationalist diplomacy by recalling prominent Irish political figures like James Stephen, Charles Parnell, and Arthur Griffith (*U* 8.457, 462).[28] Evidently, Bloom is preoccupied with the Irish struggle and Irish nationalism just before lunch time, and so his way of identifying with the Irish cause takes the shape of repudiating the English national food consumed at the Burton: "Roast beef and cabbage" (*U* 8.668). O'Kane Mara discusses the mutuality between food and Irish identity-formation in relation to Stephen Dedalus and not Bloom, but her claim that in *Ulysses* food and eating attempt to pave "access both to Irishness of a sort and to essential, if impossible, masculinity"[29] describes Bloom's experience as well. According to this reading, Bloom's refusal to join the company of meat-eaters at the Burton exhibits a rejection of animal flesh as the material expression of British rule; his disgust, therefore, performs an Irish resistance to British imperialism.

And yet, the scene complicates an association between Bloom's disgust with meat and his identification with the Irish cause because, at the Burton, Bloom is explicitly appalled by the customers and *their* table manners. This brings about Biltekoff's second set of ideas regulating nutritional habits: class values. She writes that eating well has become a guiding principle for a desired social status. Through food,

> members of the "thinking classes" could distinguish themselves from those in the laboring class, who seemed to lack the intelligence and will to eat what was good for them rather than what they liked.[30]

Accordingly, Bloom is repulsed by the eating of meat not because he ideologically rejects flesh-eating on grounds of its association with British ideal masculinity, but because the *eaters* clearly lack middle-class cultural finesse.

> Perched on high stools by the bar, hats shoved back, at the tables calling for more bread no charge, swilling, wolfing gobfuls of sloppy food, their eyes bulging, wiping wetted moustaches. [. . .] A man spitting back on his plate: halfmasticated gristle: gums: no teeth to chewchewchew it. (*U* 8.654–60)

Spencer reports that at "the beginning of the century the vegetarian movement had become solidly middle class" since vegetarianism required "enough income to afford abundance of food, so that some foods might be sacrificed."[31] This was especially so in Bloom's Dublin. Adkins writes: "In Dublin, vegetarianism was publicly represented by an 'advanced-circle' of middle-class, mainly Anglo-Irish intellectuals affiliated with the Celtic revival. [. . .] For the revivalists, vegetarianism did not primarily reflect a concern with animal welfare, so much as it was a spiritual and political practice."[32] Indicating that the motivation for middle-class practitioners of vegetarianism was not a personal distaste to animal cruelty, Adkins reinforces the view that diet (here, a vegetarian diet) is a socioeconomic construct. Another valid interpretation, therefore, is that Bloom rejects meat consumption as a typical low-class diet. However, while Adkins claims that Bloom reluctantly identifies "with the brutish eaters of the Burton,"[33] I believe that Bloom cannot identify with the diners insofar as he is disgusted by their manners.

Adkins's claim rests, it seems, on the allusion to Robert Burns's poem: "See ourselves as others see us" (*U* 8.139). While the pronoun "ourselves" may potentially align Bloom with the party of meat-eaters, it more likely refers to the eaters' lack of self-awareness: They do not realize how crude their table manners are, precisely because they lack middle-class education and social etiquette. It seems to me that Bloom is offended less by the consumption of beasts and more by the bestiality of the consumers: "See the animals feed" (*U* 8.651–52). Dehumanizing terminology persists when Bloom compares the crowd to ruminants, "old chap picking his tootles. Slight spasm, full, chewing the cud" (*U* 8.674–75), suggesting Bloom's sense of class superiority that historically associates with vegetarian ideals. Fittingly, when Bloom leaves Burton's place, he denounces not the meat, but the men: "Out. I hate dirty eaters" (*U* 8.696). With "See the animals feed," Bloom differentiates himself from the "dirty" crowd of men. As an observer, not a participant, he views the feeding animals/men from a position of superiority.

Flicka Small addresses Bloom's sense of superiority, proposing that "when Bloom chooses to eat a cheese sandwich, he is temporarily endorsing a group that does not kill flesh and thereby feels superior."[34] Middle-class Bloom can afford selectivity in food, as he does when he leaves the Burton and enters Davy Byrne's place instead. He can choose what to eat and drink for lunch; these "savage" men, perhaps, cannot. Bloom's disgust readily establishes his estrangement from the crowd on basis of class values and thus demonstrates the popular perception of vegetarians as "not able to relate to the working classes."[35] Indeed, at Davy Byrne's "[n]ice quiet bar" (*U* 8.822), Bloom savors a Gorgonzola sandwich and a glass of Burgundy. The wine, especially, is one consumable that does not address Bloom's nutritional needs but that Bloom *can afford* to have: "Nice wine it is. Taste better because I'm not thirsty" (*U* 8.851).

If the glass of wine is not meant to quench Bloom's thirst, then it serves a different purpose, namely, to reinforce Bloom's attempt to distinguish himself from the mass of uncultured people. It is only after being repelled by the customers at the Burton that Bloom rationalizes the benefits of eating vegetable food and begins to contemplate the nutritional and moral aspects of a vegetarian diet. "After all there's a lot in that vegetarian fine flavor of things from the earth garlic of course it stinks after Italian organgrinders crisp of onions mushrooms truffles. Pain to the animal too" (*U* 8.720–22). Only after fleeing away from the meat-eating *men,* he resolves that vegetarianism is morally preferable to meat eating: "He entered Davy Byrne's. Moral pub" (*U* 8.732).

The several possible interpretations for the seemingly mundane experience of eating lunch reveals the abundance of culturally constructed motives that shape individual diets in the culture reflected in *Ulysses.* As I have demonstrated, interpretive strategies from food studies provide the students with tools for exposing the possible motivations for Bloom's choice of meal. The purpose of the class discussion is not to pinpoint a single reason for Bloom's aversion to meat-eaters but to explore the complex layers of meaning within the text while forming a personal connection to food-related themes. But this is not all. Precisely because food studies do not solve the confusion surrounding Bloom's brief hour of meat avoidance but rather reinforce Joyce's encyclopedic project, then a reading of "Lestrygonians" highlights the coexistence of a variety of histories, traditions, and cultural values that inform individual experiences, particularly, individual eating habits.

That personal food intake reflects the political and economic factors prevalent in our own culture is itself thought-provoking. An important question arises: If our food choices are influenced by cultural factors, does it not suggest that our thoughts, politics, and social views, can also be manipulated? This holds particular significance in Israeli university classrooms. In Israel, the education system, mainstream media, and other state policies, are dedicated to perpetuating racist ideologies alongside Jewish supremacy. Individuals are under the impression they are autonomous thinkers yet are guided to endorse the agendas of those in control.

One such agenda, that has served Israeli state apparatuses throughout the years, is that Israel is a democracy. However, the reality of Israel's military control of the West Bank and permanent siege of the Gaza Strip prove that this description is inaccurate and politically charged. Magid Shihade articulates the ideology informing the narrative of Israel democracy:

> What we hear today is that Israel is "the only democracy in the region," as well as "a villa in a jungle." Following this line of thought, one cannot but see Israel as a Frontier, an open frontier for Western hegemony, power, domination of those who are considered part of the East, a jungle.[36]

Discriminatory ideologies and practices challenge Israel's self-definition as a democracy and, in turn, foster misunderstandings of concepts like "democracy," "the right to defend," and "military occupation." Thus, the state perpetuates this confusion by implementing selective democratic procedures while using educational and media platforms to train people to believe that Israel is a fully functioning democracy.

Applying principles of food studies in analyzing *Ulysses*, I aim to help the students engage with the novel, while communicating the idea that our freedom of thought is often compromised—that we have been conditioned not to think independently. I frequently remind my students that when we fail to think for ourselves, others will do the thinking for us. While I cannot dictate what my students should think, or what to eat, I can use *Ulysses* and food studies as tools to encourage critical thinking and intellectual autonomy. Joyce's modernist writing style and chaotic thematic arrangements already encourages a recognition in the instability of meaning that, in turn, frustrates established dogmas. Together with the complex histories and ideologies attached to foodstuffs and their consumption, representations of eating in *Ulysses* encourage a conversation, a debate between opposing ideas, and a realization that our personal choices are often dictated by political forces. As a teacher of literature, I see it as my responsibility to reveal the passive patterns in my students' thinking. It is my hope that if I can show students how cultural forces shape our diets, I can also help them recognize how government and institutional powers attempt to manipulate our thoughts.[37]

Notes

1. By "Israel," I mean the borders agreed upon by Israel, Egypt, Jordan, Lebanon, and Syria, and established in the 1949 Armistice Agreement. For a specification of the borders, see Google.
2. By "Palestine," I refer to the Israeli-occupied West Bank, East Jerusalem, and the Gaza Strip.
3. The desire to engage with universal issues rather than with the local ones is intertwined with a long-standing indoctrination of a one-sided narrative that has led many Israelis to overlook or suppress awareness of the racist and divisive policies enacted by Israeli governments over the years. I will return to the topic of indoctrination at the end of this discussion.
4. James Joyce, *Ulysses*, ed. Hans Walter Gabler, et al. (New York: Random House, 1984), 4.1–5. Hereafter cited parenthetically in the text as *U* followed by episode and line number.
5. Marguerite M. Regan, "'Weggebobbles and Fruit': Bloom's Vegetarian Impulses," *Texas Studies in Literature and Language* 51, no. 4 (2009): 463–75.

6   Regan, "Bloom's Vegetarian Impulses," 473.
7   Peter Adkins, "The Eyes of That Cow: Eating Animals and Theorizing Vegetarianism in James Joyce's *Ulysses*," in *Joyce, Animals and the NonHuman,* ed. Katherine Ebury, *Humanities* 6, no. 3 (2017), MDPI, https://doi.org/10.3390/h6030046.
8   For an interesting account on the encyclopedic nature of *Ulysses,* see Simone Rebora's "Encyclopedic Novel Revisited: Joyce's Role in a Disputed Literary Genre," in *Joyce Studies in Italy: Joyce's Fiction and the Rise of the Novel,* ed. Franca Ruggieri (Rome: Editoriale Anicia, 2017).
9   Rod Preece, *Sins of the Flesh: A History of Ethical Vegetarian Thought* (Vancouver: UBC Press, 2008), 26.
10 Colin Spencer, *Vegetarianism: A History* (London: Grub Street, 2000), 231–37.
11 Spencer, *Vegetarianism,* 216.
12 Preece, *Sins of the Flesh,* 269.
13 Preece, *Sins of the Flesh,* 270.
14 *Punch, or The London Charivari,* vols. 14–15 (Punch Publications Ltd., 1848), https://www.google.co.uk/books/edition/_/zP8CAAAAIAAJ?hl=en&gbpv=0.
15 Spencer, *Vegetarianism,* 274.
16 Vicki Mahaffey effectively summarizes the appealing nature of linguistic ambiguity in *Ulysses,* arguing that the novel "works through inclusion rather than opposition, because it offers readers (or audiences) choices among possible meanings" and that, therefore, "play is both radically democratic and potentially threatening to the established order." Mahaffey, *States of Desire: Wilde, Yeats, Joyce, and the Irish Experiment* (New York: Oxford University Press, 1998), 4.
17 Tristram Stuart, *The Bloodless Revolution: A Cultural History of Vegetarianism from 1600 to Modern Times* (New York: W. W. Norton and Co., 2008), 419.
18 Stuart, *Bloodless Revolution,* 423.
19 Emma-Jayne Abbots, *The Agency of Eating: Mediation, Food and the Body,* Contemporary Food Studies, ed. David Goodman and Michael K. Goodman (London: Bloomsbury, 2017), chap. 6.
20 For evaluating the popularity of BuzzFeed through stock data, see *Wall Street Journal,* October 8, 2021, https://www.wsj.com/market-data/quotes/BZFD.
21 Hannah Marder, *BuzzFeed,* October 5, 2022; Jordynnbrown01, *BuzzFeed,* October 3, 2022; Bumblebee, *BuzzFeed,* September 26, 2022.
22 Charlotte Biltekoff, *Eating Right in America: The Cultural Politics of Food and Health* (Durham: Duke University Press, 2013), 7.
23 Preece, *Sins of the Flesh,* 270.
24 Alvin Jackson, *Ireland 1798–1998: War, Peace, and Beyond.* 2nd ed. (Hoboken, NJ: Wiley-Blackwell, 2010), 69.
25 James Joyce, *The Critical Writings of James Joyce,* ed. Ellsworth Mason and Richard Ellmann (New York: Viking, 1959), 167.
26 Corey Wrenn discusses England's use of Ireland's vegetable-based diet, reporting that the dehumanization of the Irish by imperialist narratives looked to "this vegetarianism as a marker of inferiority." Wrenn, "Vegan Geographies in Ireland," in *The Routledge Handbook of Vegan Studies,* ed. Laura Wright (New York: Routledge: Taylor and Francis Group, 2021), 397.

27 Miriam O'Kane Mara, "James Joyce and the Politics of Food," *New Hibernia Review* 13, no. 4 (2009): 95.
28 For a comprehensive discussion on the differences between aggressive and constitutional resistance, see James Fairhall, "'Sunflawered' Humanity in *Finnegans Wake*: Nature, Existential Shame and Transcendence," in *Eco-Joyce: The Environmental Imagination of James Joyce,* ed. Robert Brazeau and Derek Gladwin (Cork: Cork University Press, 2014), 18–19.
29 O'Kane Mara, "Politics of Food," 102.
30 Biltekoff, *Eating Right in America,* 99.
31 Spencer, *Vegetarianism,* 276.
32 Adkins, "Theorizing Vegetarianism," 2.
33 Adkins, "Theorizing Vegetarianism," 7.
34 Flicka Small, "'Know Me Come Eat With Me': What Food Says About Leopold Bloom," in *"Tickling the Palate": Gastronomy in Irish Literature and Culture,* ed. Máirtín Mac Con Iomaire and Eamon Maher (Bern: Peter Lang, 2014), 41.
35 Spencer, *Vegetarianism,* 279.
36 Magid Shihade, "Reflection on Elia Zureik's *Israel's Colonial Project in Palestine: A Brutal Pursuit,*" *Arab Studies Quarterly* 38, no. 4 (2016): 711.
37 This chapter was written during a judicial overhaul in Israel and revised in the time that followed October 7, 2023. Teaching in a university classroom in the Faculty of Humanities requires, in my opinion, addressing the political and social realities that surrounded these events. As a person and a human-rights activist, it is my hope that a true and actual democracy will finally emerge in our troubled region, and that all people from the Mediterranean Sea to the Jordan River, will live in equality and fairness, and be entitled to human and civil rights.

Bibliography

Abbots, Emma-Jayne. *The Agency of Eating: Mediation, Food and the Body.* Contemporary Food Studies: Economy, Culture and Politics. Series editors David Goodman and Michael K. Goodman. London: Bloomsbury, 2017.

Adkins, Peter. "The Eyes of That Cow: Eating Animals and Theorizing Vegetarianism in James Joyce's *Ulysses.*" In *Joyce, Animals and the NonHuman,* edited by Katherine Ebury. *Humanities* 6, no. 3 (2017), MDPI. https://doi.org/10.3390/h6030046.

Biltekoff, Charlotte. *Eating Right in America: The Cultural Politics of Food and Health.* Durham: Duke University Press, 2013.

Bumblebee. "Choose Your Favorite Snacks And I'll Guess If You're An Old Soul Or Not." *BuzzFeed,* September 26, 2022. https://www.buzzfeed.com/zjupri99/favorite-snacks-checklist-quiz.

Fairhall, James. "'Sunflawered' Humanity in *Finnegans Wake*: Nature, Existential Shame and Transcendence." In *Eco-Joyce: The Environmental Imagination of James Joyce,* edited by Robert Brazeau and Derek Gladwin, 231–45. Cork: Cork University Press, 2014.

Jackson, Alvin. *Ireland 1798–1998: War, Peace, and Beyond*. 2nd edition. Hoboken, NJ: Wiley-Blackwell, 2010.
Jordynnbrown01. "Which Plant-Based Milk Are You Based On What You Eat In A Day?" *BuzzFeed*, October 3, 2022. https://www.buzzfeed.com/jordynnbrown01/plant-based-milk-quiz.
Joyce, James. *The Critical Writings of James Joyce*. Edited by Ellsworth Mason and Richard Ellmann (New York: Viking, 1959).
Joyce, James. *Ulysses*. Edited by Hans Walter Gabler, et al. New York: Random House, 1984.
Kodat, Catherine Gunther. "Pulp Fictions: Reading Faulkner for the 21st Century." *Faulkner Journal* 12, no. 2 (1997): 69–86. JSTOR.
Mahaffey, Vicki. *States of Desire: Wilde, Yeats, Joyce, and the Irish Experiment*. New York: Oxford University Press, 1998.
Marder, Hannah. "Don't Be Weirded Out When We Know Exactly What Career You Should Pursue Based On Your Choice In Animated Food." *BuzzFeed*, October 5, 2022. https://www.buzzfeed.com/hannahmarder/order-an-animated-feast-and-well-give-you-a-career.
O'Kane Mara, Miriam. "James Joyce and the Politics of Food." *New Hibernia Review* 13, no. 4 (2009): 94–110. JSTOR.
Preece, Rod. *Sins of the Flesh: A History of Ethical Vegetarian Thought*. Vancouver: UBC Press, 2008.
Punch, or The London Charivari. Volumes 14–15. Punch Publications Limited, 1848. https://www.google.co.uk/books/edition/_/zP8CAAAAIAAJ?hl=en&gbpv=0.
Rebora, Simone. "Encyclopedic Novel Revisited: Joyce's Role in a Disputed Literary Genre." *Joyce Studies in Italy: Joyce's Fiction and the Rise of the Novel*. Edited by Franca Ruggieri, 147–68. Roma: Editoriale Anicia, 2017.
Regan, Marguerite M. "'Weggebobbles and Fruit': Bloom's Vegetarian Impulses." *Texas Studies in Literature and Language* 51, no. 4 (2009): 463–75. JSTOR.
Shihade, Magid. "Reflection on Elia Zureik's *Israel's Colonial Project in Palestine: A Brutal Pursuit*." *Arab Studies Quarterly* 38, no. 4 (2016): 709–13. JSTOR.
Small, Flicka. "'Know Me Come Eat With Me': What Food Says about Leopold Bloom." In *"Tickling the Palate": Gastronomy in Irish Literature and Culture*, edited by Máirtín Mac Con Iomaire and Eamon Maher, 35–46. Reimagining Ireland 57. Bern: Peter Lang, 2014.
Spencer, Colin. *Vegetarianism: A History*. London: Grub Street, 2000.
Stuart, Tristram. *The Bloodless Revolution: A Cultural History of Vegetarianism from 1600 to Modern Times*. New York: W. W. Norton and Co., 2008.
Wrenn, Corey. "Vegan Geographies in Ireland." In *The Routledge Handbook of Vegan Studies*, edited by Laura Wright, 394–406. New York: Routledge: Taylor and Francis Group, 2021.

9

Teaching the Wakean Sentence

Paul Fagan

In this chapter, I outline some approaches and activities for teaching *Finnegans Wake* at the level of the sentence. Of course, there are many levels of understanding and interpretation that students will require to develop an appreciation of James Joyce's avant-garde final work. These include the *Wake*'s fluid characters, settings, and environments; its evocations of night and dreaming; its Viconian, cyclical structure and thematics of fall and regeneration; its intertextual links to diverse texts and traditions; its skewed relationship to national, planetary, and universal histories and contexts; its composition history and cultural legacy.[1] When I teach the novel, I dedicate sessions to each of these topics that pair front-loaded contextualization and selected secondary literature with group close readings of passages in which characters or environments are connected to specific themes or intertextual clusters.[2] Nevertheless, I have found that all of these dimensions of the text will teach better if the class first develops methods for reading the work's strange language.

The present chapter details my approach to teaching this first lesson, in which I introduce linguistic concepts and guide group work to spotlight some ways in which the *Wake*'s radically experimental language maps onto English syntax, morphology, and punctuation. The purpose is to offer students both concrete techniques for reading the *Wake* and bases for broader reflection on how "nonsense" or avant-garde language might generate semantic and pragmatic meanings. Especially for students who are new to the *Wake*, the arc from bewilderment to a sense that the text can yield understandings through learnable reading strategies (even as we must insist that they do not *solve* the text's meaning, nor *resolve* its obscurities) can be a rewarding experience that provides a firm basis for working closely with the text in subsequent sessions.

Preparatory Discussion

In advance of our first session, I ask students to familiarize themselves with the following three sentences from episodes 1.1 and 1.3 of *Finnegans Wake*:[3]

1. The "Oftwhile" sentence (*FW* 4.30–5.4)
2. The "Cod" sentence (*FW* 54.23–55.2)
3. The "Lord's own day" sentence (*FW* 51.21–52.6)

I also bring handouts of these sentences and the first verse of Lewis Carroll's "Jabberwocky," as I will want the students to be able to mark them in group work.

After the necessary preliminaries, I ask for a volunteer to read aloud the first sentence:

> Oftwhile balbulous, mithre ahead, with goodly trowel in grasp and ivoroiled overalls which he habitacularly fondseed, like Haroun Childeric Eggeberth he would caligulate by multiplicables the alltitude and malltitude until he seesaw by neatlight of the liquor wheretwin 'twas born, his roundhead staple of other days to rise in undress maisonry upstanded (joygrantit!), a waalworth of a skyerscape of most eyeful hoyth entowerly, erigenating from next to nothing and celescalating the himals and all, hierarchitectitiptitoploftical, with a burning bush abob off its baubletop and with larrons o'toolers clittering up and tombles a'buckets clottering down. (*FW* 4.30–5.4)

To ground our debate in the students' responses to the text, I ask them about their first impressions of this excerpt, guiding them not yet to analyze the text but rather to share their own readerly experiences, whether they be curiosity, comicality, confusion, or annoyance (or some combination of these or other emotions). It is helpful to make clear that bafflement and even frustration are legitimate (and anticipated) responses to this text, and to encourage the group to reflect on their apprehension and incomprehension as part of the efferent and aesthetic reading experience. This discussion will create a useful baseline for measuring our progress by the end of the session.

To transition the discussion to the lesson's focus, I cite Louise Bogan's proposition that "before one starts hating or loving or floating off upon [the language of *Finnegans Wake*], the attention might be bent toward discovering what it is, and how it works."[4] Through this quote, I invite students to reflect on whether they consider the sentence to be meaningful or nonsense, or something inbetween. Drawing on these responses, I place the diversity of opinion about the *Wake*'s language into three general categories, showing that students who voice any of these positions may be supported by the work's critical reception, and even by direct quotes from the *Wake* that echo (and perhaps ironize) these stances.

(1) ***Finnegans Wake* is not written in any language.** This view is articulated representatively by Sean O'Faoláin, who contends that readers of the *Wake*'s "meaningless scrawls [...] cannot be expected to understand them as language."[5] Indeed, at points in the text, the *Wake*'s narrators appear to concur with the charge that this text "is nat language at any sinse of the world" (*FW* 83.12), or *not language in any sense of the word*. Yet, in our discussion we can consider that, while unorthodox, this quote is basically parsable and interpretable: this *does* appear to be language in *some* sense of the word, and we can note that with the exception of "nat" and "sinse," the line is composed of recognizable English words, even if they are deployed in an unorthodox fashion (as in the use of "world" to suggest the near-homophone "word").

(2) ***Finnegans Wake* is written in a new language.** Representative of this view is Arnold Bennett's assertion that the work is "written in James Joyce's new language, invented by himself."[6] A Wakean narrator at one juncture asks, reflexively: "[a]re we speachin d'anglas landadge or are you sprakin sea Djoytsch?" (*FW* 485.12–13); or, are we speaking English ("d'anglas landadge"), Deutsch ("Djoytsch"), a mix of languages (English, German, French), or quite simply speaking "Joyce" (a near-homophone of the nonce word "Djoytsch")?

(3) ***Finnegans Wake* largely adheres to the rules of the English language.** In her 1939 review, Bogan asserts that the *Wake*'s "language is not gibberish," in so far as it evidently "has rules and conventions."[7] Katie Wales anchors this assertion to a specific set of rules and conventions when she deems the book's vernacular "a universal language based on English,"[8] while Sam Slote asserts that Wakean peregrinism (its incorporation of features of other languages) "operates upon an (apparently) English syntax and lexicon,"[9] and Allen B. Ruch observes that Joyce's malleable "fusion of portmanteau words, stylistic parodies and complex puns" is sustained by "a language that's basically English."[10] Supporting this view, a Wakean narrator assures us in lexically and grammatically clear language at the book's outset that "here English might be seen" (*FW* 13.1).

Once students have discussed their intuitions in relation to these three possibilities, I announce my intention to outline a case for the third option: that one strategy for reading the *Wake*'s eccentric language is to explore whether a given sentence is syntactically and semantically predictable based on the rules and codes of the English language. In the next part of our session, we will explore the syntactic and morphemic adherence of the "Oftwhile" sentence to the English code alongside its lexical deviance. This approach requires the introduction of some core linguistic and discursive concepts about the function of syntax and morphology.

Syntactic Predictability

Students are asked to share their understanding of what constitutes a language and what distinguishes one language from another. Gathering together the expressed views, I propose that languages are differentiated linguistically by appeal to their distinct grammars—the logical and structural rules that preside over the composition of sentences—and lexicons, although they may exhibit a lesser or greater degree of lexical similarity depending on the genetic relationship between the languages and their political histories.

As a predominantly *analytic* language, English uses syntax to convey subject-object distinction. As such, its Subject-Verb-Object (SVO) word order is crucial to understanding a given utterance, to the point that "the dog bites the man" bears a decidedly different meaning to "the man bites the dog," and the subject-object distinction of the deviant formulation "bites the man the dog" is unclear. This is not the case in predominantly *synthetic* languages, in which the subject-object distinction is encoded through inflection, so that word order possesses less semantic significance. In German, for instance, both "der Hund beißt den Mann" (SVO) and "den Mann beißt der Hund" (OVS) are permissible syntactic constructions to express the meaning of "the dog bites the man" (albeit, with a different emphasis), owing to the fact that the determiners ("der" and "den") are inflected to distinguish the sentence's subject from its object regardless of word order. Thus, in contrast with a highly *synthetic* language in which an intelligible sentence is formed morphologically so that items may be placed in a largely arbitrary sequence—as in the Latin variants "canis mordet hominem," "hominem canis mordet," and so on—semantic meaning in English is predominantly married to its SVO syntax.

These factors result in a significant degree of syntactic predictability in English sentences, as the opening word largely determines what follows. According to Dwight L. Bolinger's concept of "linear modification," before a speaker begins an utterance, the possibilities of what they will communicate are practically infinite; when the first word of a syntactically adherent utterance is chosen, the possibilities are vastly reduced.[11] By the logic of this theory, if the opening word of an utterance is a subject noun phrase, for example, a verb shall have to follow at some point, regardless of how many hypotactic subclauses succeed it. To demonstrate the point that even nonlexical (or "nonsense") utterances can be syntactically predictable (if not semantically decipherable), I here introduce Charles Kay Ogden and Ivor Armstrong Richards's analysis of the sentence "the gostak distims the doshes." Ogden and Richards show that even as the nonce words are indecipherable—nothing in the English lexicon will apparently help us to anchor "gostaks" or "doshes" to referents in the external world—it is possible to describe the relationships between the terms owing to the sentence's syntax: the *gostak* (subject noun) is that which *distims* (verb) the *doshes* (object).[12]

Working with these concepts of linear modification and syntactic predictability, students are invited to parse the "Oftwhile" sentence by ascertaining whether it conforms to the *analytical* syntax of English. Here, I encourage them with Tony Thwaites's advice that "sometimes the only way to follow the structure of a *Wake* sentence is to keep one's finger firmly on the grammatical subject until the verb arrives."[13] In the discussion that follows, students share their findings, and I draw attention to the following points if they don't arise organically.

With reference to Bolinger's principle of linear modification, the sentence's first word should introduce a certain degree of syntactic predictability. The opening item, "Oftwhile," appears to be a compound of the temporal adverb "oft" (or "often") and the conjunction "while." Students may identify a relationship with the archaic term "oftenwhiles" (meaning oftentimes), or perceive a latent comma separating the adverb from the conjunction ("Oft[,] while"). In either case, the opening word appears to introduce a temporal adverb and initiate a subordinate clause. Following Thwaites's principle, we can hold our finger on the opening adverb "oft" until we find the subject and predicate to which it relates. Indeed, after a number of digressive clauses further modifying the subordinate "while balbulous" clause, we discover the SVO core structure to which the opening temporal adverb relates, with the assertion that "oft[,] [. . .] he *[subject]* would caligulate *[verb]* by multiplicables *[means]* the alltitude and malltitude *[object]*." Next, we find the lexical conjunction "until" introducing a new clause that likewise follows an SVO syntax and modifies the previous clause by stating that this "caligulation" would occur "until he *[subject]* seesaw *[verb]* by neatlight *[means]* [. . .] his roundhead staple *[object]* [. . .] rise *[verb]*."

While the nonlexical items remain obscure (what does it mean, exactly, to "caligulate" a "malltitude"?), students should start to see an identifiable pattern emerge: The sentence follows the syntactically predictable process of couching SVO clauses in modifying subclauses. Importantly, these dependent clauses can be recognized by their clear lexical markings, through English conjunctions such as "while," "like," "until," and "and." These lexical items afford us insight into the grammatical categorization of nonlexical items, but they also allow us to distinguish clauses, and further separate them into independent and dependent clauses, so that the syntactic thrust of the line can be parsed. If this approach is continued all the way through, the core sentence could be inferred as: "Oft[,] [...] he would caligulate [...] the alltitude and malltitude until he [...]saw [...] his roundhead staple [...] rise." While still uncertain how to attach semantic or pragmatic significance to the line's nonlexical terms, we observe that a core *analytic* English syntax guides our scheme of interpretation, despite the line's many disorienting hypotactic digressions.

Semantic Predictability

Having established that the line is hypotactically extravagant but syntactically predictable, I turn the discussion to whether the Wakean sentence is semantically predictable according to the rules of English morphology. Here, a volunteer reads the first verse of Lewis Carroll's nonsense poem "Jabberwocky" from the handout as an illustrative point of comparison:

> 'Twas brillig, and the slithy toves
> Did gyre and gimble in the wabe:
> All mimsy were the borogoves
> And the mome raths outgrabe.

The key takeaways from our discussion of syntactical predictability can be reinforced by noting that the verse's standard English conjunctions ("and"), prepositions ("in"), and determiners ("the") are non-referential function words that express grammatical relationships. Thus, the nonce words can be categorized speculatively as prenominal adjectives ("slithy," "mimsy," "mome"), nouns ("toves," "wabe," "raths"), verbs ("gyre," "gimble"), and the syntax suggests a specific relationship: the "toves" performed a series of actions (they "gyred" and "gimbled") in a particular place ("in the wabe").

H. G. Widdowson cautions that while we can thus classify these nonce words, "grammatical evidence" is not the only grounds for interpreting their meaning: "Although these words are not part of the normal vocabulary of English, they resemble words that are, and so we treat them as lexical items and assign them meaning accordingly."[14] To develop this point, Widdowson draws on the Carrollian concept of *portmanteaux* (known in linguistics as "blends"), which Ingo Plag defines as "combin[ing] two [...] words into one, deleting material from one or both of the source words."[15] Widdowson continues:

> Thus, "brillig" can be said to suggest "brilliant/bright" [and] "slithy,"
> "slimy/lithe" [...]. Other people will no doubt read the lines differently,
> but they will do so by assigning some meaning or other to the lexical
> items. [...] Meaning may not be fully determined by lexis, but given a
> collection of words, [...] we can always infer *some* figment of a proposition.[16]

Indeed, Jean-Jacques Lecercle asserts that "what is chiefly imitated [in 'Jabberwocky'] is the regular derivation of words"[17] according to two principles of word-formation:

1. *Charabia*: the coinage of possible words by exploiting the possibilities offered by the phonotactics and morphotactics of a given language;
2. *Baragouin*: the phonetic approximation of foreign lexical items.[18]

Having set up these ideas, I point out morphological clues as to the categories of the nonce terms and their relationships in "Jabberwocky." For *charabia*, I note the English adjectival suffix "-y" in "slithy" and "mimsy," and the plural noun suffix ("-s") in "toves" and "raths."[19] For *baragouin*, I identify the German adjectival suffix "-ig" in "brillig." Thus a method for interpreting the Wakean sentence—even if only for *some* figment of a proposition—is to gloss its words according to the rules of English morphology.

I begin by spotlighting an exemplary syntactical clause from the "Oftwhile" sentence that uses *charabia*. I highlight that "and ivoroil*ed* overall*s* which he habitacular*ly* fondse*ed*" contains words and morphemes that serve standard lexical functions: "and" (clausal conjunction); "-ed" (adjective); "-s" (plural noun); "which" (relative pronoun); "-ly" (adverb); "-ed" (regular past tense suffix). Indeed, submitting the clause to the rules of English syntax, we can even discern the different functions of the "-ed" suffix that identifies "ivoroiled" as an adjective (preceding the noun "overalls") and the "-ed" suffix that establishes "fondseed" as a verb (preceded by the adverb "habitacularly"). Thus glossed, the clause exhibits a consistent observance of the morphemic rules of the English linguistic code, with the metalinguistic non-referential features—prepositions, conjunctions, determiners, pronouns, prefixes, suffixes—all presented standardly, as in Carroll's poem.

With these coordinates in hand, groups are assigned a single neologism from the "Oftwhile" sentence—for purposes of demonstration, let us suppose these are "entowerly" and "balbulous"—and invited to consider it morphologically, reflecting on the following questions: (1) How can the word be broken down into its smallest parts (stems, root words, prefixes, suffixes, phonemes)? (2) Can these morphemic elements help us to define the grammatical categorization of the nonlexical signs? (3) Based on these observations, is the word a *portmanteau*, *charabia*, or *baragouin*?

After their group work, I ask students to share their findings. We might note that the nonlexical "entowerly," is constructed by the same morphological means as a standard English adverb, with a bound prefix (*en-*) and suffix (*-ly*) around a free stem (*-tower-*). Thus, it is an example of *charabia*, as it coins a syntactically and semantically predictable new word through lawful combinations using the phono- and morpho-tactics of the English language. The other group might observe that "balbulous" takes the adjectival "-ous" suffix. Given its position in a subordinate clause (as we have previously discussed), we may consider "balbulous" as indicating an attribute of the subject (*oft, while he was balbulous, he would . . .*). Yet, "balbul-" cannot easily be glossed as an English root or stem. Students may note or be pointed to "balbulous" as a near-homophone of both the English *bibulous* (addicted to drinking) and the Latin *balbus* (stuttering). In the latter case, it can be identified as an instance of *baragouin,* and a number of other foreign lexical and morphemic elements may be discerned in words such as "maisonry" (French *maison,* "house"), "himals" (German *Himmel,* "sky" or "heaven"), and "erigenating" (Greek *êrigeneia,* "early-born" or "Dawn"). I will usually finish the discussion by asking the groups to identify a portmanteau in the line, with "celescalating" presenting the most obvious example, as a blend of "escalating" and "celestial."

Teachers might like to use these terms as jumping off points for discussing the *Wake*'s more commonly noted use of punning (treating homophones as though they were synonyms) to suggest multiple meanings at once: "entowerly" as a near-homophone of "entirely" that introduces the image of the tower; "balbulous" as evoking both drinking and stuttering; "celescalating" suggesting "ascending to the heavens." These glosses can be combined with the previous syntactic parsing to develop a reading of the sentence that links it to the scene's broader thematic imagery of the stuttering Finnegan falling drunkenly from the tower he is building up into the heavens (like the Tower of Babel). But the point I want the students to come away with is how English syntax and morphology can be crucial points of orientation for reading the Wakean sentence and building blocks upon which to justify and develop these broader readings of plot, imagery, and theme.

Punctuation (Parentheses)

Derek Attridge notes the difficulty of distinguishing "what is central from what is digressive" in the *Wake*'s prolix, hypotactic sentences.[20] Standardly, sentences use parentheses to mark the text inside the brackets as "explanatory, less important, or even at a different narrative level."[21] Thus, in the last part of the session we explore how parentheses might help to distinguish core from digression and establish hierarchies of relevance in the Wakean sentence.[22]

I ask students to find and highlight all of the parentheses in the second sample sentence. When completed, they should have highlighted four opening and four closing brackets, thus:

> Meggeg, m'gay chapjappy fellow, I call our univalse to witness, as sicker as moyliffey eggs is known by our good househalters from yorehunderts of mamooth to be which they commercially are in ahoy high British quarters (conventional!) my guesthouse and cowhaendel credits will immediately stand ohoh open as straight as that neighbouring monument's fabrication before the hygienic gllll (this was where the reverent sabboth and bottlebreaker with firbalk forthstretched touched upon his tricoloured boater, which he uplifted by its pickledhoopy (he gave Stetson one and a penny for it) whileas oleaginosity of ancestralolosis sgocciolated down the both pendencies of his mutsohito liptails (Sencapetulo, a more modestuous conciliabulite never curled a torn pocketmouth), cordially inwiting the adullescence who he was wising up to do in like manner what all did so as he was able to add) lobe before the Great Schoolmaster's. (*FW* 54.23–55.2; emphasis mine)

Testing the hypothesis that the brackets can help to distinguish the sentence's central core from its digressive envelope, I ask the students to apply Thwaites's principle to the sentence's punctuation by putting their finger on the opening bracket and waiting for the closing bracket, paying attention also to parentheses within parentheses.

The first instance—"(conventional!)"—should pose no problem, but the task becomes more complex once we come to the peculiar "gllll (." If carefully move past the nested parentheses within parentheses—"(he gave Stetson one and a penny for it)" and "(Sencapetulo [. . .] pocketmouth)"—we will find that the corresponding closed bracket is ") lobe." If we cross or white out the intervening parentheses, what we are presented with is "gllll ([. . .]) lobe." Students might first speculate on the meaning, before I suggest that what we have here is an unusual case of parentheses within a single word: namely, "gllll-lobe," or "globe." Time permitting, I might walk the class through a reading of this line, in which the speaker, while drawing out his pronunciation of the word "globe," lifts his hat (he "touched upon his tricoloured boater, which he uplifted") and gestures for the audience to raise their hats in a similar fashion ("cordially inwiting the adullescence [. . .] to do in like manner") and waiting for them all to comply so that he can finish his enunciation of the word globe:

"what all did so as he was able to add) lobe." Here, Joyce's unorthodox use of parentheses works to capture the simultaneity of speech, gesture, and reaction. However, the primary outcome of the task should be that students learn to use parentheses and other punctuation clues to uncover the core syntactic unit of the Wakean sentence.

Conclusion

To reinforce the skills that the class is designed to teach, I issue a homework assignment in which students are tasked with parsing and glossing the third sample Wakean sentence by paying close attention to its syntax, morphology, and punctuation:

> It was the Lord's own day for damp (to wait for a postponed regatta's eventualising is not of Battlecock Shettledore—Juxta—Mare only) and the request for a fully armed explanation was put (in Loo of Pat) to the porty (a native of the sisterisle—Meathman or Meccan?—by his brogue, exrace eyes, lokil calour and lucal odour which are said to have been average clownturkish (though the capelist's voiced nasal liquids and the way he sneezed at zees haul us back to the craogs and bryns of the Silurian Ordovices) who, the lesser pilgrimage accomplished, had made, pats' and pigs' older inselt, the south-east bluffs of the stranger stepshore, a *regifugium persecutorum*, hence hindquarters) as he paused at evenchime for some or so minutes (hit the pipe, dannyboy! Time to won, barmon. I'll take ten to win.) amid the devil's one duldrum (Apple by her blossom window and Charlotte at her toss panomancy his sole admirers, his only tearts in store) for a fragrend culubosh during his weekend pastime of executing with Anny Oakley deadliness (the consummatory pairs of provocatives, of which remained provokingly but two, the ones he fell for, Lili and Tutu, cork em!) empties which had not very long before contained Reid's family (you ruad that before, soaky, but all the bottles in sodemd histry will not soften your bloodathirst!) stout. (*FW* 51.21–52.06)

This can be assigned as individual homework, or, ideally, set up as a discussion forum in the e-learning platform for students to work on together.

Using the practices we have discussed in class—identifying lexical markers, following the logic of linear modification, parsing the line's syntax, glossing the nonce words morphologically, identifying *portmanteaux, charabia*, and *baragouin*, and using parentheses to distinguish core from digression—students will likely uncover some variation of this core syntactic unit:

> the request for a fully armed explanation was put [. . .] to the porty [. . .] as he paused at evenchime [. . .] for a fragrend culubosh during his weekend pastime of executing [. . .] empties which had not very long before contained Reid's family [. . .] stout.

An advantage of assigning the task as online group work is that it will furnish the students with the time and opportunity to produce an array of "false" starts and leads, which will yield productively contradictory readings. And these can be used to emphasize a key point at the outset of the next session when the group reflects on this task: namely, as David Hayman insists, the *Wake*'s "tenuous narratives" may only be accessed through "the dense weave of a language designed as much to shield as to reveal them."[23] Thus, while the class's goal is to give students concrete, helpful, and learnable strategies for reading the Wakean sentence, these cannot, ultimately, fix the meaning of Joyce's "devious" language, which constantly "conceals and reveals" its obscure "secrets."[24]

Notes

1 See Margot Norris, "Teaching *Finnegans Wake* Between Domestication and Deconstruction," *James Joyce Quarterly* 39, no. 1 (Fall 2001): 113–21; Paul K. Saint-Amour, "Late Joyce and His Legacies: Teaching *Finnegans Wake* and Its Aftertale," *James Joyce Quarterly* 39, no. 1 (Fall 2001): 123–34; Kimberly J. Devlin, "Attempting to Teach *Finnegans Wake*: Reading Strategies and Interpretive Arguments for Newcomers," *Joyce Studies Annual* (2009): 159–87.
2 For instance, "The Cad in the Park" episode to introduce HCE and thematics of Irish literary and political conflict; I.8 to introduce ALP and ecocritical approaches; "The Ondt and the Gracehoper" to introduce Shem and Shaun and the *Wake*'s interfaces with philosophical traditions.
3 James Joyce, *Finnegans Wake* (New York: Viking, 1959). All future references are to this edition and will be cited parenthetically in the text.
4 Louise Bogan, "*Finnegans Wake*," *Nation* 148 (May 6, 1939): 533–35, qtd. in Robert H. Deming, *James Joyce: The Critical Heritage* (London: Barnes and Noble, 1970), 665.
5 Sean O'Faoláin, "Style and the Limitations of Speech," *Criterion* 8, no. 30 (September 1928), qtd. in Deming, *James Joyce*, 391–92.
6 Arnold Bennett, "Comment," *London Evening Standard*, September 19, 1929, 7; qtd. in Deming, *James Joyce*, 404.
7 Bogan, "*Finnegans Wake*," 665.
8 Katie Wales, *The Language of James Joyce* (Basingstoke: Macmillan, 1992), 136.
9 Sam Slote, "No Symbols Where None Intended: Derrida's War at *Finnegans Wake*," in *James Joyce and the Difference of Language*, ed. Laurent Milesi (Cambridge: Cambridge University Press, 2003), 196.
10 Allen B. Ruch, "Joyce Works: *Finnegans Wake*," *Shipwreck Library*, https://shipwrecklibrary.com/joyce/joyce-works-fw/.

11 Dwight L. Bolinger, *Forms of English: Accent, Morpheme, Order* (Cambridge: Harvard University Press, 1965), 281.
12 Charles Kay Ogden and Ivor Armstrong Richards, *The Meaning of Meaning: A Study of the Influence of Language Upon Thought and of the Science of Symbolism*, ed. W. Terrence Gordon (London: Routledge, 1994), 46.
13 Tony Thwaites, *Joycean Temporalities: Debts, Promises, and Countersignatures* (Gainesville: University Press of Florida, 2001), 168.
14 H. G. Widdowson, *Linguistics* (Oxford: Oxford University Press, 2007), 54.
15 Ingo Plag, *Word-Formation in English* (Cambridge: Cambridge University Press, 2003), 122.
16 Widdowson, *Linguistics*, 54.
17 Jean-Jacques Lecercle, *The Philosophy of Nonsense: The Intuitions of Victorian Nonsense Literature* (London: Routledge, 1994), 40.
18 Jean-Jacques Lecercle, *The Violence of Language* (London: Routledge, 1990), 4.
19 See Lecercle, *Philosophy of Nonsense*, 21.
20 Derek Attridge, *Peculiar Language: Literature as Difference from the Renaissance to James Joyce* (London: Routledge, 2004), 212.
21 Edward A. Levenston, *The Stuff of Literature: Physical Aspects of Texts and Their Relation to Literary Meaning* (Albany: State University of New York Press, 1992), 65.
22 On the *Wake*'s use of punctuation, see Paul Fagan, "'(hic sunt lennones!)': Reading and Misreading the *Wake*'s Signs of Suspicion," in *Doubtful Points: Joyce and Punctuation*, ed. Tim Conley and Elizabeth Bonapfel, 116–35 (Amsterdam: Brill-Rodopi, 2014); and Elizabeth M. Bonapfel, "Joyce's Punctuation and the Evolution of Narrative in *Finnegans Wake*," *Journal of Modern Literature* 42, no. 4 (Summer 2019): 54–73.
23 David Hayman, *The Wake in Transit* (Ithaca: Cornell University Press, 1990), 42.
24 Margot Norris, *The Decentered Universe of "Finnegans Wake": A Structuralist Argument* (Baltimore: John Hopkins University Press, 1976), 120.

Bibliography

Attridge, Derek. *Peculiar Language: Literature as Difference from the Renaissance to James Joyce*. London: Routledge, 2004.
Bolinger, Dwight L. *Forms of English: Accent, Morpheme, Order*. Cambridge: Harvard University Press, 1965.
Bonapfel, Elizabeth M. "Joyce's Punctuation and the Evolution of Narrative in *Finnegans Wake*." *Journal of Modern Literature* 42, no. 4 (Summer 2019): 54–73.
Deming, Robert H. *James Joyce: The Critical Heritage*. London: Barnes and Noble, 1970.
Devlin, Kimberly J. "Attempting to Teach *Finnegans Wake*: Reading Strategies and Interpretive Arguments for Newcomers." *Joyce Studies Annual* (2009): 159–87.
Fagan, Paul. "'(hic sunt lennones!)': Reading and Misreading the *Wake*'s Signs of Suspicion." In *Doubtful Points: Joyce and Punctuation*, edited by Tim Conley and Elizabeth Bonapfel, 116–35. Amsterdam: Brill-Rodopi, 2014.
Hayman, David. *The Wake in Transit*. Ithaca: Cornell University Press, 1990.

Joyce, James. *Finnegans Wake*. New York: Viking Press, 1959.
Lecercle, Jean-Jacques. *The Philosophy of Nonsense: The Intuitions of Victorian Nonsense Literature*. London: Routledge, 1994.
Lecercle, Jean-Jacques. *The Violence of Language*. London: Routledge, 1990.
Levenston, Edward A. *The Stuff of Literature: Physical Aspects of Texts and Their Relation to Literary Meaning*. Albany: State University of New York Press, 1992.
Norris, Margot. *The Decentered Universe of "Finnegans Wake": A Structuralist Argument*. Baltimore: John Hopkins University Press, 1976.
Norris, Margot. "Teaching *Finnegans Wake* Between Domestication and Deconstruction." *James Joyce Quarterly* 39, no. 1 (Fall 2001): 113–21.
Ogden, Charles Kay, and Ivor Armstrong Richards. *The Meaning of Meaning: A Study of the Influence of Language Upon Thought and of the Science of Symbolism*, edited by W. Terrence Gordon. London: Routledge, 1994.
Plag, Ingo. *Word-Formation in English*. Cambridge: Cambridge University Press, 2003.
Ruch, Allen B. "Joyce Works: *Finnegans Wake*." *Shipwreck Library*. https://shipwrecklibrary.com/joyce/joyce-works-fw/.
Saint-Amour, Paul K. "Late Joyce and His Legacies: Teaching *Finnegans Wake* and Its Aftertale." *James Joyce Quarterly* 39, no. 1 (Fall 2001): 123–34.
Slote, Sam. "No Symbols Where None Intended: Derrida's War at *Finnegans Wake*." In *James Joyce and the Difference of Language*, edited by Laurent Milesi, 195–207. Cambridge: Cambridge University Press, 2003.
Thwaites, Tony. *Joycean Temporalities: Debts, Promises, and Countersignatures*. Gainesville: University Press of Florida, 2001.
Wales, Katie. *The Language of James Joyce*. Basingstoke: Macmillan, 1992.
Widdowson, H. G. *Linguistics*. Oxford: Oxford University Press, 2007.

10

Teaching *Finnegans Wake*

Reading, Performing, and Creating

GREGORY ERICKSON

The Class

This chapter will focus on an undergraduate seminar I teach at New York University titled "Reading, Performing, and Creating *Finnegans Wake*." When people find out that I teach undergraduate courses on James Joyce they often ask, sometimes in jest, if I teach *Finnegans Wake* to undergraduates too. Yes, I answer, to their surprise, and not just to literature majors, but to students across the university. While it is unusual to build a whole undergraduate course around *Finnegans Wake*, and even more so, one that is not aimed exclusively at English majors, I have also found that the study of *Finnegans Wake* addresses issues relevant to students interested in education, philosophy, history, the arts, and other disciplines. The answers to *how* I teach the course are, at least superficially, easy: We read short sections, we read together, and much of the course is devoted to works of art or performances inspired by or depicting *Finnegans Wake*.

I have enjoyed teaching it, but it was in writing this chapter that I thought more deeply about *why* I think the course structure works and why teaching the *Wake* in this artistic context is important. The answer, I think, comes down to the relationship between three words in my title and the productive tensions between how we project meaning onto them: reading, performing, and creating. My teaching of *Finnegans Wake* is more rooted in creativity, performance, and pleasure than in claiming, imparting, or acquiring any sort of mastery. Although I would not describe this class as a model of radical pedagogy, it does, implicitly and through practice, follow many of the precepts: alternative grading practices, class dialogue, giving power to the students, and challenging the hierarchical model of knowledge in which the professor imparts facts, interpretations, and wisdom. Most importantly, the very practice of the class is based on the idea that knowledge and culture are always changing.

When students ask how they can psychologically prepare for a semester "reading" a text that seems complete gibberish to them, I tell the story of being on a cross-country flight with a bored-looking businessman sitting in front of me, who asked if I had anything to read. The only book I had in my bag was a copy of the *Wake*, so I gave that to him, but warned that it was a "really weird book." As I sat in my seat grading papers, I could hear him reading out loud under his breath. He slowly read a line at a time, page by page. After over an hour, he turned and handed it back to me, dismissively saying that it "made no sense." But *something* had kept him concentrating, reading intently, and had kept him entertained with a book that he had never heard of and that "made no sense." He had instinctively known to sound out words, to experience the *Wake* physically and sonically as well as mentally.

What kept him interested? Was it the sound of the words as he spoke them to himself? The strange visual experience of reading words that looked and sounded like English but were not? I didn't ask him, but to me it remains a good example of how *Finnegans Wake* can be an experience in defamiliarization, rather than comprehension, yet can hold our attention. That, I tell students, is how we will try to read the *Wake*—by paying attention to sounds, bodies, and images as well as the process of parsing out and making meaning. The course builds on the idea that *Finnegans Wake* is not just a book for experts or literature scholars, and that the experience of engaging in different ways with its style, content, and difficulty can be a practice of individual and collaborative thinking, learning, and artistic creating. Rather than seeing it as a dauntingly difficult text for scholars only, I have found that a study of *Finnegans Wake* by and with curious, inexperienced readers can be a way to open questions about the nature of books, why and how we read, the productivity of the interdisciplinary college classroom, and what experimental forms of artistic communication might have to offer.

My practice of teaching this class is part interdisciplinary seminar, part reading group, and part arts workshop. Half of the class is devoted to the work itself. We read short sections of the *Wake* in concert with various commentaries, histories, and annotations, exploring possible "meanings" that the text suggests. The other half of the course engages with artistic pieces that have been inspired by or that incorporate elements of *Finnegans Wake*. We listen to classical, jazz, and popular music ranging from John Cage to DJ Spooky. We look at Derek Pyle's massive online project "Waywords and Meansigns," in which he has curated the whole of *Finnegans Wake* being set to music more than twice in styles varying from techno to metal.[1] For a week on visual art, we look at works like Stephen Crow's "*Wake* in Progress," László Moholy-Nagy's *Wake* diagram, concrete poetry, the Book of Kells, and critical writings from Christa-Maria Lerm Hayes. We read and watch theater performances by Adam Harvey, Ciceil L. Gross, and Olwen Fouéré, and study dance pieces by Pilobolus and Merce Cunningham. We also look at artistic projects by previous students that work within all of these same genres. In each case, we use art to facilitate questions about the role of literature, language, representation, difficulty, ritual, and performance. Students study these pieces, read critical texts about them, and in turn create and present their own creative works. Class requirements include an analytical paper, an oral presentation, and their own creative work or work in progress.

Welcome to *Finnegans Wake*

Before we even read a word together, I find out what interested the students in taking the class and what skills and expertise they may have. Some are English or Irish Studies majors or have heard of the book's reputation. Others are drawn to the studying and making of interdisciplinary experimental art. Some of the students will come to the class having read *Dubliners, Portrait,* or *Ulysses* and are eager to read further. And others are just curious without any context. I reassure them that this is the blend that I want, that the class works better when there are no expectations and when we all start from different places. In order to empower those who have never read Joyce before, I ask a series of questions intended to determine what tools we have as a reading community, and to identify authorities in reading and discussion that are not me. These include:

- Who speaks or reads a language other than English?
- Who is Irish? Catholic?
- Who knows a lot of Shakespeare? Swift? The Bible?
- Who is a musician? Who is a painter? A poet? An actor? A dancer?
- Who knows lots of Irish songs or dirty limericks?

Each of these knowledge areas, I tell them, will be important to our process as a class. I make it clear that *Finnegans Wake* will not feel like normal "reading," or what they are used to, but also that it will help us think about what the acts and practices of reading involve, and to ask if any kind of reading is "normal."

As much as I am tempted to throw students into reading the book at the top of the course to see what their varying expertise comes up with, I have found that doing so mostly results in frustration or confusion, so I want to give them a few things to hold on to first. I find it important to give them a few basic tools to help them create their own meanings from the text, but I also think it offers an important model of how we interact with primary texts. *Finnegans Wake*, I explain, is a text that one never really "begins" or "finishes." In that way, it is not unlike other important texts, which one never approaches as a blank slate (I might use Genesis, *Hamlet*, or *Harry Potter* as examples), and I want students to have and discuss the experience of beginning but having already begun. *Finnegans Wake*, of course, dramatizes this idea of nonlinear reading, as it "begins" with a lowercase letter, ends with the word "the," and constantly reminds us that it is a story "retaled," and that it is a "meandertale" of "reredos."[2]

We start with the title—*Finnegans Wake*—and some familiar questions: Who is Finnegan? Why no apostrophe? Are there many Finnegans? Okay, keep thinking. What else might it mean? Could it mean to finish again? And what does that mean in a title? Usually students, with a little prodding, are able to come up with three or four meanings for the word "wake:" to wake up, to be enlightened, to leave a wake behind you, and a funeral ritual. Lately, there is often some play on the word "woke," and how we might bring that into our discussion, and if that would even be relevant or allowed. This immediately throws us into the question of authorial intent or anachronistic interpretations—questions that today's students think about very differently than they might have even ten or fifteen years ago. They are more aware that to read a novel in 2023 that was finished in 1939 is necessarily a negotiation of time and of multiple cultural horizons. We are, after all, always reading in the wake of the novel.

Since this is a course rooted in intersecting artistic disciplines, it makes sense to initially think about the title through the Irish song "Finnegan's Wake," from which the novel takes its name. We listen to the song in class and think about its themes of music, death, life, and whiskey. The song, as Joyce readers know, is about one Tim Finnegan, who was born "with the love of the liquor." One morning, when he was "rather full," he "fell from the ladder and he broke his skull." His friends hold a wake for him, which erupts into a drunken fight, and when a bucket of whiskey is thrown, it misses its target:

> The liquor scattered over Tim
> Tim revives, see how he rises
> Timothy rising from the bed
> Said "Whirl your whiskey around like blazes
> Thundering Jesus, do you think I'm dead?"

Students are quick to point to connections between alcohol and resurrection, which they already see as a possible theme in our upcoming readings, and they also start thinking about the role of music in literature. More than just a source for the title, the song offers a place to start asking generative questions: Does it matter if we know the song before reading? Does the *melody* change how we read the title? The book is full of quotations from and references to songs, and it even creates a few of its own. Is it important, we ask, that we know, learn, or sing these melodies, and how might that change the reading process?

To provide a foundation for their reading, I introduce the main characters—reading can be difficult when we "don't know whose hue" (*FW* 227.25)—and that a big question in the book is, as Joyce scholar Adaline Glasheen writes, "Who is who when everybody is somebody else."[3] I do a quick run-through of Humphry Chimpden Earwicker (Here Comes Everybody or HCE), Anna Livia Plurabelle (ALP or the River Liffey), and their children Shem (brain), Shaun (body), and Isabel. Each character, I briefly demonstrate, can stand for other characters and historical figures throughout the novel; readers and critics are not always in agreement about what character is speaking or is being represented. I then briefly introduce the plot by giving them four main plot points:

1. Something naughty is done (maybe) by the main patriarchal character (HCE) in Phoenix Park (maybe) and is observed (perhaps).
2. Many people talk about this incident in different forms (gossip, rumor, songs, dreams, news reports, histories).
3. His wife (ALP) writes a letter to exonerate him.
4. The younger generation gradually takes the place of the old.

I give few details on any of these plot points, except to say that—like the main characters—they will be revisited and remixed in different ways throughout the novel. We also talk about how different forms of art create structures of repetition and difference that are similar to these: for example, theme and variation or remixes in music, repeated performances in live theater, the nature of a rehearsal, and the aesthetics of film and photography.

Although art, music, and theater are an important part of the course, at some point we need to just start reading and thinking about the text itself, which most of the students have thus far only glanced at. Because this is a text of "punns and reedles" (*FW* 239.35–36), I begin with showing them a few specific words: What might "laughtears" mean? Or "cryzy?" These are easy for students—happy and sad at the same time, crying and crazy. "Godinpotty" is a little stranger, but they usually get at some sort of combination of divinity, blasphemy, and an English Garden Party.

These examples, they see, are just a combination of words or a portmanteau—like Brexit or brunch, chillax or cosplay. Students are quick to give other examples from meme culture or hip-hop (crunk). Once we agree that words will mean (and perhaps always do mean) multiple things—or, as Joyce writes, "two thinks at a time"—a fun place to dive in is to look at how the *Wake* adapts the lyrics to the song "Finnegan's Wake." In the song, we hear that Tim Finnegan was "laid out upon the bed / with a gallon of whiskey at his feet /and a barrel of porter at his head." In Joyce's version, we read that "they laid him brawdawn alanglast bed. With a bockalips of finisky fore his feet. And a barrowload of guenesis hoer his head" (*FW* 6.26–27). Students are already able to see the religious reference of combining Guinness and Genesis and the reference to the apocalypse (a bockalips), which seems to be both the finale and a bit finicky ("finisky"). This then brings us back to the title of the song and the book, with their realization that it was already about biblical beginnings and endings before we even started.

It is important to me that this first class ends with a communal performance, and the last activity of our introductory class is always the first thunderword, found on the first page and used to represent the fall (or Fall) of Tim Finnegan, of HCE, of Wall Street, of Humpty Dumpty, and of Adam and humankind:

> bababadalgharaghtakamminarronnkonnbronntonnerrontuonnt-
> hunntrovarrhounawnskawnt
>   oohoohoordenenthurnul.

To guide students through, I consult Joycegeek.com, created by the actor and Joycean Adam Harvey, and its video series "Don't Panic: It's only *Finnegans Wake*," in which he takes watchers through each thunderword, step by step.[4] After first pronouncing the word a couple of times as the words and letters flow across the screen, prompting viewers to pronounce them along with him, Harvey then begins by pointing out that opening "bababadal" is often taken to refer to the Tower of Babel. From there the rest of the word is made out of words of thunder:

> kaminari (Japanese)
> karak (Hindi)
> brontaô (German)
> tonnerre (French)
> tuono (Italian)
> aska (Swedish)
> tórnach (Italian)
> trovão (Portuguese)
> todenen (Danish)

I encourage my own students to say the individual words and finally the whole thunderword along with Harvey, which they start to enjoy as they recite and, of course, laugh together. As this is the last activity of the first class, it is not unusual to have students reciting the word as they leave the classroom, already bonding together over the multilinguistic creativity, theatricality, and silliness that will sustain the class over the course of the semester.

Finnegans Wake and the Arts

The conclusion of the first class reinforces that I want students to recognize the emphasis on *performance* as well as reading at the beginning of the course. While they may originally think of the art as a way of *illustrating* or *representing* the book, I want them to develop a more creative and performative way of engaging with texts. In some ways, the class is a form of performance studies without the label. The influential performance studies scholar Richard Schechner explains that, while performance studies used archives and texts extensively (books, photographs, images, archives), the "dedicated focus is on the 'repertory,' namely, what people do in the activity of their doing it."[5] It is this act of "doing it" that I will keep bringing us back to in the class, whatever that "it" might be at that particular moment.

For Dwight Conquergood, what is radical about performance studies is that it embraces:

> Both written scholarship and creative work, texts and performance. . . . Printed texts are too important and powerful for us to cede that form of scholarship. But it is not enough. We also engage in creative work that stands alongside and in metonymic tension with conventional scholarship.[6]

Although Conquergood is not talking exactly about the kind of teaching I am doing, his words are a perfect encapsulation of what my course attempts to do. Beginning with our group's recitations of the first thunderword, the art, music, and performances that we study, share, and produce in the class both expand the idea of what *Finnegans Wake* is and challenge much of the scholarship and methodology that surrounds the study of the text.

In the next class, we take a shot at reading, or, better yet, at *performing*, the first page. I have them read it out loud and start to work through some possible meanings. I encourage them to use Roland McHugh's annotations or online sources (such as fweet.org) or Google and Wikipedia. Nothing is off limits in this class, I say, it is all one big network of knowledge and possible meanings, and they should feel free to try anything out. Books, laptops, dictionaries, guidebooks, and phones are all welcome at the table. Reading this first page, even my class of non-experienced Joyce readers is able to arrive at the themes of flowing waters and history, rises and falls, and references to the Bible. They are excited when they get to the (now familiar) thunderword—usually reading it out loud together—and start interpreting the themes of thunder and falling back into the lines they have just read.

From this point on, the course progresses in an alternating fashion: one week focuses on passages from the book and the following week looks at a different art form. Our readings are taken from some of the more familiar passages from the *Wake* as well as ones that lend themselves to visual, sonic, or theatrical possibilities: "Mamafesta," the "Museyroom," the "Riddles," "The Ballad of Persse O'Reilly," and the "The Ondt and the Gracehoper."[7] I pair these readings with Richard Ellmann's chapter "The Making of *Finnegans Wake*" and with sections from a *Wake* guidebook, which might be Edmund Epstein's *A Guide Through "Finnegans Wake"* or John Gordon's *"Finnegans Wake": A Plot Summary*.[8]

On more art-focused weeks, we work through film, music, dance, visual art, and theater. More important, though, than the actual works of art we look at are the ways that we, as a class, think through them in relation to the *Wake*. I try to choose works that are not traditional "settings" of the text to music, nor are they, for the most part "illustrations." In other words, the works challenge the idea that the primary literary text must be primary. This idea emerges organically during our discussions and debates and reflects back on our discussions during the weeks we focus on the *Wake* itself. Or, as more than one student has told me, the class makes the phrase "the *Wake* itself" problematic. Can *Finnegans Wake* exist on its own? What does it mean to assume any text's autonomous existence? As one student wrote in an informal response paper, "I have only one book in my backpack and yet I feel like it contains everything I've ever done or thought. And I have neither read nor understand any of it."

Since many of the students in the class are interested and conversant in film and film aesthetics, I often begin by showing Mary Ellen Bute's 1966 black-and-white film version of *Finnegans Wake*, titled *Passages from James Joyce's "Finnegans Wake."* The film uses subtitles to capture some of the language complexities and double meanings, and mostly uses a conventional camera style, but occasionally switches between animations, manipulations of drawings and paintings in front of the camera, double exposures, and old film clips that run forward, backward, and upside down. Even students beginning to read the book are able to engage with the film and to talk about various choices that a film adaptation would have to make. They notice, for example, that the film centers on the main character HCE and his dream world much more obviously than the book seems to. Some see this as a filmmaker's choice, and others wonder if it points to their own misreading of the novel. Another comment that is often made early in the discussion is that the film can be watched in ninety minutes, while the book is very dense, and 628 pages long. This observation leads to an interesting discussion on the nature and autonomy of a book or of a work of art, which is a question of borders that is also part of the experiences of reading the *Wake* itself.

In class, we might watch the opening of the film together. It begins with scrolling words that provide basic background and describe the overlapping and intersecting characters. We then see the sun rise over the River Liffey. And the opening minutes feature water: the river and a bay. As a narrator intones the opening words of the novel—which we also see printed on the screen—the images of water alternate with a couple in bed. A harp glissando and gentle flute introduce the voice of HCE who describes "jogging along in a dream." He wakes, gazes fondly at his wife, and then, as we hear a thunderclap and hear the thunderword spoken, we see images of his fall woven in with Humpty Dumpty, the collapse of buildings (and civilization), paintings of hell, and HCE in a coffin. Fall, indeed. It is very 1960s in its style, at which students laugh, but this scene, and others we discuss, echoes, enhances, alters, or parallels the book in intriguing ways. Usually, the concepts that students bring up in their reaction pieces relate to narrative structure, character development, or the idea of time. They note that the film self-reflexively plays with time by having characters see themselves on TV or in pictures at an earlier age or they appear dressed of an earlier era.

The class does not have a single shared syllabus. Unlike most of my other classes, I make it a point in this class that students are not always expected to read, see, or listen to the same supporting or secondary material as the other students; in other words, we come to class bringing different critical backgrounds. I assign some students critical texts, reviews, or historical context, but others I do not. I try to establish that the context behind the text is always in flux. I want the class itself to mimic reading *Finnegans Wake* where we might stop to research a word or a reference, but often just keep going. So, for example, in the film unit, some of the students read Patrick A. McCarthy's "*Finnegans Wake* on Film," where he points out that "the puns are often funnier when we can see the punsters, and in the film this effect is enhanced by the use of captions," and that "at the very end of the credits, however, we are left with Joyce's final word, 'the,' isolated on the screen—a nice touch."[9] Other students learn that the film is based on Mary Manning's 1957 *Passages from "Finnegans Wake,"* that the film won a Cannes Film Festival prize in 1965, or that Bute had spent twenty-four years synchronizing music and abstract animation.[10] Students interested in making biographical connections to Joyce and film can read about how he was interested in early cinema and had even owned a movie theater in Dublin. Others may search the text itself for film-related words such as "movietone" (*FW* 62.9) or "longshots" (*FW* 221.22). All of these different perspectives are then brought into our discussion. Like reading *Finnegans Wake*, or like any kind of reading, it becomes clear in this course that no two readers are ever really perceiving the same text.

To get them thinking creatively at the outset, I ask students to write about how they might create their own film version of *Finnegans Wake*. Like all the other assignments in this class, I let them work alone or collaboratively. One student, Michael Abraham, wrote:

> If I were to create a cinematic adaptation of the *Wake*, the focus would be on the text itself. A single narrator would read the text from top to bottom in order, while footage from the history of cinema—everything from Woody Allen to *Keeping Up with the Kardashians* to *Casablanca*—would be timed to the audio. In offering visuals that the audience is overly familiar with, the visuals would call attention to themselves as visuals, highlighting the text and attempting to represent both its foreignness and affinities for Western culture since the novel's publication.

We talk in class about how having a single actor speak the lines of a character might limit the overlapping multiple personalities that we perceive in reading the book, or if seeing words on the screen might add a connection to the book. We inevitably talk about other books that have been adapted into films and how this both is and is not like *Lord of the Rings*, *One Flew Over the Cuckoos Nest*, or *The Unbearable Lightness of Being*. While critics of the film in the 1960s often focused on how successfully (or not) it captured the book, students today—trained on multiverse narratives in books, graphic novels, films, and video games—are more apt to see the film and book in an open dialogue, with neither necessarily the original nor the canonical.

While the film gives students perhaps a clearer narrative or plot than they can find anywhere in the book itself, John Cage's sound piece "Roaratorio, an Irish circus on *Finnegans Wake*" (1979) offers no discernible plot or characters (or even structure) at all. "Roaratorio" is a sixty-minute piece, originally written for radio, that is "based" on *Finnegans Wake*. It consists of four layers of sounds totaling sixty-two tracks: first, the voice of Cage himself speech-singing a text adapted from *Finnegans Wake*; second, a collection of field recordings Cage took from places mentioned in the book; third, a collection of sounds mentioned in the book; and fourth, where Cage recorded Irish folk musicians and added their pieces to the mix. Cage used chance operations to make editing and mixing choices, intentionally eliminating the role of the composer or arranger. The spoken text of the piece is Cage's text, "Writing for the Second Time Through *Finnegans Wake*," a series of mesostics based on passages from the text. But this seemingly organized description does not capture the experience of the piece. "Roaratorio" opens with sounds of water, Cage reading almost imperceptibly in the background, and then the sound of an Irish fiddle. The piece then seems to wander aimlessly and then kind of just stops when you are not paying attention.

When my students listen to the piece, they have various reactions, but within the context of the course, they tend to focus on one main question: Does this really have anything to do with *Finnegans Wake*? If they come from a traditional English-class mindset, it is hard for them to see random chance operation, indecipherable language, and unidentifiable sounds as either a form of critique or as a text they can critique. After listening to "Roaratorio," student Paul Pinson wrote that he "felt the chaos of Cage's piece only brought out the most obvious effect of *Finnegans Wake*—I'd be more satisfied if the sounds, voice, and music would drift into brief moments of tunefulness and order." In writing this, Paul was trying to find something in the listening that he had found in the text, even in just reading the *Wake* for a week or so—he wanted that movement of clarity, where you realize that a word like "riverrun" could mean the Liffey river, as well as the flow of time and flux of history (and perhaps reverend).[11] As difficult as it is, readers of the *Wake* delight in these moments of unfolding meanings. Cage's music resists those kinds of experiences.

In class, students would often point to the intentional "randomness" of Cage's music, as opposed to what they were starting to see as the very carefully structured and crafted text. Are these two pieces—*Finnegans Wake* and "Roaratorio"—then, opposite types of art? Two kinds of "reading?" (We might, somewhat reductively think of it as a modernist versus postmodernist aesthetic.) One reading practice, based on our first day of class, is to dig into commentaries, guides, and dictionaries—to work through one word at a time until some sort of meaning starts to emerge. But the other possibility for reading is based more on what they might learn from a piece like Cage's "Roaratorio." A way to envelop yourself in the *Wake* without necessarily looking for a traditional sort of "meaning." I steer the class toward two questions here: the first asks if this tension changes how we read and understand the *Wake,* and the second asks what this awareness says about the composition process and the tools that Cage and Joyce both work with.

We then apply these two questions to various other pieces of music connected to the *Wake,* listening to pieces by Milton Babbitt, Phil Minton, DJ Spooky, and Neal Kosaly-Meyer. These composers each work with the themes and words of the *Wake* in radically different ways—each asserting through repetition, difficulty, and structure (or lack of it), various sonic representations of elements of the text. Derek Pyle's online project "Waywords and Meansigns," for most of the students, uses text settings and music they are better able to discuss, as it leans toward rock, metal, and electronica, and we talk more about how the music changes how we process the language. Pyle's take on Joyce and music often speaks to students who feel that they identify more with the music than with literature or literary criticism. For Pyle, "Joycean music is not merely exegesis, but a form of artistic collaboration/co-creation, with blurred lines of authorship."[12] This kind of thinking frees students up in talking and writing about music, as well as the text when they return to it. To be given permission to "experience" a text in multiple ways, and without always having to analyze or interpret along what they feel are predetermined patterns and strategies, creates a different kind of classroom dynamic where ideas are more likely to be tried out and experimented with.

In the unit on visual art, I usually let the students search on their own and bring in some images they find to discuss. Another way I might begin is to look at the cover art of their *Finnegans Wake* texts, which are usually the 1999 Penguin edition with art from the Book of Kells on the cover that combines scripture, speech, music, and Celtic designs in an image that students enjoy digging into. We then might turn to Stephen Crow's "Wake in Progress" (which is, sadly, no longer in progress—he stopped in 2018), where he attempted to illustrate every page of *Finnegans Wake*. Crow's drawings cast the *Wake*'s words in different styles of illustration, ranging from Matisse-style cutouts to old-timey cartoons to images based on the Book of Kells. His artwork plays off the words and their meanings at the same time as it visually plays with historical styles.

Other examples that we may discuss in class include László Moholy-Nagy's well-known diagram of the themes of *Finnegans Wake*, with Joyce positioned as the pivotal point of a wheel-like structure. Moholy-Nagy draws four concentric circles that represent Giambattisata Vico's theory of history, and columns on the left showing various "levels" such as familial, historical, mythological, biblical, etcetera. We also see columns representing main characters HCE, ALP, and their children, alongside alter egos below the label. Does this kind of visual mapping help make sense of the text? What are other familiar literary maps or graphs? Does it have any meaning without the context of the plot of the book?

We might also look at previous student artwork, and some students will read essays by Christa-Maria Lerm Hayes on *Finnegans Wake* and visual art, where she writes that "one can certainly speak of influence in the sense that Joyce was instrumental in triggering artists to create works in the ways they did, but inspiration is a term better suited to acknowledging the multi-dimensionality of the relationship."[13] Giving students the freedom to be "inspired" rather than to be "influenced," I again ask them how they would go about creating visual art around *Finnegans Wake*. Emma Hickey wrote:

If I were to visually depict *Finnegans Wake* I think I would create a series of standard images and then combine them in interesting ways. What I mean is, one of the things that interests me so much about *Wake* is its effort to be about everything by combining characters that are really stand-ins for everyone. In that way, the characters are very broad but they encompass so many themes. I'd try to visually represent this by using basic geometric shapes—one for each character—and then combining them in a series of different images. The images could each represent a theme, but I'm not sure that would be as interesting as simply making wildly different pictures using the same basic shapes.

Comments like Hickey's lead the class into thinking about how a graphic novel representation would use combinations of words and images, rather than reproducing full passages; we then experiment with what that might look like.

In this way, our discussions are similar to an essay by Yaeli Greenblatt that pushes back on scholars like John Bishop who have argued that *Finnegans Wake* resists visual interpretation. For Bishop, the dreamscape of the *Wake* does "not simply [resist] visualization, but actively encourages its reader not to visualize much in its pages."[14] Greenblatt looks at works that don't necessarily "visualize" in any literal or even interpretive sense, but that by "directing the reader's perception towards the materiality of textual objects . . . brings to light Joyce's emphasis on the visuality of text, typography, and the physical dimensions of the novel."[15] As we do in my class, he looks at the recently published illustrated editions of the *Wake* fables, "The Ondt and the Gracehoper" (2014) and "The Mookse and the Gripes" (2018) by Thomas McNally, and shows how McNally borrows ideas from Joyce's typographic experiments in the *Wake* for his images.

The world of dance offers a chance to return to Cage through Merce Cunningham's dance version of "Roaratorio," which we watch together and then discuss how Cunningham's choreography resists interpretation in the same ways that Cage's music does. To watch Cunningham's "Roaratorio" (for example, a 1986 live version available on YouTube) is to see dancers running on and off the stage and dancing alone, often unaware of other dancers or of the music and sounds from Cage's piece that are playing. They dance short jigs and reels that occasionally match up with the Irish music that fades in and out, but they also dance in characteristically random Cunningham styles that seem completely separate from the music and sound. I ask students to keep a log of their thoughts as they view the piece—to write them down next to the time in the piece when it occurred to them. We can then "perform" sections of the piece in class, in real time, with students reading out their comment at the point in time that they had noted it. Almost always, in the first few minutes of the piece, several students will have written a comment something like, "Wait, what are they dancing *to*?" Or as one student wrote after class, "I feel like I am listening to sounds that have *something* to do with *Finnegans Wake* and watching dancers that have *something* to do with the sounds, but I can't figure either out."

To watch any Cage/Cunningham collaboration is to question your own experience of perceiving art; typical questions that ask why a passage is where it is or what a word or image means, turn into more self-reflexive questions, such as what and why one notices certain events over others. It turns into a meditation on our own experience in a frame of space and time. For Pyle, "John Cage and Merce Cunningham's Roaratorio may be inspired by *Finnegans Wake*, and while few people would claim to have 'read' the book after viewing a performance, Roaratorio viewers might assert having 'experienced' the *Wake*."[16] Cage and Cunningham's work challenges students who have learned to think of music and dance as rooted in steady rhythm, as conveyors of emotion, and as a "universal language." Once we let go of these assumptions, the experience of watching or listening to "Roaratorio" becomes something we can compare to the experience of reading *Finnegans Wake*, even if, as we noted earlier, the intent of the creators seems to pull in opposite directions.

The other dance work I like to use is "ReJoyce—A Pilobolus *Finnegans Wake*," which was performed in 1993 by the dance group Pilobolus and is available on YouTube. The dance opens with sounds of thunder and of a violin tuning. The set is empty, except for a huge white moon hanging over the stage. Then, a man tumbles slowly to the stage, hanging in the air above the ground. My students immediately recognize this as the beginning scene of the novel, but their main interest is in seeing how this scene turns into the five main characters—as they wonder in what way a dance version is either more or less abstract than the written. Can literal bodies on a stage represent the plurality of a character who has elements of an Irish father, husband, and pub owner everyman, mythical giant, Hebrew patriarch, and medieval knight?

Theater is the most obvious connection to reading for most students and, for that reason, we focus on it last. Each class meeting takes on an element of theater, and, in addition to reciting in different voices and accents, students naturally start to imagine acting or staging the scenes that we read out loud. In our unit on theater, I give students different assignments and different pieces to look at. From the 1960s *The Coach with the Six Insides*, to the much less literal and more playful 1996 *Nine Characters in Search of a Wake*, to current companies like Boston's HCE players, we read and perform sections and talk about theories of adaptation.

I live and teach in New York, so if I am lucky or plan far enough ahead, I can take students to see a performance, such as when the class saw Olwen Fouéré's *riverrun* monologue at the Brooklyn Academy of Music in 2014. In addition to seeing and discussing this dramatic and beautiful rendering of the long ALP monologue that concludes the book, we spent time studying the reaction of the New York critics, scholars, and Joyceans. *The New York Times* review wrote that "hourlong piece animates and activates the text without making much sense of it."[17] We read other reactions from critics and scholars, most of whom drew connections between Fouéré's performance and the "text itself" and made assumptions that my students were more than ready to engage with and even challenge by this point in the semester. "What if we see her performance as something separate from the book?" they ask. And "What if we look at audience reactions instead of the stage?" At the same time, students comment that after seeing her performance, reading the last pages of the novel seemed easier and made more sense.

New readers to the *Wake* always ask me how Joyce wrote in this style, and so I spend part of one class taking them through Joyce's drafting. I do this partly to introduce the field of genetic criticism and partly to keep us thinking about creative processes. But I also hope to further emphasize the point that there are multiple ways of reading and multiple layers of text to think about. Relying heavily on Finn Fordham's analysis in *Lots of Fun at "Finnegans Wake,"* I look at a passage from an early draft in which we see Shem using a dye to write on his own body: a covering of words (in an early version) that "slowly unfolded universal history & that self which he hid from the world grew darker & darker in outlook." We look at various subsequent versions in which this relatively clear, all-English statement becomes gradually longer and more obtuse, growing from the nineteen words above to over sixty, and now including words such as "squidself," "squirtscreened," and "doriangrayer." I point out how such clear (if reductive) concepts as "universal history" become the complex negotiations contained in the more difficult (if more accurate) "marryvoising moodmoulded cyclewheeling history."[18] In other words, this revised "history" is one not so easy to understand, but a more fluid one shaped by cycles, shifts, voices, and moods.

It is a history, then, like *Finnegans Wake* itself, like the process of reading; and, like the performances and art we experience throughout this class, that is about challenging the assumed stability of such concepts as time or self or book. Most important for my class is how this exercise brings us back to the question of what it means to read. Should we use the "meanings" of the early drafts to inform our readings of the published versions? Or should we now see these drafts as multiple versions in themselves? For a roomful of undergraduates from different backgrounds, educations, and majors, these questions speak in multiple ways, and I ask students to apply them to their own disciplines and interests. How important are intent or creative drafts in the legal profession, for example? Or does the study of multiple and plural meanings and versions change how we understand theories of education?

From the Students

The last few weeks of the course are devoted to workshopping and presenting the students' creative projects. I often combine the class sessions with an informal evening *Wake* reading group and an evening class session specifically for the performance-based presentations. Some theater and some dance, the majority of the projects are music. Often borrowing on "Waywords and Meansigns," they combine sections with music; the more successful music projects, however, do more than just set the words to the music. One of the more creative musical projects came from students Isaac Slone, Anna Waterman, and Sofia Kapur, who put together a suite of songs that they sang accompanied by guitar and ending with electronics. The song cycle opens with Waterman intoning the words "O! Tell me all about Anna Livia" from 1.8 in a melancholic, ceremonial tone. She then combines this statement with the biblical description of ALP found a few chapters earlier, "haloed be her eve, her sing time sung, her rill be run, unhemmed as it is uneven." In splicing together the voices of the gossipy washerwoman and the reverent worshipper, the opening captures two views of the multifaceted subject, and also combines gossip with religion in a very *Wakean* sense. In the next section, the pace picks up: Slone starts playing a chord progression that sounds like an Irish pub song, and Kapur and Waterman begin to chant and sing the remainder of the ALP passage: "Tuck up your sleeves and loosen your talktapes. Don't butt me—hike!—when you bend. Whatever it was they threed to make of you, they tried to two in the Fiendish Park. Look at the shirt of him! Look at the dirt of him! Look at the reppe, he's a routy old rappe." This section works like conversational, festive lyrics of an Irish folk song, featuring a narrative thread, multiple voices, and authoritative commands for the group.

From here on, their piece progresses more or less through two hundred years of music history as they sing sections of ALP's confessional song. They begin in an old Irish ballad style, singing wistfully and soft. When, about halfway through the song, ALP goes from ruminating about her marriage to having a series of sexual fantasies, they mark this change by emphasizing the line "bore down like he used to" as an intermediary between the two sentiments and between musical styles. The song then switches into a sexy blues jam and shows an entirely different sensibility of ALP. Waterman and Kapur alternate parts, in an attempt, as they say, to show the conflicting sides of ALP and demonstrate her "plurability." The next section skips a few generations and jumps into 1960s America to capture the description of ALP as a water goddess. Next, they use music from *Grease* to play on "tell me more, tell me ev'ry little thing," combining *Finnegans Wake* with the melody and words of a 1970s musical set in the 1950s, which is a move that sends us spinning in time in a very *Wake*-like sense. Slone then transitions into rap, beginning with Joyce's words "Hustle along, why can't you? Spit on the urn while it's hot," a phrase that scans very well in a 4/4 hip-hop groove. Finally, they bring the song to an end in the twenty-first century by using a website that translates words into rhythmic and melodic sound effects. They play a computer robotic voice reading the last lines of the ALP chapter over and over, as Kapur and Waterman slump dramatically to the ground. Overall, their song cycle comments on, but also performs, the way that the *Wake* plays with history, borrows sounds and style, and shifts from one style to the other in mid-sentence.

For readers and teachers of *Finnegans Wake*, one challenge is balancing the emphasis on single words and phrases with an awareness of the work as a whole. In other words, how do we negotiate between close reading, textual analysis, and the acceptance (or denial) of an autonomous coherent book itself? Modern physics provides an interesting analogy in that its two major theories—general relativity and quantum physics—study, on the one hand, stars and galaxies, and, on the other, atoms and subatomic particles. While these two theories underlie the scientific progress that has explained the expansion of the universe and the fundamental structure of matter, they are mutually incompatible, and they cannot both be right at the same time.[19] Similarly, when we are reading the *Wake*, are we looking at the whole world, a map of it, or just at HCE's shirt? This problem of being unable to perceive the micro and macro at once is a central concern in reading and discussing the *Wake*, because in each minute analysis of a phrase or word there are assumptions about the entirety of the work itself. For students encountering the *Wake* for the first-time and longtime readers alike, it is often tempting to get drawn into an expanding discussion of a single phrase and lose sight of the book itself.

Hannah Baek, an undergraduate whose specialization was East Asian studies, created a piece out of knitted and felted wool yarn that offers a perspective on this problem. Titling her work "The Knitbook" (a play on Joyce's term "Night Book" for the *Wake*), the piece represents the 628 pages of the book in 628 rows of knitting. [see fig. 1] Baek writes that this medium "can allow us to

Figure 10.1. "Knitbook" by Hannah Baek, New York University Class of 2017. Photograph by Hudson Carter.

conceptualize the progression and shape of the novel in ways that a physical book cannot." She uses the color blue to track the progression of the plot from day to night to day again, with a flash of yellow to signal the break of dawn. She then color-codes passages and themes within the progression: dark teal points to ALP (the Mamafesta, the letter within the Ricorso section), black and white symbolizes the duality in the passages focusing on the twins (Shaun's chapter, Night lessons), and pink and green indicate the more often-read passages that we studied in my class (the Museyroom, Mookse and the Gripes, the Ondt and the Grasshopper, and so on). Baek captures the *Wake* as a structure and moves away from the overemphasis of the word or the phrase, but her work also features the minute in its page-by-page color-coded summations. Between these alternating reading practices, her piece recognizes the experience of a first-time reader as it highlights the familiar passages that were studied more closely than others. The piece as a whole allows us to see the whole book, the placement and special relationships of these passages, and the circular logic of the narrative.

Throughout the semester, students have had a chance to rethink the power of their own creativity by confronting difficult ways of reading and perceiving that are new to them. They have also learned the importance of reading and thinking in collaboration, as students stay in touch with each other, maintain relationships and working groups, and often return, even years later, to a *Finnegans Wake* reading group that I help run. Other students continue working on their artistic projects, or with the collaborative connections that have formed during the class. The majority of the students, of course, may never read another word of the *Wake* again. Yet, what I hope lasts is a sense of embracing the difficult and the odd in ways that can encourage creative, communal, if not always logical solutions. As one student wrote at the end of their final project: "I had an amazing experience and feel incredibly grateful to have worked with such talented, funny and inspiring people. *Finnegans Wake* has definitely created some new friendships."

Notes

1. Or, if we are lucky, Derek comes to our class to talk about it.
2. James Joyce, *Finnegans Wake*, reissue ed. (London: Penguin, 1999), 3.18, 18.23, 18.30. All future references are to this edition and will be cited parenthetically in the text.
3. Adaline Glasheen, *A Second Census of "Finnegans Wake"* (Evanston: Northwestern University Press, 1963), lx–lxvi.
4. Adam Harvey, "DON'T PANIC: it's only Finnegans Wake—thunderword #1," YouTube, October 8, 2014, https://www.youtube.com/watch?v=TV3vT5nW_I4.
5. Richard Schechner, *Performance Studies: An Introduction,* 4th ed. (New York: Routledge, 2020), 1.
6. Dwight Conquergood qtd. in Schechner, *Performance Studies,* 30.
7. My selected passages—slightly different each time I teach the course—more or less follow Sebastian Knowles's suggestions in his article "*Finnegans Wake* for Dummies," *James Joyce Quarterly* 46, no. 1 (Fall 2008): 97–111.
8. See John Gordon, *"Finnegans Wake": A Plot Summary* (Syracuse: Syracuse University Press, 1986); Edmund Lloyd Epstein, *A Guide through "Finnegans Wake"* (Gainesville: University Press of Florida, 2010).
9. Patrick A. McCarthy, "*Finnegans Wake* on Film," *Flashpoint* 12 (Summer 2009), https://www.flashpointmag.com/pmfilm.htm.
10. Mary Manning, *Passages From "Finnegans Wake" by James Joyce: A Free Adaptation For the Theater* (Cambridge: Harvard University Press, 1957).
11. And, as someone always points out, Riverrun is the seat of House Tully in *Game of Thrones* and the New World plantation in *Outlander.*
12. Derek Pyle, "Static Crooning Consciousness Expansion: Musical Undergrounds Respond to James Joyce," *European Joyce Studies: James Joyce and the Arts* 29 (April 2020): 107, https://doi.org/10.1163/9789004426191_009.
13. Christa-Maria Lerm Hayes, *Joyce in Art: Visual Art Inspired by James Joyce* (Dublin: Lilliput Press, 2004), 8.
14. John Biship qtd. in Yaeli Greenblatt, "'Our eyes demand their turn': The Materiality of the Joycean Image and Illustrations of Finnegans Wake," *European Joyce Studies: James Joyce and the Arts* 29 (April 2020): 152, https://doi.org/10.1163/9789004426191_013.
15. Greenblatt, "'Our eye demands their turn,'" 152.

16   Pyle, "Static Crooning Consciousness Expansion," 105.
17   Alexis Soloski, "In Lilting Singsong, Dublin's Burbling Essence," *The New York Times*, September 18, 2014, https://www.nytimes.com/2014/09/19/theater/joycean-character-comes-alive-in-riverrun.html.
18   Finn Fordham, *Lots of Fun at "Finnegans Wake": Unravelling Universals* (Oxford: Oxford University Press, 2007), 39–65.
19   Brian Greene, *The Elegant Universe: Superstrings, Hidden Dimensions, and the Quest for the Ultimate Theory*, 2nd ed. (New York: Vintage Books, 2000), 3–4.

Bibliography

Fordham, Finn. *Lots of Fun at "Finnegans Wake": Unravelling Universals*. Oxford: Oxford University Press, 2007.

Glasheen, Adaline. *A Second Census of "Finnegans Wake."* Evanston: Northwestern University Press, 1963.

Greenblatt, Yaeli. "'Our eyes demand their turn': The Materiality of the Joycean Image and Illustrations of *Finnegans Wake*." *European Joyce Studies: James Joyce and the Arts* 29 (April 2020): 151–65. https://doi.org/10.1163/9789004426191_013.

Greene, Brian. *The Elegant Universe: Superstrings, Hidden Dimensions, and the Quest for the Ultimate Theory*. 2nd ed. New York: Vintage Books, 2000.

Harvey, Adam. "DON'T PANIC: it's only Finnegans Wake—thunderword #1." YouTube, October 8, 2014. https://www.youtube.com/watch?v=TV3vT5nW_I4.

Joyce, James. *Finnegans Wake*. Reissue edition. London: Penguin, 1999.

Knowles, Sebastian D. G. "*Finnegans Wake* for Dummies." *James Joyce Quarterly* 46, no. 1 (Fall 2008): 97–111.

Lerm Hayes, Christa-Maria. *Joyce in Art: Visual Art Inspired by James Joyce*. Dublin: Lilliput Press, 2004.

McCarthy, Patrick A. "*Finnegans Wake* on Film." *Flashpoint* 12 (Summer 2009). https://www.flashpointmag.com/pmfilm.htm.

Pyle, Derek. "Static Crooning Consciousness Expansion: Musical Undergrounds Respond to James Joyce." *European Joyce Studies: James Joyce and the Arts* 29 (April 2020): 96–110. https://doi.org/10.1163/9789004426191_009.

Schechner, Richard. *Performance Studies: An Introduction*. 4th edition. New York: Routledge, 2020.

Soloski, Alexis. "In Lilting Singsong, Dublin's Burbling Essence." *The New York Times*, September 18, 2014. https://www.nytimes.com/2014/09/19/theater/joycean-character-comes-alive-in-riverrun.html.

11

Preparing to Teach *Exiles*

A. NICHOLAS FARGNOLI

An Apology

Teaching plays in a classroom setting may be akin to viewing Georgia O'Keeffe's *Grey Blue & Black—Pink Circle* or Wassily Kandinsky's *Yellow-Red-Blue* in monochrome. Something essential is missing: the perspective color provides. Figuratively, the same might be said of plays. Without the perspective of dramatic color, a play loses the vitality and vividness that actors, stage setting, movement, and other performative features provide. But not all is lost in a classroom. A play is always more than its performance. Its literature and dramatic coloring appear in ways other than performance. As literary texts, plays provoke thought, analysis, discussion, and interpretation.

Joyce himself seems to have practiced such an approach in his late teens, three years before he sketched out his own definition of dramatic art in March 1903.[1] In two separate but topically connected essays in 1900, "Drama and Life," a paper he delivered to the Literary and Historical Society at University College, Dublin, and in his first published piece, "Ibsen's New Drama" that appeared in the prestigious *Fortnightly Review,* Joyce framed his arguments from the perspective of the literary nature of drama. In "Drama and Life," he asserts that Shakespeare is "above all else a literary artist" whose dramatic works are "literature in dialogue."[2] In "Ibsen's New Drama," Joyce, focusing on *When We Dead Awaken,* gets to the very heart of the matter. Though he includes of necessity a discussion of the characters and action of the play, his real interest is with the essence and meaning of drama, with "what primarily rivets our attention" incited by "either the perception of a great truth, or the opening up of a great question, or a great conflict that is almost independent of the conflicting actors."[3] Joyce did not abandon these ideas when writing *Exiles.*

Plays can and should be studied as literature and, like any other literary genre, they demand literary analysis. With or without performance, they are expressions of human experience and worthy of serious scholarly discourse. *Exiles* fixes our attention on the struggle with confronting the great truths we all face: freedom, friendship, love, trust, honesty, doubt, betrayal, and other intricacies of intimate relations. Though these themes are found throughout Joyce's works, they are center stage in *Exiles* and critically examined here to provide interpretative possibilities to be considered by anyone teaching the play. Non-Joycean instructors—and perhaps even novice Joyceans—may need foundational information, but not pedagogical methods, to prepare classes in a manner suitable to them. The divisions in this chapter contain material to consider and adapt, such as distinguishing between studying a play and viewing a performance, framing the compositional history of *Exiles* within Joyce's artistic development, offering a summary analysis of characters and themes, and suggesting in-class assignments concentrated on dramatic readings of selected passages to engage students in the rigors of performative interpretation based on close analysis of dialogue and stage directions.

Program Notes: Title and Compositional Background

The term *exile* is familiar to everyone, but not everybody has had the personal experience of being an exile, that is the experience of being compelled to leave one's homeland either by coercion or choice. If compelled by choice, self-imposed exiles perceive conditions in their native land as unfavorable or intolerable and hopeless. Whatever the specific motivating factors may be, their decisions offer them promise and freedom. Joyce's self-imposed exile, or, as he referred to it in a 1905 letter to his brother Stanislaus, "voluntary exile," gave him the freedom to pursue the personal and professional life he believed was not possible to him in Ireland.[4] In "The Holy Office," a broadside written several months before this letter to Stanislaus, Joyce clearly indicates the sense of literary alienation or personal exile he was facing at that time, a condition that appears to be one of the determinants behind his decision to leave Dublin and one of the reasons for the play's title. With very little money and few possessions, Joyce left Ireland with Nora Barnacle in October 1904. Like Richard Rowan and Bertha in *Exiles*, Joyce and Nora were unmarried when they departed, but unlike Richard and Bertha, Joyce and Nora never again returned to reside in Ireland.

Joyce was an exile for most of his life and for virtually his entire literary career. This experience, as Michael Patrick Gillespie carefully examines in *James Joyce and the Exilic Imagination*, permanently shaped Joyce's literary sensitivities and affords readers an interpretative perspective on his works.[5] The title of Gillespie's chapter on Joyce's play, "Re-Viewing Richard: Nostalgia and Rancor in *Exiles*," exemplifies the focus his study places on the antithetical emotions of rancor and nostalgia in Joyce's works and the oscillating perspectives these emotions afford the viewer or reader. Another concern for our purposes in teaching *Exiles*, as Gillespie underscores, is the distinction between drama and fiction as genres, the latter of which is more than likely the avenue we take before turning to *Exiles*. Accordingly, and unwittingly, we may be inclined to judge the merits of the play and its characters from the bias of a narrative perspective to which we have become accustomed by reading Joyce's fiction, but, Gillespie cautions, applying the same interpretative approach we use when reading his fiction can easily alter our "comprehension of a work in a markedly dissimilar genre."[6] Padraic Colum, in his review of the play when it was first published, mirrors that attitude: "Mr. Joyce may return to the drama and bring into it some of the discoveries that make his narrative so startling. Meanwhile, *Exiles* would make it appear that narrative is his peculiar domain."[7]

The play might not meet the expectations of some readers who concentrate on Joyce's fiction, but the absence of narrative should not be a stumbling block and certainly ought not be the single virtue used to judge *Exiles*. This question of narrative importance needs to be critically considered when teaching the play and when surveying initial reviews and later critical essays, most of which are based on reading and not seeing *Exiles*. Adversely contrasting the play to Joyce's fiction may be the wrong place to start. An initial negative tone is self-defeating. Unfavorable opinions, however, are not to be dismissed when reviewing critical assessment, and yet they should not determine the worth of the play either.

Since its publication in 1918, the merits of *Exiles* have been mixed, sometimes in the same articles and reviews.[8] Unfortunately, for one reason or another much of the negative criticism lingers in the forefront and conditions our judgment. One of the most dismissive of all opinions centers on its being unoriginal and a failed imitation of Ibsen. Ezra Pound, who read *Exiles* two years before it was published, wrote that "*if* there were an Ibsen stage in full blast, Mr. Joyce's play would go on at once. But we get only trivialized Ibsen."[9] In one stroke, Pound brushed off what Joyce actually accomplished in writing *Exiles*, but to be fair, Pound at this time did not have the hindsight that we have today with the publication of *Ulysses*, *Finnegans Wake*, and Joyce's letters, nor did he have access to relevant biographical material, all of which help contextualize the play within the history of Joyce's artistic development and output.[10] A. Walton Litz explains that Joyce put aside the early stages of composing *Ulysses* to write *Exiles*, and by doing so "he exorcised the spectre of Ibsen," but, Litz discerns, of greater significance is that Joyce "dramatized in the play a personal experience of sexual jealousy, thus preparing the way for objective treatment of Bloom's jealousy and cuckoldry."[11] *Exiles* is more than merely a transitional piece, however. It realized for Joyce the dramatic value he professed in "Ibsen's New Drama."

John MacNicholas has edited *Exiles* and written extensively on it.[12] His thorough assessment of its critical reception and performance history and his insights into its dramatic structure provide a solid and necessary foundation for anyone teaching the play.[13] Readers of Joyce know that one of the distinguishing characteristics of his literary style is ambiguity or indeterminacy. If *Exiles* is examined carefully, according to MacNicholas, whatever ambiguity the play appears to present, particularly in relation to the question of sexual consummation between Robert Hand and Bertha in the second act, is not dramatic weakness, as some may judge, but a strength and a clear departure from the kind of dramatic resolution found in Ibsen.[14] In this respect, Joyce is decisively defining his approach to writing drama fourteen years after his first attempts when he was in his late teens and reading Ibsen.

To expand upon Litz's observation regarding Joyce's personal experience dramatized in *Exiles,* one can speculate that the play may also be dramatizing Joyce's final farewell to Ireland, a farewell coupled with a profound sense of loss. Vicariously through the protagonist, Richard Rowan, Joyce may have imagined a return with his family and the problematic reception a writer like him would have received. But in fact, the return might not have been all that imagined. He was in Ireland with Nora and their children from mid-July through mid-September of 1912, the same year in which *Exiles* takes place (June 1912). While in Dublin, Joyce, after several years of failed negotiations with publishers, failed again to get *Dubliners* published.

Disappointed and embittered, Joyce left his homeland for good, and on his way back to Trieste wrote "Gas from a Burner," a broadside satirizing the publisher, George Roberts, for deciding at the last minute not to publish the collection, and the printer, John Falconer, for destroying the sheets that had already been printed.[15] Another minor detail that may have merged with Joyce's disposition at the time of writing *Exiles* can be found in the poem "Tutto é Sciolto" ("All is lost now") that he composed in July 1914. The poem's title, taken from an aria in Vincenzo Bellini's opera *La sonnambula (The Sleepwalker),* reveals Joyce's feelings of loss further intensified by the poem's last lines that indicate his failure in initiating an affair with one of his women students. This combined experience of loss and failure may have contributed to the dramatic uncertainty of a consummated sexual encounter between Robert and Bertha.

Another incident that occurred in Joyce's life two or three years prior to his writing "Tutto é Sciolto," Richard Ellmann suggests, had a meaningful bearing on portraying Robert Hand as a betrayer and depicting Richard Rowan as a schemer.[16] Roberto Prezioso, a close Triestine friend of Joyce and editor of the newspaper, *Il Piccolo della Sera*, attempted to initiate an affair with Nora. She told Joyce, who then confronted Prezioso, and their friendship came to an end. Ironically, the offended Joyce, according to Nora's biographer, Brenda Maddox, had encouraged Nora to pursue such advances,[17] but unlike Bertha, who, after telling Richard of Robert's overtures, was to decide on her own, Nora did not have that choice. If Roberto Prezioso served as a model for Robert Hand (both share the same first name, both are betrayers), Joyce himself served as a model for Richard Rowan. In act two, Richard divulges to Robert the yearning he had to be betrayed by him and Bertha, but it was to be done openly, honestly, and freely. Robert, however, is not the only betrayer in the play. Richard admits to his infidelity when he was living in Italy, an inevitable outcome of the freedom he professes and the burden it places on the individual.

Thematic Synopsis

On a late June afternoon in 1912, *Exiles* opens in the sitting room of Richard Rowan's home in Merrion, a well-to-do but fictitious suburb of Dublin. Three months prior, Richard returned from Italy where he was living for nine years with Bertha, his common-law wife, and where Archie, their eight-year-old son, was born. Their return was occasioned by the death of Richard's estranged mother and the inheritance his father arranged to take effect at this time. Because of Bertha's lower social standing, Richard's mother never approved of her.

The first extended conversation of the play occurs between Richard and Beatrice Justice, the woman with whom he corresponded during eight of his nine years in Italy. Among other themes yet to appear (betrayal, infidelity, and doubt), their conversation introduces those of freedom, suffering, and the play's overarching theme of the vulnerability of relationships. Referring to his mother, Richard expresses his sense of loss and suffering:

> She drove me away. On account of her I lived years in exile and poverty too or near it. I never accepted the doles she sent me through the bank. I waited too. Not for her death but for some understanding of me, her own son, her own flesh and blood. That never came. (37)

Richard's refusal to live on his mother's generosity anticipates his attitude toward Robert Hand in act two when Robert surrenders Bertha to him. "Angry or not," Richard says to Robert, "I will not live on your generosity" (113). The pun on Robert's surname should not be overlooked. He is willing to hand Bertha over to Richard as though he were disposing of an inconsequential possession. He confirms this attitude in act three when he says to Richard that he failed, and that Bertha is his. Robert is a Judas figure and ultimately willing to betray them both: his friendship with Richard and his professed love for Bertha.

The opening scene contains other background information that emerges from the conversation between Beatrice and Bertha. Beatrice is a Protestant, who was once engaged to her journalist cousin Robert Hand, Richard's longtime friend and neighbor. A moment before Robert arrives, Beatrice perceives that something has changed Richard since his return. Evidence of this change appears when Richard hurriedly ends their conversation and slips out to avoid Robert. In the last act of the play, Bertha, too, recognizes a change in Richard and, when the opportunity arises, confronts Beatrice as the cause. Although no explicit single reason is disclosed, various factors may have precipitated this change. Richard is now a published author, who with Robert's determined efforts is poised to receive a position at the university. As the play reveals, Richard not only notices Robert's obvious affection for Bertha but is informed of it by her. Even before Richard and Bertha left for Italy, he was aware of Robert's unfulfilled feelings toward her.

When Robert enters carrying red roses for Bertha, he is surprised to meet his cousin. Their brief and pointless conversation, which comes to an end when Archie and Bertha return home, captures the detachment between two individuals who once were very close. After Beatrice leaves to give the boy a piano lesson, Robert and Bertha's conversation provides insight into his intentions and Bertha's indecision. The intimacy of their behavior (handholding, embracing, kissing) displays more of Robert's sexual longings for Bertha than hers for him. As her comments and stage directions indicate, Bertha's reaction signals both confusion and uncertainty; she promises nothing to Robert. This hesitation is a form of doubt and foreshadows her indecisiveness at the end of this act and the dramatic uncertainty at the end of the next act. Though not primarily associated with Bertha, the theme of doubt reaches its high point in Richard's last words when, at the end of the play, he speaks of his "deep wound of doubt which can never be healed" (176). What is not uncertain or doubtful, however, is Robert's goal to pursue Bertha and convince Richard to accept a position at the university. An unsettled—and perhaps unsettling—issue in the play is Richard's treatment of Bertha. Unconsciously, he may be echoing his own mother's attitude toward her and at the same time his mother's lack of empathy toward him.

The extended conversation between Richard and Bertha after Robert leaves reveals unrealized sexual tensions and Richard's awareness of Robert's advances toward her. She informs him that Robert planned their meeting to take place at the same hour as Richard's interview with the vice-chancellor of the university.

Although Bertha has ambivalent feelings about going to Robert's cottage, she is not unclear about characterizing Richard as demonic: "The work of a devil to turn [Robert] against me as you tried to turn my own child against me. Only you did not succeed" (83). In her anger, Bertha accuses Richard of trying to turn everyone against her and of loving Beatrice, with whom she knew he was corresponding while in Italy. Rebuking Richard for the freedom he ostensibly gives her, Bertha skeptically views it as his justification to pursue Beatrice. At the end of the act, Bertha must decide on her own whether or not to visit Robert:

BERTHA
Tell me not to go and I will not.

RICHARD
(*without looking at her*) Decide yourself.

BERTHA
Will you blame me then?

RICHARD
(*excitedly*) No, no! I will not blame you.
You are free. I cannot blame you. (90)

The burden of freedom can be oppressive and easily stymie or paralyze decision-making, but for Richard it is blameless and comes with impunity.

The first act can be interpreted as a prelude foreshadowing central themes that become more and more apparent as the play progresses. It initiates the type of behavior Joyce explained in his notes: *Exiles* "is three cat and mouse acts."[18] In the same paragraph, he also commented on Bertha's "mental paralyses." Though these notes lend perspective and offer insights into Joyce's objectives, they should be read judiciously. The cat-and-mouse reference, however, is a particularly apt metaphor. Richard Rowan appears to share the cunning and clever traits of a Mr. Mistoffelees figure, to borrow from T. S. Eliot's *Old Possum's Book of Practical Cats*.[19] In one way or another, Richard directs the action of the play, at times from behind the scenes as in act two when he leaves Robert and Bertha alone in the cottage. In this same act, Bertha admits as much to him: "There is one person in all this who is not a fool. And that is you. I am though. And [Robert] is" (117). With the possible exception of the third act when Bertha asserts herself, Richard controls the conversation by dominating its subject.

The second act takes place in Robert Hand's cottage in Ranelagh, a Dublin suburb, and concentrates on Robert's relationship with Bertha and his effort at winning her away from Richard. Anxiously awaiting her arrival, Robert is taken by surprise when Richard, and not Bertha, appears. In their conversation that further develops the unresolved themes of freedom, fidelity, and friendship, Richard explains that she had earlier in the day spoken to him about their rendezvous. The cat-and-mouse image becomes even more evident in the following conversation:

> RICHARD
> Your advances to her, little by little, day after day, looks, whispers. (*with a nervous movement of the hands*) Insomma, wooing.
>
> ROBERT
> (*bewildered*) But how do you know all this?
>
> RICHARD
> She told me.
>
> ROBERT
> This afternoon?
>
> RICHARD
> No. Time after time, as it happened.
>
> ROBERT
> You knew? From her? (RICHARD *nods*) You were watching us all the time?
>
> RICHARD
> (*very coldly*) I was watching you. (95–96)

Much of the dialogue between Richard and Robert in this act takes on what Zack Bowen identifies as a confessional scene, one of many throughout the play.[20] As in a confession, the dialogue is direct, stark, and even unforgiving. Richard explains to Robert that he told Bertha of his infidelity and concealed nothing, preferring the absolute truth of having her know him as he is; by extension he expects the same between the two of them. Before their conversation ends, Richard wants Robert to know him as he is:

> RICHARD
> (*quickly and harshly*) Wait. One thing more. For you too must know me as I am—now.
>
> ROBERT
> More? Is there more?
>
> RICHARD
> I told you that when I saw your eyes this afternoon I felt sad. Your humility and confusion, I felt, united you to me in brotherhood. *(he turns half round towards him)* At that moment I felt our whole life together in the past and I longed to put my arm around your neck.

ROBERT

(deeply and suddenly touched) It is noble of you, Richard, to forgive me like this.

RICHARD

(struggling with himself) I told you that I wished you not to do anything false and secret against me—against our friendship, against her; not to steal her from me, craftily, secretly, meanly—in the dark, in the night—you, Robert, my friend. (109)

This concluding part of their discussion, according to Bowen, suggests unrealized homosexuality; sharing one another "by sharing the same woman is a classic homosexual strategy."[21] Joyce perhaps drew this idea from the Prezioso incident, but, according to Maddox, he may have been unaware of Prezioso's bisexuality; however, he was not unaware of troilism, arguably discernible here in *Exiles*.[22] The possibility of this type of homosexual activity seems to be hinted at again when Richard says to Bertha that she may be both his and Robert's. The ambiguous use of the first-person plural objective pronoun in his comment—"You have drawn us near together" (118)—is telling. The reader or viewer cannot be certain as to whether Richard means Robert and him alone or the three of them together. An echo of homosexuality might also be heard in what Bertha says to Richard at the very end of the play. Caressing his hand, she says: "It is not true that I want to drive everyone from you. I want to bring you close together—you and [Robert]. Speak to me. Speak out all your heart to me: what you feel and what you suffer" (175).

When Bertha finally does arrive at the Ranelagh cottage, Robert becomes unnerved and sneaks out into the garden in the rain, leaving Richard to answer the door. In the brief but awkward conversation that ensues, the question of trust, a concept inextricably linked to freedom and fidelity, surfaces between them. For Richard, it betrays his apodictic belief in absolute freedom; for Bertha, her persistent suspicion of Richard's romantic involvement with Beatrice, whom she mockingly depicts as "Her ladyship" (116). Once Richard leaves, Robert reenters and begins to question Bertha about her motives and Richard's knowledge of their relationship. To his dismay, she admits that she told him everything. The issue of suffering in reference to Richard reemerges. Though Bertha denies that he suffers, Robert does not. The act concludes without giving us any clear evidence of any sexual activities that may have transpired between Robert and Bertha.

The setting of the third act circles back to the drawing room of Richard Rowan's home. A noticeable shift in mood characterized by a serene sadness offers momentary relief from the intensity of the previous act and a transition to the animated conversations yet to occur in this act. In the early morning, Bertha is alone when Brigid, the Rowans' elderly servant whom Richard continues to employ, comes in to start dusting. Startled to find Bertha up at this time, Brigid senses that something is upsetting her and ingenuously questions Bertha about Richard:

> BRIGID
> (*comes towards her and leans over the back of a chair*)
> Are you fretting yourself, ma'am, about anything?
>
> BERTHA
> No, Brigid.
>
> BRIGID
> Don't be. He was always like that, meandering off by himself somewhere. He's a curious bird, Master Richard, and always was. Sure there isn't a turn in him I don't know. Are you fretting now maybe because he does be in there (*pointing to the study*) half the night at his books? Leave him alone. He'll come back to you again. Sure he thinks the sun shines out of your face, ma'am.
>
> BERTHA
> (*sadly*) That time is gone. (141)

Remembering Richard's excitement when he first started seeing Bertha, Brigid encourages her to be patient and hopeful. Her comments contain dramatic irony.[23] By saying that Richard meanders off, Brigid unknowingly uses a metaphor that, one may argue, conjures up in Bertha's memory his moments of infidelity in Italy and reignites her suspicions of his involvement with Beatrice. In saying that Richard will come back to her on his own, Brigid ironically anticipates Bertha's last words in the play, her impassioned appeal to Richard to return to her. She may have sown the seeds of this idea in Bertha's mind.

As Archie leaves to go with the milkman on his route, Beatrice arrives with a copy of the morning newspaper containing Robert's piece on Richard, titled *A Distinguished Irishman*. Though reluctant to see her at this moment, Bertha becomes especially interested in what she says about Robert and Richard and noticeably dismayed to find out that Robert is leaving. Her reaction causes Beatrice to question why this news is so upsetting. Readers and viewers can only speculate on Bertha's motives and on whether they relate to what transpired between her and Robert the previous night. Beatrice, however, conjectures that a rift may have occurred between the two friends and feels partly responsible because of her role in encouraging Richard to return to Ireland. Picking up on this admission, Bertha charges Beatrice with being the single reason for his return and for the change that has recently occurred in him. Bertha is also determined to find out why Robert decided to leave without saying anything to her, so she writes a note to be delivered to him. In the end, the conversation between the two women ends up being cathartic. Bertha offers friendship and comments, "It is so strange that we spoke like this now. But I always wanted to. Did you?" Beatrice replies, "I think I did too" (159).

At one point during the exchange between Bertha and Beatrice, Richard returns from a morning walk on the strand and reads a portion of Robert's newspaper article before going into his study. After Beatrice leaves, he comes out and is confronted by Bertha, who triggers a conversation that touches upon the play's central themes of doubt, freedom, love, and betrayal. Ironically, this encounter has Richard accusing Bertha of driving everyone away from him, the very opposite of her complaint in act one. More so in this act than elsewhere in *Exiles*, Bertha asserts herself. Intent on pursuing certain issues with Beatrice, Richard, and Robert, she dominates the conversations with them. When speaking with Richard before Robert's arrival, she blames him for making her, Beatrice, and his own mother unhappy, and rues the day she met him. Her earlier conversation with Beatrice may have been a warm-up for this even more cathartic one with Richard.

Their argument eventually pivots on a dominant theme in the play, that of freedom:

RICHARD
(*bitterly*) I am in the way, is it? You would like to be free now. You have only to say the word.

BERTHA
(*proudly*) Whenever you like I am ready.

RICHARD
So that you could meet your lover—freely.

BERTHA
Yes.

RICHARD
Night after night?

BERTHA
(*gazing before her and speaking with intense passion*) To meet my lover! (*holding out her arms before her*) My lover! Yes! My lover! (162)

No one definitively knows Bertha's thoughts when she speaks these words and gestures with her arms. On one level, they are directed toward Richard and ostensively express her intentions; such an interpretation may be supported by Bertha's last comments to him at the close of the play. On another level, spoken in the heat of passion, they may be a momentary mockery of what once was but is no more; this interpretation seems to be supported by Bertha's response to Brigid at the beginning of the act where her sense of loss is obvious. Immediately after this incident with Richard, she breaks down in tears, and being told by him that she is free is no comfort. She feels estranged and more abandoned now than ever before. "You do not understand anything in me," she says to Richard, "not one thing in my heart or soul. A stranger! I am living with a stranger!" (163).

At this point, Robert knocks on the door and Richard retreats to his study. Bertha reproaches him for not having told her of his decision to leave and insists that he speak the truth of the night before to Richard. As uncomfortable as that may be for Robert, Bertha is seeking reconciliation between the two friends, a goal she also appears to be seeking between herself and Richard. After she calls Richard out of his study, Robert confesses that he failed with her, but that confession is no relief to Richard, who instinctively is doubtful as he is suspicious of those who say they love him. He explains to Robert that while he was walking on the strand earlier in the morning, he heard those voices telling him to despair. To despair, Richard could never do lest he abandon his unwavering belief in doubt, even if this doubt leads to pain and suffering.

After Archie comes in through a window—a moment of comic relief and brief transition to the final scene—Robert takes him for something to eat, leaving Bertha and Richard alone. In the last conversation of the play, Bertha once more avows that she has always been faithful to him and, perhaps for the first time in their relationship, speaks of her suffering and sadness when they were living in Rome. Bertha's resolve manifests itself throughout this act and culminates in the play's last words. Richard tells her that he suffers a "deep wound of doubt" in his soul for her. Speaking softly in a comforting way, she responds by asking him to come back again as her lover.

Exiles ends without a definite resolution. The future relationship between Richard and Bertha is uncertain as are the relationships between them and Robert and Beatrice, but this uncertainty underscores the dramatic focus Joyce stressed in his essay on Ibsen. He directs our attention away from the characters and onto the conflicts between them. This shift, however, does not preclude character study. The personalities of the four main characters and their interactions with one another invite literary analysis and a critique of Joyce's notes to the play where he comments on each of the characters.

Adding Color to the Canvas

Although the play's three acts are not structurally divided into scenes, they do provide self-contained segments that can be read aloud and examined by students in the classroom. This type of engagement offers opportunities to analyze closely the nuances in the characters' conversations and interpretative possibilities these subtleties afford. At the same time, students should consider the dramaturgical role of the play's extensive stage directions and their impact on uncovering behind-the-scenes details that lend insights into each character's personality. Dramatic readings can give students an academic understanding of the complexities actors and directors face when deciding on a performance.[24] After all, a performance on stage or a dramatic reading in the classroom is an interpretation. *Exiles* is a psychologically penetrating work that fastens our attention on the perennial questions we face in the intimate web of personal relationships.

Notes

1 See James Joyce, "Paris Notebook," in *The Critical Writings of James Joyce*, ed. Ellsworth Mason and Richard Ellmann, 143–46 (New York: Viking, 1959), where he explains "that art is dramatic whereby the artist sets forth the image in immediate relation to others" (145).
2 Joyce, "Drama and Life," in *Critical Writings*, 39.
3 Joyce, "Ibsen's New Drama," in *Critical Writings*, 63. During this period when Joyce was expressing his ideas about drama and Ibsen, he also turned to writing *A Brilliant Career* and *Dream Stuff*, two plays that have not survived.
4 Joyce's "voluntary exile" from *Letters of James Joyce*, vols. 2 and 3, ed. Richard Ellmann (New York: Viking Press, 1966), 2.84. In act three of *Exiles*, Richard Rowan reads an excerpt from Robert Hand's article on him that includes the following lines: "There is an economic and there is a spiritual exile. There are those who left her to seek the bread by which men live and there are others, nay, her most favoured children, who left her to seek in other lands that food of the spirit by which a nation of human beings is sustained in life" (155–56). These lines reflect ideas Joyce incorporated in "La Cometa dell 'Home Rule,'" a 1910 piece written in Italian for *Il Piccolo della Sera*; see "The Home Rule Comet," in *Critical Writings*, 209–13. The biblical allusion to the teaching that we do not live on bread alone is obvious; see Deuteronomy 8:3 and Matthew 4:4.
5 Michael Patrick Gillespie, *James Joyce and the Exilic Imagination* (Gainesville: University Press of Florida, 2015). In his perceptive study, Gillespie marks a clear distinction between exile and emigration (4–5) and rightly notes that the hermeneutical possibilities of Joyce's experience of exile have received insufficient scholarly attention (31).

6. Gillespie, *Exilic Imagination*, 88.
7. Padraic Colum, "James Joyce as Dramatist," in *James Joyce*, vol. 1, ed. Robert H. Deming (New York: Barnes and Noble, 1970), 144.
8. Written in Trieste during 1914 and 1915, *Exiles* was published in 1918, two years after the publication of *A Portrait of the Artist as a Young Man*. From February 1914 through September 1915, *Portrait* was being serialized in *The Egoist*. Joyce intentionally waited to publish the play until after the novel appeared in book form.
9. Ezra Pound, "Mr. James Joyce and the Modern Stage," in *James Joyce*, vol. 1, ed. Robert H. Deming (New York: Barnes and Noble, 1970), 134. The review was first published in *The Drama* 6 (February 1916): 122–32.
10. Seventeen years after his review, Pound wrote: "*Exiles* is a bad play with a serious content; . . . the play's many excellences are those of a novelist not of a dramatist. It was a necessary step. Joyce had to write something of that kind before he cd. write *Ulysses*." See Forrest Read, *Pound/Joyce: The Letters of Ezra Pound to James Joyce* (New York: New Directions, 1967), 249–50.
11. A. Walton Litz, *The Art of James Joyce* (London: Oxford University Press, 1961), 4. Also see B. J. Tysdahl, *Joyce and Ibsen: A Study in Literary Influence* (New York: Humanities Press, 1968), where he writes: "*Exiles* is sometimes seen as a landmark in Joyce's relations to Ibsen—as far as *Exiles* apprenticeship, after the play artistic independence" (101).
12. See John MacNicholas's edition of the play in *Exiles: A Critical Edition*, ed. A. Nicholas Fargnoli and Michael Patrick Gillespie (Gainesville: University Press of Florida, 2016); page references to *Exiles* are to this edition hereafter cited parenthetically in the text.
13. See John MacNicholas, "The Stage History of *Exiles*," *James Joyce Quarterly* 19 (Fall 1981): 9–26, where he evaluates the negative criticism of the play in relation to the successes of its performances.
14. John MacNicholas, "Joyce's *Exiles*: The Argument for Doubt," *James Joyce Quarterly* 11 (Fall 1973): 33–34.
15. For an overview of what transpired, see Richard Ellmann, *James Joyce* (New York: Oxford University Press, 1982), 328–38, and Gordon Bowker, *James Joyce: A New Biography* (New York: Farrar, Straus and Giroux, 2011), 201–5.
16. Ellmann, *James Joyce*, 316–17, 356. According to Ellmann, "Joyce was half-responsible for Prezioso's conduct, in an experiment at being author of his own life as well as of his work" (357).
17. Brenda Maddox, *Nora: The Real Life of Molly Bloom* (Boston: Houghton Mifflin, 1988), 115–16. Nora, Maddox writes, "was profoundly puzzled to find Joyce pushing her toward the very deception he said he most feared" (115).
18. James Joyce, *Exiles* (New York: Viking, 1951), 123. Joyce's notes appear in this edition; for a brief commentary on them, see "A Note on Joyce's Notes for the Play," in *Exiles: A Critical Edition*, ed. Fargnoli and Gillespie, 182–87.
19. T. S. Eliot, *The Complete Poems and Plays: 1909–1950* (New York: Harcourt, Brace and World, 1952), 161–62.
20. Zack Bowen, "*Exiles*: The Confessional Mode," *James Joyce Quarterly* 29 (Spring 1992): 581–86.

21 Bowen, "*Exiles:* The Confessional Mode," 584.
22 Maddox, *Nora*, 115. Also, see Ellmann, *James Joyce*, 316.
23 Brigid's remark that Richard "thinks the sun shines out of your face," according to Ellmann in *James Joyce* (316), had its origin in Prezioso's remark to Nora: "*Il sole s'è levato per Lei*" ("The sun has risen for you"). In her interior monologue, Molly remembers Bloom saying to her, "the sun shines for you." (See *Ulysses,* ed. Hans Walter Gabler [New York: Random House, 1986], 18.1571–72.)
24 For a discussion on performing *Exiles*, see "Directing and Acting in *Exiles*: An Interview with Richard Nash," in *Exiles: A Critical Edition,* ed. Fargnoli and Gillespie, 329–39. In explaining his decisions, Nash is in effect offering interpretations of the play.

Bibliography

Bowen, Zack. "*Exiles:* The Confessional Mode." *James Joyce Quarterly* 29 (Spring 1992): 581–86.
Bowker, Gordon. *James Joyce: A New Biography.* New York: Farrar, Straus and Giroux, 2011.
Colum, Padraic. "James Joyce as Dramatist." In *James Joyce,* vol. 1. Edited by Robert H. Deming. New York: Barnes and Noble, 1970.
Eliot, T. S. *The Complete Poems and Plays: 1909–1950.* New York: Harcourt, Brace and World, 1952.
Ellmann, Richard. *James Joyce.* Rev. ed. New York: Oxford University Press, 1982.
Fargnoli, A. Nicholas, and Michael Patrick Gillespie, eds. *Exiles: A Critical Edition.* Gainesville: University Press of Florida, 2016.
Gillespie, Michael Patrick. *James Joyce and the Exilic Imagination.* Gainesville: University Press of Florida, 2015.
Joyce, James. *The Critical Writings of James Joyce.* Edited by Ellsworth Mason and Richard Ellmann. New York: Viking, 1959.
Joyce, James. *Exiles,* ed. John MacNicholas, in *"Exiles": A Critical Edition,* edited by A. Nicholas Fargnoli and Michael Patrick Gillespie, 23–176. Gainesville: University Press of Florida, 2016.
Joyce, James. *Letters of James Joyce.* Vol. 1. Edited by Stuart Gilbert. New York: Viking Press, 1957.
Joyce, James. *Letters of James Joyce.* Vols. 2 and 3. Edited by Richard Ellmann. New York: Viking Press, 1966.
Joyce, James. *Ulysses.* Edited by Hans Walter Gabler, et al. New York: Random House, 1986.
Litz, A. Walton. *The Art of James Joyce.* London: Oxford University Press, 1961.
MacNicholas, John. "Joyce's *Exiles:* The Argument for Doubt." *James Joyce Quarterly* 11 (Fall 1973): 33–40.
MacNicholas, John. "The Stage History of *Exiles.*" *James Joyce Quarterly* 19 (Fall 1981): 9–26.
Maddox, Brenda. *Nora: The Real Life of Molly Bloom.* Boston: Houghton Mifflin, 1988.

Pound, Ezra. "Mr. James Joyce and the Modern Stage." In *James Joyce,* vol. 1, edited by Robert H. Deming, 133–35. New York: Barnes and Noble, 1970.
Read, Forrest, ed. *Pound/Joyce: The Letters of Ezra Pound to James Joyce.* New York: New Directions, 1970.
Tysdahl, B. J. *Joyce and Ibsen: A Study in Literary Influence.* New York: Humanities Press, 1968.

II

Extracurricular Joyce

12

Teaching Joyce's Poetry

MARGOT NORRIS

I retired from my position as Chancellor's Professor at the University of California, Irvine, three years after my sweet husband Rowland Davis suffered a stroke in 2008. I loved teaching, and for the first three years after his stroke, I fortunately had a teaching sabbatical and a limited number of courses, since I was able to use credits assigned to me for committee work and other university chores. But when the credits ran out and I would have to return to teaching full time, four or five classes a year, I realized I could no longer do it. What if I was teaching one of my undergraduate classes with 140 students and Rowland suffered another stroke? No, it was impossible, and so I retired.

I missed teaching and explored what other options I might have. And living in Laguna Beach, California, I had an excellent opportunity. Our city is home to a senior center whose multiple services include instruction in yoga, bingo, and meditation, but also in more academic projects such as music appreciation and writer's workshops for older and retired individuals. Scheduling is flexible, and I quickly realized that my best program would be to offer four courses of two hours in length, once a month in January, February, March, and April, on the topic of early twentieth-century English and American literature.

In one of my early classes, I focused on T. S. Eliot's *The Waste Land*, Gertrude Stein's *The Autobiography of Alice B. Toklas*, D. H. Lawrence's *Lady Chatterley's Lover*, and Nella Larsen's *Quicksand*. Each class began with a lecture and was followed by a discussion—and the students loved it. And a few years later I ventured into my specialty, the work of James Joyce, and offered classes on Joyce's short stories in *Dubliners, A Portrait of the Artist as a Young Man, Ulysses*, and even an introduction to Joyce's difficult *Finnegans Wake*. However, since the pandemic, classes are no longer offered at the center but are attended mainly on computers on Zoom.

So, I began thinking about what to teach in a possible upcoming class in the spring of 2023. I had just recently taught Joyce's work, so another class on

Joyce was not really plausible. But after thinking and thinking, I found nothing else new that particularly appealed to me. And then a wild idea popped into my mind. Joyce wrote some poems, didn't he? Yes, he did, although they are rarely mentioned in Joyce discussions. What would it be like to offer a class on "The Poetry of James Joyce"?

My first exploration of this topic was somewhat discouraging. I had a copy of the 1969 Viking Press edition of James Joyce's *Collected Poems* on my shelves, and when I leafed through it, I felt it difficult to believe that the author of the brilliant *Ulysses* and *Finnegans Wake* had written these simple, if lyrical verses. "Strings in the earth and air / Make music sweet; / Strings by the river where / The willows meet."[1] Yes, a lovely sound, but is there more? I decided it wouldn't be a good idea to just start with the poems without offering a fuller introduction into the history of Joyce's writing of these poems, and here Richard Ellmann's biography, *James Joyce,* turned out to be a blessing.

Ellmann reports that Joyce began writing both poetry and prose while still in his early years at Belvedere College, with prose sketches titled *Silhouettes* and his first collection of poems called *Moods.*[2] By the time Joyce was in his late teens, he put together a collection of his poems and prose and began to try to make himself known to writers in Dublin literary circles. He showed them to people like George Russell and W. B. Yeats, who wrote him a complimentary letter telling him "You have a very delicate talent but I cannot say whether for prose or verse." But Yeats also conceded that Joyce's "technique in verse is much better than the technique of any young Dublin man I have met during my time."[3]

Two years later Joyce's friend Arthur Symons published one of his poems, "probably 'Silently she's combing'" in the *Saturday Review,*[4] and eventually through a recommendation helped him get *Chamber Music* published in 1908—making it James Joyce's first book publication. Symons also wrote the first review of the book in *The Nation,* calling the poems "delicate and musical."[5] Eventually both W. B. Yeats and Ezra Pound were impressed by some of the poems in *Chamber Music,* particularly the one that begins "I hear an army charging upon the land" and Pound was willing to use it in an anthology he was publishing.[6] And so Joyce's poetry eventually became a legitimate and meaningful part of his canon.

Having explored the history of the creation and final initial publication of *Chamber Music,* it became time for me to begin working myself through the poems, as best as I could, keeping in mind what attention I should draw to my students, and what issues might arise for discussion. Inevitably I began at the beginning, and so played in my mind with verse 1, "Strings in the earth and air / Make music sweet; / Strings by the river where / The willows meet" (*CP* 9). The setting is nature, outdoors, near a river, perhaps the Liffey, but the sound is not merely the sound of nature but something cultural, as though produced by lyrical art. And so, a figure is introduced, not necessarily human but more likely figurative: "There's music along the river / For Love wanders there, / Pale flowers on his mantle, / Dark leaves on his hair." Nature is now given signs and colors of living vegetation, pale flowers and dark leaves, and movement and motion. "Love," however, is a human attribute, and the music produced is no longer the sound of nature but a human production by a "head to the music bent, / And fingers straying / Upon an instrument." Verse 2 now veers from nature into a more human environment: "The twilight turns from amethyst / To deep and deeper blue, / The lamp fills with a pale green glow / The trees of the avenue" (*CP* 10). We appear to be on a street where the sound of an old piano playing makes us imagine a woman as "She bends upon the yellow keys" with her head inclining. And we now enter her mind, with "Shy thoughts and grave wide eyes and hands" as the twilight gets darker. Verse 3 begins at daylight, "When all things repose do you alone / Awake to hear the sweet harps play" (*CP* 11). And in verse 4 the narrative ends with the woman awake, hearing "One who is singing by your gate. / His song is softer than the dew / And he is come to visit you." And the verse ends with the producer of the four verses identifying himself as the male Lover, "Tis I that am your visitant" (*CP* 12).

Would my retired students in my senior center class produce this reading of the first four verses of *Chamber Music*? Possibly not, and after my introduction, I would commence by having assorted students read each of the first four verses aloud and then asking the others what they thought of them, what to make of them. My discussion above could be helpful in answering or inserting questions that arise in their discussion, and at the end, I could give them my own narrative, if it has not already come together in the class discussion. It would probably be helpful to set a limit of sorts for discussion—perhaps fifteen to twenty minutes for each verse so that the first class could then continue with another section of *Chamber Music*.

As we move along into other parts of the collection, we might also consider the question of how gender might affect reading and interpretation and response to the poems. Verse 5, like the ending of the first four verses, begins with lines that appear to identify the speaker as male: "Lean out of the window, / Goldenhair, / I heard you singing / A merry air" (*CP* 13). Here the speaker appears indoors, while the singing is clearly outdoors: "I have left my book, / I have left my room, / For I heard you singing / Through the gloom" (*CP* 11). In a 1982 collection of essays titled *Women in Joyce,* Robert Boyle, S. J., offers a chapter on "The Women Hidden in James Joyce's *Chamber Music*," in which he gives us a more detailed interpretation of these lines.[7] He writes, "'I have left . . . I have left' probably echoes the leaving of father and mother to cleave to a wife."[8] There is no clear indication of this, although the verse does suggest that the effect of the singing is to draw the male speaker out of his home, perhaps away from his parents, and into another space outdoors where a woman can be heard singing. But the singing woman appears to be indoors too, and must be asked to "Lean out of the window" so that he can see her.

In discussing a somewhat later verse, verse 8, Boyle offers a more poetic response to the first lines, "Who goes amid the green wood / With springtide all adorning her? / Who goes amid the merry green wood / To make it merrier?" He writes, "Her light and love make the whole woodland gleam with a fire, soft and golden, far superior to the fire he left behind," and goes on to describe "her" as "light also in her movements, graceful, virginal, calling forth all that is beautiful and good in nature" (*CP* 12). Students discussing these poems might also be open to another characteristic of the poetic: the quality and effect of sound and rhythm and melody and their effects on the reader. I would be tempted to ask them to take a look at, and then read aloud, the second stanza of verse 13.

What sounds do they hear, and what makes them melodic? They would surely notice the repetition of both words and sounds in "Now, wind, of your good courtesy / I pray you go, / And come into her little garden / And sing at her window." The repetition of asking a 'wind' to approach a 'window' takes two words with totally different meanings and brings them together not only narratively but also sonically. And then the additional echo of "sing" is placed into the fourth line. This is a particularly significant issue for Jolanta Wawrzycka, as she discusses her experience translating the verses of *Chamber Music* into Polish.[9] She begins with the first stanza of verse 20: "In the dark pine-wood / I would we lay, / In deep cool shadow / At noon of day." She then explains that "where Joyce's first stanza resonates with elongated vowels in '-w**oo**d,' 'w**ou**ld,' 'w**e**,' 'd**ee**p,' 'c**oo**l,' and 'n**oo**n' and dipthongs in 'l**ay**,' 'shad**ow**,' and 'd**ay**,' my translation reproduces these sounds through elongation, dipthongs, and triphthongs."[10] Although I don't know the Polish words into which she translates these words in the verse, she certainly draws our attention to their sound.

Wawrzycka then goes on to make a similar point about the sibilants in the second stanza of verse 20, and if we pay attention to the sound of the consonants that begin and end some of the first and last words in the stanza, we can see her point. The text gives us "How sweet to lie there, / Sweet to kiss, / Where the great pine-forest / Enaisled is!" and we can see the repetition of the "s" sound in "**s**weet," '**S**weet,' and 'ki**ss**,' and at the end of 'pine-fore**s**t,' and the last word '**is**.' It would certainly be interesting to use these examples to show students how sound in poetry is not just a matter of rhyming last words in the lines of stanzas, but sounds in other places as well.

As the verses of *Chamber Music* progress, they will slowly—very slowly—begin to move beyond their joyful beginning and become more complex not only in their composition but also in their spirit and their mood. The "Winds of May" begin verse 9 joyfully, dancing "a ring-around in glee." But the foam of the sea seems to obstruct emotional vision, obliging the voice to ask, "Saw you my true love anywhere?" and ending without a resolution, and with a worry: "Love is unhappy when love is away." But the next verse (10) gives us a male voice singing "in the hollow," and while conceding that "the time of dreaming / Dreams is over," still sends a positive message forward, "As lover to lover/ Sweetheart, I come." Three verses later, verse 13, the male speaker still pursues her on a difficult journey, "over the dark lands," running upon the sea, determined that "seas and land shall not divide us / My love and me." He begs the wind to sing at her window, letting her know that he is on the way, and that although he is not yet there, "soon will your true love be with you, / Soon, O soon." By verse 16, he is still not there but still looking forward to their reunion in a cool valley where they will go, a "cool and pleasant" valley, and "there, love, will we stay."

This hopeful wish comes to a surprising blow in the next verse, 17, which introduces a topic that has not come to light before in the series and produces a bit of a shock. "Because your voice was at my side / I gave him pain," it begins. Is this still the male voice from before speaking, and if so, is he still speaking to a woman, telling her that the pain may have been caused "Because within my hand I held / Your hand again"? This suggests that while he was holding the singing woman's hand, another male saw them together and was hurt by what he saw. The speaker then makes a sad and sorrowful confession: "There is no word nor any sign / Can make amend—/ He is a stranger to me now / Who was my friend." This is also how Robert Boyle constructs the scene, as one where the vision of a couple holding hands suggests betrayal to a man who sees them: "Her singing voice and willful hand have effectively destroyed his friendship with a man who was once at his side."[11]

This turn toward sadness and sorrow is worrisome with respect to how students who are senior citizens would respond to this change in the continuity of the verses. Would they handle it better than undergraduates, or find it unnecessarily depressing? The best tactic in dealing with such concerns might be to focus their attention on how much more complicated the words have become in some places, and the role virtually unknown mythic figures begin to play in the verses' meaning. In verse 22 we get the word "imprisonment" at the beginning of the first line, then "prisoner" at the end of the first stanza, and "prisoned" at the end of the second. Curiously, the speaker gives the word a positive spirit right from the start—"Of that so sweet imprisonment / My soul, dearest, is fain"—"fain" in the sense of pleased and willing, making it clear that he likes having "soft arms" holding him and keeping him from leaving. But having "interwoven arms" make love "tremulous" suggests an embrace that might produce nervous shaking and quivering rather than comfort and peace, leaving the ending of the verse ambiguous: "But sleep to dreamier sleep be wed / Where soul with soul lies prisoned."

Who feels imprisoned here—the speaker, the embraced lover, or both? This could make for an interesting discussion in a class. Things get even darker a few verses later when verse 27 begins "Though I thy Mithridates were, / Framed to defy the poison-dart." Students will probably have to go to Wikipedia to look up "Mithridates," and learn that he was an "effective, ambitious and ruthless ruler" who waged "several hard-fought but ultimately unsuccessful wars . . . to break Roman dominion over Asia and the Hellenic world." He also apparently developed an immunity to poisons by "ingesting sub-lethal" doses—another strange bit of information that may however help explain why the poem's figure is able to "defy the poison-dart."

The students will have to figure out why the lover would describe himself in this way to the one he loves, and why he would "confess / The malice of thy tenderness." How and why is her tenderness—if his lover is female—malicious, or why does he say or feel that it is? Does he confess that his lips are capable of producing elegant and antique phrases—or that he is too smart to do this? And has he never known a love of the kind produced by poets in their verses, and neither "a love where may not be / Ever so little falsity"—or does this imply that all the love he has ever known has always been burdened by some falsity? I have to confess that the complexity and ambiguity of this poem is so rich that I have no clear explanation, and I would hope that whatever class I teach would help me to get a fix on this.

"Gentle lady, do not sing / Sad songs about the end of love" begins verse 28, but this is, in a sense, *Chamber Music*'s announcement of the ending of the verses, which is contorted with the end of love. "Dear heart, why will you use me so?" the beginning of the next verse asks, and asks again at the end, "Alas! why will you use me so?" The ending of love and poetry will be illuminated by weather, beginning with "wild winds" in verse 29, then "the summer wind" two verses later, and in the next verse with rain that "has fallen all the day." The winds continue in the next verse (33) "whistling merrily," but the leaves begin to fall, and in the next verse "the voice of winter / Is heard at the door." This is followed in the next verse by the speaker now hearing the "noise of waters / Making moan," accompanied by the "grey winds, the cold winds are blowing" and now the end is nigh. The last verse of *Chamber Music* (36) ends militarily, with the words "I hear an army charging upon the land." According to Ellmann, it was praised by Yeats in a note to the secretary of the Royal Literary Fund as evidence of Joyce's "beautiful gift": "There is a poem on the last page of his *Chamber Music* which will, I believe, live. It is a technical and emotional masterpiece."[12]

It is difficult to know if this last verse expresses Joyce's own emotions or if it is his design to end the series loudly, powerfully, in an emotional crescendo. The army "charging upon the land" begins with the "thunder of horses plunging" with the force of "fluttering whips" of "arrogant" "charioteers" clad in "black armour." But they appear to be the nightmare of a speaker who concedes that he moans in his sleep as they "cleave the gloom of dreams, a blinding flame / Clanging, clanging upon the heart as upon an anvil." And the last poem brings love to an end: "My heart, have you no wisdom thus to despair? / My love, my love, my love, why have you left me alone?" *Chamber Music* here brings us to a sad and powerful ending after a long and complex journey of poetic love.

Joyce's next set of poetry consisted of a collection of thirteen verses that came into existence and were published at a difficult time in Joyce's life. Joyce had begun working on the complicated writing that he initially called a *Work in Progress*, but that later became known as *Finnegans Wake*. This new project was initially treated with both great caution and some outright rejection by contemporaries, and Joyce apparently hoped to appease Pound's criticism by "showing him the manuscript of the thirteen poems he had written since *Chamber Music*." According to Ellmann, Pound told Joyce that "They belong in the Bible or in the family album with the portraits," and when Joyce asked Pound if he thought "they are worth printing at any time," Pound replied, "No, I don't."[13] In the end it was a recent friend, Archibald MacLeish, who praised the poems and encouraged Joyce "to have his poems published under the modest title of *Pomes Penyeach*."[14]

The title "pomes" rather than "poems" may refer also to the French word *pommes* for apples, and the Wikipedia article connects this title to the first poem, "Tilly," since a tilly may refer to an extra serving, offering thirteen items rather than twelve in the expression "a baker's dozen," and accounting for the thirteen poems in *Pomes Penyeach*. Critic Lee Spinks offers some possible background to the poems when he describes how a decade earlier the married Joyce developed a crush, of sorts, on a woman named Amalia Popper, with whom he had some "furtive meetings" and "intense conversation" and who inspired him to write some of the verses that became part of *Pomes Penyeach*. The relationship "petered out gently a year after it began," but may possibly be reflected in some of the "love's language" in the volume's verses.[15] I would think that my senior students might very much enjoy the collection's first poem "Tilly," which begins with the narrator telling us "He travels after a winter sun," suggesting that the sorrowful ending of *Chamber Music* may now be reversed. But this is not yet to be, although the male figure certainly gives the cattle he is urging "along a cold red road" the promise that "home is warm," and that they, or perhaps only he, will tonight "stretch full by the fire." But "Tilly" ends with the voice conceding "I bleed by the black stream / For my torn bough"—a broken branch that Chester Anderson describes as a "deeply evocative archetypal image."[16]

The second poem in this series makes its difficulty clear right at the outset with its title, "Watching the Needleboats at San Sabra." What are "needleboats" and what or where is "San Sabra"? There are other problems in the verse with such lines as "Vainly your loveblown bannerets mourn!" I looked up "banneret," and it turns out to be a "medieval knight." What do medieval knights have to do with "young hearts crying" and "prairie grasses sighing"? Since I have no idea what to make of this poem is it worth giving it to my senior students to explore and discuss? I bet they would research the mysterious words and places and begin playing with them in relation to the lines in the poem.

Other verses in *Pomes Penyeach* are equally problematic, including the rather simple and lovely verse "A Flower Given to My Daughter." Carol Loeb Shloss describes the poem as speaking "of a beauty symbolically passed from one generation to another," but without conceding until later that it refers to Joyce's daughter Lucia and her mother.[17] Women are described in the verse as frail and delicate, "Frail the white roses and frail are / Her hands that gave," presumably to a "blueveined child," "Rosefrail and fair," with a "wonder wild / In gentle eyes" (*CP* 49). Shloss suggests that the verse refers to "the infant Lucia" who, as an adult in 1929, created lettrines or large ornamental letters to illustrate *Pomes Penyeach*.[18] It is not difficult to believe that this verse had a personal meaning for Joyce, and, if so, this does give it a very special status in the collection. But even before I researched this information, and before I saw any personal connection to Joyce, the verse still felt caring and poetically lovely to me.

The next verse, "She Weeps Over Rahoon," begins "Rain on Rahoon falls softly, softly falling, / Where my dark lover lies." If we look up "Rahoon," we learn that it is a suburb of the city of Galway, and the location of a Rahoon cemetery, which is apparently where Joyce's wife Nora's early admirer Michael Bodkin was buried. Richard Ellmann's biography of Joyce notes that Joyce, on August 20, 1912, expressed in the poem "what he felt to be her thoughts about her dead lover and her living one."[19] This explains why the Rahoon poem is narrated by a female voice—highly unusual in Joyce's poetry, as we have seen—as though she were hearing the voice of her dead lover: "Sad is his voice that calls me, sadly calling, / At grey moonrise." A moving image, certainly, and this time clearly linked to a personal experience within Joyce's family.

The next verse in *Pomes Penyeach* has a title in another language: "Tutto è sciolto," translated in the notes in the *Chamber Music and Other Poems* 1917 Alma Books edition eight as "All is undone" in Italian.[20] The note traces the line to Vincenzo Bellini's 1831 opera *La sonnambula*. The poem clearly refers to a girl's or a woman's "clear young eyes' soft look, the candid brow / The fragrant hair," but nothing more is told to us about her except that "the dear love she yielded with a sigh / Was all but thine?" (87). To whom did the female figure yield her love—and who is the speaker or narrator who tells us this ambiguous and complex incident or memory? Probably the best issue to ask students to address when discussing this verse is precisely its concealments of everything, its figures, who they are, its setting, its timing—present or past, its narrator, and what that concealment itself is intended to mean? I would want to suggest that there is no answer to these questions, but that we might want to consider if its ambiguity is precisely the point, and if so, does this give the verse any strength or power, or any intrigue in and of itself?

The one thing this verse does support is the theme of love and lovers that has so far started this series of verses and will continue, and the Italian theme will continue as well in the next verse, "On the Beach at Fontana." "Fontana" appears to be an Italian word for "fountain." But while the most well-known fountain in Italy may be the Trevi Fountain, a baroque sculpture in Rome, that would not work well with the title's reference to a "beach," and the poem's mention of a "crazy pier," a "senile sea," and a "grey sea." The notes in the Alma Books edition calls *Fontana* the "Fountain of the Four Continents" located in the "Piazza Unita d'Italia" in the city of Trieste, which apparently opens onto a harbor (*CM* 87). That works better with the "whining wind" in the verse, and the coldness and chill that apparently causes the narrator of this verse to touch a male's "trembling fine-boned shoulder" and "boyish arm." The location and the weather together work to make the emotion in this verse still one of affection, presumably a woman's affection, but one that is affected by fear and a "deep unending / Ache of love."

But we are not yet finished with the effects of Italian, because the next verse, titled "Simples," gives us an Italian introduction with the words "*O bella bionda, / sei come l'onda!*" The Alma Books notes translate this epigraph as "Beautiful blonde, / you are like a wave!" and tells us it is adapted from a "Trentine folk song" in which a speaker tells a female figure that he likes the way she wears her locks because she wears them like a wave of the sea (87). Joyce was clearly familiar with this song, given his entry of its Italian words into the beginning of the poem, and we can see its appearance in the beginning of the second stanza: "A moon-dew stars her hanging hair / And moonlight kisses her young brow." In the first stanza of the verse the moon also "a web of silence weaves / In the still garden where a child / Gathers the simple salad leaves." The speaker gives the impression of being a man watching a girl in a garden gathering greens while singing a song, "*Fair as the wave is, fair, art thou!*" and he seems to wish he does not hear her because he needs to shield his heart from the effect of hearing her "childish croon."

So how does all this relate to the title of the verse, "Simples," which also does not appear to be entirely simple? Apparently, the plural "simples" is used to convey something that is very straightforward and uncomplicated, and at the same time also refers to medicinal herbs. Is that what the young girl is harvesting with her uncomplicated gestures while singing her uncomplicated verse? If so, the enigma becomes why this troubles the male speaker, and makes him wish he cannot hear her, when all he would need to do is describe the simple scene of a young girl gathering herbs while singing a little song. There is a hidden emotion implied in the way he speaks, something like desire or lust, and it makes us wish we could simply have gotten this simple image with nothing to complicate its simplicity.

The three next verses that follow in *Pomes Penyeach* are focused strongly on nature rather than on individual persons. The verse "Flood" begins with "rock-vine clusters" that lift and sway upon "lambent waters." In the next stanza the "waste of waters" is described as an animal of sorts that sways "and uplifts its weedy mane." The mood of both verses is brooding, and now the day is given a persona as a "brooding day stares down upon the sea / In dull disdain." The third stanza of "Flood" addresses a "golden vine," and tells it to "uplift" and "sway" its "clustered fruits to love's full flood." But the flood is now made an expression of love, whose emotional products are "lambent," glowing with a soft radiance, but also "vast and ruthless" in its "Incertitude." Students are now going to have to clearly discuss what effects uncommon words like "lambent" are going to have on readers? Are they designed to make readers feel not very smart, a little ignorant—and, if so, why?

These questions will not go away because the next verse, "Nightpiece," introduces more uncommon words, like "sin-dark," "thurible," "star knell," and "voidward." It would be good to ask students what they make of these words as they appear in phrases in the poem, and to ask if these odd words remind them of more common ones. The website "Eleanor Heag-Shenandoah" offers a copy of "Nightpiece" along with an analysis, in which she sees it presenting a "night sky" as a "sindark nave" or physical place of worship inhabited by angels like the "Seraphim" in the verse. She concedes that "sindark" is one of Joyce's neologisms but offers no interpretation. On the other hand, "thurible" turns out to be an acceptable word for an apparatus used to contain and spread burning incense during church services. She does not tackle "star knell" or "voidward," but, given the religious allusions she offers for the poem, we can begin to imagine these words in her larger context of a dark night sky as a heaven filled with stars and clouds and lights—but no moon—moving across the nightscape with sounds, perhaps thunder, moving upward toward the void of the space above.

It is difficult to find comments on one of the last pieces of *Pomes Penyeach*, a verse titled "A Memory of the Players in a Mirror at Midnight." One of the few helpful notes I found when trying to research this poem was offered on the website of a composer, located as "'A Memory of the Players in a Mirror at Midnight' Henry Dehlinger," who tells us that the poem most likely "refers to the English Players, a Zurich-based amateur theatrical company with which Joyce was involved during World War I." He describes the verse as underscoring "the anguish of aging" that "achieves its clarity of expression through its precise images." What is helpful about this explanation is that it gives us a possible perspective on what is otherwise a rather negative description of the players, whoever they may be, and one that evokes sympathy rather than scorn in the reader.

The opening lines of the poem, "They mouth love's language," does indeed suggest actors speaking lines from a play, rather than their own personal feelings. And their acting is extremely emotive, "Gnash / The thirteen teeth / Your lean jaws grin with," and possibly brutal, "Lash/ Your itch and quailing, nude greed of the flesh" (57). If it is a conflict between lovers that the actors are performing in this play, it deliberately spoils any sentimentality of a love story: "Love's breath in you is stale, worded or sung" and "Harsh of tongue." And the second stanza makes clear that the real-life actors who are performing this scene would not desire romance with the figure in the play: "None / Will choose her what you see to mouth upon."

The second to the last poem in *Pomes Penyeach* is titled "Bahnhofstrasse," a German word for a train station, and refers to "A street in Zurich where Joyce suffered his first attack of glaucoma," according to the notes in the Alma Books edition of the *Pomes* collection (*CM* 87). And the first line does indeed refer to eyes that have begun to "mock" their seer by making vision difficult, especially when it gets dark: "The eyes that mock me sign the way / Whereto I pass at eve of day." It is difficult to know or guess if students without this background information would have any way of imagining that the poem refers to problems that old age can confer on normal eyesight. "Ah star of evil! star of pain! / Highhearted youth comes not again."

And youth will indeed not come "Again!" the first word of the last verse of *Pomes Penyeach*, titled "A Prayer." We appear to hear the voice of a dying man pleading most passionately in his last lines, "Take me, save me, soothe me, O spare me!" in response to the voice calling him at the beginning to "*Come, give, yield all your strength to me!"* The voice is highly evocative of one facing the disappearing options at the very end of life, suffering "submission's misery," dreading "the cold touch," "the threatening head," the breathing of a low word "on my breaking brain." And he calls for the spirit to "*Come!* I yield," and finally to "Take me, save me, soothe me, O spare me!" which it presumably cannot and will not do. But if we think back on the collection of verses in *Pomes Penyeach*, with so many moments of comfort and joy, we've been given a poetic journey through a busy and good life, with all of life's ups and downs but many things for which we might be happy and grateful. There was the warm home in "Tilly," and the wild wonder in the gentle eyes of a blue-veined child in "A Flower Given to My Daughter." There has been sadness too, of course, the sad voice calling in "She Weeps over Rahoon," and the fear of an unending ache of love on the "Beach at Fontana." And then more lovely and happy moments when we see a child gathering simple salad leaves in a garden and singing an air in "Simples." Occasionally we learn of a "sullen day," when ruthless water sways, and yet suddenly a golden vine uplifts clustered fruits in "Flood." But as we near the end, we do hear those gnashing teeth in that grim performance of those "Players in a Mirror at Midnight," and the star of evil and star of pain warning that highhearted youth comes not again in the German "Bahnhofstrasse."

Yes, it has been a complex human journey ending in "A Prayer" at the end of the collection, with that dying voice pleading the mysterious "subduer" of life not to leave him. And, here, even after he is gone, we have not left him. And, finally, given Joyce's own delightful sense of humor, perhaps we should end the discussion of *Pomes Penyeach* with a verse tribute that Joyce wrote in 1933, and that is published as a footnote in Ellmann's biography of Joyce:

Pennipomes Twoguineaseach
Sing a song of shillings
A guinea cannot buy
Thirteen tiny pomikins
Bobbing in a pie.

The printers' pie was published
And the pomes began to sing
And wasn't Herbert Hughesius
as happy as a king.
    J. J.[21]

The only remaining poem published along with *Chamber Music* and *Pomes Penyeach* in the 1969 edition of Joyce's *Collected Poems* is the one titled "Ecce Puer." I would love to have the students lead and pursue the discussion of this verse without any input from me, but there is some crucial information needed to fully understand this verse, and students will need it to get to the heart of it. Since these are senior citizens, they would probably look things up on the web or elsewhere, and those using the 2017 Alma Books edition of Joyce's poems would learn that the translation of "Ecce Puer" is "Behold the Boy" (*CM* 94). And in addition, the notes tell us that the poem was written on February 15, 1932, presumably the day Joyce's grandson Stephen was born, and nine days after the death of Joyce's father. This would explain the moving contradictions in the poem's first stanza: "Of the dark past / A child is born / With joy and grief / My heart is torn." Why grief? We would be inclined to ask this before reading the next stanza, but its first two lines, "Calm in his cradle / The living lies," begin to give us a worrisome clue that something else is going on besides the child's birth. For if the child is "the living," then will there also be "the dead"?

The third stanza has a mysterious but moving line—"Young life is breathed / On the glass." Is the mother holding a child near a window and its breath creates a mist on the glass? Or does it breathe on the glass of a bottle of milk that will be used to feed it? Whatever the context, the meaning is simple and clear: the child is alive and has vitality and has thereby brought new life into the world. But even as a child is born, death is also occurring in the world: "A child is sleeping: / An old man gone." No doubt many people on this earth suffer the terrible emotional conflict produced by having a child born into a family near the same time that a close family member passes away. And they may indeed experience the anguish that the poem's last two lines evoke—a feeling of guilt for feeling tremendous joy at the same time as experiencing the death of a loved one. "A child is sleeping: / An old man gone. / O, father forsaken, / Forgive your son!" (*CM* 63). I must say that I personally feel that none of Joyce's writing has ever let me feel closer to his personal emotion, to Joyce's feeling on a day nine days after his father's death, than these lines.

If our class will be the regular two-hour classes for four months, we would certainly not be able to get to and discuss all of the poems in *Chamber Music* and *Pomes Penyeach*. I will therefore need to consider whether to ask to have an additional fifth class scheduled, or whether to wait and see if it might be better to simply schedule another separate class. And down the line, more classes could be offered to deal with additional Joyce poetry and perhaps Joyce essays or translations or letters or other off-beat work of his. The Alma Books collection of the poetry includes a "selection of uncollected poems" that feature eighteen additional works, some of them very brief, but some also substantial, including "Epilogue to Ibsen's *Ghosts*," "O Come-All-Ye, by a Thanksgiving Turkey," "The Holy Office," and "Gas from a Burner." That alone is quite a collection and would certainly make for some interesting discussion. This again makes it surprising that Joyce's poetry, often not mentioned at all in critical books about Joyce's work, has not received much more attention over the years. So, we'll have to see if student enthusiasm might spur more interest in the future to this body of the famous James Joyce's work.

Notes

1. James Joyce, *Collected Poems* (New York: Viking Press, 1969), 9. References to this edition will be cited parenthetically in the text as *CP* followed by page number.
2. Richard Ellmann, *James Joyce* (Oxford: Oxford University Press, 1983), 50.
3. Ellmann, *James Joyce,* 104.
4. Ellmann, *James Joyce,* 149.
5. Ellmann, *James Joyce,* 260.
6. Ellmann, *James Joyce,* 350
7. Robert Boyle, S. J. "The Women Hidden in James Joyce's *Chamber Music,*" in *Women in Joyce,* ed. Suzette Henke and Elaine Unkeless, 3–30 (Urbana: University of Illinois Press, 1982).
8. Boyle, "Women Hidden."
9. Jolanta Wawrzycka, "'Mute chime and mute peak': Notes on Translating Silences in *Chamber Music*." In *James Joyce's Silences,* ed. Jolanta Wawrzycka and Serenella Zanotti (London: Bloomsbury Academic, 2020).
10. Wawrzycka, "Notes on Translating Silences," 194.
11. Boyle, "Women Hidden," 13.
12. William Butler Yeats, qtd. in Ellmann, *James Joyce*, 391.
13. Ellmann, *James Joyce*, 591.
14. Ellmann, *James Joyce*, 591.
15. Lee Spinks, *James Joyce: A Critical Guide* (Edinburgh: Edinburgh University Press, 2009), 29.
16. Chester G. Anderson, *James Joyce and His World* (London: Thames and Hudson, 1967), 114.
17. Carol Loeb Shloss, *Lucia Joyce: To Dance in the Wake* (New York: Picador, 2005), 61.
18. Shloss, *Lucia Joyce,* 115.
19. Ellmann, *James Joyce*, 325.
20. James Joyce, *Chamber Music and Other Poems* (Richmond, UK: Alma Books, 2017), 87. References to this edition will be cited parenthetically in the text as *CM* followed by page number.
21. Ellmann, *James Joyce*, 619. Epigraph source: Rachel Sagner Buurma and Laura Heffernan, *The Teaching Archive: A New History for Literary Study* (Chicago: University of Chicago Press, 2021), 213.

Bibliography

Anderson, Chester G. *James Joyce and His World.* London: Thames and Hudson, 1967.
Boyle, Robert, S. J. "The Women Hidden in James Joyce's *Chamber Music*." In *Women in Joyce,* edited by Suzette Henke and Elaine Unkeless, 3–30. Urbana: University of Illinois Press, 1982.
Eliot, T. S. *The Waste Land and Other Poems.* Norton Critical Edition. Edited by Michael North. New York: Norton, 2022.
Ellmann, Richard. *James Joyce.* Oxford: Oxford University Press, 1983.
Joyce, James. *A Portrait of the Artist as a Young Man.* Edited by Seamus Deane. New York: Penguin, 2003.
Joyce, James. *Chamber Music and Other Poems.* Richmond, UK: Alma Books Ltd., 2017.
Joyce, James. *Collected Poems.* New York: Viking Press, 1969.
Joyce, James. *Dubliners:* Norton Critical Edition. Edited by Margot Norris. New York: Norton, 2006.
Joyce, James. *Finnegans Wake.* Reissue edition. New York: Penguin, 1999.
Joyce, James. *Ulysses.* Edited by Hans Walter Gabler, et al. New York: Vintage, 1986.
Larsen, Nella. *Quicksand.* Norton Critical Edition. Edited by Carla Kaplan. New York: Norton, 2019.
Lawrence, D. H. *Lady Chatterley's Lover.* New York: Penguin, 2008.
Shloss, Carol Loeb. *Lucia Joyce: To Dance in the Wake.* New York: Picador, 2005.
Spinks, Lee. *James Joyce: A Critical Guide.* Edinburgh: Edinburgh University Press, 2009.
Stein, Gertrude. *The Autobiography of Alice B. Toklas.* New York: Vintage, 1990.
Wawrzycka, Jolanta. "'Mute chime and mute peal': Notes on Translating Silences in *Chamber Music*." In *James Joyce's Silences,* edited by Jolanta Wawrzycka and Serenella Zanotti, 191–207. London: Bloomsbury Academic, 2020.

13

Teaching *Ulysses* in Nonacademic Spaces

Jonathan Goldman

> *Literary study was not a long-ago elite formation . . . it was often cultivated alongside or even as part of vocational education. The disciplinary shape of English bears the marks of this history, but it will be visible to us and to others only once we see classrooms at vocational programs, night schools, community colleges, and technical institutions as part of our intellectual genealogies.*
> Rachel Sagner Buurma and Laura Heffernan, from *The Teaching Archive*

Joyce is read outside of formal academic structures, studied outside of formal academic structures, so taught outside of formal academic structures—possibly with greater consequence now than ever before. In the twenty-first century, a time when long-embattled humanities disciplines seem more embattled than ever—a crisis largely foisted upon them by draconian budget cuts and neoliberal policy, implemented often without regard for evidence and always without regard for results outside of the redistribution of funding—the nonacademic spaces where teachers of James Joyce ply their trade take on particular significance. Rachel Sagner Buurma and Laura Heffernan argue in *The Teaching Archive* that pedagogy in general is as significant as research and critical writings in the history of literary study, and should occupy, but have not occupied, a major part of any evaluation of the field. They catalog pedagogical situations outside of elite institutions, "vocational programs," etcetera, as particularly under-scrutinized. This essay aims to supplement their list, widen our view of Joyce studies by widening our view of the spaces of Joyce pedagogy. Courses focused solely on Joyce, *Ulysses* courses particularly, have flourished in bookstores, library lounges, cafés and restaurants, living rooms, Irish consulates, and cultural centers. Taught by academics and academic outsiders, they serve students who have signed up to study Joyce not for grades but for—well, I will discuss what for. These nonacademic sites are part of the "intellectual genealogy" of Joyce's legacy, as are, of course, the virtual zones that host online Joyce courses for the un-matriculated.

Nonacademic study has deep roots in Joyce. As Buurma and Heffernan note, in 1942 Edmund Wilson opened his Smith College course about Joyce to the general population of western Massachusetts, creating a classroom that "cut across multiple publics," as it "strove for the effect of a decent railway station bar."[1] An early Joyce champion, Wilson taught the class as an insistently democratic, polyvocal enterprise—contradicting the oft-bruited-about lament that US academics, specifically, are responsible for reserving Joyce for elite readers. Wilson's handwritten lecture notes and drafts show his intent to familiarize, to domesticate, the author, New Criticism be damned. His first note reads: "Joyce: family man."[2] Simultaneously, he promotes Joyce as master manipulator of language: "The use of Language in Joyce is precise and intense in a way that is hardly to be found in the work of any other novelist."[3] Wilson's lecture goes on to offer several pages of comparisons to Virgil and Dante. His teaching notes treat Joyce as human, the writing as superhuman, the literary context as one of classicism, not experiment, serving to both rationalize and ease the way for studying the author's work.

I teach *Ulysses* outside of accredited educational systems, almost exclusively outside of accredited educational systems. One of my students recently labeled me a "sherpa," helping the class climb Mount *Ulysses;* I have seen myself as, variously, resident expert, tour guide, and cheerleader for *Ulysses* in nonacademic courses—a term that, along with "classes," I am using capaciously. In this chapter, I will reflect on this work, occasionally invoking colleagues in parallel roles who shared their thoughts with me,[4] and touching upon my experiences with those nominally untaught classes, *Ulysses* reading groups. Vibrant elements in the Joyce readerly universe, nonacademic spaces should be interrogated like any other Joyce material. In their complicated relationships with issues of equity and class, cultural capital, prestige, whiteness, labor, and the gulf between the academic and the not, these spaces have much to tell us. Because their teachers and students are free from the stakes of grading, and the students unburdened by concerns about progressing toward degrees and professions, it is tempting to idealize nonacademic courses, consider them as somehow pure. I contend that, rather, they should be read as zones of negotiation, conflict, and harm—like any classroom, and for that matter any public space.

On Not Teaching *Ulysses*

In my second year of graduate school, I taught *Ulysses* cover to cover, chapter by chapter, the first time I did so in a university setting—and the last. (How that came about is a story for another time.) In my early postgraduate career, I taught only excerpts of the novel, very rarely: a few chapters in the one grad seminar I led in a prior job, a chapter or a few passages snuck into modern novel classes and Irish lit surveys. At New York Tech, where I have taught since 2008, these occasions have been infrequent, because of programming demands, needs of the student body, and contours of the department. Our literature faculty are by necessity generalists plus composition and ESL instructors for our undergraduates, many of whom are first-generation college students, immigrants, or techies who have been told for years that they are good at STEM, bad at writing. In our literature seminars, we are ultimately remedial reading comprehension and writing coaches. I, like countless instructors throughout the academy, am devoted to this work, and gratified by its rewards—while I also lament not being able to add some of the texts I study most fervently to the syllabus. Our students are eager for a challenge, but not one that defeats them from the start. In my infrequently run Irish literature and modernism courses, books such as *Normal People* (2018) or *Passing* (1929) represent unfamiliar forms of reading—and, some students tell me, constitute the first novels they have ever read. Joyce's *Dubliners* stories, heavily anthologized and understood as his most accessible works, stump many of them. The foreignness of "Araby" and "Eveline" generate real puzzlement; "The Dead" is so dense that it drives more students than usual straight to consulting overly simplistic study aids that result in contorted, nonsensical, plagiarism. In this environment, I sometimes assign a short section of *Ulysses*, rationalizing that all readers can derive something out of the text, and a few of my students have responded with enthusiasm; for one, it seems to have been life-altering. However, for me to devote much time to the novel, more than a class meeting, would be doing most of my students a disservice. I would lose too many of them, depriving them of practice developing their reading and analytical skills. *Ulysses* would serve not as a whetstone, but an obstacle.

The irony here is that these are readers whom I would like to see interested in Joyce, to share the rewards of engaging with *Ulysses*, and whose perspectives would widen my own appreciation for it. But students at schools such as mine who want to read *Ulysses* are probably out of luck. University courses that include *Ulysses*, much less focus largely on it, are likely dwindling along with literary study here at the crisis stage of twenty-first-century liberal arts. Terry Eagleton, contributing to the bibliography of laments about the neoliberalization of higher ed, writes that "humanities above all . . . are being pushed to the wall. . . . If English departments survive at all, it may simply be to teach business students the use of the semicolon, which was not quite what Northrop Frye and Lionel Trilling had in mind."[5] Hyperbole aside, and notwithstanding the fact that English programs at elite institutions continue to thrive, it is clear that many university teachers and students do not have a chance to dig into *Ulysses*.

Some whose academic programs preclude *Ulysses* find their way to nonacademic courses. In metropolitan centers and online, these courses are offered by institutions and individuals, seeming to flower particularly as the novel's centenary approached, which coincided with a global pandemic that had many people staying home, getting accustomed to online video interactions and discussions, and finding extra time on their hands. A poll of users of Patrick Hastings's "Ulysses Guide" website reveals a two-to-one ratio of nonacademic-course to academic-course readers, which, granted, partly reflects who is driven to online guidance, and who answers poll questions, but certainly suggests a robust culture of classes outside the academy.[6] Someday a scholar should attempt a comprehensive list of nonacademic courses, but in the meantime, here are some examples: Caroline Elbay has led "*Ulysses* for all" at the James Joyce Centre in Dublin since 2014. Jesse Meyers teaches courses on the novel for retirement communities, libraries, and community organizations in Connecticut, the Hudson Valley area of New York, and New York City. At the 92nd Street YM-YWHA in New York City, the late Michael Groden taught an annual Joyce class, frequently focusing solely on *Ulysses*. He was midway through a remote version of the *Ulysses* course at the time of his 2021 passing; Phillip Weinstein led the remaining sessions. Across the East River from the 92Y, Rebecca Ariel Porte teaches *Ulysses* for Brooklyn's School for Social Research. Over the last decade, Robert Berry has taught his "A Pint of *Ulysses*" and courses on creating visual art through *Ulysses* in and around his Philadelphia environs, including some associated with the Rosenbach Museum—for whom Nicholas Fargnoli has also taught the novel. Susan Bazargan has led *Ulysses* classes for the Newberry Library in Chicago, and—bookstores!—Christopher Griffin for Politics and Prose Books in Washington, DC, and Barry Devine at Third Place Books in Seattle. In Buenos Aires, writer and Joyce scholar Carlos Gamerro quit the badly underfunded Argentine university system to set up his own mini-school of sorts, making sure to include *Ulysses* courses in his catalog.

That is where I came in. A few years ago, Gamerro, his schedule full, sent my way a student who wanted a *Ulysses* tutorial. I, by coincidence temporarily situated in Buenos Aires, jumped at the chance, happy to revisit the novel and share my enthusiasm for it. Back home in New York City, more such opportunities arose, so that for several years, in addition to occasional one-off opportunities, I led groups that met weekly, February through June. These were the eighteen-week *Ulysses* course variety, one chapter per meeting, starting after Joyce's birthday and concluding in time for Bloomsday. The hook of a course-ending Bloomsday celebration appeals to many of these students. Berry and Elbay plot their classes similarly, though both have radically experimented with assigning the early chapters by hour, reading temporally rather than sequentially: episodes 1 and 4 one week, 2 and 5 the next, then 3 and 6.

My courses have met in apartments, cafés, and public atriums, and when the pandemic hit in March 2020, that group continued on Zoom. I take great pleasure in the meetings in public, such as those at the Lincoln Center Atrium, where over the years many passersby and those seated nearby eavesdropped, some quite animatedly. Eating and drinking establishments also provide this perk but are risky options. For one group's first meeting, the organizer chose a restaurant with terrible lighting, and I had forgotten my reading glasses, and I could not eat the food they had ordered for me because I was talking so much, and it was raining outside, and my shoes were uncomfortable.

Some details about the formation of these groups: In one case, the boss of a small real estate firm recruited me online, arranged the course, and strong-armed, it seemed, several of his employees to join. (About half of those who attended participated enthusiastically—the rest, not.) Another group had connected via a social media site and decided, apparently after much debate, to recruit a teacher. After our course started, their listing continued to attract participants, some proposing widely different approaches to the course; the group soon took down their post, not wanting to disrupt our momentum through the novel. A queer women's book club that had been reading together for years over elaborate dinner parties reached out to me to lead them through a couple meetings about *Ulysses*. More recently, I was hired for more formal classes by two different cultural organizations, the Irish Arts Center and the 92nd Street Y—the latter honoring me by having me take over Groden's role. For these groups, I teach condensed versions of the course, addressing multiple chapters per session.

My motivations for teaching *Ulysses* courses are roughly divisible into benefits for myself and to the world around me. Professionally, I relish the incentive to continue my engagement with *Ulysses*, which mitigates the novel's near absence in my university teaching. Rereading, discussing with the students, keeping up with new annotations and research, all help me maintain a scholarly connection, whereas previously, for a few years there, I would arrive at conferences and be slapped in the face by how long it had been since I had opened it, how much catching up I had compared to some of my colleagues. Add to all this the personal pleasure, the boost to my sense of self-actualization provided by including a favorite text in one's teaching life. If readers of this essay are wondering why I would need external impetus to reread the book, then perhaps they have stronger self-discipline or time management skills than mine.

Other motivations are directed outward. I have faith in this activity, in reading *Ulysses* with nonacademic students—for its benefit to the world, for the novel's power to shape. There are ideological and humanist reasons for teaching literature generally, for having entered the professoriate, and of course these reasons apply here. Reading, writing, analyzing skills, I believe, can lead to a more informed, more critical citizenry (even if not for all citizens). Reading closely compels an attention to language that underpins the development of writing skills—still essential in professional spheres, and often what my university pupils most need to improve. But nonacademic *Ulysses* courses offer additional satisfactions and opportunities. The students in these classes tend to appreciate the adulting that Leopold and Molly Bloom must perform, the concerns of parenthood, long-term romantic partnerships, aging, financial security, usually having led several decades of grown-up lives. That they are carving time out of those lives to take the course adds intensity to their efforts, and gratification in their progress. Most teachers of *Ulysses* know the pleasure of seeing a reader arrive at the realization they are going to get through the novel, for real. There is particular satisfaction when that student was previously unsure that they would, having fallen short in the past. So, at the end of each course, I distribute makeshift certificates, signing off that they have completed *Ulysses;* the primitive aesthetics of the document do not detract from my message that this is a real achievement.

Nonacademic courses grant a wider population the option of participating in the Joyce community, letting more people place themselves in the category of *Ulysses* reader. This goal—to include more readers, particularly those who may not have had the opportunity previously—is shared by others whom I informally polled. Elbay comments that her motivation is to "'democratise' the book and give it back to the people (away from the perceived 'ivory towers' of academia)."[7] The concern with de-elite-ifying the spaces, and the population, of *Ulysses* readership motivates me, as it motivated Wilson, and as it has motivated the countless projects to make the text more accessible, whether through guidebooks, reedited texts, or the recent waves of websites, podcasts, online video mini-lectures—and still more books intending to be the essential guide to the perplexed *Ulysses* reader. The tension between commonality and an elitism linked to academia has long been an undercurrent in the Joyce world, dating at least to Patrick Kavanagh's assertion that Joyce was "killed" by a "Harvard thesis."[8]

Who Takes *Ulysses* Now?

Teaching *Ulysses* in nonacademic courses immediately fulfills the function, expressed by Elbay, of countering the novel's identification with academia. These courses literally promote reading the book outside of academe. This de-academicizing is made complicated, somewhat by the presence of teachers such as me whose professional identities are intertwined with academic work. Furthermore, while teachers such as, for example, Berry and Meyers, are largely situated outside the academy, they rely on generations of scholarly treatments formulated within universities and are thus enmeshed in the academic world. We are establishing *Ulysses* study out of the university, but are we bringing the university's invisible structures and ideologies with us? The shadow of the academy opens to debate the degree to which nonacademic courses constitute an inherently democratizing pursuit.

One might approach the debate by considering the student bodies of these courses. My own nonacademic students over the years constitute too small a sample to be seen as dispositive, but my impressions of them may be a useful steppingstone, and my informal sense of their demographics is roughly matched by reports from others I informally consulted. In many ways, my first Argentine student was typical: She was a late-thirty-something professional in a social services administrative job, with enough job and personal flexibility to carve out two hours of her weekly schedule. She was Jewish but not practicing, with a well-educated, upper-middle-class upbringing. She had recently taken Gamerro's course on Homer and was committed to filling other gaps in her familiarity with literature. Like her, many of my nonacademic students have tended to be a generation past their college years, or two, just as often, and sometimes three. I seem to have taught multiple psychiatrists, lawyers, a few professors in other fields, one graduate student in anthropology. These intellectual laborers outnumber both the artists and those in management, real estate, accounting, and public relations, but not by much. The shared feature among them is their position of access. To enroll in a nonacademic *Ulysses* course, one must possess the necessary leisure time and the financial resources to pay. (The cost varies widely from course to course.) However, this does not mean that these classes are only for elites. Many of the students are the adults who did not have this exact resource—access—during their university years; as undergraduates, they lacked the latitude or opportunity to pursue humanistic studies, to take literature courses, to read novels. Providing such readers a space for studying *Ulysses* is intellectual equity work, from this perspective.

From other perspectives, it is not. While I do not survey my students in terms of ethnicity, nationality, and gender identification, I unscientifically gauge my nonacademic groups to be far less diverse than my university courses—admittedly something of a high bar. Black and Brown students are particularly underrepresented—something also reported by the other teachers I consulted. It should not be surprising, given the historical Jewish and Irish presence in New York City, that many participants have been Jewish, and that many are of Irish descent, some Irish-born NYC transplants. A significant number of the latter express interest in the novel as an aspect of their Irish heritage to which they have not been able to connect. They speak of embarrassment at not having read *Ulysses* yet, impending trips to Ireland and Joyce walking tours, and the desire to be prepared for Bloomsday; they have attended Bloomsday celebrations in their past and are finally getting around to really understanding what's going on. Some mention a sense of obligation to previous generations of their family. At times, these students have evinced a kind of conservatism, with intentions around reading *Ulysses* that go beyond cultural pride and take on sinister connotations, rhetorically related to racial exceptionalism, also to notions of whiteness and even white supremacy. In this, the nonacademic spaces mirror concerns in Irish literary study generally; Anne Mulhall writes of concerns with the field's "whiteness, its conservatism, and its elitist and hierarchical attachments."[9]

This is in no way to claim that individual students harbor malevolent, racist intentions when enrolling in Joyce reading groups. Rather, my experiences have reminded me to be alert to the infelicitous use that the culture at large can derive from something like Joyce courses, which lionize a specific writer who is male, and white—and of a heritage, Irish, about which the world makes claims of literary/linguistic superiority, a form of Irish exceptionalism. Of course, any slippage into an implied racism/nationalism/conservatism is a more sinister matter than that of cultural capital, and its handling in the moment a more fraught affair. A teaching opportunity, to be sure, one that raises the issue of fulfilling the expectations of these students versus a pedagogical inclination to use literature as a social good. They may not have signed up, so to speak, for a theoretical challenge to their inherent mindset, and may resist too didactic a response. The "Cyclops" episode is one spot I have found productive in navigating this issue. Through the Citizen, Joyce shows one effect of colonization on the colonized subject: how subjugation leads to essentialist, racialized views of Irishness, which lead to essentialist views of masculinity, of nations, of history, of violence. Exploring such moments becomes a way for students to rethink their own training when it comes to Irish identity. It is a strategy for confronting my students' ideological stances, but indirectly—though I do eventually slip in my pointed tagline that the Citizen aims to "make Ireland great again."

As Mulhall notes, the elitism issue and the whiteness issue overlap. Perhaps of larger import than the demographics of nonacademic students is to consider whether the goal of a "democratized" *Ulysses* is possible given the way the novel has become popularly synonymous with exclusivity. Sean Latham writes of the book's "deep entanglement in the interlinked economies of symbolic and cultural capital, rendering its identity as an aesthetic object indistinguishable from its iconic status."[10] Put bluntly: Is it possible to teach *Ulysses* without participating in the ossification of intellectual class? Are nonacademic *Ulysses* courses challenging the class implications of reading *Ulysses* by widening the scope of the audience, or are they expanding the numbers of readers who can appropriate the cultural capital of the book, reinforcing intellectual caste systems? I submit that the approach to teaching nonacademic courses is where we can answer the question in the former, optimistic sense.

Teaching *Ulysses* in Nonacademic Spaces

How to teach *Ulysses* at all is a familiar question in the Joyce world. Recently, in a Joyce social media group, prominent Joyce scholar Fritz Senn mused, and asked,

> I am always wondering what some of us mean by "teaching" *Ulysses* as one of their activities. After more than a century of dealing with *Ulysses* facing new readers, it never occurred to me that I was "teaching" the book. What exactly would one be doing?[11]

Senn likely had many answers in mind, and part of his point was to reconsider our terminology around *Ulysses* pedagogy, how the idea of "teaching *Ulysses*" could invoke a scene of hidden knowledge imparted from master to acolyte. Senn's implication seems to be that *Ulysses* should be read with a sense of self-discovery, that readers should determine their experience of the text, and thus the book should be taught by an absent presence, sitting back, paring his fingernails. It is an unassailable proposition, in a way, and the ensuing comments did not assail it, although a couple comments (one from me) pointed out that Senn himself has provided a model for teaching the book—one that I have found dovetails particularly with my teaching in nonacademic spaces.

I often tell my students that although I am a longtime Joyce scholar, I do not consider myself an expert. I do not remember what all the allusions invoke, I do not always remember a character's history, or every detail of the Blooms' lives. I have not mastered Irish history, Catholic theosophy, or colonial capitalist economics. To forestall accusations of false modesty, I tell them that I am an expert in reading without understanding every word that one is reading, and reading on to see whether the matters clear up, or just to get to more secure footing. I am an expert, I tell them, in helping others do the same. This spiel is an invitation for them to think of the novel as approachable. That said, I do not soft-pedal its difficulty, avoiding the mistake that Stephen Dedalus makes in *Ulysses*, saying a math equation is simple when for his student it is not. I tell new readers that there is no shame in skimming parts of the novel they find impenetrable. Come back to that some other day, I tell them; don't do something that takes away your enjoyment. I usually say this when episode 14 is looming.

I have found my role to be an odd combination of tour guide, as I have said, and cheerleader for Joyce readers. I am also a sometime hype man for Joyce's text, punctuating a class meeting by marveling at its achievement. My prototypes for ushering readers through the novel are the *Ulysses* lectures of Senn and my undergraduate mentor John Bishop, whose teaching mannerisms and intonation are burned into my brain and occasionally take over my body; I will never be able to read the words *"For Raoul!"* without hearing his guttural, mock-sensual performance, and I will never be able to pronounce them without channeling it. From these models, I adopted the strategy of always foregrounding the nuts and bolts of the narrative, as these matters can be difficult to track amid the diffuse narrative. I clarify how characters are moving through space, interacting with one another and the objects of their world. Of course, students appreciate being walked through some of the questions particular to Joyce's style: Who is thinking? Who is speaking? Who is narrating? And then on to: How does the idiom of this section register differently than others? These are compelling matters for all of us. But I prefer to start with the physical. Who is positioned where? What does the space look like? Often these details are wherein profundity lies, as exemplified by Bloom's movements among his peers. He is last to enter the funeral carriage, not quite part of the "we all" spoken by Martin Cunningham (*U* 6.8); a moment later Simon Dedalus salutes Blazes Boylan, pushing his way into Bloom's personal space (*U* 6.198).[12] In the newspaper office, no one makes room for Bloom, who is forced to stand awkwardly in the doorway until the doorknob hits him in the back (*U* 7.280). My specific approach is to ask questions that remind students of what they have read and perhaps absorbed, encouraging students to think that they would have noticed this had they just realized that an nth degree more attention at that moment would have thus rewarded them. That said, in the course of recapping the plot and untangling the narrative voices, I do more talking than I'd like, for the sake of efficiency.

To counteract the sense that I am handing the students an authorized reading, I find ways to authorize theirs. They read passages we are going to discuss aloud and select passages in advance they want the class to scrutinize. I have experimented with having students sign up to be our resident experts in topics of their choice: Catholicism, Irish nationalist politics, 1900-era popular songs, etcetera. Elbay, whose course has an online component, uses breakout rooms, small group discussions, in every session, resulting in strong engagement and student self-licensing. Berry invites guests with scholarly pedigrees to his course meetings and stages conversations with them, to show students that differently devoted Joyce readers come at the book from different angles.

Berry's strategy is partly based on the notion that nonacademic students want to hear voices of authority, of experience. Indeed, it turns out the majority of my adult students, *pace* Senn, want to be "taught" *Ulysses*, and, *pace* my protestations, desire the imprint of expertise, want their teacher to evince an air of mastery over the book. But teach a reader *Ulysses*, they read it for one day; teach a reader to read *Ulysses*, they read it for life. If *Ulysses* teaches us to read itself, as is often asserted,[13] then my role is to teach students to recognize how the novel teaches us to read itself. When I point out the links between disparate moments in the novel, then students start looking for such patterns themselves. I point out that Stephen Dedalus's imagined diatribe of Simon against his in-laws turns out to be dead-on when we read Simon's rant that is three chapters later, but in the same hour of the day, then students learn to look for such patterns. Similarly, if I signal details that are legendary *Ulysses* elements for the Joyce community—Throwaway, MacIntosh, potato, rumpled stockings—then students may start to feel that they, too, can be part of a community, can assert authority over their reading.

In search of guidance and expertise, many students avail themselves of contextual resources. Here I again take on the role of tour guide, or perhaps reference librarian, helping sift through the wealth of material, though some students are more apprised of what is available. Often, my job is to talk about approaches to reading *Ulysses*. How much to consult the annotations? How to use Homer? As many of the students do not have literature in their academic background, are not steeped in the theoretical underpinnings of the field, tensions can arise between the readings of *Ulysses* that we want to do, and mainstream understandings that to study literature is to ask, What does it mean? What was the author's intention? The nonacademic teacher of *Ulysses* also needs to be ready to listen with grace to occasional readings far afield of the standard critical understandings of the text. We have to deal with the disappointment of readers who, often accustomed to being authorities in their own line of intellectual work, can be frustrated to learn that they have misread, misunderstood, a plot point or stylistic tic.

In nonacademic courses, much more than in my university teaching, I model a combination of analytical and affective responses to the text. I learned this from Bishop, whom I remember telling his class of twentyish-year-old college students that we would read *Ulysses* one way now, another way later in life, after getting married, and differently yet after getting divorced. In recent years, I have talked about how becoming a parent deepens my appreciation for the depictions of Leopold and Molly Bloom, how they think about their children, both the living and the dead. This attitude invites students to integrate their personal reactions to the narrative with their understanding of the novel.

Wild Card: Reading Groups

I had been teaching informal, off-the-record *Ulysses* courses for a couple years when I was named vice president of the James Joyce Society. My subsequent ascent to the presidency occurred mid-pandemic, just before the centenary of *Ulysses*'s 1922 publication in one volume. In 2022, as newly minted leader of the organization, I chose to have the Joyce Society capitalize on the *Ulysses* buzz, rather than doing so personally. I did not set up my own course; I set up a JJS *Ulysses* reading group, both for the enjoyment of current members and to attract newcomers. I felt compunction about taking business away from online courses, but I reconciled this by noting that there were many other free online groups available to readers—for example Dublin's "Joyceborough" that originated at Sweny's pharmacy, and groups based in Montreal, and at the Fort Washington branch of the New York Public Library. I reminded myself that the Joyce Society group would be a very different animal from privately run courses, with no teacher. There were plenty of *Ulysses* readers to go around in the centenary year.

The group launched in February 2022. I took on the role of organizer and summarizer-in-chief and recruited a series of "expert" facilitators for many of the chapters, some Joyce Society members, some international colleagues whom I knew would kill it. I played facilitator for the episodes where there were no guest leaders. Seventy-five participants logged on the first week; over the course of eighteen Zoom sessions we consistently had about sixty people, never dropping below fifty for a meeting. A surprising majority of these consistently joined in the discussions, both out loud and of course in our busy chatboxes. The group mixed longtime scholars, longtime enthusiasts and first-time adventurers; this last category—I insisted repeatedly—needed to be our focus. That was hard to maintain, at times. The numerous Joyce lifers sometimes wound up dominating discussion, and in two-person dialogues for stretches. Only a couple times did a longtime Joycean struggle to respond generously to neophyte questions whose answers were obvious to them. Part of my job, as I saw it, was to steer us away from these situations, or gently ask my colleague to stand down. In general, the veteran *Ulysses* devotees and I worked hard to keep the discussion inclusive.

The combination of old and new readers among the group produced compelling moments. For example, during our discussion of "Penelope," the guest leader that day, Keri Walsh, began the session by offering a historical overview of how the episode has been read in gender-oriented criticism, emphasizing the evolution of those readings alongside stages of feminism. Walsh then asked the group members whether they found the chapter liberating, progressive, problematic, etcetera—where they placed it in relation to their own sense of feminism. Several first-time *Ulysses* readers, while acknowledging Joyce's egalitarian impulses, critiqued the chapter on various counts, including its reinscription of the feminine as corporeal. A couple of the longtime readers objected to the objections, strongly. One seemed rankled by the insinuation that the limitations of Joyce's feminism would color our readings and had a couple others supporting her arguments in the chat. The division between these responses was not gendered—all the responses I am informally cataloging here were from women—nor did it seem to align with age; it was rooted in experience and personal identification with reading *Ulysses*. What Margot Norris would call "virgin" readers sharply criticized the notion that Molly Bloom's monologue represents a feminist triumph, whereas the "veteran" (Norris, again) readers were inclined to be generous with its shortcomings.[14]

This moment of schism between *Ulysses* readers old and new does not signal, to me, that reading group participants disregard the authority of accredited Joyce scholars in their midst. On the contrary, in my experience visiting such courses, one or two more experienced voices are usually treated with deference, though it is not always clear why. Furthermore, *Ulysses* reading groups often bring in a ringer for a session or two; I have been that ringer, showing up either as a hired gun or as a favor to folks who seemed nice.

Teaching *Ulysses* and Academic Privilege

As a tenured professor, and a straight white male, I have myriad privileges within the academy, more without, and my opportunity to teach non-university *Ulysses* courses constitutes yet another. That these courses mitigate research disadvantages rendered by my particular job position illuminates those disadvantages and a problematic system. The academic profession is often seen in terms of haves (tenure-track/tenured positions) and have-nots (contingent faculty, the precariat). The truth is more complicated. While job security is, for most, the single most desirable goal, scholars can be contingent and well-funded—that is, possessing an elite research post-doc, while tenure, on the other hand, does not always correlate to adequate research support, research time. Nor does it guarantee, as I demonstrate above using myself as an example, synergy between one's research interests and teaching materials—a synergy that, assuming that professors' intense interest with the materials results in exciting and provocative pedagogy, benefits students and faculty alike.

Scattered throughout the academy are professors blessed with benefits of tenure, but curtailed in their options for teaching materials, deprived of those explorations alongside their students, and at a disadvantage in comparison with faculty in R1 institutions. This stratification calcifies over time. The advantages of posts more conducive to research facilitate professional achievements, which lead to more advantages—grants, visits to archives, invitations to publish—that widen the gap. What the academy generally treats as merit—the scholar's strong work justifies their elite job—is actually academic opportunity. The scholar's elite job allows them to produce strong work, which leads to more opportunities, which facilitates more strong work. Kudos to the academics who continue to make use of their advantages to produce vital research, but let's not forget that they have certain legs up on a large swatch of their colleagues.

Teaching *Ulysses* nonacademically therefore constitutes a weird form of intellectual labor. I did not anticipate that my lifelong enthusiasm for *Ulysses* would translate into a marketable side-gig, but here we are. With *Ulysses* largely absent from my university courses, I take on nonacademic teaching, what is the equivalent of overload—extra classes—to include the book in my pedagogical life. I consider myself fortunate that nonacademic courses have become a fixture of the Joyce world, especially in NYC. While my primary employment has conditions that roughly match those of many academics all over the world, my ability to teach *Ulysses* allows me to financially benefit from the incredible amount of wealth that surrounds me in New York City, to carve off a tiny piece of that wealth. Most of my academic peers do not have comparable opportunities. Will these courses continue to run, creating opportunities for myself and others? That is up to us. If teachers can find ways to support twenty-first-century readers as they make their way through *Ulysses*, we will chip away at its reputation as reserved for the elite and nourish the novel's reputation as a transformative readerly experience, hopefully for generations to come.

Notes

1 Buurma and Heffernan, *Teaching Archive*, 152.
2 Lecture notes from An Introduction to James Joyce: English 30 by Edmund Wilson, fall 1942, YCAL MSS 187, box 163, folder 40–48, Edmund Wilson Papers, Beinecke Rare Book and Manuscript Library, Yale University Library, New Haven, CT, 24.
3 Wilson, lecture notes, Edmund Wilson Papers, 15.
4 I am grateful to Robert Berry, Caroline Elbay, Nicholas Fargnoli, and Jesse Meyers for corresponding with me about this topic.

5. Terry Eagleton, "The Slow Death of the University," *Chronicle of Higher Education*, April 6, 2015, https://www.chronicle.com/article/the-slow-death-of-the-university/.
6. Note the number of visitors to Patrick Hastings's site, which show a gradual increase over the years 2019–2021, peaking between February and June 2022. I am grateful to Hastings for sharing his unpublished data in multiple emails between April and June 2024.
7. Caroline Elbay, email message to author, June 6, 2023.
8. Patrick Kavanagh, "Who Killed James Joyce?" (1951), in *Irish Writing in the Twentieth Century: A Reader,* ed. David Pierce (Cork: Cork University Press, 2001), 650.
9. Anne Mulhall, "The Ends of Irish Studies? On Whiteness, Academia, and Activism," *Irish University Review* 50, no. 1 (2020): 94–111.
10. Sean Latham, *Am I a Snob?: Modernism and the Novel* (Ithaca, NY: Cornell University Press, 2008), 119.
11. Fritz Senn (fritz.senn.33), "I am always wondering what some of us mean . . ." Facebook, May, 19, 2022.
12. James Joyce, *Ulysses,* ed. Hans Walter Gabler (New York: Vintage, 1984).
13. Daniel R. Schwarz, "'Tell Us in Plain Words': An Introduction to Reading Joyce's *Ulysses*," *Journal of Narrative Technique* 17, no. 1 (1987): 25–38.
14. Margot Norris, *Virgin and Veteran Readings of "Ulysses"* (New York: Palgrave MacMillan, 2011).

Bibliography

Buurma, Rachel Sagner, and Laura Heffernan. *The Teaching Archive: A New History for Literary Study.* Chicago: University of Chicago Press, 2021.

Eagleton, Terry. "The Slow Death of the University." *Chronicle of Higher Education,* April 6, 2015. https://www.chronicle.com/article/the-slow-death-of-the-university/.

Hastings, Patrick. "Who Reads *Ulysses?*" Paper presented at the International James Joyce Symposium, Dublin, Ireland, June 13, 2022.

Joyce, James. *Ulysses.* Edited by Hans Walter Gabler, et al. New York: Vintage, 1984.

Kavanagh, Patrick. "Who Killed James Joyce?" (1951). In *Irish Writing in the Twentieth Century: A Reader,* edited by David Pierce, 650. Cork: Cork University Press, 2001.

Latham, Sean. *Am I a Snob?: Modernism and the Novel.* Ithaca, NY: Cornell University Press, 2018.

Mulhall, Anne. "The Ends of Irish Studies? On Whiteness, Academia, and Activism." *Irish University Review* 50, no. 1 (2020): 94–111.

Norris, Margot. *Virgin and Veteran Readings of "Ulysses."* New York: Palgrave Macmillan, 2011.

Schwarz, Daniel R. "'Tell Us in Plain Words': An Introduction to Reading Joyce's *Ulysses.*" *Journal of Narrative Technique* 17, no. 1 (1987): 25–38.

Wilson, Edmund. Edmund Wilson Papers. Beineke Rare Book and Manuscript Library, Yale University Library, New Haven, CT.

14

"At their joggerfry"

Joyce, Dublin, and City-as-Text

GREG WINSTON

Teaching Joyce in the twenty-first century with an emphasis on geography offers pedagogical opportunities and intellectual benefits. It can familiarize new readers with places that have symbolic resonance within the fiction and cultural relevance beyond it. Even students who have never been to Dublin can form impressions of it from Joyce's local references and spatial descriptions, which can enhance their understanding of atmosphere as a component of setting whose undercurrents flow to and from social, cultural, and political contexts. Geography is integral to Joyce from the start: Even the simple title *Dubliners* intuitively suggests the place makes the people, and people become their place. The stories explore the evolving variety of this implicit interconnection.

Geography is a fundamental frame for teaching Joyce but also complex and multifaceted. It was controversial in Joyce's Ireland, as school subject, military project, and political tool—cultural contexts all reflected in his fiction. They suggest a confluence of narrative with spatial thinking that has deep cultural roots: A specific genre of early Irish literature even articulates the link between story and landscape—a tradition Joyce's modernism emulates and updates. In effect, Joyce's city and texts are connected by a two-way street: Readers' expanding awareness of Dublin's ever-changing cityscape runs parallel to their increasing familiarity with Joyce's texts. In this essay I examine how Joyce represents the stakes and contexts of learning geography in colonial Ireland and reflect on my parallel experience of learning Joyce and Dublin. I conclude with ideas for how faculty and students might pair Dublin's streets with Joyce's texts.

Stumbling On Joyce

Once upon a time and a very good time it was, when the Celtic Tiger was a cub and I was pulling pints in Stoneybatter and making sandwiches on Wicklow Street, I stumbled upon James Joyce. Walking through Dublin city centre one night, my left foot slid over something icy smooth, while my right came to a full stop. I barely managed to stay upright, then looked down to see what almost upended me. Set in the sidewalk was a shiny portrait, about two feet square, of a man in mid-stride. His arm, leg, and bowler hat were worn smooth from contact with countless feet before mine. My American sneaker had slipped on the polished profile of Leopold Bloom (for it was he) set in a commemorative brass plaque "proudly sponsored by Cantrell and Cochrane (Dublin) Limited," which associated the spot where I stood with Bloom's fictional perambulation in *Ulysses* (fig. 14.1).

My chance misstep came in a time when the city had finally begun to memorialize Joyce as Joyce had the city. After decades of being at best unacknowledged and at worst persona non grata in Dublin, the tide had turned so that by the end of the twentieth century elements of Joyce's fictional geography were being mapped back onto the city in a myriad of ways. These ranged from intellectually obsessed to commercially opportunistic. A number of locations and landmarks—most having histories that long predated their mention in Joyce—suddenly acquired new significance for their fleeting reference in Joyce's writing or indelible influence on his life.[1]

The brass plaque I had come upon—and around a dozen others like it—embedded the Joycean imaginary within Dublin's concrete reality. These sidewalk signifiers extend *Ulysses*'s narrative circuitry and transactional economy. It might even be said the drinks company's tribute to the novel works out a belated payment for an outstanding debt: Walking down Westland Row in "Lotus Eaters," Bloom notices among the "multicolored hoardings" of advertisements one for "Cantrell and Cochrane's Ginger Ale (Aromatic)."[2] Seven decades after *Ulysses*'s publication, the ad canvasser Bloom probably would have relished how the streetside plaques were a perfect fusion of literary imagination and commercial reality in their dual promotion of book and beverage. The convergence of art and industry seemed appropriate to a postmodern media landscape then awash in product placement, the not-so-subtle marketing technique whereby household brands surface in cultural or cinematic texts. (I learned later that Joyce gave considerable thought to advertisement and promotional strategies, in both his life and fiction.)[3] Were it not for the sponsorship of Cantrell and Cochrane, I might have never become a reader of Joyce—at least not one who

Figure 14.1. Dublin city centre *Ulysses* sidewalk plaque. Photograph by Eytan6, "*Ulysses* Plaque Dublin, episode 7. Aeolus," Wikimedia Commons, June 15, 2009. https://es.m.wikipedia.org/wiki/Archivo:Ulysses_Plaque_Dublin.JPG. Image unaltered from original.

would seek out the intersections of Joyce's fiction with the intersections of Dublin streets.

As a teenager in the 1980s, I was drawn to an Ireland that was suddenly punching well above its weight in music and film. I first visited Dublin near the end of that decade expecting the city of *The Commitments* or *My Left Foot*, but soon I was searching for Joyce. In more than three decades since, I've found myself gazing at the imperturbable faces of the houses on North Richmond Street, searching the backstreets of Dalkey for Mr. Deasy's school, hiking high amid the rhododendrons of Howth Head, and diving into the scrotum-tightening sea at the Forty Foot. So much of Dublin and environs—streets and parks, museums and monuments, art and architecture—bears tangible traces or enduring details of Joyce's books. Sometimes, the correlations of city and text seem to persist almost miraculously through a century of intense change. Yet, other moments show the contemporary city has paved over, built anew, or otherwise severed its link to Joyce's urban simulacrum. But even the disappointment of a lost connection can be an appropriate legacy for fiction that frequently turns on the meaningful absence or inconclusive gap.

Geography Lessons

When I teach Joyce with an emphasis on geography, I start by showing students how the topic had become contentious in Ireland at the turn of the twentieth century. Nationalist newspapers pointed to lack or failure of instruction in the subject in Irish schools. For example, in September 1899, *The United Irishman* ran a column titled "Learning Geography," written by Calraide—a pseudonym used by publisher Arthur Griffith (fig. 14.2). It relates the experience of a hypothetical Irish student, Tom, who, eager to learn geography, finds his enthusiasm stifled by three successive National Schools. Griffith describes maps so "antique" and textbooks so Anglocentric, arbitrary, or inaccurate, that by "the end of his course" Tom "had but a confused outline of the world in his head."[4] Griffith's remedy for such confusion: refocus on the local. Instead of a world atlas or Mercator projection, he recommends "each school . . . have a map of its own district . . . on which the houses, roads, fields, and every prominent feature are marked so as to be easily identified by the pupils when the teacher has explained the purpose of a map."[5]

Griffith, for his part, does not explain the purpose of a map, but he does suggest how to *re*-purpose one. He wants schools to obtain the six-inch-to-one-mile Ordnance Survey townland sheets "coloured as near as practicable to nature."[6] Produced by the British military in Ireland starting in the 1830s, the survey maps were intended for purposes of colonial administration, land valuation, and military occupation, but not education. Griffith recommends hanging two survey townland sheets in every local school so students might learn to identify their own surroundings, then proceed to the map of their county, and, eventually, to "the map of Ireland, beyond which, to the majority of Irish scholars, it is not *necessary* to go."[7] This highly localized way of learning geography would not only replace a National School curriculum that had students memorize names and facts of remote locations; the new approach, Griffith argues, could "awaken a far different interest."[8] Such a cryptic and revolutionary assertion seems apropos for the Sinn Féin founder.

Such articles were a fixture of the *United Irishman,* and as a longtime reader of Griffith's paper Joyce would have read many along these lines. Their overt reference to the Ordnance Survey came in response to the long-standing projects of British cartographic revisioning of Ireland: the surveying, mapping, and renaming implemented by army sapper units. The survey fit within the broader, systematic project of the British Empire to leverage geographic knowledge for purposes of conquest and colonization. To those ends, the ostensibly objective science often betrayed politicized strategies and problematic tendencies and

LEARNING GEOGRAPHY.

One of the first things we learn is Geography. The youngster just learning to toddle about is as eager and persevering a student of geography as the Stanleys and Nansens, who, with much the same objects as the youngster, go poking around into every out-of-the-way corner of the world. Prohibitions and warnings are alike thrown away on the young as on the older explorer, who will learn only from personal experience. Failures don't daunt him. Let him drop on his head down half a flight of stairs, and when his plasters are beginning to curl at the edges you will find him proudly squatted on the landing above the scene of his last defeat, possibly daring the stairs to throw him again. As he grows up the spirit of exploration grows with him. Long before he knows what history or literature is, when still his whole learning consists of the prayers he knows by rote, and the fairy and ghost stories he has heard, he makes out for himself a notion of the world from his own very limited views of it, and perhaps fills up the blank beyond out of the kingdoms of fairy-

Wash, and the mouth of the Thames, which he got off to the air of "Let Erin Remember." He was thoroughly disgusted on reading that the Thames was twenty miles longer than his old friend the Shannon, and he stoutly maintained that "the Shannon was measured in Irish miles, and besides that, they dug the Thames out purposely to make it big, while he heard that the Government were always trying to drain away the Shannon and other Irish rivers so as they wouldn't be as long as the English ones." But coming of age to earn result fees, Tom was promoted to a higher school, where he was crammed at high pressure, from a big atlas and geography, first with a string of definitions, and then with a set of countries for each year, which he was to disgorge, as required at the examinations. And at the end of his course he had but a confused outline of the world in his head, and knew as much about India or Africa as about Ireland.

How many thousands there are who have gone through some such course, and arrived at much the same result. In fact, this is the best the present system of teaching can offer, no attempt being made to teach local

Figure 14.2. "Learning Geography," *The United Irishman,* 2 September 1899. From *The United Irishman,* 1899. Used under Creative Commons Attribution-Noncommercial-No Derivative Works 3.0 Unported License.

Figure 14.3. The former St. Joseph's National School, Dorset Street. Photograph by Gareth Collins. Published by John Hunt, *The Joyce Project* at joyceproject.com. http://m.joyceproject.com/notes/040002nationalschool.html. Used under Creative Commons Attribution-Noncommercial-No Derivative Works 3.0 Unported License.

became what David Livingstone calls a "contested enterprise."[9] Griffith takes this as a given in his argument to revise Ireland's school geography curriculum; he does not aim to resolve the controversy so much as harness it to an advanced-nationalist agenda.

Joyce portrays two of his prominent fictional characters with regard to this fraught context and liberating potential for school geography. Readers first meet Bloom in the "Calypso" episode and follow him to the butcher shop. He passes St. Joseph's National School (fig. 14.3) and hears the morning lesson through an open window: "Inishturk. Inishark. Inishboffin. At their joggerfry. Mine. Slieve Bloom" (*U* 58). The moment raises essential questions of curricular content and cultural identity. Reciting names of Co. Mayo and Galway islands, the students forge a connection from urban, anglicized Dublin to the rural western Gaeltacht. Their toponymic recitation leads Bloom to recall his own personalized geography lesson—the mountains that share his name ("Mine. Slieve Bloom").

The fact that Slieve Bloom is geologically Ireland's oldest mountain range connotes a sense of rootedness and belonging that is ultimately at odds with the citizen's bigoted attempt in "Cyclops" to marginalize Bloom along the intersecting lines of race, religion, culture, and nationality.[10] Such individuated geographic self-definition simultaneously counters imperial dispossession and nativist assumptions about Irish identity. The moment demonstrates the reality of geography as a controversial and politicized discourse, while at the same time underscoring its potential for individual liberation and empowerment, particularly in education.[11] If Joyce echoes Griffith's avowed interest in a revised school geography curriculum, he also suggests a more expansive purpose and inclusive project.

This possibility is foreshadowed in the schooldays segment of chapter 1 of *A Portrait of the Artist as a Young Man*. Stephen Dedalus, much like Griffith's fictional student Tom, grows frustrated at a geography assignment based on distant locations: "He opened the geography book to study the lesson; but he could not learn the names of places in America. Still they were all different places that had those different names."[12] Stephen's dissatisfaction prompts the famous act of writing wherein he places himself within an expanding concentric array that extends from the geographic to the extraterrestrial:

Stephen Dedalus
Class of Elements
Clongowes Wood College
Sallins
County Kildare
Ireland

Europe
The World
The Universe. (*P* 27)

Marjorie Howes notes the absence of the United Kingdom from this list, a meaningful omission that sets Ireland in a European frame.[13] Given *Portrait*'s first publication in December 1916, the parallel assertions of selfhood and nationhood suggest an echo of the Proclamation of the Republic made eight months earlier on Dublin's Sackville Street.

Fading empire and emerging nation are only part of the picture. Significantly, this moment comes not through indirect narration but direct replication of Stephen's writing where else but on the flyleaf of an unnamed geography book, presumably in response to what is or is not contained within. In effect, Stephen revises the Irish geography curriculum through an intentional and individuating exercise in spatial perspective and self-awareness that he deems more appropriate to his own identity and relevant to his unfolding experience than either the information in his textbook or the random and remote facts he learns from Dante Riordan, distant and arbitrary arcana such as "where the Mozambique Channel was and what was the longest river in America and what was the name of the highest mountain in the moon" (*P* 22–23). As it does for Bloom and the Dorset Street students, geography becomes for Stephen a means of resituating oneself—in his case amid not just local and national, but global, continental, and cosmological scales, moving well above and beyond the narrow parameters imposed by imperial schoolbooks.[14]

Walkabouts

Chapter 2 of *Portrait* initiates a more deliberate and localized geographic awareness with the narrator's account of walking as social and recreational activity, at least for the Dedalus men:

> On Sundays Stephen with his father and his granduncle took their constitutional. The old man was a nimble walker in spite of his corns and often ten or twelve miles of the road were covered. The little village of Stillorgan was the parting of the ways. Either they went to the left towards the Dublin mountains or along the Goatstown road and thence into Dundrum, coming home by Sandyford. (*P* 64)

Retracing their steps out and back from Blackrock today, one finds suburban sprawl of tract housing, business parks, and industrial estates has overtaken the once-quiet country lanes. Stillorgan is now a dense cluster of shops and homes that is difficult to distinguish from Sandyford. Dundrum town centre is a major traffic intersection overlaid by a suspension bridge for the LUAS tram system; walking is hardly possible there, at least not in the rural, recreational sense *Portrait* describes. The eastern and western boundaries are practically impassable for walkers, since the N31 and M50 motorways bisect the route. What Stephen, his father, and Uncle Charles explored so freely is now virtually inaccessible on foot. Any expectation of re-creating their pastoral experience of south Co. Dublin seems bound for ironic disappointment. Still, comparing the novel's description to today's reality offers important lessons in the city's outward expansion over the past century, which all but swallowed up formerly distinct villages and quaint crossroads. With a longer temporal view of spatial change and urbanization, we might read many moments of *Portrait* as contributing to a *bildung* of the city that runs parallel to that of the artist.

Another function of walking emerges later in chapter 2 when the Dedalus family moves from suburban Blackrock to Dublin, and Stephen begins his solo explorations of the "gloomy foggy city" (*P* 67). Orienting himself to his new surroundings, he gradually moves from short, tentative loops to extended perambulation: "In the beginning he contented himself with circling timidly round the neighboring square or, at most, going half way down one of the side streets: but when he had made a skeleton map of the city in his mind, he followed boldly one of its central lines until he reached the customhouse" (*P* 67–68). Like any new arrival or emigre, tourist or transplant, Stephen's mental map and real movements slowly extend in direct proportion to his comfort level with the new surroundings.

Looking back, I realize my own first forays across Dublin in some sense replicated Stephen's gradualist strategy. Moreover, I used some of the same points of reference. Given the semi-autobiographical basis of the book, the "neighboring square" can be identified as Mountjoy, located nearly equidistant between the Joyces' first Dublin addresses at Fitzgibbon and Hardwicke Streets in 1893–94.[15] When, not much older than Stephen, I first visited the city in 1989 and 1991, I lived in youth hostels and basement bedsits a few blocks from Mountjoy Square. As I ranged further out each day into unfamiliar surrounding neighborhoods, down long blocks of indistinguishable rowhouses, the green space of that "neighboring square" was confirmation I had found my way back. Like Stephen, I soon grew bold enough to follow those "central lines" of Gardiner or O'Connell Streets to the Custom House.

Remember (if you are old enough or imagine if you are not), this was well over a decade before there would be a cellphone with GPS in every pocket. When learning their way around a new city in the twenty-first century, it is a rare thing for anyone to make "a skeleton map" of it in their mind. Most university students today have never known a world without digital maps or navigation apps. All the more reason for them to try to see how Stephen learns to see the "new and complex sensation" (*P* 67) of Dublin. I encourage my students to try Stephen's approach of walking and memorizing new spaces when visiting any new city or town.[16] We begin by defining "skeleton map," usually agreeing on a kind of rough mind's-eye sketch; over time and successive observations, the observer adds more detail to their mind-map. Discussion turns to what happens when we challenge ourselves to learn new places without the assistance of Google Earth or Apple maps. Some students who follow through with the digital-free walkabout report being pleasantly surprised at the additional attention and focus they give their surroundings; they notice more and different things when apps are turned off and senses tune in to more of their urban environment. Even if they momentarily get sidetracked or lose their bearings, they discover a place on their own terms. Like Dedalus in Dublin, or his mythic namesake in the labyrinth, they learn to make their own unmediated way. I do not expect anyone to surrender their smartphone for good but hope this simple thought experiment might bring readers closer to this character's acclimation to urban space via walking and memory.

Walking in *Portrait* incorporates something else that will interest anyone exploring connections between literature and urban geography: its ability to fasten reading onto reality. Stephen does this by projecting notable moments from his favorite books onto the Dublin cityscape. An ardent fan of *The Count of Monte Cristo*, during those weekend walks with Uncle Charles, Stephen associates a house on the mountain road beyond Blackrock with "another Mercedes," an allusion to the former fiancée of Dumas's protagonist (*P* 65). By the final chapter of *Portrait*, he extends this imaginative habit to "[h]is morning walk across the city" from Lower Drumcondra to UCD, connecting authors, genres, and themes of his personal canon to specific details of the surroundings:

> [T]he rainladen trees of the avenue evoked in him, as always, memories of the girls and women in the plays of Gerhart Hauptmann. . . . and he foreknew that as he passed the sloblands of Fairview he would think of the cloistral silverveined prose of Newman, that as he walked along the North Strand Road, glancing idly at the windows of the provision shops, he would recall the dark humour of Guido Cavalcanti and smile, that as he went by Baird's stonecutting works in Talbot Place the spirit of Ibsen would blow through him like a keen wind, a spirit of wayward boyish beauty, and that passing a grimy marinedealer's shop beyond the Liffey he would repeat the song by Ben Jonson which begins: *I was not wearier where I lay*. (P 154–55)

Stephen's pedestrian perspective aligns Dublin's mundane economies and parochial locations with a cosmopolitan array of writers and texts. Bernard Benstock notes how the moment has Stephen connect the "drab reality of Dublin" with English and European literary heritage.[17] The non-Dublin literary connections seem counterintuitive, if not deliberately contrarian, during the highwater mark of the Irish Literary Revival. Yet, if they have scant connection with Dublin, the five writers have everything to do with the young artist's emerging tastes and aesthetic interests. Moreover, the associations suggest a capacity to re-imagine the city out of its subaltern status and into a pan-European literary context; doing so, they imply an ambition that *Portrait* itself reach offshore audiences. In its decolonizing project, Stephen's list concludes rather counterintuitively with Ben Jonson, among the most quintessentially English of poets, and also known for doing his fair share of walking through England and Scotland. Still, to admire Jonson by associating his work with a "grimy marinedealer's shop" near the Liffey instead of the lush gardens of Penshurst or other Elizabethan manor houses enshrined in his verse effects a creative reclaiming of English poetry and revisioning of literary geography that is all in a morning's walk.

So much of Dublin for young Stephen has been altered or effaced by the past century that retracing his steps to look for the Dublin of *Portrait* or other Joyce texts today might seem a futile task. In many ways—social, economic, demographic, architectural—it is a completely different city. That might have already been the case by the time the book was published in December 1916. Just seven months earlier, the Easter Rising had leveled most of Dublin city centre and some outlying neighborhoods. A century of steady, if less dramatic, changes followed: tenement clearances in the 1920s, urban renewal and public housing projects during the 1960s and 1970s, and a heavy influx of global capital spearheaded intensive redevelopment projects from Temple Bar to the Docklands starting from the 1990s. Despite so much erasure and transformation, exploring twenty-first-century Dublin can still enrich and expand our reading of Joyce.

"The carriage rattled swiftly along Blessington street. Over the stones" (*U* 97)

During my first months in Dublin, I would begin to know *Ulysses* beyond those slippery sidewalk plaques. People had variously described the book to me as challenging, nonsensical, delightful, and unreadable, and at many moments in my first reading I didn't disagree with those descriptions. What kept me persevering with *Ulysses* was finding in it a sort of primer to my new surroundings.

Its narrative complexity and stylistic chaos contained the street names, landmarks, accents and attitudes that I, a Dublin newcomer, encountered directly each day beyond my door.

I came to understand how my walk home from the city centre overlapped with the two prominent northbound routes of the novel: the morning funeral procession and the late-night return to 7 Eccles St. I came up O'Connell Street to Rutland Square and Cavendish Row, on up to Dorset, Blessington, and Berkeley Streets to the North Circular Road, like the carriage bringing Bloom, Simon Dedalus, and friends to Paddy Dignam's funeral at Glasnevin. When I read "Ithaca," I discovered my occasional jaywalking shortcut through the traffic circus at Hardwicke Place turned out to be the same efficient radius Bloom and Stephen trace in their walk from the cabman's shelter. Navigating the city by the book and reading the book by the city increased my confidence and enjoyment for both. Not unlike the boys of St. Joseph's National School, I was "at my joggerfry."

"Wash quit and don't be dabbling" (*Finnegans Wake* 196)

My initial experience of the city also included some moments of remarkable continuity—past to present, fiction to reality—in which Joyce's Dublin seemed to persist not only in urban spaces but the routines and personalities of the city some eight decades on. While still getting my bearings in *Ulysses*, I had come across anthologized excerpts of *Finnegans Wake*, and, starting with the Anna Livia Plurabelle chapter, had begun to grasp some of the mythical and musical elements. I especially adored the dialogue of the Liffey washerwomen: "Well you know or don't you kennet or haven't I told you every telling has a taling and that's the he and the she of it. Look, look, the dusk is growing! My branches lofty are taking root. . . . In kingdome gone or power to come or gloria be to them farther? Allalivial, allaluvial!"[18]

My Phibsboro flat was without a washer/dryer, so I went weekly to the laundromat down the block. The women who ran it worked tirelessly and talked incessantly to one another. The radio always played songs from their day: Tom Jones's "It's Not Unusual" and Dusty Springfield's "Son of a Preacher Man." The *Dublin by Lamplight* laundry this was not. Generally cheerful and easygoing, the managers could quickly turn on anyone who stepped out of line. They could assume the tough presence of barroom bouncers to eject a drunk or sternly shoo away neighborhood kids who pawed the machines for loose change. They were also quick to pounce on anyone who was slow to move their clothes from washer to dryer. There were loads of customers and commercial wash, and not a moment to waste.

One day, returning well past my dryer cycle, I feared the worst. I thought I could squeeze in a grocery trip to Quinnsworth (a block away) and return before the buzzer. I could already feel the managers' hostile glares and expected I would soon be collecting my clothes from the four corners of the room, if not the sidewalk of the North Circular Road. I would likely be banned for life, or at least the rest of the summer. I saw myself, at the same time the next week, a creature driven and derided by laundry, my eyes burning with anguish and anger and looking for a new place to wash and dry.

Fortunately, it didn't go that way. Instead, I came back to find my clothes neatly folded and stacked on the table. "It's no worry, love. They're all set right here for youse. We just needed the dryer. We knew ye must have got held up." Expecting to be persona non grata, I now felt trusted, even protected, by these two Northside matriarchs. In that moment, it seemed the whole city opened right up to me. To this day, whenever I return to *Finnegans Wake*, it is their lilt and laughter that echoes for me in the beautiful and timeless banter of the washerwomen. I half expect to return to Phibsboro one day to find them metamorphosed to tree and stone.

"a day's miching" (*Dubliners* 11)

During the 2012 International Joyce Foundation symposium in Dublin, I decided to skip the afternoon sessions and, like the two adventurers in "An Encounter," make a trek to the Pigeon House. Since the boys never actually get there, the Pigeon House is one of the gaps or ellipses in *Dubliners* that always made me curious. Did it have meaning as an unreached destination in the story? It also seemed like an absent presence in the contemporary cityscape, since no Dubliner I asked ever seemed to know the first thing about it. I found only a few brief references to it in history books: a former naval fort, like the Martello Towers, built to defend Dublin Bay against Napoleonic invasion. Before that it had been the site of a hotel and tavern serving travelers departing or arriving at the port of Dublin. It did not house pigeons—at least not by design—but took its name from Joseph Pidgeon, the late eighteenth-century entrepreneur and architect of the hotel scheme. (Somewhere along the way the D was forgotten, as was the man behind the name.)

At the time "An Encounter" takes place, the mid-1890s, according to James's brother Stanislaus, the Pigeon House was at the eastern edge of the city's working waterfront. Today it is in a less-accessible area of the south Dublin docks, a narrow strip of scrap yards and freight facilities. Not sure I would be able or permitted to navigate those postindustrial spaces, I opted to approach from the

Figure 14.4. Poolbeg Stacks seen from Sandymount Strand. Photography by Dan Heap, Poolbeg Generating Station stacks, Dublin 2014. https://en.wikipedia.org/wiki/Peter_Pearson_%28painter,_born_1955%29#/media/File:Poolbeg_Generating_Station_stacks,_Dublin_2014_(12889481224).jpg. Image unaltered from original.

south, working my way up from the Sandymount side. It was a breezy day, and a few kite surfers raced across the water as I made my way around swerve of shore and bend of bay to Irishtown Nature Park. I followed the trail through the sand dunes at Shellybanks Beach and onto the tarmac of Pigeon House Road. I recalled the narrator's motivating credo from "An Encounter": "Real adventures do not happen to people who remain at home; they must be sought abroad."[19]

The iconic red-and-white stripes of the twin Poolbeg Stacks dominated the skyline ahead, signifying I was nearing my goal (fig. 14.4). The road came to a T, and I found myself facing a tall gray security fence that partially contained an unruly hedgerow; a solid granite building was visible beyond the fence. I had reached my destination. The Pigeon House stands as an intriguing eighteenth-century relic between its two modern industrial neighbors, a wastewater treatment plant and Poolbeg power station (fig. 14.5). As I approached, a security guard emerged from the station gatehouse to ask what I was doing. "Sightseeing," I replied, and he seemed puzzled but satisfied enough with the answer. He told me few people came out this way, and even fewer tourists. He usually dealt with young kids from Ringsend or Irishtown skipping school to sneak around the old building. (I knew of at least two who never made it that far.) So that explained why the building was locked and its ground-floor windows boarded up. Unfortunately, I wouldn't be going inside.

In the years after my visit, the Pigeon House was opened up and renovated into a performance space, the Pigeon House Lab. It hosted the Dublin Theatre Festival and a 2017 ANU production of Louise Lowe's *The Sin Eaters*, a play that raised powerful questions about sexuality, gender, and violence in Ireland, topics familiar to readers of "An Encounter." More specifically, *The Sin Eaters* confronted the issue of reproductive rights, just seven months prior to the national referendum on abortion. The issue was underscored by the location, as the production amounted to what one reviewer called a "site-specific immersive theater" by leveraging the enduring ignominy of this location "where long ago the B&I [ferry] slipped out by the North Wall, leaving and returning with women seeking abortions . . . nothing has changed as newer, larger boats carrying even more women, undertake the very same journey today."[20]

With the COVID-19 pandemic, the Pigeon House was shut once more, presumably going as silent as on the day I visited, when the only sounds came from a few cars on their way to the Great South Wall, some seagulls circling above, and, sure enough, a flock of pigeons congregating on the roofline. When the security guard returned to his perch, I circled the building to snap photos from different angles. I ate the last of the biscuits and chocolate in my pack and, taking a last look at the Pigeon House, wondered what distance, if any, separates abiding interest from recurring folly. Then I retraced my steps to Sandymount Strand.

Looking for Joyce's Dublin in the twenty-first-century city can enrich even a mundane errand or cross-town commute. It can also reveal how Joyce's writing lives on in our own lived experience. His fiction invites connection to Dublin in its past or knowing the city in an eternally unfolding present tense—one subject to change with successive generations of readers. Recall how *Ulysses* defines the city not by cartography or physical infrastructure, but by a dynamic, collective continuity: "Cityful passing away, other cityful coming, passing away too: other coming on, passing on. Houses, lines of houses, streets, miles of pavements, piledup bricks, stones. Changing hands" (*U* 164). Those fortunate enough to follow the threads from Joyce's fiction to today's Dublin might be doing so in an era even more rapidly and aggressively transformational than Joyce's own. Reading Joyce's "joggerfry" reveals illuminating connections and inspires innovative interpretations. And if these should lead to occasional inconclusive meanings or solipsistic quests . . . well, those might be among the most Joycean experiences of all.

Figure 14.5. The Pigeon House. Photograph by Gareth Collins. Published by John Hunt, *The Joyce Project* at joyceproject.com. http://m.joyceproject.com/notes/030004pigeonhouse.html. Used under Creative Commons Attribution-Noncommercial-No Derivative Works 3.0 Unported License.

Dublin City as Text

In *Teaching Literature in the Real World,* Patrick Collier argues for a realigned pedagogy "that activates consciousness and metacognition" in undergraduate literature classrooms.[21] Instead of content-cramming studies of the traditional canon, Collier outlines a method-based approach to emphasize skills of advanced reading comprehension and advanced literacy. Such a recommended course correction for literary studies articulates what is already underway in English programs at many, if not most, non-elite institutions, and is more in line with the needs, values, and expectations of most twenty-first century students.

In recent years, the new pedagogical approach of City as Text™ has emphasized similar habits of mind with its dual focus on critical reading of literature and urban landscapes. City as Text not only teaches literature in the real world but also teaches students to read the real world like literature. As Bernice Braid explains, City as Text can teach students how to "regard the world as a book to be read and to see their journey through it as a mapper's task of charting the personal paths they take to uncover and discover what is out there."[22] In this regard, it has potential to inspire intellectual insight and personal growth that extend well past the college or university years.

Its multidisciplinary emphasis draws from literary studies, cultural studies, and related disciplines whose methodologies and critical inquiry center on textual close reading, analysis, and interpretation. Its pairing of active observation with rigorous reading directly aligns City as Text with the discipline that provides its cognitive centerpiece and eponymous metaphor. Whether interpreting classic stories or contemporary streets, decoding landscape paintings or landscaped gardens, engaged readers and critical observers employ similar strategies. They formulate questions, observe details, and gather evidence; note patterns and detect anomalies in textual forms; contextualize, historicize, and synthesize facts; classify and categorize details; generate interpretations and synthesize arguments from their findings.

In a course unit on Boston film, Julie Levinson offers a template for connecting a text-based humanities course to the City-as-Text pedagogy.[23] The assignment sequence sends her Babson College students out to explore city neighborhoods, then juxtapose their field observations with the neighborhoods' cinematic representations. Levinson values the "cognitive mapping" of the City-as-Text approach for how it "compels students to be active participants in and shapers of the course rather than passive recipients of pre-existing knowledge" and for how it "decenters and relocates the site of instruction; here, the urban space is a wall-less classroom in which students experience a dynamic interaction between their knowledge, observations, and interactions."[24]

Applying the City-as-Text approach to Joyce's "joggerfry" and Dublin's geography offers a similar opportunity for critical close reading of places represented in the text and the contemporary city as text. Like Levinson's film-class assignment, which encourages "[s]tudents to consider how the experience of a place compares to the perspectives fostered by cultural products," the juxtaposition challenges students to be discerning observers of a new environment as well as the cultural or artistic depictions it inspires.[25] While filming locations for movies made in Boston circa 2000–2010 may not have changed as much as the Dublin places Joyce referenced a century ago, students' actual and intellectual legwork is equivalent and offers potentially similar challenges and benefits. A comparative critique of one's observations and perceptions of a place with depictions of that place in the "cultural products" that are Joyce's fiction provides a point of access and relatability to texts whose historical or cultural remoteness might otherwise make them daunting or inaccessible to many students.

Below is a sample City-as-Text assignment sequence for a course unit on Joyce and Dublin. It could be adapted to a Joyce seminar, Irish Studies class, or general-education literature or humanities course in a semester-long study abroad program or shorter travel course. This group project is intended to help students new to Dublin familiarize themselves with the city while they engage in interpretive study of Joyce's fiction in its social, historical, and geographic contexts. Combining textual interpretation, spatial analysis, and ethnographic observation, the project builds from the premise that examining our own first-hand experiences of a place alongside cultural representations of it can lead to a more in-depth awareness and critical scrutiny of both perceived and imagined geographies. These assignments can be taught as a complete sequence of walkabout/presentation/essay, or as pairings of walkabout/presentation or walkabout/essay assignments. The essay can be written individually or by a team.

A Joyce and City-as-Text Assignment Sequence

Overview

Your team will engage in parallel studies of Dublin locations and their representations in James Joyce's fiction. You will explore, observe, analyze, and argue about the material and social realities of Dublin today relative to its portrayal by Joyce a century ago. The project consists of three assignments: walkabout, presentation, and essay.

Preparation

Site selection: Your team (2 to 5 students, depending on class size) selects a geographic location or landmark in or around Dublin that has significance in a Joyce text from the course reading list. It should be a place whose proper name appears in the text. It could be a street, neighborhood, monument, or building. It can be part of the natural environment (Sandymount Strand), built environment (Eccles Street), or a combination of the two (Phoenix Park). It might be a place characters go (the National Library in *Ulysses*) or one they imagine or mention but do not reach (the Pigeon House in "An Encounter"). If not overtly referenced in the text, it should somehow be identifiable through its associated details or context.

Some potential City-as-Text locations in Joyce's major works:

Dubliners: North Richmond Street, Hardwicke Street, Chapelizod, Ushers Island, Phoenix Park, Gresham Hotel.
A Portrait: Bray, Blackrock, Clongowes, Belvedere, Stephen's Green, Findlater's Church, North Great George's Street, Mountjoy Square.
Ulysses: Sandymount Strand, Westland Row, Glasnevin Cemetery, Eccles Street. Sandycove, National Library, National Museum, Grafton Street, Davy Byrnes Pub, Arbour Hill.
Finnegans Wake: Chapelizod, River Liffey, Howth Head, Phoenix Park.

Textual Analysis and Prewriting: Reread the passage(s) in which your location is referenced and described. What denotations are included? What connotations are conveyed? What is the role or function of the place in the narrative? How do characters use, engage with, or talk about the place? Are there conflicting views of it or a shared meaning? What overall impression emerges around it? Beyond a literal setting, does it have symbolic significance? Does it relate in any way to Dublin or Irish history?

Draft a page of writing to convey your group's overall interpretation of Joyce's portrayal of the place.

Walkabout

Next, compare Joyce's representation to your experience of the place today. Spend a day (midmorning to late afternoon) in your location and its surrounding neighborhood. Walk around and pick a comfortable spot from which to observe. Public spaces like parks and bus stops are ideal locations, as are restaurants, pubs, and shops. Be mindful of the presence you project. Obey any posted rules or policies and obtain permission from business or property owners if you are spending time in commercial or private space.

Joyce scholar Claire Culleton notes the "frenzied activity going on above and beneath the surface" of *Dubliners* to make the case that we should pay as much regard to motion and movement in the book as to paralysis and stasis.[26] Any Dublin walkabout with Joyce in mind is as much about the experience of moving around in the neighborhood as making observations from a fixed location. Therefore, make a point of circulating through the streets to consider the different perspective that movement provides.

Have each teammate contribute to your geographic inventory of the area. Write notes, compile lists, sketch images, and make maps. Take photos or videos on your cell phone. (If you include people outside your group, be sure to ask their permission to be filmed or photographed.) Aim to record your first impressions and emerging sense of the place throughout your visit. How does your route compare with descriptions of the place in Joyce's writing or the movements of Joyce's characters? Is it possible to retrace their steps? Why or why not? What details remain the same after all this time? What has changed?

Interactions/Interviews: Strike up conversations with residents, business owners, or passersby to learn who lives, works, or visits there. Let them know you are university students working on a project and looking for impressions or opinions of the area. Some questions to ask: How long have you lived here? Where do you work? What are the major occupations and businesses in the area? How do people here spend their leisure or free time? What are the oldest, newest, or most remarkable places to visit in the neighborhood?

Presentation

After your walkabout, join your team in a debriefing session to compile notes and observations. Look for distinct connections, themes, or patterns. Tie your field observations back to your reading of Joyce's text. How do your observations and conclusions about the place compare to its portrayal in Joyce's fiction? Present your findings in a fifteen-minute talk to the class. Assign equal time to each teammate and aim for a structure that builds around your main points or conclusions. Emphasize the comparative nature of the project by anchoring your presentation in slides or handouts that incorporate key conclusions and specific evidence from both literary analysis and city walkabout.

Essay

Combine your textual analysis, field observations, and additional secondary-source research in a 1200+ word essay that synthesizes social, historical, geographic, and literary (that is, Joycean) significance of the location. This thesis-driven, evidence-based essay should interpret the Joycean text and Dublin City-as-Text via multiple disciplinary frames.

Notes

1 The Martello Tower at Sandycove was reopened as the Joyce Tower and Museum. The house at 15 Usher's Island, home to Joyce's great-aunts and his setting for "The Dead," was a filming location for John Huston's 1987 cinematic adaptation of the story. At the time of this writing, it sits vacant.
2 James Joyce, *Ulysses* (New York: Vintage International, 1990), 76. Quotations from *Ulysses* are from this edition, hereafter cited parenthetically in the text.
3 See Daniel Gunn, "Beware of Imitations: Advertisement as Reflexive Commentary in *Ulysses*"; Jennifer Wicke, "Modernity Must Advertise: Aura, Desire, and Decolonization in Joyce"; and Garry Leonard, *Advertising and Commodity Culture in Joyce*.
4 Calraide, "Learning Geography," *United Irishman*, September 2, 1899, p. 2.
5 Calraide, "Learning Geography," 2.
6 Calraide, "Learning Geography," 2.
7 Calraide, "Learning Geography," 2.
8 Calraide, "Learning Geography," 2.
9 David Livingstone, *The Geographical Tradition: Episodes in the History of a Contested Enterprise* (London: Wiley-Blackwell, 1993).
10 "Mine. Slieve Bloom," a silent thought of Bloom's inner monologue, anticipates his vocalized affirmation of Irish identity and courageous counter in "Cyclops" to the citizen's anti-Semitic, blood-and-soil nationalism: "Ireland. I was born here. Ireland" (*U* 331).

11. It follows a direct reference to Griffith amid signifiers of Irish politics, media, and urban space: "What Arthur Griffith said about the headpiece over the *Freeman* leader: a homerule sun rising up in the northwest from the laneway behind the bank of Ireland" (*U* 57).
12. James Joyce, *A Portrait of the Artist as a Young Man,* ed. R. B. Kershner (New York: Bedford/St. Martin's, 1993), 26. Hereafter cited parenthetically in the text.
13. See Marjorie Howes, "'Goodbye Ireland, I'm Going to Gort': Geography, Scale, and Narrating the Nation," in *Semicolonial Joyce,* ed. Derek Attridge and Marjorie Howes, 58–77 (Cambridge: Cambridge University Press, 2000).
14. Two textbooks are named in *Portrait,* Richmal Mangnall's *Questions* and Samuel Goodrich's *Peter Parley's Tales,* implying Anglo-American cultural hegemony over Irish education. See Greg Winston, "Stephen's Schoolbooks: The Problem of Geography in A Young Nation," *Etudes Irlandaises* 30, no. 1 (2005): 83–99.
15. Vivien Igoe, *James Joyce's Dublin Houses and Nora Barnacle's Galway* (Dublin: Lilliput Press, 2007), 46–47.
16. Since a visit to Dublin is not always possible, some good alternative resources for learning the Dublin-Joycean cityscape include Ian Gunn and Clive Hart's *James Joyce's Dublin, the Mapping* Dubliners *Project,* and the virtual-reality *Joycestick: The Gamification of* Ulysses.
17. Bernard Benstock, *James Joyce: The Undiscover'd Country* (Dublin: Gill and MacMillan, 1977), 102.
18. James Joyce, *Finnegans Wake* (New York: Penguin, 1967), 213.
19. James Joyce, *Dubliners,* ed. Terence Brown (New York: Penguin, 1992), 12.
20. Chris O'Rourke, "Dublin Theatre Festival 2017: *The Sin Eaters,*" *Arts Review,* September 29, 2017. https://www.theartsreview.com/single-post/2017/09/29/Dublin-Theatre-Festival-2017-The-Sin-Eaters.
21. Patrick Collier, *Teaching Literature in the Real World: A Practical Guide* (London: Bloomsbury Academic, 2021), 24.
22. Bernice Braid, "City as Text," in *Place as Text: Approaches to Active Learning,* ed. Bernice Braid and Ada Long (National Collegiate Honors Council, 2010), 53.
23. Julie Levinson, "City as Text: A Teaching Resource Document" (Brighton: Harvard Business School Publishing, 2016), 11–15.
24. Levinson, "City as Text," 5.
25. Levinson's assignment ultimately leads students to examine "the repercussions of knowing about something primarily through secondary texts or through popular culture." "City as Text," 11.
26. Claire Culleton, "Thin End of the Wedge: How Things Start in *Dubliners,*" in *Rethinking Joyce's "Dubliners,"* ed. Claire Culleton and Ellen Scheible (Cham, Che.: Palgrave Macmillan, 2017), 12.

Bibliography

Benstock, Bernard. *James Joyce: The Undiscover'd Country.* Dublin: Gill and MacMillan, 1977.

Braid, Bernice. "City as Text." In *Place as Text: Approaches to Active Learning,* edited by Bernice Braid and Ada Long, 51–54. National Collegiate Honors Council, 2010.

Calraide. "Learning Geography," *United Irishman,* September 2, 1899.

Collier, Patrick. *Teaching Literature in the Real World: A Practical Guide* (London: Bloomsbury Academic, 2021).

Collins, Gareth. "National Schools." *The Joyce Project: Ulysses/Calypso.* http://m.joyceproject.com/notes/040002nationalschool.html.

Culleton, Claire "Thin End of the Wedge: How Things Start in *Dubliners.*" In *Rethinking Joyce's "Dubliners,"* edited by Claire Culleton and Ellen Scheible, 9–32. Cham, Che.: Palgrave Macmillan, 2017.

Gunn, Daniel. "Beware of Imitations: Advertisement as Reflexive Commentary in *Ulysses.*" *Twentieth Century Literature* 42, no. 4 (Winter 1996): 481–93.

Gunn, Ian, and Clive Hart. *James Joyce's Dublin.* New York: Thames and Hudson, 2004.

Howes, Marjorie. "'Goodbye Ireland, I'm Going to Gort': Geography, Scale, and Narrating the Nation." In *Semicolonial Joyce,* edited by Derek Attridge and Marjorie Howes, 58–77. Cambridge: Cambridge University Press, 2000.

Huston, John, dir. *The Dead.* Vestron, 1987. 1 hr., 23 min.

Igoe, Vivien. *James Joyce's Dublin Houses and Nora Barnacle's Galway* (Dublin: Lilliput, 2007).

Joyce, James. *A Portrait of the Artist as a Young Man.* Edited by R. B. Kershner. New York: Bedford/St. Martin's, 1993.

Joyce, James. *Dubliners.* Edited by Terence Brown. New York: Penguin, 1992.

Joyce, James. *Finnegans Wake.* New York: Penguin, 1967.

Joyce, James. *Ulysses.* New York: Vintage International, 1990.

Joycestick: The Gamification of "Ulysses." Directed by Joseph Nugent. Boston College, 2017.

Leonard, Garry. *Advertising and Commodity Culture in Joyce.* Florida James Joyce Series. Gainesville: University Press of Florida, 1998.

Levinson, Julie. "City as Text: A Teaching Resource Document." Brighton: Harvard Business School Publishing, 2016.

Livingstone, David. *The Geographical Tradition: Episodes in the History of a Contested Enterprise.* London: Wiley-Blackwell, 1993.

Mulliken, Jasmine. *Mapping Dubliners Project.* http://mappingdubliners.org.

O'Rourke, Chris. "Dublin Theatre Festival 2017: The Sin Eaters." *The Arts Review,* September 29, 2017. https://www.theartsreview.com/single-post/2017/09/29/Dublin-Theatre-Festival-2017-The-Sin-Eaters.

"Poolbeg Stacks." Wikimedia Commons. https://commons.wikimedia.org/wiki/File:Poolbeg_Generating_Station_stacks,_Dublin_2014_(12889481224).jpg

"Ulysses Plaque Dublin." Wikimedia Commons. https://commons.wikimedia.org/wiki/File:Ulysses_Plaque_Dublin.JPG.

Wicke, Jennifer. "Modernity Must Advertise: Aura, Desire, and Decolonization in Joyce." *James Joyce Quarterly* 50, no. 2 (Fall 2012–Winter 2013): 203–21.

Winston, Greg. "Stephen's Schoolbooks: The Problem of Geography in A Young Nation," *Etudes Irlandaises* 30, no. 1 (2005): 83–99.

15

Teaching Art Through the Prism of *Ulysses*

Robert Berry

A Simple Disclaimer

Whenever beginning a new course for readers of James Joyce's *Ulysses*, I greet my students with the same disclaimer that seems prudent to use here; I come to the novel as an outsider.

This is to explain that I have never studied Joyce or modernist literature in college or in any other kind of formalized classroom environment. I also hold no degree in teaching nor creative writing that might qualify or commend my understanding of the novel or of its significant role in history. My own background of study is in pictorial arts and art history. I left the university before completing my degree in that area of study and to take up a career as a painter, illustrator, and, eventually, a cartoonist.

I believe it is important to make this known to people from the very beginning. Any credentials I have that might make me seem a worthwhile teacher of this book come from over fifteen years of self-directed research that I have done for the purpose of translating *Ulysses* into a visual form. I feel that my students (and anyone reading this chapter) should have the opportunity to know that I come to the task of teaching the novel from a completely different skill set than most of my colleagues and, I believe, an outsider's perspective on my own goals for teaching. I prefer to think of my role in the classroom as having an opportunity to teach art through the prism of *Ulysses*.

My Own Experiences

Currently I teach the novel in three rather different classroom environments: (1) at the University of Pennsylvania as an undergraduate course in the English department alongside my good friend and colleague Paul Saint-Amour; (2) at the Rosenbach Museum and Library where, during the COVID-19 pandemic,

I created an online course of study; and (3) at the Penn Studio School of Pennsylvania in which most of the students identify themselves as artists or writers. All three of these venues provide me with a completely different cross section of interested students and many opportunities to examine those students' needs. *Ulysses* is famously considered to be a book that opens doors to a wide number of topics. Trying to answer questions from engaged students who come from a variety of backgrounds forces me to go further into my research and my approach to the novel as an artist; in many ways teaching students to read *Ulysses* results in teaching myself how to draw it.

The class that Paul and I teach at UPenn is part of our English department's "Critical/Creative Disciplines," a very small subset of undergraduate courses in which students are encouraged to make something new out of something they have studied. For the first half of the semester the students are immersed in reading and discussing the novel alongside short critical papers from the history of Joyce studies. Then, in the final half of the class, they team up with other class members to create an artwork of some kind that is born from their interaction with the novel as well as their own creative or academic interests. We have had portable museums of the "Proteus" and "Circe" episodes, story-driven video games about the Bloom marriage, apocryphal episodes about Bloom and Stephen's first meeting, experimental soundscapes for each of the many scenes and sections of the novel, fake conspiracy websites related to the role of "The Arranger," tabloid fashion magazines dedicated to the women of *Ulysses*, and many other unique works of art that have pushed the students to go beyond their classroom discussion of the novel and to experiment freely with what they have learned.

For my nonaccredited courses, I have been using an eighteen-week format of synchronous and nonsynchronous teaching. During the first few months of the COVID-19 outbreak here in the United States (February to May of 2020), I wrote and recorded sixty short video lectures on *Ulysses*. They vary in length from five to twenty minutes and can be listened to by students online as a podcast or video. This is supplemented by a live Zoom meeting each week in which students can discuss the themes and mysteries of the novel alongside any troubles they might have encountered while reading it. These live sessions are quite informal and have more of the character of a guided book club reading—a method I much prefer to cold lecturing. Often I invite guests, friends from the Joycean community, and I find that this gives students a much greater ease in enjoying the novel.

But my earliest experiences in trying to understand and communicate some of the novel's many complexities come from my work on ULYSSES *"seen,"* a project I began with a handful of friends in 2008. The goal of that project was to create a digital graphic novel version of *Ulysses* that would serve as a gateway to its annotations, provide online support through an open readers' guide, and one day (we hoped), bring a new audience back into the text itself. We created three chapters of the adaptation and readers' guide exclusively for the premier of Apple's iPad in 2010. While that material is no longer available in the iPad format, I have continued with work on the adaptation and, at the time of this writing, I have storyboarded, drawn, or painted over 1,100 pages of comics that seek to render Joyce's novel into a faithfully visualized form for new and returning readers alike.

I should point out that my work on *ULYSSES "seen"* or any other illustrated Joyce projects are not the subject of this chapter and also not something that I bring into the classroom; my goals as a teacher are quite different from my goals as an artist. When I make decisions about how to depict a scene, those are my decisions, made from careful research, certainly, but also made in respect to my feelings about art in my time and possibilities or restrictions of the media (comics). As any careful and considerate illustrator, actor, or director can tell you, illuminating the text of a story can cause complications for the reader. We are given the job of visualizing the characters and scenes and may, through our own imaginative lens, potentially narrow the imagination of the reader. My Molly Bloom is not, nor should she be, every reader's Molly Bloom. Illustrators make choices that readers may accept or deny, but we still need to make them in accordance with our own vision of the story we are trying to adapt.

Teachers of any novel should, I believe, work in quite the opposite direction; our job is to open up the imagination of our students as they first encounter the novel and aid them through any barriers that the text itself might present. My own art school background has left me quite aware of the danger in showing my own work to students, and so I shy away from it in my classes. The goal of teaching, for me, is set upon having students imagine the scenes and characters in their own way using whatever tools they have toward this purpose.

For this I rely a lot more on the students' interest in writing rather than my own background in illustration. I have a classroom assignment at the end of "Calypso" in which I ask students to come up with clever portmanteaus or adjectives for how they see Mr. Bloom in comparison to Stephen from the previous three episodes. Later, after teaching the "Circe" episode, I ask them to revisit and amend these descriptions. Many times, this leads to the very desirable result of the students projecting their own likes or dislikes with Bloom (and the novel) into these conversations; this simple exercise makes the reading become less static for the students and encourages them to bring their own imagination into the experience. Realizing how much they have learned about the characters' growth helps students to get past the sometimes-difficult veneer of styles in *Ulysses;* they become more engaged with unraveling the novel's mysteries and how close reading can make the experience more enjoyable.

Just Who Is Reading *Ulysses*?

If we are to have any useful conversations about teaching the novel in our own time, then that would certainly require some examination into who is reading it. Who are our students now, and just what interests them about *Ulysses?* After one hundred years of fame (or infamy) as one of English literature's most difficult books, why are people still picking it up in increasing numbers?

When we teach *Ulysses* at the undergraduate level in the university, our classroom is filled with (mostly) young readers, many (but never all) of whom declare English literature as their major or minor field of study. But we also see a good percentage of students from other disciplines who are attracted to the class by the book's reputation for being challenging and complex. Curiosity regarding that reputation, I believe, is a key factor in capturing the interest of younger readers who are (in most cases) experiencing the novel for the first time.

When I teach *Ulysses* outside of the university in nonaccredited courses, I encounter a very different set of students. Many of these, as with the university students, are first-time readers drawn by the book's reputation. But in many cases, these first-time readers, tending to be middle-aged or a bit older, have tried to read the novel before and have either given up or somehow came to believe that they couldn't understand it. Personally, I find these readers will often become some of my most engaged students; they have paid money to have someone help them solve a book of puzzles that they couldn't quite manage to put down or ignore.

Some smaller percentage of students in the online courses are frequent readers of the novel: "Joyceheads," as I like to call them. I have found over the years that *Ulysses* has a very dedicated and nonacademic fan base and that most of them enjoy any chance they can get to read the book again in an informal setting with new fans. This group of students comes from a wide variety of backgrounds and always lends a fresh flavor to the class. But beginning any discussion of "Who Is Reading *Ulysses* Now?" I believe we should remember that this book, more than any other modernist fiction that I'm immediately aware of, has a quite loyal following of devotees and evangelists. That engagement from the fans continues to be a strong attractor of new readers.

Why Are They Reading?

Many first- or second-time readers see the book as part of their personal "bucket list," a kind of X Game of English literature prompted by its reputation. As teachers and lifelong fans of the novel, it is often too easy for us to see that motivation as disingenuous: that reading *Ulysses* should not simply be an accomplishment or a milestone but should, hopefully, force a change in one's very habits of reading. I've found that people who take one of my courses motivated purely by the challenge of conquering the novel often become my most engaged students; there is a keen desire in them to argue with accepted theories and to wonder about the elaborate house of cards that one hundred years of Joyce studies might have to offer. I believe that kind of mistrust of accepted authority can be a healthy place to start any conversation.

In the very first class meeting, we examine the notes on the word "chrysostomos."[1] I do this because I want the students to become aware of the weight of research and criticism that this book has inspired and endured. There are some students who, from that beginning, form an opinion for themselves on just how important that research and criticism may or may not be to their own enjoyment of the novel. This allows us to talk further about the novel's place in culture as well as our position to it as modern readers. Do we need to know about the status of "écriture féminine" in 1922 in order to enjoy the Molly monologue? Some students will say "no" to this at first, only to find themselves wanting to connect to those theories more on a return reading. This willingness on the part of my students to "challenge the book back" brings important conversations into the classroom that often inform my own ideas about the novel and how to continue teaching it. Almost without exception those students who come to *Ulysses* with some kind of axe to grind (and make it through the course) come away with an interest in all of the research, speculations, biographical information, and genitive evidence that Joyce studies offer to so many of us. Those discussions and arguments are a great part of the experience, and a challenging book is, after all, only as interesting as the conversation it prompts in us.

If there are readers who are drawn to this book because of its challenges, there are also a number of them who come to it through their heritage. Joyce and his family had a complex relationship with Ireland, of course, but that hasn't dimmed the importance of *Ulysses* among the Irish diaspora. It is well regarded not only as "one of the great works of English literature" but, and perhaps more importantly, also as a great work of Irish fiction. I've had many students over the years who have taken my course because of their own "Irishness." I've heard stories of parents or grandparents who would quote the book and how, by reading it for the first time, sons and daughters would feel closer to family members whom they had lost. I've sat in Irish pubs in different parts of the world as readers would raise their glass and say, "I was blue mouldy for want of that pint. God I could hear it hit the pit of my stomach with a click."[2] So in examining the motivations of new readers we should never forget that this book, for good and for bad, is deeply associated with many readers' own Irish heritage and sense of community.

The "Irishness" of *Ulysses* brings up another aspect of the book's appeal for today's reader: it is a very good teaching tool in the examination of postcolonial fiction. There are many authors who can speak more clearly to that point than I, but I have noticed a great interest among foreign students that I have had over the years, particularly those from countries that were formerly part of the British Empire, who choose the novel not simply because of its challenges to the reader but because of its position in history. I try to include this thread of conversation in our discussion of many of the novel's episodes. Unlike the worlds of Charles Dickens or Virginia Woolf, Joyce's world is that of an oppressed people seeking to maintain their unique culture and language in the face of colonization by a foreign power. If the study of collapsing colonialism can tell us anything about the subtle power dynamics of the current world, then *Ulysses* does so with its frank portrayal of a variety of characters who are all caught up in "the Irish Question."

What Reading Might Tell Them

Beyond the reasons that may draw a new audience to *Ulysses*, there is an equally long and troubling list of reasons why many of today's readers may be averse to the challenge. While there are so many ways in which it is a groundbreaking novel, *Ulysses* is also very much a novel of its time; there are a number of very important features of the narrative that are now anachronistic, and many themes, attitudes, and situations that are now old-fashioned at best and may indeed be considered culturally insulting. *Ulysses* is very much a book filled with white men talking, drinking, and trying to figure out the world through their own perspectives and desires. On the surface *Ulysses* does not seem to be a book that concerns itself with the inclusion of other voices and insights.

Or does it?

Some teachers and Joyce fans will make a case that the episodes "Nausicaä" and "Penelope" are the author's genuine attempt to understand the cultural imprint of literature, popular magazines, fashion, and psychology on the psyche of young girls and women at the time. Certainly, Gerty and Molly have asserted their importance in understanding the roles and small freedoms of women in the early part of the twentieth century. Women and women's rights are in no way lacking from the history of how we have talked about this book in the past.

There are some who might say that *Ulysses* is very much a book about navigating a modern marriage. Students can learn a lot about loss and grief from the Blooms' story as well as a lot about patience and acceptance. Faced with troubles at home and a series of microaggressions from the neighbors who surround him, Bloom becomes a model for pacificism in a world that stands on the brink of war (and is written in a time when war is coming again). Otherwise uncomfortable conversations of fidelity, loyalty, open sexuality, acceptance, and revenge can be found among my students through their study of this book. Some will embrace those conversations and others will not; I find that to be just another example of the novel's continuing power to challenge its readers.

But teaching *Ulysses* now rather than when I first began studying it nearly two decades ago, I'm drawn more and more to the mystery of Leopold Bloom: Is he a Jew or isn't he? Joyce plays very freely with the answer to this, and I point that out repeatedly to new students. He is and he isn't. It is situational and something Bloom himself both claims and denies. It brings us not only to the question of "what does it mean to be Jewish?" but to the much broader discussion of how we define ourselves when confronted with how others may see us. Who knew that a book written over one hundred years ago could present us with thoughtful conversations about the identity issues that are so important to our world today?

But *Ulysses* is a book that is always teaching us something new. For all of my classes, students are required to purchase the Gifford and Seidman *"Ulysses" Annotated*, which I feel is essential for going down the rabbit hole of mysteries that the novel presents us with.[3] We discuss *Ulysses* very openly as an encyclopedic novel filled with a very purposeful command that its readers continually go deeper. I warn them that by reading *Ulysses* they will learn more about the Catholic Church and her heresiarchs, Irish tram lines to Dublin's neighborhoods, Dante, *Don Giovanni*, Shakespeare, Celtic mysticism, women's undergarments, the nature of consubstantiality, the speed of bodies falling, the angle of the sun over Sackville Street on a summer afternoon, the Freemasons, the Invincibles, "*the Man who Broke the Bank at Monte Carlo*," Aristotle, Socrates, Moses, Averroes, Moses Maimonides, the Orange Lodges, the Ballast Ball, the principle of parallax, foot-and-mouth disease in cattle, and the cycles of human birth than they ever would have expected. Learning to read *Ulysses* carefully is a lesson in applied research; the allusions are very specific and, if you do the work, the puzzles pay off marvelously.

What Reading *Ulysses* Might Tell Them About Themselves

Not every reader enjoys doing this kind of work, and I'm very quick to point that out to friends and students who are new to the book. Not everyone who enjoys reading does so out of challenge or a thirst for research. Not everyone looking for a good story wants to read seven hundred pages of annotations or spend hours in a classroom trying to explain it. It is quite possible to love reading and absolutely hate reading the work of James Joyce. Joyce was said to be looking for "that ideal reader suffering from an ideal insomnia"[4] and, though I definitely fall into that description myself, I don't for one minute believe that *Ulysses* is a book for everyone. Not everyone stays with it, and not everyone should expect themselves to.

My job, in both the accredited and nonaccredited classes, is to encourage my students to find ways into the novel and to coach them along to the task of thinking about it in relation to their own lives. I prefer to do this in group conversations that allow students to speak about any frustrations they may be having. It is not always easy to get students to feel comfortable with this kind of sharing, but the classroom environment is all the better when it occurs. The advantage of the classroom conversations is that they allow us to have a shared experience of being challenged. There is so much material to teach in any episode of this novel, but I feel that some of our best conversations come when students are unafraid of asking questions. Lectures can only anticipate familiar questions. To really open up a new readership for this book our first responsibility should be to look for new questions. When students wish to move beyond our conversations and the scope of my own lectures, I have many options to offer them. There are now a great number of open-source books and websites they can be directed to that cover particularly intricate areas of Joyce study. *Ulysses* has, as I've said before, a very engaged fandom, and that has produced a lot of opportunities for new readers to find their way in—both good and bad ways perhaps, but the doors for study are more open now than they have ever been. I believe that the most important part of my job as a teacher is in letting students speak to one another about the difficulties they may share in the reading—to let them know that not enjoying *Ulysses* is by no means a failure and not, by any means, a measure of their intelligence.

To my mind, this is the greatest obstacle for us as teachers of *Ulysses:* the prevailing idea that the successful reading of this novel somehow qualifies a person's intelligence. I can think of no more damaging force on the impact of art in a culture than to have it relegated to serving as a hallmark of taste, intelligence, or society.

What Reading *Ulysses* Might Tell Us About Ourselves

From the very start of all my courses, I nudge my students along with the idea that Joyce was likely very much smarter than they are and, once faced with that knowledge, they should just get over it. We read this book together, I tell them, considering it to be a great work in the history of literature and a singular work of genius. We seek out the mysteries of its method, the ornate and idiosyncratic elements of its structure, and the lyrical beauty of its language for our own enjoyment and for the conversations it can promote among us. We do this because that is what we expect from any serious study of a work of art: that it should challenge us in unique ways that will teach us more about ourselves. Why is it that so many take the challenges of this book not as a pleasure, as they might some other work of art, but as a question of their own intelligence?

If we are standing together looking at a still-life painting by Paul Cezanne we shouldn't be asking ourselves, "I wonder if I draw better than he does?" That is a question only for art students and, I can say from personal experience, the only useful answer is "why should that matter?" Cezanne should have us talking together about so many other things, not the least of which is the relative unimportance of drawing itself.

In my forty years as a working studio artist, I've learned that exploring and challenging my own method is the constant difficulty and (dubious) triumph of my art. If, through the examination and conversations regarding this one book, I can impart that to students then, well, that is the pleasure I get from teaching it.

Adapting Our Methods of Teaching

In our course of study at UPenn, Paul and I try to get our students to work past the challenges and puzzles in *Ulysses* to see some of the structures and methods Joyce uses. We try to move rapidly through the explanation of styles (which is so important for understanding the later episodes) and get at the technique exhibited by the choice of those styles. And this examination of Joyce's method pays off for the students in their group projects; they form very focused, and unique, working methods for themselves and learn the difficulties and triumphs of seeing their own chosen methods applied to a creative project.

As grateful as I am for the opportunity to work with the students at UPenn, my approach to teaching the nonaccredited classes has changed quite a bit over the past three or four years. *Ulysses* courses at the Rosenbach Museum, prior to the COVID-19 pandemic, were in person and met for ninety-minute sessions held monthly over a span of ten months. These informal sessions, taught by myself and many other Philadelphia-based Joyceans, were intended to engage new and returning readers of the novel and build a supportive community for better understanding a complex novel. But that format, as you might imagine, was not nearly as immersive as one would like; spanning just ten meetings meant we would sometimes try to cover three episodes of *Ulysses* in ninety minutes. Many students had deeper questions than the course plan would allow.

I believed at the time (as I do now) that a teacher should never underestimate the engagement that students will show when the classroom environment encourages them to ask deeper questions. Students in nonaccredited courses should be given as much opportunity to dig into the material as they might find in a university program. In this way we begin to "democratize *Ulysses*" and expose it to new readers as a significant and vital work of art rather than a subject for purely academic study. I knew that many students at the Rosenbach were deeply interested in more than our old class format could provide. The trick was in finding a way to meet their interest.

The development of a blended model for synchronous and asynchronous learning is, of course, not something new. But I don't think any of us realized just how quickly the world would embrace it after the COVID-19 pandemic. Once the lockdown forced the Rosenbach to build an online program, I prepared a series of sixty short lectures for release over Google Classroom as video, audio, or text files. These lectures, averaging about three lectures to each episode of the novel and lasting no longer than twenty minutes, were set into three major categories: (1) "What to Watch Out For," which served as a kind of simple synopsis that indicates some of the important details within each episode; (2) "Little Lectures," where I could spend more focused time on topics like verisimilitude, consubstantiality, autobiography, and many other important elements of Joyce's method; and (3) "Big Ideas," which dealt directly with explanations of major themes like paternity, "the Arranger," Irish history, parallax, montage, and consubstantiality (again). These are accompanied by a selection of PDFs and links to outside reading as well as a short quiz for each episode intended to show students some of the subtle details that return later in the novel. Google Classroom also has a very user-friendly discussion thread in which I and my students can place links to related material or ask questions of one another.

We also changed the duration of nonaccredited classes. For the past three years I've been running eighteen-week courses (set between Joyce's birthday and Bloomsday) exclusively online. Students are able to view the lectures on their own time, and we then get together over Zoom for ninety minutes each week to talk through our reading of the novel. During those calls I'm available to answer questions they have about the book or my lectures, but I warn them that this live session is intended for them to engage with one another and bring their own feelings into the conversation. We often drill down into the text itself by doing short readings that make the students more comfortable with the beauty and cadence of Joyce's writing as spoken word.

In many ways the amount of material offered in these nonaccredited classes is even greater than what the students at UPenn are expected to read (though their reading time is shorter and includes mandatory additional reading, the writing of term papers, and the development of final projects). I am constantly amazed to find how engaged the nonaccredited students are, how far they are willing to take the study of this novel, and the conversations that come from our time together.

One last thing worth mentioning on this topic: These online classes have given me the opportunity to work with students from all over the world and from many different age groups, cultural backgrounds, and points of interest—all intersecting in the reading of *Ulysses*. Google Classroom and YouTube (where the class recordings are stored) provide very decent analytics that describe who is viewing the material and the amount of time they spend doing so. In a group of twenty online students I'm happy to see fifteen or so stay with me for the whole eighteen weeks. It's still *Ulysses* after all, and not everyone makes it to the other side. But those fifteen, even if they don't make all the Zoom calls, spend time on all the lectures and watch all the recorded sessions. Like any online class, there are many who prefer to keep their cameras off and really don't speak up much unless called upon. I found this difficult to understand at first: Why would anyone want to know more about this book but not actively talk about it? But many do. As teachers we have to accept that students, particularly in the online environment that comes directly into their homes, have different ways of engaging now and it's our responsibility to reach them on their own ground. The old models for measuring class participation seem to be changing.

Staying Fresh

I began this piece by stating that it is my goal to teach art through the prism of *Ulysses*. I won't say that I planned that from the very start, of course, but instead that it came from recognizing my own goals as a teacher. Last year I had the opportunity to teach the novel at a small online school here in Philadelphia, the Penn Studio School. Still a very new institution, which formed itself during the first year of the COVID-19 pandemic, the Penn Studio School became a place for artists and instructors to work with students during the lockdown. There are many fine painters and craftspeople there from the Philadelphia area, and I was honored to be the first person asked to teach a course about a book.

But it is an art school, and I was aware that would mean a unique shift in who my students would be. We closed enrollment at thirty students, and, as expected, almost all of them identified themselves as artists or writers of some kind. They were largely younger than my Rosenbach students, and many of them had professional careers that they managed alongside their interest in art. There was more online marketing for the course at Penn Studio School, and therefore we had students from a wider area outside of Philadelphia; many from the United States, but some from Europe and Asia and even as far away as Australia. I knew that I would have to make some changes in my usual method to keep them engaged for the coming eighteen weeks.

Undoubtedly a lesson learned from Joyce, I've grown to accept the idea that constraint is a catalyst to creative growth. I always set fresh conditions for myself as a cartoonist with every new episode of ULYSSES "seen" and have tried to maintain that manner of thinking in any illustration project I've taken on. It seemed appropriate to apply it again to my teaching.

While my online recorded lectures would remain the same, I decided to add a new wrinkle to our weekly meetings. Each week I would find a different artist or work of art to discuss that I felt might coincide with the episode of *Ulysses* we were to discuss. I put two further conditions on this method: (1) I would not spend more than twenty minutes talking about the art or artist; and (2) I would only prepare it a few hours ahead of time.

This was not, by any means, an art history class. Taking more than twenty minutes to introduce an artist or their position within art history would take us too far off topic. Likewise, by waiting until the last few hours before selecting an artist I found myself thinking only in terms of how their work would fuel our discussion. The choice of artist had to be made in service of what I thought the class needed to think about next. Think about encountering *Ulysses* as we might if it were a central painting in a museum collection. The other paintings that might be chosen to surround it should offer context.

These kinds of comparisons allowed me to go a bit deeper into examining *Ulysses* as a singular work of art than I ever have before. I hoped to be reaching out to this new set of students on a ground where I felt they might be more comfortable; I won't deny that this was part of my plan. But I believe these lectures were more successful because I was able to easily draw from my own experiences and bring my students into deeper conversations. My feelings on art, like those of any artist, are unique. By bringing them into the study of *Ulysses*, I was able to step more easily into that outsider role that I feel is a big part of what I bring to teaching. It allowed me to share my views on art while at the same time showing how my work with *Ulysses* has shaped those views.

Because the editors have kindly asked me to share more of that experience here, I will list some of those artists with their corresponding episodes and topic of discussion. It feels right to end this with some thoughts on the approach that I've found worked best for me.

1) "Telemachus"—Piet Mondrian's *Composition II in Red, Blue, and Yellow,* 1930;. Mondrian is an excellent place to begin. What we know of the work is what we've seen and heard as it has become popularized. What must it have been like to discover this painting without history's window? Would we recognize in it the qualities of arrangement or design that make it an important work? How much does the reputation of a work of art alter the experience of it?

2) "Nestor"—Théodore Géricault's *Raft of the Medusa,* 1819. A history lesson, but what remains of its cultural significance after the event has been forgotten? Géricault questioned survivors and even had a life-size replica built in his studio to employ a unique journalistic integrity. There are political themes within the work lost to modern viewers. How might some of the artist's intent be subsumed by the response of history's audience?

3) "Proteus"—Joseph Cornell's *Untitled ("Fountain of Youth"),* circa 1959. How is the working of consciousness depicted? The hand of the artist becomes less visible (and less important) than how the eye and mind arrange things. How is this like the isolation of the poet Stephen and of Joyce's unique way of presenting that to readers?

4) "Calypso"—Édouard Manet's *Boating,* 1874. A brief history of the changing marketplace for art that ushered impressionism into fashion. The bourgeois tastes of the times, the development of avenues in Paris, and tram lines to her suburbs bring about a sharp turn in subject matter. As we switch to the domestic life of Mr. Bloom can we also see how drastically Joyce alters the expectations of the reader? Are these domestic subjects still important, still heroic?

5) "Lotus Eaters"—Gustav Bauernfeind's *Market at Jaffa,* 1877. Orientalism was still a very popular bourgeois fashion in Bloom's time and is mentioned quite often in the novel. Bauernfeind's work, like tourist postcards of Colonialism, presents us with opportunities to discuss this fashion alongside its prevailing racism. How does Joyce seem to feel about it at the time of his writing?

6) "Hades"—Lucian Freud's *Benefits Supervisor Sleeping,* 1995. As we start to move out of the interior monologue method, I always feel a discussion must be had about realism. That label means entirely different things in different art disciplines; painters and authors and filmmakers all have very specific and unique ideas of the techniques of realism, and they vary greatly from what most people think of when they hear the word applied. Freud's work is particularly useful here to discuss the idea of verisimilitude, which Joyce uses so well in this episode. But is that realism?

7) "Aeolus"—Marcel Duchamp's, *L.H.O.O.Q.*, 1919. The comparison between the Irish and Jewish peoples is a major theme and given its most direct presentation in this episode. But the speech that is used for that presentation is not Joyce's own writing. It seems important to begin a conversation about "appropriation" in art.

8) "Lestrygonians"—Gustav Klimt's *Judith,* 1901. Klimt's work presents us with an excellent opportunity to discuss Sensualism in relation to this episode. Most students are quite surprised by how radical Klimt's work was and how, like Joyce, it was engaged in the overthrow of Victorian prudery.

9) "Scylla and Charybdis"—Æ's *Bathers,* 1918. It would seem unfair to use anyone other than George William Russell for discussion of this episode. I chose one that was from the same period of *Ulysses* but lacks the overt mysticism of better-known work. While a great amount of class time is better spent on "The Hamlet Theory," it seems important to also talk to students about the old guard literati who Stephen is trying to impress.

10) "Wandering Rocks"—Louise Nevelson's *Lunar Landscape,* 1959–1960. Most of my lectures on this episode discuss it like the opening of a watch face to reveal the inner mechanisms. We see how gears revolve, touch, and continue on their path. Nevelson's puzzle-like sculptures, often made from found objects that have been disguised so that we no longer consider their old purposes, seem a good presentation of that idea. It is here that I like to discuss the differences between stories and vignettes. When we see so many of the forces at play in an episode like "Rocks," are we so engaged by sorting them into distinct units that we lose sight of the whole mechanism?

11) "Sirens"—Richard Hamilton's *Bronze by Gold* (year unknown). Hamilton's series of drawings and etchings are wonderful, and it's a shame he never completed enough for an illustrated version of the novel. I mostly bring this one into class so we have a chance to discuss depiction: Can any one style of work be useful in depicting scenes from a novel that is increasingly based on changing styles?

12) "Cyclops"—John Sloan's *McSorley's Bar,* 1912. Sloan's work in what was called "the Ashcan School" of New York painters is a favorite of mine. Their goal was to capture some of the less glamorous elements of urban life and heroicize the common man. His painting from McSorley's gives students a glimpse into the scene at Barney Keirnan's but also gives us a chance to discuss the social order of men drinking.

13) "Nausicaä"—Willem De Kooning's *Woman III,* 1953. Is the depiction of Gerty a commentary on young girls? Is the depiction itself sexist? What are the responsibilities of an artist when it comes to the politics of depiction?

14) "Oxen of the Sun"—Robert Rauschenberg's *Canyon,* 1959. The "combine paintings" (and many of the screen prints) of Rauschenberg present us with the idea of a narrative that seems somehow lost underneath its style of presentation. They seem to have a connective thread, some idea running through them, that constantly is at risk of being overwhelmed by the playfulness of their depiction. I like to begin talking with students about that here before showing just how detailed and rigorous Joyce's method was for the "Oxen" episode. Joyce brings his playfulness only into the mimicry of style. Everything here is in service to method and process. That kind of constraint, I feel, makes it much easier to explain the rushing, wild style of the final pages and sets us up for discussions of *Finnegans Wake.*

15) "Circe"—Salvador Dalí's *Soft Construction with Boiled Beans (Premonition of Civil War),* 1936. Few painters are as useful to our conversations about *Ulysses* as Dalí; if someone has done good work with comparing the two of them, please let me know. In many ways the painter is a dark mirror to the author, a willful charlatan who knew no separation between art and living. I often explain to students that Joyce often made his marriage a laboratory for his art and often vice versa. Dalí made no such distinctions. *Soft Construction* has an interesting history and shows us some evidence of Dalí fudging its completion date to show himself as being more prophetic. But it very clearly operates in the same kind of dreamspace as the "Circe" episode and has all of the hyperbolic sexuality that both artists are regarded for. There is so much to talk about with this episode that, for me, the biggest danger of using Dalí comes from talking too much about Dalí.

16) "Eumaeus"—Cindy Sherman's *Untitled Film Still #23,* 1977–1980. One could use any or all of the work of Cindy Sherman to engage students with a deeper understanding of "Eumaeus." The big idea that new readers of the novel must wrestle with in this episode is disguise and identity. When I first thought about using artists as talking points, Sherman is the first one that came to mind. The compelling argument for using anything from the Film Still Series is how often people are fooled into believing they have seen the movies these photos come from, how engaged they are with trying to remember and sort a false memory. Much of the chatter about "Eumaeus" for new readers of *Ulysses* seems to involve how this may be Joyce writing in the style of Bloom. I find that a good conversation around Sherman's work and the subtle play between identity and the artist quickly restores Bloom's mystery and Joyce's genius.

17) "Ithaca"—René Magritte's *The Treachery of Images,* 1929. The best that I have found to approach conversations about the style of "Ithaca" is to expose students to the idea of the counterfactual. A catechism has its well-known history of passing on preserved and sustained ideas through recitation. Much of our

modern education has (thankfully!) moved beyond that method, but I believe it to be so embedded in our understanding of Joyce as a "recovering Catholic" that new readers don't recognize the irony of its use here. *The Treachery of Images,* the very famous one with the pipe, is a textbook exercise in counterfactuality. The image is a very realistic painting of a pipe. Written in an equally controlled cursive hand below the image is the clear statement, "this is not a pipe." Are the roles of the two interlocutors separate identities in "Ithaca"? Are the painter and the commentator different roles in Magritte's creation "Treachery"? If not, then who is the hand that assembles these differing perspectives?

18) "Penelope"—Henry Moore's *Large Reclining Figure,* 1984. Any talk we have to modern readers about "Penelope" involves the idea of "écriture féminine" just as it must. It also engages us with discussions about depiction (again!) and the male viewpoint on "who women are." Moore's sculptures give us the idea of an "earth mother," which so many of our conversations revolve around. It is, yes, a very male-centered view, but it is surprisingly well in line with the ideas of a kind of rolling, turning, grounded-but-not-pointed arrangement écriture féminine was experimenting with in Joyce's time. Is it a fair depiction of a woman's interior thinking? I do not know. How do we place discussions of nonbinary identity alongside this kind of thinking? If "Penelope" is "the indispensable countersign to Bloom's passport to eternity,"[5] what does that tell us of the relationship between partners of any sexual orientation today?

Notes

1   James Joyce, *Ulysses,* ed. Hans Walter Gabler (New York: Vintage, 1986), 3.
2   Joyce, *Ulysses,* 245.
3   Don Gifford and Robert J. Seidman, *"Ulysses" Annotated: Notes for James Joyce's "Ulysses"* (Berkeley: University of California Press, 1988).
4   James Joyce, *Finnegans Wake* (New York: Penguin, 1999), 120.
5   James Joyce, *Letters of James Joyce,* vol. 1, ed. Stuart Gilbert (New York: Viking, 1957), 160.

16

Teaching *Dubliners* in Prison

Michael Patrick Gillespie

It may seem to demonstrate a keen grasp of the obvious to assert that teaching in a prison involves a student population and an academic environment very different from what one would find in a typical college classroom. In fact, the truth is that it does, and it doesn't, for, as Algernon Moncrieff says in *The Importance of Being Earnest*, "the truth is rarely pure and never simple." While the environmental disparity between traditional instruction and prison teaching can be profound—physically, emotionally, and pedagogically—striking similarities in terms of students' interests, enthusiasms, and abilities obtain as well.

Over the past year, I have learned that teaching in the penal system requires that one first come to grips with what is different and what is the same about classroom instruction in prison. To convey the pedagogical experience of teaching James Joyce's *Dubliners* to incarcerated students, I feel the need first to clarify the context in which that instruction took place. I will go into some detail because my experience in prison gave me a profound sense of how little I knew or understood.

Before entering the Everglades Correctional Institution (hereafter referenced as ECI), located on the edge of the Everglades fifteen miles west of downtown Miami, I had never been inside a correctional facility. Up to that point, my conception of prison life had been shaped primarily by cinematic representations, and I quickly found that they gave me no more sense of what life in detention was like than did movies about the war in Vietnam convey what combat experience was like. I am sure on entering a penal institution that many feel the same sort of confusion that Dorothy expressed when she first arrived in Oz—"Toto, I've a feeling we're not in Kansas anymore."

Let me extend the analog to state that like Oz, absence and presence equally clarify prison life. Obvious physical institutional markers set off areas where inmates are incarcerated—locked doors, secured rooms, and barbed wire fences. Other mundane aspects of domestic life that we have come to take for granted are markedly different in any penal institution. There is no air-conditioning in any of the living areas. Any reader who sees that as only a minor inconvenience has never been in South Florida in September where temperatures are always in the nineties and the humidity is rarely below 75 percent. For a clearer sense of it, imagine what trying to sleep in a sauna would be like. In contrast, overnight temperatures in January can drop into the '50s and '60s. For Northerners that would seem balmy winter weather. However, I assure you that for locals it is indeed a hardship. There are no provisions for heating in the dormitory areas, and when the cold raises the need for extra blankets, inmates are given the same aluminum sheets that are used by EMT personnel at the scenes of accidents.

Physical discomfort, however, is by no means as significant as the psychological hardships experienced in prison. By that I do not mean anything like the melodramatic brutality sensationalized in prison films. Rather, the emotional constraints placed on inmates, though much more understated, are far more enduring.

At ECI I was struck by the subtle oppressiveness of its psychological environment of incarceration, strikingly different from what most of us experience in our daily lives. The prison world embodies the pointless existence and the inability to exert control over one's environment. One sees this condition summed up in Estragon's opening lines in Samuel Beckett's play *Waiting for Godot*: "Nothing to be done." While inmates do not exist in an environment as physically desolate as the setting of Beckett's play, even when given jobs as cooks, cleaners, librarians, or in other prison tasks, inmates do little more than play out the same kind of existence endured by Beckett's characters.

The incarcerated live frozen in time. Prison life is a paradigmatic postmodern world. Rules, not morality, govern their behavior. They follow a daily schedule organized around the twin concepts of order and routine. There is no grand plan beyond achieving physical comfort, and no specific aspirations beyond attaining resignation. It is a world of appetites and materiality. As in any other postmodern world, metaphysics is an alien conception. One comes to understand *Waiting for Godot* by discerning the complexity inherent in a world characterized by absence. I went through the same process of apprehension as I sought to comprehend life in a prison community. Even there, however, the structure is more complex than it might at first seem.

ECI is designated as an accelerated state prison. That means that its inmate population consists of men who have not had a disciplinary report for five years. (Again, if that seems a fairly easy condition to meet, ask yourself how long you have gone without a spouse, partner, family member, or employer, fairly or unfairly, criticizing your behavior.) While it is still a prison in every sense of the word, the men much prefer serving their sentences at ECI to being in any of the more restrictive institutions, some of them notorious, that stretch across the state. Furthermore, because they know that with any perceived lapse in their adherence to prison rules or routines they could very easily be sent to a place with even harsher conditions, the general atmosphere is one where everyone knows the rules and does not wish to suffer the consequences of any perceived lapse in adhering to them.

Significantly, even with the enhanced access to benefits, like the educational opportunities available at ECI, there are few if any programs provided to the inmates directly by state government. A punitive philosophy undergirds the prison ethos. Like air-conditioning and extra blankets, such programs are seen as luxuries for which the citizens of Florida should not have to pay.

In keeping with this attitude, there is often suspicion of any efforts to bring humanity into the prison. Before anyone can undertake a project to enhance the lives of inmates, one must go through screening by the Department of Corrections, which serves as an often suspicious gatekeeper. The dedicated work of idealistic individuals committed to social justice implemented the opportunities for instruction in which I have been able to participate, and I would be remiss if I continued without first mentioning the broad efforts of the unique organization responsible for doing so much for the students and teachers who have participated in its programs.

Exchange for Change is a private nonprofit organization founded in 2014 by Kathie Klarreich to provide academic instruction to inmates of various penal institutions in Miami-Dade County. Although it is run on a shoestring and, like Blanche DuBois, always depends upon the kindness of strangers, Exchange for Change has had a powerful impact on prison communities in South Florida. It facilitates classes for men, women, and juvenile offenders at three South Florida prisons (Everglades Correctional Institution, Everglades ReEntry, and Homestead Correctional Institution), as well as Miami-Dade County jails, a youth residential center, a work-release center, and a state prison in central Florida. Every semester, Kathie and her staff solicit volunteers to teach a variety of courses—journalism, acting, filmmaking, yoga, and a number of other subjects. (Despite the eclectic nature of the offerings, there is a concerted effort to incorporate some writing component, from journals to analytic assignments, into every class.) Exchange for Change staff coordinate instructional logistics in all these institutions. They arrange for visits by politicians and others. And they generally ensure that all of the faculty keep a positive attitude and remember how fortunate we are to be doing what we do.[1]

While understanding the atmosphere of the prison is important, an account of the students' nature is essential, but necessarily subjective. As I attempt to describe my students, I readily admit that my knowledge of the students in my ECI class is limited. I only see my students for the two hours per week and for several hours at the end of the semester when all of the classes gathered for a graduation celebration featuring poems, raps, storytelling, and pizza (a rare and greatly appreciated treat). All of this provides the same sort of stilted impressions that characterize our views of the students we teach outside the ECI environment.

Nonetheless, a number of demographic details are obvious to even a casual observer. At ECI there are the usual sampling of races, though I do not know the proportionate breakdown. Men at ECI seem to range in ages from their early thirties to their mid-sixties, though any number may have led prematurely aging lives. Some of these men are serving life sentences without parole. Others are there for a fixed number of years. Some allude to homes to which they will return. One noted that he will be deported to Colombia as soon as he has served his term. It is difficult to discern by looking at them why they have been incarcerated, and frankly I never have wanted to know.[2]

Before turning to the classroom experience, however, it would be useful to get a clearer picture of the prison ethos that informs the students' lives. What then is life in prison like for them? At ECI it is beige and blue. A range of one-story buildings (with the hurricane threat constant in South Florida, only the brave and the reckless erect edifices that have more than one floor) with their paint faded into a uniform dreariness cover the landscape. Although there are few palm trees, there are a few flower beds, and the sky is generally Florida blue. Were it not for the twenty-foot fence topped by barbed wire surrounding the facility, it would resemble a small Sunbelt community that has shriveled after a new highway diverted traffic from it.

The inhabitants of the facility, with a few exceptions, are all in blue. The guards, although the name they prefer is prison officers, wear dark blue uniforms. The incarcerated men, for this is a men's prison, wear loose fitting, baby blue, short sleeve pullover shirts and baggy pants of the same color. Civilian staff wear sports coats or casual business attire. Even from a distance, one immediately recognizes and labels the individuals one sees. Clothes, posture, even the pace while walking immediately puts one in a category.

This is particularly true with inmates. When they walk down the asphalt street that serves as the main thoroughfare, they walk on either edge. The center of the road is reserved for non-prisoners. The prison officers whom they encounter are aloof, tense, harried, and underpaid. The students are routinely treated like objects, self-propelled pieces of furniture moved from one place to another and under the complete control of others.

They look like a group of men one might encounter in the stands at a high school football game. Their ages range from early seventies to mid-twenties.

A good number have tattoos. Many are white. More are Black. And there are fewer Hispanics than one usually sees in South Florida. Some are professional people like lawyers. Some have owned businesses. Others were raised in ordinary middle-class homes, while others grew up in extreme poverty. Some lived in cities, and others in rural areas. Almost all are extremely reserved, but at the same time they are most polite. While generally wary, they respond to friendliness. Above all, they are individuals who experience continual confinement and a near total absence of control over their lives.

My own experiences begin with the security checks, a defining element of prison routine. When one arrives on the prison grounds, there are a number of steps to go through before entering the facility. After parking my car, I open the trunk, put in my cell phone, my wallet, and anything I have with me that I will not use during the course of instruction. I approach the building where visitor screening occurs. Standing outside and speaking through a narrow window opening, I give my prison identification number, surrender my driver's license, and move to the inspection area.

It is very much like a TSA screening at an airport. I empty the contents of my pockets into a plastic bin. I take off my belt, coat, and shoes. I walk through a metal detector, and then, with my legs spread and my palms against a glass wall, I am physically searched as is every other non-staff person who wishes to enter the facility. Only after all this is accomplished to the satisfaction of the supervising prison officer, am I granted admission to the facility. This routine is repeated without variation for every visit.

After walking through the intake building, I move toward the library where my class is held. I walk on an asphalt road with parallel yellow lines, each about two feet from each edge of the road. Inmates are only permitted on the edges of the road set off by those lines. They are never allowed to walk in the center of the road.

I am most conspicuous as I cross the open area on my way to class. I have no uniform of any sort, and I am not one of the staff with whom the inmates are already familiar. Prisoners see me with reserved curiosity, though they are always polite and respond often with wariness to my greetings. Most prison officers remain aloof and acknowledge my presence only when unable to avoid doing so.

In the classroom, one encounters students with a range of educational backgrounds—from those who have not finished high school to those with postbaccalaureate degrees. Likewise writing skills vary. However, I found that the students were very open to direction, and even those who lacked a strong educational background were able to understand directions for constructing effective analytical essays. Certainly, in any population one would expect to encounter individuals with learning disabilities. I did have one such student in one of my classes. He proved to be one of the hardest workers, turning in far more assignments than required, and he participated fully in all discussions.

One constant in any of the classes is the high level of student engagement. Lively discussions stood at the center of our examinations of the stories in *Dubliners,* and I was often surprised when I called on someone who seemed to be disconnected from the class discussions by how much he understood and by all that he had to contribute. Although they express it in different ways, always wary of giving away too much, I found that the students are universally gratified to have their opinions valued, as well they should be. The men in my classes, no matter what their IQs or academic backgrounds, are very careful readers who often raise questions about texts that neither I nor previous students with whom I had discussed particular works had considered. They are often anxious to present their views, yet at the same time they show a great deal of respect for others. They not only relish presenting their views they also enjoy being part of an intellectual exchange.

Classes can be and usually are interrupted without warning or apology. Prison officers peremptorily "call out" students as it suits them. When told to leave the classroom, the students move silently and without question into the hallway where formal and informal counts are taken. The prison officers are often curt to a point just short of abusiveness. However, no one considers challenging the treatment. Such temerity would produce only additional unpleasantness. If there is a mistake made in the tally, the counts are repeated until an accurate number is arrived at.

There may or may not be a whiteboard in a classroom, but even if there is, one must bring a marker and something with which to erase the board. The teacher must provide all reading materials for the students. Some do have access to tablets that supposedly can provide electronic versions, but the devices are unreliable as is the software. Wi-Fi support is sporadic and strictly controlled by the prison authorities, and if an inmate is allowed access to send an email there is a charge for the service. Assignments are all handwritten, and students must be clever in finding materials upon which to write. Most of the inconveniences are small, and almost all could easily be remedied. They remain in place out of a lack of institutional concern and perhaps as a reminder to the students, should they need one, of the precarious nature of their privileged position.

I have been offering courses at ECI since the fall of 2021. When I began teaching, I did not know what authors or what form of writing would appeal to my students. I chose to use short stories because I felt we could have a self-contained discussion on one per class. I selected James Baldwin's *Going to Meet the Man* for my first semester's teaching because I thought, mistakenly, that most of my students would be Black and that these stories would have a greater resonance than others. I realize now how simplistic my assumptions were.

Here's an anecdote that underscores what I mean. On the first day of my first class, a course devoted to discussing the short stories of James Baldwin's *Going to Meet the Man,* I spent most of the period talking about how the course was structured, how we read (analyze) everything we encounter, and how experiences, values, assumptions, and background shape all of our judgments. When I finished and asked for questions or comments, one of the students raised his hand and said: "You know, to be perfectly honest, I expected you to be Black." To which I replied, "You know, to be perfectly honest, I'm often mistaken for Denzel Washington" (a remark that would have surprised both Denzel Washington and my Irish grandparents). The exchange got a good laugh, and the questioner turned out to be one of my best students in a class that was excellent across the board.

Moments like that illustrate how teaching at ECI has come to mean a great deal to me, but not because of any impulse toward self-satisfaction. I do not uplift my students. They enhance me. I tell each class at the beginning of every semester that what I am doing I am doing for selfish reasons. It is an exhilarating, affirming, and stimulating experience to have them in class participating as they do, and I hope in the following pages to be able to give you some sense of why this is so.

The class had a voracious curiosity, wide-ranging intellectual interests, and an openness to whatever they encountered although that does not preclude a certain wariness and a low tolerance for insincerity balanced by wry senses of humor. After a successful course on James Baldwin, due entirely to the energy, enthusiasm, and openness of the students, I tried something that I thought would be more exotic. In the spring of 2022, I taught James Joyce's fiction, and those experiences form the subject of this essay. In the fall of 2022, as I write this essay, I am teaching the short stories of Lebanese-Cuban-American writer Ana Menendez, to give students yet another perspective of complex ideas.[3]

As noted above, in many ways ECI students are like those whom one hopes to find in any university in the country. They are highly motivated. They stand open to a range of views—even those that challenge assumptions that they already hold. They read the material with great care and keep up with the assignments.

I conduct classes in a dialectic fashion, so most of the talking is done by the students guided by questions that I ask relating to the material we are reading. The tone and topic of all questions mirror those I would ask in any college class I might teach, and the discussions rise to the level that one would expect from any college course. Written work varies in quality, but the effort is never in doubt. In reading the assignments, I apply the same standards I would use in any class, and I generally come away with the same range of responses, in terms of intellectual quality, that I would expect in any university setting. In short, while the physical surroundings are severely limited, the engagement of students in the ECI classes matches that which one finds in most institutions of higher learning.

Wherever the classroom may be located, teaching *Dubliners* presented certain challenges relating to the social and cultural context of the stories and the background necessary to provide students with a full understanding of the stories is no different from that needed by my classes at Florida International University (FIU) or for that matter at any other school where *Dubliners* is taught. (I have provided the syllabus we used for the course at the end of my chapter.) The striking difference, however, lies in the resources. My ECI students cannot Google the answers to questions that pop up in class. They cannot turn to Wikipedia to flesh out information on a particular topic. And the reference works in the prison library, when available, are at best limited.

Nonetheless, a number of points need clarification. Dublin at the turn of the last century is a world foreign to us all. The layout of the city is unfamiliar to most readers. The numerous landmarks to which Joyce continually alludes—the Pigeon House, St. Stephen's Green, the River Liffey, and many others—need explanation and often some elaboration.

The lower-middle-class, urban Catholic ethos that most of Joyce's characters inhabit stands as equally baffling to contemporary readers. The near-homogeneous society of Joyce's Dublin does not resonate with the experiences of many. Further, even for those students raised in a city, the rhythm of 1900 Dublin—with horse traffic, noises, and smells literally and metaphorically foreign to them—stands as an experience difficult initially at least to comprehend. Boarding house life requires some glossing as does the practice of political canvassing. While fairs like Araby and gatherings like the Morkans' Christmas party have approximate contemporary analogs that make them easier to grasp, even these events need some glossing.

It can hardly be surprising that the complexities of pre–Vatican II Catholicism, not so much as a theological position but rather as a social conditioner, are as difficult to fathom for those students who come from a Catholic background as for those who do not. Primarily, the sense of discipline and control that Joyce's Dubliners felt is not a feeling that many contemporary readers have experienced, at least in terms of religion. When the narrative tells them that Mrs. Mooney plans her confrontation with Bob Doran in order to make the short twelve at the procathedral, it is necessary to explain not only the obligation Catholics have to attend Mass every Sunday but also the expectations of neighbors for whom the ritual observance had as much social significance as would the outward profession of faith. It is also helpful to explain why St. Mary's Catholic Church is a procathedral and St. Patrick's Church of Ireland is a cathedral. Clarifying these religious-related aspects of ordinary life also elucidates the social significance of Mr. Duffy's adamant atheism in "A Painful Case." Of course, the businessman's retreat to which Tom Kiernan is dragged in "Grace" also needs some explanation, particularly his vehement opposition to the inclusion of candles in the service. And some explanations of the jumbled liturgical references appearing in "The Dead" and elsewhere can enhance the stories' complexities to readers unaware of the embedded irony.

Needless to say, a background discussion of Irish history becomes essential to clarify issues that arise in many of the stories as would be the case for students in any American university. While a synopsis of the controversy surrounding Charles Stewart Parnell will come to mind as necessary background to "Ivy Day in the Committee Room," others though perhaps less direct in their evocation of the Irish ethos nonetheless need glossing. The details of the Irish Literary Revival necessarily add to a student's understanding of the complex crosscurrents at work in "A Mother." And, that knowledge in addition to a clear sense of the rising nationalism and the forces behind it provide important insights into the significance in "The Dead" of Gabriel Conroy's unwillingness to travel to the west of Ireland and of Molly Ivors's playful but barbed designation of him as a "West Briton."

As sometimes occurs in university classes, the foundational abilities students brought to the class covered a broad spectrum, and the scope of our discussions had to be adjusted accordingly. This delicate process is familiar to any teacher. Too much adjustment will make the material seem simplistic to the bright students; too little will make portions of the discussion incomprehensible to others.

More significantly, ECI students lack any meaningful control of their time. That meant I could not be sure that all were able to complete the reading assignments for any particular class day. Consequently, I began most of my classes at ECI with a brief summary of the story under discussion as a way of refreshing the memory of any student who had a less than full recollection of the narrative and needed me to fill in some of the gaps regarding cultural, social, historical, and geographic details shaping the particular story. This exercise also provided an implicit invitation, more often than not accepted, to the students to raise questions about the context of the story that was not entirely clear to them. To my embarrassment, I found that as my students singled out one of these cultural details, perfectly obvious to anyone reading the story, I found that they were issues that even in my repeated readings I had overlooked.

Both the glossing of details and the acknowledgment of blind spots proved to be useful ways to start the conversation. As is the case in all of my courses at FIU, my classes at ECI are structured on a dialectic method that points to ambiguous moments within each reading and that asks students to consider their engagement with these moments and to develop a sense of the features in the narrative that led them to their various opinions. From the first day of class onward, I made it clear that I would call on each member of the class at least once every time we meet. (So as not to embarrass someone, I let the class know that individuals could tell me privately if they are unprepared to participate. Students did not come forward in large numbers, but it helped a few avoid awkward public moments.)

After beginning with a general introduction that I hoped would clarify any contextual ambiguities, I would propose a question, broadly related to central issues in the story under consideration, that I wanted to use as a springboard for the class exchanges. I let them think about it, making notes for four to five minutes, and then began the discussion. This helps avoid the danger of the suffocating silence that can occur when a class begins with absolutely no response to the first question and thereby more than likely makes any subsequent discussion a strained and painful process. Once students have begun to talk, it becomes easy to move to more specific topics and to raise issues likely to produce a range of contradictory responses, all of which moves the discussion forward.

Students at ECI were very comfortable with this format. I would move the discussion forward periodically by introducing new questions and calling on those who had not already volunteered opinions. In this fashion, most of the class time was occupied by the students' responses to my questions and to issues that other members of the class had raised during the discussion. It became quickly evident that even the seemingly most withdrawn of the ECI students had an informed opinion, and none seemed reluctant to express it. (In fact, as in all my other classes, the challenge was to hold the most eager students at bay until I had a chance to call on each of the other class members.)

Two key factors drove this high level of participation. As noted above, ECI students are very careful readers, and so they nearly always had a very full awareness of what has gone on in the narratives. A clichéd explanation for this condition would simply fall back on the idea that because they seemingly have a great deal of time on their hands, they would of course spend it going over the material. To a certain degree that may be true, but that assumption overlooks a much more important point. In prison, observation and assessment is an important skill to develop in a foreign environment with protocols for behavior that need to be intuited rather than learned from a manual. Acquiring this skill to navigate social situations well prepares ECI students for literary analysis.

Further, the dialectic process provided students with a welcome counter to the dominant tone of their exchanges with the prison staff. The ethos of almost any penal institution, by design or by default, enforces a sense of the valuelessness of the incarcerated individuals. Their ideas, opinions, and aspirations are of no concern to the prison staff, and acknowledging them would only complicate interactions, particularly because all interactions between staff and inmates rest on the enforcement of discipline. Effacing the possibility of alternative interpretations simplifies the enforcement of the prison's everyday routine.

Conversely, class discussions did not simply demonstrate the students' abilities to hold opinions. The weekly interchanges created a sense of community and an awareness of a wide range of attitudes. (I was quite amazed, for example, when a student from my Baldwin class told me about a conversation on sexuality in "The Outing" that he and another student had while waiting in line for lunch.) Student interactions provided immediate reinforcement of an individual's abilities, underscoring the sense his ideas had value. This in turn increased their eagerness to participate, but it had another effect, equally important, as well. Seeing their own views validated encouraged in them a tolerance for the ideas of others, even when the student clearly did not agree with those positions. Further, students seemed to have a heightened sensitivity to the power of their words. Topics of race, gender, political affiliations—all potential powder kegs in a traditional university classroom setting—can be engaged vigorously but with respect for alternative attitudes.

While evidence of the students' levels of skill at engaging in-class discussions could come quickly and easily, evaluating written work proved to be more challenging. A stark difference from their writing and the digitally generated, spell-checked essays submitted by my FIU students emerged immediately. ECI students wrote their essays on sheets of blank paper with ballpoint pens. Few had dictionaries and there were no programs for checking spelling, no autofill, no suggestions for improving grammar, or choices for synonyms to alter the rhythm of their prose.

Assessing the context of the essays presented another challenge. While a number of my students were extremely bright, in any class at ECI, one is confronted with a range of educational backgrounds from those who dropped out of high school to those with advanced degrees. I asked students to write on just under half of the work we have read. (They were allowed to choose which.) I offered a prompt for each story to get some started, but I also allowed any student to take any opinion he had and to write a paper on it. Of course, they do not have the material resources available to support composition work. There are no Writing Centers in the prison, and pre-submission conferences with the instructor are impossible because of the way their lives are regimented.

Nonetheless, students manage to produce insightful work in two to three pages. Some admittedly do not rise above the level of plot summary. However—spoiler alert—that occurs in an inordinate number of essays submitted in traditional college classes. Others take issues and respond to them in an intelligent and insightful fashion. A few write stunningly good analyses. In short, the responses come very close to replicating what I see in my FIU classes and what I suspect most instructors see in theirs.

A refreshing difference does obtain regarding ECI student responses to my evaluations of the writings and those I found, in my own experience and that of colleagues, characteristic of university students. The men in my ECI class were interested in all of the comments. They read them carefully. They took criticism of their writing and analytic abilities to heart, and they were delighted when I pointed out significant improvement. All this came from a simple desire to develop intellectually. The exercises they undertook were not aimed at earning a particular grade but at demonstrating their abilities and at finding ways to improve them.

I began this essay by noting what a privilege it is to teach students at ECI. I do not mean this to denigrate my FIU students or indeed students whom I have taught at other schools. However, in closing I want to underscore the unique traits that contribute to the rewarding experience that teaching at ECI has been. Students are gratified at being taken seriously—indeed at being treated like human beings—and the intensity of that gratitude makes me both humbled and full of joy. One of the things that students often repeat is that none wish to spend the rest of their life being judged by the worst thing they have ever done. While that sentiment in no way absolves any from the responsibility for their behavior, it does underscore the complexity of their lives.

The time I spent reading *Dubliners* with them enhanced my understanding of Joyce's work, but it did more. It gave concrete proof of the power of art. It showed how creativity touches all of us. And it gave me a full sense of the imaginative impact of works to which we have devoted our lives.

James Joyce's *Dubliners*

Spring Semester 2022, ECI, Mondays 3:00–5:00 p.m.
Michael Patrick Gillespie

<u>Course Description</u>: We will read and discuss the short stories written by the Irish author James Joyce and published in the collection entitled *Dubliners*. The approach to instruction will be based on a form of literary analysis that emphasizes individual interpretations supported by evidence from the text. By

design, the dialectic approach eschews the lecture format. Instead, it focuses on questions by the instructor answered through extended discussion by the students.

<u>Course Requirements</u>: Read the assigned material before each class. Be prepared to answer questions that arise in the discussion. Each student will be called upon at least once to contribute to the class discussion. To receive Continuing Education Credit from FIU, students must write at least six essays, two to three pages long, over the course of the semester.

<u>Paper Structure</u>: The paper is organized around an opinion, not a statement of fact. It focuses on one element in the work under consideration, and it does not try to cover all aspects of the narrative. It presents an argument not a summary. It is developed through a series of examples and logical arguments to show the validity of the opinion. Here is an outline of a generic paper.

- Opening paragraph states the thesis or central idea and explains any terms that need clarification: Goldilocks is an evil creature. By evil I mean someone who takes pleasure in harming others simply for the sake of harming them.
- Paragraph two presents evidence to support the thesis: Goldilocks willfully disobeys her parents by going into the woods. This causes great suffering for her parents, but she doesn't seem to care.
- Paragraph three continues presenting evidence and showing the logic of what it proves: She invades the home of the three bears with no concern for their privacy. This reflects a selfishness that disregards the feelings of others.
- Paragraph four gives a final bit of evidence to establish the validity of the argument: She consumes their food, spoiling what she does not eat, with no thought for the welfare of the three bears.
- Concluding paragraph: Contrary to popular belief Goldilocks is neither a heroine nor a victim. She is a victimizer.

When taken together the elements in this structure outline the reasons for supporting the thesis. A reader like myself can judge the essay sound and valid even if I disagree with the assumption upon which it is founded, Goldilocks as evil.

<u>Course Objectives</u>: Students will learn the format for interpretive argumentation—forming an opinion, finding examples to illustrate it, explaining how the examples support your views. This format will apply both to the discussions and to the papers so that by the end of the course students will have acquired verbal and written skills of argumentation.

Course Schedule:

Week	Reading	Writing Prompt
1.	Introduction	
2.	"The Sisters"	Does the unnamed narrator's opinion of Father Flynn change over the course of the story?
3.	"An Encounter"	What do the boys understand about "the queer old josser"?
4.	"Araby"	Look at the last line. Why is the narrator embarrassed?
5.	"Eveline"	What does Eveline fear?
6.	"Two Gallants"	Are these men predators?
7.	"The Boarding House"	Is Mrs. Doran a sympathetic character?
8.	"A Little Cloud"	Is Little Chandler a failure?
9.	"Counterparts"	Is Harrington a victim of society?
10.	"A Painful Case"	Should I feel sorry for Mr. Duffy?
11.	"A Mother"	Does Mrs. Kearny behave badly?
12.	"Grace"	Are the characters hypocrites for attending the religious service?
13.	"The Dead"	Is Gabriel Conroy a snob?
14.	"The Dead"	Does the story end optimistically or pessimistically?

Notes

1 It would be difficult to overestimate its positive impact on the individuals involved in Exchange for Change programs, but I am afraid doing full justice to its work would sound hyperbolic. I urge you instead to visit the program's website at exchangeforchange.org to see its achievements for yourself.

2 During our Exchange for Change orientation, we were told that information about each of our students was readily available online. We could in short order Google each to find out his crime, his sentence, and other related information. We were also strongly encouraged never to do so. Other teachers have told me that they had and deeply regretted doing so. Several students at different times would address this situation by saying, more or less, please do not judge me by the worst thing I have ever done in my life. Though it sounds perhaps melodramatic, it captures the burden borne by a complex individual who is continually having every aspect of his life, save one, ignored, and that one thing becomes the benchmark by which his character is judged.

3 That sentence was true when I first wrote it. However, a change has occurred that illustrates how different the prison world is from the rest of academia. Because of a schedule change, my class had to be moved from one day to another. A fellow teacher agreed to shift time slots, and all seemed to work out. However, an assistant warden refused to allow the change, offering no real explanation for the decision, so I must now defer my class until next spring. It is a minor inconvenience for me, but it underscores the often arbitrary decision-making process that controls the lives of our students and of all of the inmates at ECI.

CONTRIBUTORS

Talia Abu is an early career researcher, lecturing at Tel Aviv University and the Hebrew University of Jerusalem. She teaches mostly modernist and postmodernist texts, with a special attention to the intersections between literature and cultural studies. She is the author of *Guilt and "Finnegans Wake": From Original Sin to the Irredeemable Body*. This project, as well as her previously published work on defecation in *Finnegans Wake*, intertwine three prominent topics in literary research: the material body, the materiality of language, and affect theory.

Robert Berry, trained as a painter and cartoonist, has spent sixteen years of his life studying Joyce for *ULYSSES "seen,"* his adaptation of the text into a (very) long-form graphic novel. He publishes that work regularly in the *James Joyce Quarterly* and has taught the book, in a variety of venues, for nearly ten years. Occasionally he still gets the opportunity to paint pretty pictures that have nothing to do with any of that.

Mary M. Burke, professor of English at the University of Connecticut, is the author of *Race, Politics, and Irish America: A Gothic History*. Her first book was a cultural history of Irish Travellers, and she collaborated on the reissue edition of Juanita Casey's *The Horse of Selene*. A former NEH Irish Institute Fellow at the University of Notre Dame, she is a graduate of Trinity College Dublin and Queen's University Belfast.

Shinjini Chattopadhyay is an assistant professor at the Department of English and Comparative Literature, University of North Carolina at Chapel Hill. She completed her PhD in English at the University of Notre Dame, with minors in Irish studies and gender studies. She works on British and Irish modernisms and global anglophone literatures. Her monograph-in-progress, "Plurabilities of the City," investigates the construction of metropolitan cosmopolitanism in modernist and contemporary novels. She is published in *James Joyce Quarterly, European Joyce Studies, Joyce Studies in Italy,* and *Modernism/Modernity Print+*. She is an elected member of the board of trustees of the International James Joyce Foundation (IJJF).

Barry Devine is an associate professor of English at Heidelberg University, where he teaches British and Irish literature. His work on James Joyce appears in *The Irish*

Bildungsroman; The Cambridge Centenary Ulysses: *The 1922 Text with Essays and Notes; Joyce Studies in Italy;* and *Genetic Joyce Studies.* He is the James Joyce content editor for the *Irish Literary Supplement.*

Gregory Erickson is a professor of interdisciplinary studies at New York University's Gallatin School, where he teaches courses on modern literature, James Joyce, popular culture, and religion. He is the author of *The Absence of God in Modernist Literature; Christian Heresy, James Joyce, and the Modernist Literary Imagination: Reinventing the Word;* and *Speculative Television and the Doing and Undoing of Religion.* He is the coauthor, with Richard Santana, of *Religion and Popular Culture: Rescripting the Sacred;* and the coeditor, with Bernard Schweizer, of the collection *Reading Heresy: Religion and Dissent in Literature and Art.* He is also a professional trombone player.

Paul Fagan is a research fellow at the Ludwig Maximilian University of Munich and the Principal Investigator of the Research Ireland project *Celibacy in Irish Women's Writing, 1860s–1950s* (GOIPD/2022/634) at Maynooth University. Paul is a cofounder of the International Flann O'Brien Society, a founding general editor of the *Journal of Flann O'Brien Studies,* and an elected member of the International James Joyce Foundation Board of Trustees. He is the editor of *Finnegans Wake—Human and Nonhuman Histories; Irish Modernisms: Gaps, Conjectures, Possibilities;* and five essay collections on Flann O'Brien, as well as the special issues *Stage Irish: Performance, Identity, Cultural Circulation* and *Celibacy in Irish Women's Writing.*

A. Nicholas Fargnoli is professor of English at Molloy University, Rockville Centre, NY. His most recent book, coauthored with Michael Patrick Gillespie, is *Reading James Joyce: An Introduction.*

Michael Patrick Gillespie is a professor of English at Florida International University. He recently published, with A. Nicholas Fargnoli, *Reading James Joyce: An Introduction.*

Jonathan Goldman is a professor in the Department of Humanities at New York Institute of Technology. He is the author of *New York in the Age of Gatsby: Hidden Histories and Marginalized Figures of 1920s NYC; Modernism Is the Literature of Celebrity;* editor of *Joyce and the Law;* and coeditor of *Modernist Star Maps.* He is president of the James Joyce Society.

Zoë L. Henry is an assistant professor in the Department of English and Comparative Literature at Columbia University, where she is also affiliated with the African American and African Diaspora Studies Department. Her first book project, *The Public Interior: Modernism, Theatricality, and Interracial Aesthetics*, explores how women across a mixed-race modernist archive used the resources of the city to remain "private in public," thus desegregating the historiography of modernist literature. It develops a notion of privacy that moves beyond the domestic to intertwine with law, eros, and the psyche, arguing that privacy's denial to Black and mixed-race women can be understood as an afterlife of slavery, unfolding in the twentieth-century metropolis as in our own, post-Roe moment. Her work has appeared or is forthcoming in *Modern Fiction Studies*, *Modernism/modernity Print Plus*, *Feminist Modernist Studies*, the *Virginia Woolf Miscellany*, and the *Oxford Handbook of Queer Modernisms*, as well as in edited volumes on such authors as Joseph Conrad and Virginia Woolf.

Barbara M. Hoffmann teaches in the Department of Writing Studies at the University of Miami. Before returning to higher education in 2011, she taught high school English for a decade in the Boston area, including teaching Joyce in her AP Literature classes. As a PhD student, she served as the managing editor of the *James Joyce Literary Supplement* from 2014 to 2016 and has published on *Portrait* in various media. Her main interests are Joyce, Irish convicts in Australia, and contemporary Australian fiction. She is currently vice president of the American Association of Australasian Literary Studies.

Lloyd Meadhbh Houston is Leverhulme Early Career Fellow in English at the University of Cambridge, where they are also Senior Postdoctoral Researcher at Trinity College. They are the author of *Irish Modernism and the Politics of Sexual Health* and a range of articles and chapters on the medicalization of sex, queer cultural history, and the history of erotica and obscenity, and cohost of the podcast *Censored* with Dr. Aoife Bhreatnach.

Garry Leonard is a professor of literature and film at the University of Toronto. In addition to two books on James Joyce (*Reading Dubliners Again: A Lacanian Perspective* and *Advertising and Commodity Culture in Joyce*), he has published widely in such journals as *Novel*, *Modern Fiction Studies*, *College Literature*, and *Film Criticism*. His current project is entitled *History as Nightmare: Capitalist Discourse in Ulysses*.

Margot Norris is Chancellor's Professor Emerita of English in the School of Humanities at the University of California at Irvine. Her love for Joyce began with the study of *Finnegans Wake* and resulted in publishing *The Decentered Universe of Finnegans Wake* and *Joyce's Web*. She is author of *Suspicious Readings of Joyce's "Dubliners"* and a monograph on the 1967 Joseph Strick film of Joyce's *Ulysses*. She is editor of the 2006 Norton Critical Edition of Joyce's *Dubliners*.

Ellen Scheible is professor of English and director of honors at Bridgewater State University. She is the author of *Body Politics in Contemporary Irish Women's Fiction: The Literary Legacy of Mother Ireland*. Her other projects include *The Dark: A Critical Edition*, coedited with Anna Teekell; *Sally Rooney: Perspectives and Approaches*, coedited with Barry Devine; and a special issue of *LIT* on Irish women's genre fiction, coedited with Tina Morin. Her work has appeared in *New Hibernia Review*, *James Joyce Quarterly*, and *Tulsa Studies in Women's Literature*. She is coeditor, with Claire Culleton, of *Rethinking Joyce's "Dubliners"* and with Tina Morin of the 2023 *Irish University Review* special issue, "Irish Gothic Studies Today."

Julieann Veronica Ulin is associate professor of English at Florida Atlantic University, where she teaches courses on Irish literature and transatlantic modernism. She received her PhD in English from the Keough-Naughton Institute for Irish Studies at the University of Notre Dame, where she was the Edward Sorin Postdoctoral Fellow in the Humanities. She holds a MA in English from Fordham University and a BA in English from Washington and Lee University. Her work on Joyce has appeared in *James Joyce Quarterly*, *Joyce Studies Annual*, and in her book, *Medieval Invasions in Modern Irish Literature*, which explores the recurrence of twelfth-century Irish history in Ireland's modern literature.

Greg Winston is professor of English at Husson University in Bangor, Maine, and author of *Joyce and Militarism*. He was Fulbright Scholar in Anglo-Irish Literature at Queen's University Belfast in 2020.

INDEX

Page numbers in *italics* indicate figures.

Abbots, Emma-Jayne, 138
ABC of Reading (Pound), 116
Abdur-Rahman, Aliyyah, 94
Abraham, Michael, 170
Abu, Talia, 9, 131
Adams, Robert, 99
Adichie, Chimamanda Ngozi, 124
Adkins, Peter, 134, 141–42
Advertising: Araby Bazaar, 81–82; Brooke's Soap ad, *85, 86, 87;* Catholic Church slogans, 82; commodities, 80–82, 85–86, 88–89; desire and, 80; human desire and, 89, 91n17; in Joyce's writing, 78–79, 81–86, 88; transcendence and, 83, 90n15. *See also* Popular culture
The Agency of Eating (Abbots), 138
Aldridge, Ira, 106
Americanah (Adichie), 124
Antheil, George, 99, 112n29
"Araby": ChatGPT on, 60n16; church-like bazaar in, 81–82; popular culture in, 80–82, 88; teaching secondary students, 59n7; thematic frameworks, 35. *See also Dubliners*
Art: *Finnegans Wake* and, 161–63, 165, 167–69, 172; online courses, 260; teaching through *Ulysses,* 250–53, 258, 260–65
Asexual Erotics (Przybylo), 57
Asexuality, 57–58
As One Generation Tells Another (Emerick-Brown), 5
Attridge, Derek, 155
"Auprès d'un mort" (Maupassant), 35
The Autobiography of Alice B. Toklas (Stein), 199
Averill, Tim, 28n1

Babbitt, Milton, 171
Backstories: causal narratives, 45, 48–52; counter-discourse, 56–57; in *Dubliners,* 8, 44–46, 48–58, 60n14, 60n16; history of place, 59n13; literary and critical narratives, 56–57; narrative microhistories, 54; personal discussions and, 54–55; textual presence of, 56
Backus, Margot Gayle, 36
Baek, Hannah, 177–78, *178*
Baldwin, James, 271–72
Barnacle, Nora, 182, 184–85, 194n17, 195n23, 206
Bartholomae, David, 22
"Bartleby, the Scrivener" (Melville), 35
Bathers (Russell), 263
Bauernfeind, Gustav, 262
Bazargan, Susan, 217
Beckett, Samuel, 267
Bellini, Vincenzo, 184, 207
Belvedere College, 119
Benefits Supervisor Sleeping (Freud), 262
Bennett, Arnold, 150
Benstock, Bernard, 238
Berry, Robert, 10, 217, 220, 224, 227n4, 250
Biltekoff, Charlotte, 140–41, 145n20
Bishop, John, 6, 173, 223–24
Black Lives Matter movement, 63
Blackness: colonialism and, 94; connections with Irish victims, 93, 96–97, 100, 103; in *Dubliners,* 113n46; incarceration and violence, 111n10; in Ireland, 93, 95, 106–7; literary culture and, 95; in *Secret Lives of Church Ladies,* 64, 66–70, 72n4; sexual desire and, 105–6; in *Ulysses,* 8, 92–95, 97, 99–100, 105–10
Black performers, 93, 106–7, 113n42, 113n45, 113n46
"The Boarding House," 35, 45, 56
Boating (Manet), 262
Bodkin, Michael, 206
Bogan, Louise, 149–50

Bohee, George, 106–7
Bohee, James, 106–7
Bolinger, Dwight L., 151–52
Book of Kells, 163, 172
Bowen, Elizabeth, 35, 39
Bowen, Zack, 188–89
Boyle, Robert, S. J., 201–3
Braid, Berenice, 243
A Brilliant Career (Joyce), 193n3
Bronze by Gold (Hamilton), 263
Brown, Terence, 46
Brown, Will, 100–101, *101*, 102, *102*, 104–6
Bucak, Ayşe Papatya, 54
Burke, Mary M., 8, 62
Burns, Robert, 142
Burroughs, Augusten, 29n22
Bute, Mary Ellen, 168–69
Butler, Judith, 8, 35
Buurma, Rachel Sagner, 116, 214–15
BuzzFeed, 139, 145n20

Cage, John, 162, 170–71, 173–74
The Cambridge Centenary Ulysses: The 1922 Text With Essays and Notes (Flynn), 6–7
The Cambridge Companion to Modern Gothic, 36
Canonicity: backstories and, 45; Black readers and, 108; Joyce and, 3, 17, 27, 33, 40, 95, 200; reading without context, 50
Canyon (Rauschenberg), 264
Carroll, Lewis, 149, 153–54
Carson, Jan, 67, 72n15
Caruth, Cathy, 36
Catholicism: advertising slogans, 82; colonialist education system, 119–20; in *Dubliners*, 64, 67–68, 82, 273–74; in Ireland, 64, 68–69; normativity and, 39; respectability and, 68; in *Ulysses*, 256
Celibates (Moore), 35
Cesaire, Aimé, 96
Chamber Music (Joyce), 200–206, 210–11
Charters, Ann, 63–64, 66
ChatGPT, 47, 54, 60n16
Chattopadhyay, Shinjini, 8, 116
Chekhov, Anton, 66
Cheng, Vincent, 27, 94, 96, 113n50
The Child Sex Scandal and Modern Irish Literature (Backus and Valente), 36
Chopin, Kate, 18
"Circe": anthropomorphizing of objects in, 86; Blackness in, 95, 105–8; intercultural misrecognition in, 105–6; minstrelsy representations in, 105–7, 113n42; transformation in, 88. See also *Ulysses*
City as Text, 243–47, 248n25
"Clay," 34–35
Clongowes Wood College, 1, 119
The Coach with the Six Insides, 174
Collected Poems (Joyce), 200, 210
Collective trauma: college students and, 65–66; COVID-19 pandemic, 62; literature and, 65, 71; #MeToo movement, 63–64; racial violence, 62–64
Collier, Patrick, 243
Collins, Billy, 19
Collins, Wilkie, 29n22
Colonialism: British atrocities, 93, 99, 104; Catholicism and, 64, 68–69, 119–20; cosmopolitanism and, 123; cross-cultural connections, 96; educational systems, 119–22; Ireland and, 34, 64, 68–69, 123–25; Joyce on, 27, 96, 100, 117; masculinity and, 221; pedagogy and, 117; religious culture and, 69; structures of, 117
Colum, Padraic, 183
A Companion to James Joyce's "Ulysses" (Norris), 2
Composition II in Red, Blue, and Yellow (Mondrian), 262
Conley, Tim, 11n3
Conquergood, Dwight, 167
Cornell, Joseph, 262
Cosmopolitanism, 122–24, 127, 129n21
"Counterparts," 34–35, 38
Crow, Stephen, 163, 172
Culleton, Claire A., 48, 246
Cunningham, Merce, 163, 173–74
Curriculum theories: learner-centered model, 21–22; method-based approaches, 243; scaffolding, 21–22, 24–25, 27; scholar-academic model, 21–22, 24; social reconstruction, 26–27
"Cyclops": alienation in, 137; on antisemitism, 112n39; Blackness in, 95, 99–100; critique of international parallelism, 97; ecocriticism, 59n7; global liberation, 98; as inspiration for opera, 99; Irish nationalism and, 104, 113n40, 221, 234, 247n10; lynching of Will Brown, 95, 100–101, 104–5; narrative voices

in, 97–98; postcolonialism and, 98; xenophobia in, 93. *See also Ulysses*

Dalí, Salvador, 264
Davis, Rowland, 199
"The Dead": Blackness in, 113n46; character backstories, 48, 58; cosmopolitanism, 123–24, 127; creative rewriting of, 127; decolonial pedagogy, 118, 122–25; in dialogue with Willian Faulkner, 65; human body in, 34; setting for, 247n1; uplift in, 71. *See also Dubliners*
Deane, Seamus, 50, 59n12, 96
De Certeau, Michel, 113n42
Decoloniality: defined, 117; inclusive pedagogy, 8–9, 117–18, 122–24, 126–28; Joyce and, 96–97, 117–18
Decolonising Curricula and Pedagogy in Higher Education (Morreira), 117
Decolonizing the English Literary Curriculum (Mukherjee and Quayson), 118
De Kooning, Willem, 263
"The Demon Lover" (Bowen), 35, 39
Devine, Barry, 217
Dickens, Charles, 255
"Don't Panic: It's only *Finnegans Wake*," 166
Dracula (Stoker), 36
Dream Stuff (Joyce), 193n3
Dublin, Ireland: Black presence in, 95, 106–7; Catholicism in, 68; City as Text pedagogy, 245–47; expansion of city, 235–36, 238; Joycean imaginary in, 230–31, 238–42, 244–47, 247n1, 248n16; local geography, 10, 229, 236–38, 244–45; popular culture in, 78; subalternity of, 238; *Ulysses* sidewalk plaque, 231; walkabouts, 236–38, 246–47. *See also* Ireland
Dubliners: anxiety in, 60n13, 76; backstories in, 8, 44–46, 48–58, 59n13, 60n14, 60n16; *Bildung* and, 33–34; Blackness in, 113n46; Catholicism in, 64, 67–68, 82, 273–74; deficient masculinity in, 39; dialectical pedagogy, 10, 272, 275–76, 278; in dialogue with *Secret Lives*, 8, 64–71; editions of, 37–38, 46; Foundation Year teaching, 7–8, 31–40; hierarchies of empire in, 68; human body in, 34–35, 37–38; local geography, 59n13, 229, 240–42, 246–47, 273; medical science context, 38–39; narrative voice, 44–45, 48, 52; naturalism and, 38–39, 41n15; paralysis in, 37–38, 67;

popular culture in, 79–80; publication of, 70; reading aloud, 48–50; representations in, 38; scaffolding, 32, 35–36; sexuality in, 70, 73n26; teaching approaches, 5–6, 199; teaching college students, 7–8; teaching in MA programs, 46–51, 55–58; teaching in nonacademic spaces, 216; teaching in online courses, 63–64; teaching in prison systems, 10, 266, 271–79; teaching secondary students, 59n7; use of ornament, 54. *See also individual stories*
Dubliners 100 (Morris), 11n4
Duchamp, Marcel, 263
Duffy, Enda, 96

Eagleton, Terry, 216
Earle, David M., 41n8
Ecocriticism, 47, 59n7
Eco-Joyce (Lai), 59n7
Elbay, Caroline, 217, 219, 223, 227n4
Eliot, T. S., 96, 116–18, 187, 199
Ellison, Ralph, 27, 96
Ellmann, Maud, 58
Ellmann, Richard, 1, 89, 100, 184, 194n16, 195n23, 200, 205–6, 210
Emerick-Brown, Dylan, 5
"An Encounter": backstories in, 51; children and unwelcomed obedience, 54–55; compulsory sexuality in, 57; thematic frameworks, 35; trek to Pigeon House, 240–42. *See also Dubliners*
English As We Speak It in Ireland (Joyce), 121
Erickson, Gregory, 9, 161
The Ethics of Diet (Williams), 135
Eureka Studies in Teaching Short Fiction, 5
Evaristo, Bernardine, 35, 124
Eveline, 60n16, 68
Everglades Correctional Institution (ECI): arbitrary decision-making, 271, 279n3; educational opportunities, 268, 270–72, 279n1; Exchange for Change program, 268, 279n1, 279n2; inmate demographics, 269–70; physical conditions in, 266–67, 269; psychological hardships, 267; punitive philosophy, 267–70; range of backgrounds and abilities, 276–77; student engagement, 271–77; teaching *Dubliners* in, 10, 266, 271–79
Everglades ReEntry, 268
Exchange for Change, 268, 279n1, 279n2

Exiles: critical reception of, 183–84, 194n9, 194n10, 194n13; narrative in, 183; pedagogy, 9; performing, 193, 195n24; personal experience in, 183–85; publication of, 183, 194n8; relation to Ibsen, 183–84, 194n11; teaching approaches, 7, 181–83, 193; thematic synopsis, 185–92; unconditional freedom, 9

Fagan, Paul, 9, 148
Falconer, John, 184
Fanon, Frantz, 94
Fargnoli, A. Nicholas, 7, 9, 181, 217, 227n4
Faulkner, William, 65
Finnegan, Tim, 164, 166
Finnegans Wake: dance interpretations, 173–74; drafting of, 175–76; experimental language in, 148–58; film versions, 168–70; interdisciplinary approaches, 162–79; local geography, 239–40; main characters in, 165; musical approaches, 170–72, 176–77; parentheses in, 155–57; pedagogy and, 117; performing, 161–62, 167–68, 173–77, 179n7; popular culture in, 78; portmanteaux, 150, 153, 155, 157, 165–66; racial Otherness in, 92; reading groups, 162, 176, 178; semantic predictability, 153–55; sentence-level teaching, 9, 148–58; subalternity of, 96; syntactic predictability, 151–53; teaching approaches, 199; teaching college students, 161–79; thematic frameworks, 148, 158n2; thunderwords, 166–69; visual art, 9, 172–73, 177–78, *178;* "Waywords and Meansigns" project, 162, 171–72, 176
"*Finnegans Wake* on Film" (McCarthy), 169
Floyd, George, 63, 99
Flynn, Catherine, 6–7, 36
Food: bestiality of eaters, 142–43; celebrity diets, 138–39; class values, 141; identity-construction and, 139–41; Irishness and, 141, 145n26; masculinity and, 134–37, 141; meat consumption, 133–41, 143; political considerations, 140; social and cultural issues, 133–35, 138, 143; in *Ulysses,* 8, 132–36, 138–42, 144; vegetarianism, 134–43
Fordham, Finn, 175
Fouéré, Olwen, 163, 175
Foundation Year (Oxford): student research, 37, 41n9; study skills and, 31–32; teaching *Dubliners,* 7–8, 31–40

Freewriting, 75–78, 80
Freud, Lucian, 262
Freud, Sigmund, 36
Frye, Northrop, 216

Gabler, Hans Walter, 41n12
Gaelic Athletic Association, 39
Gamerro, Carlos, 217, 220
García Márquez, Gabriel, 96
"Gas from a Burner" (Joyce), 184
General Paralysis of the Insane (GPI), 38–39
Geography: City as Text pedagogy, 243–47, 248n25; Dublin city expansion, 235–36; Irish school curriculum, 232, 234–35; in Joyce's writing, 10, 229–32, 234–42, 244–46, 247n1, 273; as politicized discourse, 234; skeleton maps, 237; St. Joseph's National School, 233, 234, 239; walkabouts, 235–38
Géricault, Théodore, 262
Gifford, Don, 256
Gillespie, Michael Patrick, 10, 182–83, 193n5, 266
Gilroy, Paul, 93
Girl, Woman, Other (Evaristo), 35
Glasheen, Adaline, 165
Going to Meet the Man (Baldwin), 271–72
Goldman, Jonathan, 10, 214
GPI. *See* General Paralysis of the Insane (GPI)
Graeber, David, 35
Grant, Melissa Gira, 35
Greenblatt, Yaeli, 173
Greunig, Daniel, 100
Griffin, Christopher, 217
Griffith, Arthur, 141, 232, 234, 248n11
Groden, Michael, 100, 217–18
Gross, Ciceil L., 163
Group work: online, 158; scholar-academic curriculum model, 24; secondary students, 24–26; sentence-level teaching, 148–49, 155
Gubar, Susan, 113n47
Gunn, Ian, 248n16

Hagen, Benjamin, 128n2
Hamilton, Richard, 263
Harjo, Joy, 124
Hart, Clive, 248n16
Harvey, Adam, 163, 166
Hastings, Patrick, 217, 228n6
Hayman, David, 158

HCE players, 174
Heffernan, Laura, 116, 214–15
Henry, Zoë L., 8, 92
Herr, Cheryl, 96
Hickey, Emma, 172–73
Higher education: academic privilege, 226–27; active learning, 124–28; critical analysis skills, 125–28; decolonial pedagogy, 117–18, 123–27; elitism and, 214–16, 219–21, 227; food studies in, 132–35, 143–44; Foundation Year schemes, 31–34; inclusive pedagogy, 124–27; neoliberalization of, 214, 216; teaching Joyce, 7–8, 34, 46–47, 161–79, 250–51, 257–58; writing assignments, 126–27
Hoffmann, Barbara M., 7, 17
Hogan, Kelly A., 124–25
Homestead Correctional Institution, 268
Houston, Lloyd Meadhbh, 7–8, 31
Howarth, Peter, 116
Howes, Marjorie, 235
Human body: GPI in, 38–39; health and, 39; historical situations, 35, 37–38; paralysis in, 37–38; teaching *Dubliners*, 34–35, 37–38; in *Ulysses*, 132–33
Huston, John, 247n1

Ibsen, Henrik, 4, 183–84, 194n11
Invisible Man (Ellison), 27
Ireland: background information on, 24, 47, 274; Black presence in, 93, 95, 106–7; British colonialism and, 34, 64, 68–69, 93, 96, 117, 119, 123–25, 255; British mapping of, 232; Catholicism in, 68–69; geography curriculum, 232, 234–35; heritage resources, 26, 29n23; independence from England, 96, 100, 140–41, 146n28; mob violence in, 103; racism in, 92–94; vegetable-based diet, 140, 145n26. *See also* Dublin
Irish Homestead, 35, 37, 78–79
Irish literature: backstories in, 44–45; exceptionalism and, 221; genre courses, 62; Irish Literary Revival, 238, 274; short stories in, 63–64, 66; story and landscape in, 229
Israel: democracy narrative, 143–44, 146n37; geographic borders, 144n1; indoctrination of one-sided narrative, 132, 143, 144n3; sociopolitical complexities, 131; teaching *Ulysses*, 131–32

Jackson, Alvin, 140
Jame Joyce's Dublin (Gunn and Hart), 248n16
James Joyce (Ellmann), 195n23, 200
James Joyce (O'Brien), 2
James Joyce and the Exilic Imagination (Gillespie), 182
James Joyce Centre, 217
James Joyce Quarterly, 11n3
James Joyce Society, 225
James Joyce's "Portrait" (Pierce), 22
James Joyce's Teaching Life and Methods (Switaj), 119
Jewish students, 131–32, 143
Jones, William, 102, *103*
Jonson, Ben, 238
Joyce, James: Africanism and, 93, 95; Belvedere College, 119; Clongowes Wood College, 1, 119; colonialism and, 27, 96, 100, 117; context of works, 37; critique of white exceptionalism, 100; curriculum theories, 21; decolonial pedagogy, 125, 127; in dialogue with Philyaw, 8, 62; on dramatic art, 181, 184, 193n1, 193n3; ecocriticism, 47, 59n7; letters to Grant Richards, 47; marginalized writers and readers, 64, 96; modernism and, 76, 95, 119; neurodivergence in writing, 3, 47; pedagogy of, 1–11, 117; postcoloniality and, 27, 96–98; short stories, 5, 60n16, 64; on social issues, 3–4; teaching pedagogy, 118–19; voluntary exile, 3, 182, 184, 193n4, 193n5. *See also under individual titles*
Joyce, James. Poetry: *Chamber Music*, 200–206, 210–11; *Collected Poems*, 200, 210; "Ecce Puer," 210–11; *Moods*, 200; *Pomes Penyeach*, 205–11; teaching approaches, 9, 200–212
Joyce, P. W., 121
Joyce, Race, and Empire (Cheng), 96
Joyce, Stanislaus, 182, 240
Joycegeek.com, 166
The Joyce Project, 233
Joycestick: The Gamification of Ulysses, 248n16
Joyce Studies Annual, 6
Joyce Tower and Museum, 247n1
Judith (Klimt), 263

Kandinsky, Wassily, 181
Kapur, Sofia, 176–77
Kavanagh, Patrick, 219
Keats, John, 19

Kenner, Hugh, 79
Killeen, Terence, 98
Klarreich, Kathie, 268
Klimt, Gustav, 263
Knowles, Sebastian, 179n7
Kosaly-Meyer, Neal, 171

Lacan, Jacques, 76, 84, 86, 90n7, 90n12, 90n15, 91n17
"La Cometa dell 'Home Rule'" (Joyce), 193n4
Lady Chatterley's Lover (Lawrence), 199
Lai, Yi-Peng, 59n7
Large Reclining Figure (Moore), 265
Larkin, Philip, 60n14
Larsen, Nella, 199
La sonnambula (Bellini), 184, 207
Latham, Sean, 11n3, 37, 41n8, 221
Lavin, Mary, 64
Lawrence, D. H., 116–18, 128n2, 199
LeBlanc, Jim, 55–56
Lecercle, Jean-Jacques, 154
Leonard, Garry, 8, 75
Lerm Hayes, Christa-Maria, 163, 172
Le Roman Experimental (Zola), 36
Levinson, Julie, 244, 248n25
L.H.O.O.Q. (Duchamp), 263
Litz, A. Walton, 183–84
Living Nations, Living Words (Harjo), 124
Livingstone, David, 234
Loebeck, Agnes, 100
Looby, Christopher, 35
Lots of Fun at "Finnegans Wake" (Fordham), 175
Lowe, Louise, 242
Lunar Landscape (Nevelson), 263
Lurz, John, 6
Lynching: Black Americans, 93, 99–103; modernism, 97; in *Ulysses*, 93, 95, 97, 99–101, 103–4, 112n35; of Will Brown, 95, 100–101, *101*, 102, *102*, 104, 106; of William Jones, 102, *103*

MacLeish, Archibald, 205
MacNicholas, John, 184
Maddox, Brenda, 185, 189, 194n17
Magritte, René, 264
Mahaffey, Vicki, 36, 96, 145n16
Manet, Édouard, 262
Manganiello, Dominic, 96
Manning, Mary, 169

"The Man Who Thought Himself a Woman" (Looby), 35
Mapping Dubliners Project, 248n16
Market at Jaffa (Bauernfeind), 262
Martello Towers, 240, 247n1
Marx, Karl, 81, 86
Masculinity, 39, 52n16, 221
Maupassant, Guy du, 35, 66
McCarthy, Patrick A., 169
McDonagh, Rosaleen, 35
McHugh, Roland, 167
McNally, Thomas, 173
McSorley's Bar (Sloan), 263
Medical history, 38–39, 41n14
Medieval Invasions in Modern Irish Literature (Ulin), 44
Melville, Herman, 35
Memoir, 10
Menendez, Ana, 272
#MeToo movement, 63–64
Meyers, Jesse, 217, 220, 227n4
Mignolo, Walter, 117–18
Minton, Phil, 171
Modernism: internationalism, 97; in Joyce's writing, 76, 95, 119, 122, 144, 171, 229, 253; pedagogy and, 33, 40n3, 116; personal discussions and, 54
Modernist Journals Project, 37
Moholy-Nagy, László, 163, 172
Mondrian, Piet, 262
Moods (Joyce), 200
"The Mookse and the Gripes" (McNally), 173
The Moonstone (Collins), 29n22
Moore, George, 35
Moore, Henry, 265
Morreira, Shannon, 117
Morris, Thomas, 11n4
Morrison, Toni, 95
"A Mother," 45, 56
Motifs, 23–24
Mukherjee, Ankhi, 118
Mulhall, Anne, 221
Mullen, Jacqueline, 59n7
Mullen, Patrick, 98
The Myth of Manliness in Irish National Culture, 1880–1922 (Valente), 36, 52n16

Narrative: backstories in, 44–45, 49, 54–56, 60n16; causal, 45, 48, 50; concealment in,

44; counter-discourse, 56–57; historical situations in, 35–36; imperialist, 122, 140; motif-tracing projects, 23; obscuring marginalized, 55; in *Portrait*, 20, 22–23; spatial thinking and, 229; teaching *Exiles*, 183
Nash, Richard, 195n24
Nast, Thomas, 102, *103*
"Nestor": colonialist education system, 8–9, 120–22, 125; decolonial pedagogy, 117–18, 121–23. *See also Ulysses*
Neurodivergence, 3, 32, 47, 59n6
Nevelson, Louise, 263
The New Joyce Studies, 36
Nichols, Tyre, 99
"Nightpiece," 112n29
Nine Characters in Search of a Wake, 174
Nonacademic spaces: broad participation in, 219, 222; Irish heritage and, 221; student bodies in, 220–21; teaching Joyce's poetry in, 200–212; teaching *Ulysses* in, 214–27, 253, 257–60
Norris, Margot, 2, 9–10, 36–38, 40, 48, 55, 96, 113n46, 199, 226

O'Brien, Edna, 2–4, 11n6
O'Connor, Frank, 64
O'Faoláin, Sean, 150
O'Kane Mara, Miriam, 140–41
O'Keeffe, Georgia, 181
Ogden, Charles Kay, 152
Okorie, Melatu Uche, 124
Old Possum's Book of Practical Cats (Eliot), 187
"The Ondt and the Gracehoper" (McNally), 173
"On the Phenomenon of Bullshit Jobs" (Graeber), 35
Orr, Leonard, 96
Oxford University, 31–32, 40n2. *See also* Foundation Year (Oxford)
Ozier, Amadi, 97, 104, 113n40

"A Painful Case," 35, 53, 57
Palestine, 131, 144n2
Parnell, Charles Stewart, 141, 274
Passages from James Joyce's "Finnegans Wake," 168–69
Pedagogy: City as Text, 243–47, 248n25; decolonial, 117–18, 122–28; dialectical, 10, 272, 275–76, 278; feminist, 5, 226; freewriting, 78; geography and, 229; inclusive, 8–9, 117;

Joyce's works, 5, 7–10, 20, 117; method-based approaches, 243; modernism and, 33, 40n3, 116; nonacademic programs, 214–16; popular culture in, 8; radical strategies, 116–17
"Penelope": Blackness in, 95; Molly's mixed-race heritage in, 108–10, 113n51; popular culture in, 255; racial Otherness in, 109; reading groups, 225–26; teaching art through, 265. *See also Ulysses*
Penn Studio School, 251, 260–61
Petrosky, Anthony, 22
Philyaw, Deesha, 65–66, 70–71, 72n7, 73n27. *See also The Secret Lives of Church Ladies* (Philyaw)
The Picture of Dorian Gray (Wilde), 36
Pierce, David, 22
The Pigeon House, 240–42, *243*, 273
Pigeon House Lab, 242
Pilobolus, 163, 174
Pinson, Paul, 171
Plag, Ingo, 153
Platt, Len, 120
Playing the Whore (Grant), 35
"Poetry of Departures" (Larkin), 60n14
Pomes Penyeach (Joyce), 205–11
Poolbeg Stacks, 241, *241*
Popper, Amalia, 205
Popular culture: advertising in, 82–83, *85*, *86*, *87*, 88, 90n10, 90n15; in *Dubliners*, 79–82, 88; in Joyce's writing, 8, 75, 78, 90n10; in *Portrait*, 80, 82–83; teaching approaches, 8; in *Ulysses*, 83–84, 86
Porte, Rebecca Ariel, 217
A Portrait of the Artist as a Young Man: backstories in, 60n13; Catholicism in, 82; colonialist education system, 119; complexity of, 19–24; editions of, 29n21; geography in, 234–35; motif-tracing projects, 23–24; neurodivergence in, 47, 59n6; pedagogy and, 117; popular culture in, 80, 82–83; pre-reading questions, 22; publication of, 194n8; reading of *The Count of Monte Cristo*, 23, 47, 83, 237; scaffolded reading, 22, 24–27; student identification with Stephen, 22–23, 26–28; teaching approaches, 199; teaching secondary students, 7, 17–28, 28n1; value of words in, 83; walking in, 235–38; Word Dip, 25
The Postcolonial Bildungsroman (Roy and Ugor), 59n12

Postcolonialism: cosmopolitanism and, 122; Joyce and, 27, 96–98; *Portrait* and, 26–27; *Ulysses* and, 92, 95–96, 131, 255
Pound, Ezra, 96, 100, 116, 183, 200
Preece, Rod, 134–35, 140
Prezioso, Roberto, 185, 189, 194n16, 195n23
Proust, Marcel, 8, 44
Przybylo, Ela, 57
Pyle, Derek, 162, 171–72, 174, 179n1

Quayson, Ato, 118
Quicksand (Larsen), 199

Racial violence, 62–64, 104, 111n10
Raft of the Medusa (Géricault), 262
The Raptures (Carson), 67
Rauschenberg, Robert, 264
Reading in the Dark (Deane), 50, 59n12
Re-Covering Modernism (Earle), 41n8
"Redefining Ornament" (Bucak), 54
Regan, Marguerite M., 134
"ReJoyce—A Pilobolus *Finnegans Wake*," 174
Rethinking Joyce's "Dubliners" (Culleton and Scheible), 48, 55–56
Richards, Grant, 36, 47
Richards, Ivor Armstrong, 152
Riquelme, John Paul, 29n21, 36
"Roaratorio, an Irish circus on *Finnegans Wake*" (Cage), 170–71, 173–74
Roberts, George, 184
Rogers, Nicole, 59n6
A Room of One's Own (Woolf), 116
Rosenbach Museum and Library, 250, 258–59
Roy, Arnab Dutta, 59n12
Ruch, Allen B., 150
Running with Scissors (Burroughs), 29n22
Rusbridger, Alan, 31
Rushdie, Salman, 96
Russell, George William (Æ), 137–39, 200, 263

The Sacred Wood (Eliot), 117
Said, Edward, 18
Saint-Amour, Paul, 11n3, 96, 103, 250–51, 258
Sathy, Viji, 124–25
Saussure, Ferdinand de, 75–77
Schechner, Richard, 167
Scheible, Ellen, 11n3, 48, 64–65
Secondary students: AP Lit classes, 17–18, 21, 27, 28n3; curriculum planning, 21; developing identity, 19; group work, 24–25; literary criticism, 29n17; standardized testing, 17, 27, 28n2, 28n4; teaching *Dubliners*, 7, 59n7; teaching *Portrait of the Artist*, 7, 17–28, 28n1; YouTube and, 24. *See also* Foundation Year (Oxford)
The Secret Lives of Church Ladies (Philyaw): awards for, 64, 71n2; Biblical references in, 68–69, 72n16; church lady culture, 67, 70, 73n27; damage done by adult caretakers, 70–71; in dialogue with *Dubliners*, 8, 62, 64–71; food in, 69–70; heteronormativity structures, 67–69; naturalism and, 66; politics of respectability, 70, 73n27; publication of, 70; queer Black women in, 64, 66, 68–70, 72n4, 73n26; religious hypocrisy and, 69; sexuality in, 70, 73n26. *See also* Philyaw, Deesha
Seidman, Robert J., 256
Senghor, Léopold, 96
Senn, Fritz, 222–24
Shahjahan, Riyad A., 123
Shaw, Bernard, 138
Sherman, Cindy, 264
Shihade, Magid, 143
Shloss, Carol Loeb, 206
Short stories: innovative tradition, 66; in Irish literature, 63–64, 66; Joyce and, 5, 60n16, 64; teaching in prison systems, 271–72; thematically conventional tradition, 66. *See also Dubliners*
Showalter, Elaine, 126
Silhouettes (Joyce), 200
The Sin Eaters (Lowe), 242
"The Sisters": Biblical references, 68; character backstories, 48–50, 55–56; differing versions, 37–38, 41n12, 78–80; Lacanian theory, 90n12; mapping language in, 76; narrative style, 80; neurosyphilis symptoms, 38, 41n13; paralysis in, 37–38, 78; popular culture in, 79; reading aloud, 48–50; thematic frameworks, 35; value of words in, 78–81, 83. *See also Dubliners*
Sloan, John, 263
Slone, Isaac, 176–77
Slote, Sam, 150
Small, Flicka, 142
Social media, 2, 5–6, 138, 218, 222
Social reconstruction theory, 26–27
Soft Construction with Boiled Beans (Dalí), 264

Soul Tourists (Evaristo), 124
Soyinka, Wole, 96
Spencer, Colin, 135–36, 141
Spinks, Lee, 205
Spoo, Robert, 121
Spooky, DJ, 162, 171
Stein, Gertrude, 199
Stephen, James, 141
St. Joseph's National School, 233, 234, 239
Stockton, Carla, 28n1
Stoker, Bram, 36
The Story and Its Writer (Charters), 63
Stuart, Tristam, 138
Subalternity, 27, 96, 122, 238
Suspicious Readings of Joyce's "Dubliners" and Collaborative Dubliners (Norris), 36, 48, 55
Suter, August, 1
Svevo, Italo, 119
Swann's Way (Proust), 8, 44
Switaj, Elizabeth, 119
Symons, Arthur, 200

The Teaching Archive (Buurma and Heffernan), 116, 214
Teaching Literature (Showalter), 126
Teaching Literature in the Real World (Collier), 243
Think-Pair-Share (TPS) activities, 125–26
This Hostel Life (Okorie), 124
Thoreau, Henry David, 138
Thornton, Weldon, 99
Three Guineas (Woolf), 116
Thurman, Wallace, 96
Thwaites, Tony, 152
Townsend, Sarah, 5–6
Trauma (Caruth), 36
The Treachery of Images (Magritte), 264–65
Trilling, Lionel, 216
"Tutto é Sciolto" (Joyce), 184
"Two Gallants," 34–35, 55

Ugor, Paul, 59n12
Ulin, Julieann Veronica, 7–8, 44
Ulysses: backstories in, 60n13; Blackness in, 8, 92–95, 97, 99–100, 105–10; Black readers, 92, 94–95, 99, 103–6, 108; Catholicism in, 256; contextual resources, 224; cross-cultural connections in, 93–94, 96–97, 100, 103–4; decolonial pedagogy, 118; democratized, 221–22, 259; feminist pedagogy, 5, 226; food in, 9, 132–44; human body in, 132–33; Irish independence and, 96, 140–41; Irishness and, 254–55; Jewish Otherness in, 93; linguistic ambiguity in, 137, 145n16; local geography, 238–39, 242; lynching references, 93, 95, 97, 99–105; meat consumption in, 133–41, 143; minstrelsy representations in, 93, 97, 105–7, 113n42; narrative shifts, 84–86; neurodivergence in, 47; paradox of desire, 89, 91n16; parallactic effect in, 84–86, 89; pedagogy and, 117; popular culture in, 8, 83–84, 86; postcolonialism and, 95, 131, 255; racial Otherness in, 109; racism in, 92–95, 97, 105, 109–10; readers of, 253–56; reading groups, 9–10, 215, 221–26; self-discovery through, 222, 226, 257–58; subalternity of, 96; teaching approaches, 5–6, 199, 253, 258–60; teaching art through, 10, 250–53, 258, 260–65; teaching in Hebrew-speaking classes, 131–32; teaching in higher education, 46–47, 250–51, 257–58; teaching in nonacademic spaces, 214–27, 251, 253, 257–60; teaching in online courses, 9–10, 217, 243, 251, 259–60, 262; vegetarianism in, 134–43; writing of, 3–4. *See also* "Circe"; "Cyclops"; "Nestor"; "Penelope"
Ulysses Annotated (Gifford and Seidman), 256
"Ulysses Guide" website, 217
ULYSSES "*seen*" project, 251–52, 261
"The Uncanny" (Freud), 36
The United Irishman, 232, *233*
Unsettled (McDonagh), 35
Untitled ("Fountain of Youth") (Cornell), 262
Untitled Film Still #23 (Sherman), 264
Utell, Janine, 5

Vadde, Aarthi, 97
Valente, Joseph, 36, 52n16
Vegetarianism: Anglo-Irish relations and, 140, 145n26; cultural discourses, 135, 137; eccentricity and, 136; history of, 134–36; intellectuals and, 137–38; middle class and, 141–42; political connotations, 140–41; in *Ulysses*, 134–40, 143
Vico, Giambattisata, 172

Waiting for Godot (Beckett), 267
"*Wake* in Progress" (Crow), 163, 172
Wales, Katie, 150

Walsh, Keri, 226
The Waste Land (Eliot), 199
Waterman, Anna, 176–77
Wawrzycka, Jolanta, 202
Ways of Reading (Bartholomae and Petrosky), 22
"Waywords and Meansigns" project, 162, 171–72, 176
Weinstein, Harvey, 63
Weinstein, Phillip, 217
Weiss, Timothy, 99–100
Weldon, Thornton, 29n17
When We Dead Awaken (Ibsen), 181
Whiteness: critique of exceptionalism, 100; elitism and, 221; Gaelic League and, 93; Irish nationalists and, 93, 109, 221; minstrel performers and, 113n42; in *Ulysses*, 97–98
Widdowson, H. G., 153
Wilde, Oscar, 36
Williams, Bert, 107
Williams, Howard, 135
Wilson, Edmund, 215

Winston, Greg, 10, 229
Wolfe, Kate, 57
Woman III (De Kooning), 263
Women: exclusion from elite educational institutions, 116; impacts of colonialism, 126; in Joyce's poetry, 201, 206; popular culture and, 255; queer Black, 64, 66–70; in religious cultures, 66–69, 73n27; in *Ulysses*, 105–6, 255–56
Women in Joyce (Boyle), 201
Women's March, 63
Woolf, Virginia, 116–18, 255
Word Dip, 25, 29n22
Wrenn, Corey, 145n26
"Writing for the Second Time Through *Finnegans Wake*" (Cage), 170

Yeats, W. B., 200, 205
YouTube, 24

Zola, Émile, 36

The Florida James Joyce Series

Edited by Sam Slote

The Autobiographical Novel of Co-Consciousness: Goncharov, Woolf, and Joyce, by Galya Diment (1994)
Bloom's Old Sweet Song: Essays on Joyce and Music, by Zack Bowen (1995)
Joyce's Iritis and the Irritated Text: The Dis-lexic "Ulysses," by Roy Gottfried (1995)
Joyce, Milton, and the Theory of Influence, by Patrick Colm Hogan (1995)
Reauthorizing Joyce, by Vicki Mahaffey (paperback edition, 1995)
Shaw and Joyce: "The Last Word in Stolentelling," by Martha Fodaski Black (1995)
Bely, Joyce, and Döblin: Peripatetics in the City Novel, by Peter I. Barta (1996)
Jocoserious Joyce: The Fate of Folly in "Ulysses," by Robert H. Bell (paperback edition, 1996)
Joyce and Popular Culture, edited by R. B. Kershner (1996)
Joyce and the Jews: Culture and Texts, by Ira B. Nadel (paperback edition, 1996)
Narrative Design in "Finnegans Wake": The Wake Lock Picked, by Harry Burrell (1996)
Gender in Joyce, edited by Jolanta W. Wawrzycka and Marlena G. Corcoran (1997)
Latin and Roman Culture in Joyce, by R. J. Schork (1997)
Reading Joyce Politically, by Trevor L. Williams (1997)
Advertising and Commodity Culture in Joyce, by Garry Leonard (1998)
Greek and Hellenic Culture in Joyce, by R. J. Schork (1998)
Joyce, Joyceans, and the Rhetoric of Citation, by Eloise Knowlton (1998)
Joyce's Music and Noise: Theme and Variation in His Writings, by Jack W. Weaver (1998)
Reading Derrida Reading Joyce, by Alan Roughley (1999)
Joyce through the Ages: A Nonlinear View, edited by Michael Patrick Gillespie (1999)
Chaos Theory and James Joyce's Everyman, by Peter Francis Mackey (1999)
Joyce's Comic Portrait, by Roy Gottfried (2000)
Joyce and Hagiography: Saints Above!, by R. J. Schork (2000)
Voices and Values in Joyce's "Ulysses," by Weldon Thornton (2000)
The Dublin Helix: The Life of Language in Joyce's "Ulysses," by Sebastian D. G. Knowles (2001)
Joyce Beyond Marx: History and Desire in "Ulysses" and "Finnegans Wake," by Patrick McGee (2001)
Joyce's Metamorphosis, by Stanley Sultan (2001)
Joycean Temporalities: Debts, Promises, and Countersignatures, by Tony Thwaites (2001)
Joyce and the Victorians, by Tracey Teets Schwarze (2002)
Joyce's "Ulysses" as National Epic: Epic Mimesis and the Political History of the Nation State, by Andras Ungar (2002)
James Joyce's "Fraudstuff," by Kimberly J. Devlin (2002)
Rite of Passage in the Narratives of Dante and Joyce, by Jennifer Margaret Fraser (2002)
Joyce and the Scene of Modernity, by David Spurr (2002)
Joyce and the Early Freudians: A Synchronic Dialogue of Texts, by Jean Kimball (2003)
Twenty-First Joyce, edited by Ellen Carol Jones and Morris Beja (2004)
Joyce on the Threshold, edited by Anne Fogarty and Timothy Martin (2005)
Wake Rites: The Ancient Irish Rituals of "Finnegans Wake," by George Cinclair Gibson (2005)
"Ulysses" in Critical Perspective, edited by Michael Patrick Gillespie and A. Nicholas Fargnoli (2006)
Joyce and the Narrative Structure of Incest, by Jen Shelton (2006)
Joyce, Ireland, Britain, edited by Andrew Gibson and Len Platt (2006)

Joyce in Trieste: An Album of Risky Readings, edited by Sebastian D. G. Knowles, Geert Lernout, and John McCourt (2007)
Joyce's Rare View: The Nature of Things in "Finnegans Wake," by Richard Beckman (2007)
Joyce's Misbelief, by Roy Gottfried (2008)
James Joyce's Painful Case, by Cóilín Owens (2008; first paperback edition, 2017)
Cannibal Joyce, by Thomas Jackson Rice (2008)
Manuscript Genetics, Joyce's Know-How, Beckett's Nohow, by Dirk Van Hulle (2008)
Catholic Nostalgia in Joyce and Company, by Mary Lowe-Evans (2008)
A Guide through "Finnegans Wake," by Edmund Lloyd Epstein (2009)
Bloomsday 100: Essays on "Ulysses," edited by Morris Beja and Anne Fogarty (2009)
Joyce, Medicine, and Modernity, by Vike Martina Plock (2010; first paperback edition, 2012)
Who's Afraid of James Joyce?, by Karen R. Lawrence (2010; first paperback edition, 2012)
"Ulysses" in Focus: Genetic, Textual, and Personal Views, by Michael Groden (2010; first paperback edition, 2012)
Foundational Essays in James Joyce Studies, edited by Michael Patrick Gillespie (2011; first paperback edition, 2017)
Empire and Pilgrimage in Conrad and Joyce, by Agata Szczeszak-Brewer (2011; first paperback edition, 2017)
The Poetry of James Joyce Reconsidered, edited by Marc C. Conner (2012; first paperback edition, 2015)
The German Joyce, by Robert K. Weninger (2012; first paperback edition, 2016)
Joyce and Militarism, by Greg Winston (2012; first paperback edition, 2015)
Renascent Joyce, edited by Daniel Ferrer, Sam Slote, and André Topia (2013; first paperback edition, 2014)
Before Daybreak: "After the Race" and the Origins of Joyce's Art, by Cóilín Owens (2013; first paperback edition, 2015)
Modernists at Odds: Reconsidering Joyce and Lawrence, edited by Matthew J. Kochis and Heather L. Lusty (2015; first paperback edition, 2020)
James Joyce and the Exilic Imagination, by Michael Patrick Gillespie (2015)
The Ecology of "Finnegans Wake," by Alison Lacivita (2015; first paperback edition, 2021)
Joyce's Allmaziful Pluralities: Polyvocal Explorations of "Finnegans Wake," edited by Kimberly J. Devlin and Christine Smedley (2015; first paperback edition, 2018)
Exiles: A Critical Edition, by James Joyce, edited by A. Nicholas Fargnoli and Michael Patrick Gillespie (2016; first paperback edition, 2019)
Up to Maughty London: Joyce's Cultural Capital in the Imperial Metropolis, by Eleni Loukopoulou (2017)
Joyce and the Law, edited by Jonathan Goldman (2017; first paperback edition, 2020)
At Fault: Joyce and the Crisis of the Modern University, by Sebastian D. G. Knowles (2018; first paperback edition, 2021)
"Ulysses" Unbound: A Reader's Companion to James Joyce's "Ulysses," Third Edition, by Terence Killeen (2018)
Joyce and Geometry, by Ciaran McMorran (2020)
Panepiphanal World: James Joyce's Epiphanies, by Sangam MacDuff (2020; first paperback edition, 2020)
Language as Prayer in "Finnegans Wake," by Colleen Jaurretche (2020)
Rewriting Joyce's Europe: The Politics of Language and Visual Design, by Tekla Mecsnóber (2021)
Joyce Writing Disability, edited by Jeremy Colangelo (2022)
Joyce, Aristotle, and Aquinas, by Fran O'Rourke (2022)
Time and Identity in "Ulysses" and the "Odyssey," by Stephanie Nelson (2022)
Joyce without Borders: Circulations, Sciences, Media, and Mortal Flesh, edited by James Ramey and Norman Cheadle (2022)
An Irish-Jewish Politician, Joyce's Dublin, and "Ulysses": The Life and Times of Albert L. Altman, by Neil R. Davison (2022)

Beating the Bounds: Excess and Restraint in Joyce's Later Works, by Roy Benjamin (2023)
Genetic Joyce: Manuscripts and the Dynamics of Creation, by Daniel Ferrer (2023)
Collected Epiphanies of James Joyce: A Critical Edition, edited by Sangam MacDuff, Angus McFadzean, and Morris Beja (2024)
Guilt and "Finnegans Wake": From Original Sin to the Irredeemable Body, by Talia Abu (2025)
Sensational Joyce: The Psychology of "Ulysses," by John Gordon (2025)
Teaching James Joyce in the Twenty-First Century, edited by Barry Devine and Ellen Scheible (2025)

www.ingramcontent.com/pod-product-compliance
Lightning Source LLC
Chambersburg PA
CBHW030609230426
43661CB00053B/1907